THE GPA IRISH ARTS REVIEW

YEARBOOK 1989-90

D1332350

Cover illustration: Credence table in St. Fin Barre's Cathedral, Cork, decorated with painted herons among reeds. Detail.

Published for Ann Reihill *and* Ulli de Breffny *by* Eton Enterprises Limited, 22 Crofton Road, Dún Laoghaire, Co. Dublin, Ireland.

Irish Arts Review is sponsored by GPA Group Limited, Shannon, Ireland. *The publishers also received a grant of Stg£2,000 from the Arts Council of Northern Ireland* and a grant of Ir£500 *from the Arts Council/An Chomhairle Ealaíon* . *Other GPA sponsored events include:*
  The GPA Emerging Artists Awards (1990, 1993)
  The GPA Book Award (1989, 1992)
  The GPA International Piano Competition (1991)

ISBN 0-9513722-1-1
ISSN 0791-038X

Editor: Brian de Breffny. *Assistant Editor:* Rosemary Ryan.
Consultant Editor: Alistair Smith. *Managing Director:* Ann Reihill.
Editorial Office: Irish Arts Review, 22 Crofton Road, Dún Laoghaire, Co. Dublin, Ireland. Telephone No. 01-808415 Fax No. 01-808309
Design: Q Design, 4 Strand Road, Sandymount, Dublin 4, Ireland.
Typeset in the Republic of Ireland by Design and Art Facilities Limited, Dublin, Ireland.
Printed in Singapore by C. S. Graphics Private Limited.

Seamus Heaney kindly gave permission for a section of his recent sequence of poems in progress (entitled *Lightenings*) to be read at Brian de Breffny's funeral mass. He also kindly allows us to reprint them here.

And lightening? One meaning of that
Beyond the usual sense of alleviation,
Illumination, and so on, is this:

A phenomenal instant when the spirit flares
In pure exhilaration before death –
The good thief in us harking to the words!

So paint him on Christ's right hand, on a promontory
Scanning terrible space, so body-racked he seems
Untranslatable into the promise

That blazes on the moon-rim of his forehead,
in nail-craters on the dark side of his brain:
This day thou shalt be with Me in Paradise

Since the last edition of the GPA *Irish Arts Review Yearbook* was published in November 1988, our gifted Editor Brian de Breffny has died. He died reluctantly on February 11, 1989, after a heroic battle against cancer. This struggle was conducted over a two year period with courage, humour and dignity. He worked on this Yearbook until the week before his death and succeeded in commissioning all of it and editing most of it.

Brian de Breffny lived in Ireland for the last ten years of his life. Together with his wife Ulli he restored the beautiful Palladian house Castletown Cox, built about 1767 for the Archbishop of Cashel. There they entertained their family and friends with warmth, consideration and generosity. His friends were enriched by knowing him. He was a truly civilised man, at home in many countries and many settings. He carried his numerous talents and achievements lightly. He was stylish, kind and had a sense of fun which belied the rigour of his scholarship.

He wrote many books, most of them about the art and architecture of Ireland. Among them *The Houses of Ireland* (1973), *The Churches and Abbeys of Ireland* (1976), *Castles of Ireland* (1977) and *The Land of Ireland* (1979) still enrich our knowledge of our country and illuminate it for others. In 1983 Brian edited *Ireland, A Cultural Encyclopaedia*, published, like the others, by Thames and Hudson. While working on this project he realised there was a need for a magazine to act as a platform for the Arts in Ireland. This led, in 1984, to the birth of *Irish Arts Review* as a quarterly magazine. As his friend for ten years, and his partner in this endeavour for five years, I mourn his passing. This Yearbook and his many books are his epitaph.

Happily the *Irish Arts Review Yearbook* will continue under the editorship of Alistair Smith, Keeper of Exhibitions and Curator at the National Gallery, London, and with the sponsorship of Guinness Peat Aviation.

ANN REIHILL

CONTENTS

4   BRIAN DE BREFFNY · AN APPRECIATION

27   BOOK REVIEWS
Rosemary Ryan

29   ICONS/COSTAKIS
Hilary Pyle

30   THE DECORATION OF CORK CATHEDRAL
Hilary Pyle

35   THE LIFE AND WORK OF OISÍN KELLY
Fergus Kelly

39   UNCATALOGUED DRAWINGS IN THE KING'S
INNS LIBRARY
Anne Walsh

43   PAUL HENRY: AN IRISH PORTRAIT
Brian Kennedy

55   THE WHITE CITY–SIR JOHN LAVERY IN
TANGIER
Kenneth McConkey

63   INTERVIEW WITH ALISTAIR WILSON
John Hutchinson

67   EDWARD SMYTH, DUBLIN'S SCULPTOR
Patrick Lenehan

77   THE 'BUDDHA BUCKET' FROM THE OSEBERG
FIND
Margaret MacNamidhe

83   CASTLE COOLE, CO. FERMANAGH
George Mott

91   INTRUSIONS AND REPRESENTATIONS: THE
LANDSCAPE OF WICKLOW
John Hutchinson

100   THE PAINTINGS OF BRIAN BOURKE
Julian Campbell

107   PATRICK J. TUOHY 1894–1930
Rosemarie Mulcahy

119   PATRICK OSBORNE, AN IRISH STUCCODORE
Sean O Reilly

128   INTERVIEW WITH RICHARD GORMAN
Sanda Miller

133   SYMBOLISM IN TURN-OF-THE-CENTURY
IRISH ART
Nicola Gordon Bowe

145   JOHN SEMPLE AND HIS CHURCHES
Maurice Craig

151   THE ART-CARVING SCHOOLS IN IRELAND
Paul Larmour

158   FRENCH INFLUENCE IN LATE SEVENTEENTH
CENTURY PORTRAITS
Jane Fenlon

169   ROBERT HUNTER
Anne Crookshank

186   LOOKING BACK
An overview of the arts in Ireland over twelve months
Aidan Dunne/Liam Kelly

193   GARDEN STATUARY IN IRELAND
Patrick Bowe

200   SIR CHARLES LANYON
Paul Larmour

207   BRONZE BY GOLD, THE WORK OF IRISH
WOMEN SCULPTORS
Dorothy Walker

214   FASHION AS A GUIDE TO DATING IRISH
PORTRAITS 1660–1880
Rosemary ffolliott

233   IRISH HISTORY PAINTING
John Turpin

248   BELVEDERE HOUSE, GEM OF THE IRISH
MIDLANDS
Olive Sharkey

254   THE LYNN BROTHERS, ARCHITECT AND
SCULPTOR
Martyn Anglesea

263   BOOK REVIEWS · LATHAM ADDENDA
Ilse Hempel Lipschutz, Rosemary Ryan,
Anne Crookshank

Among Brian's many friends I think Anne and I must be unique in that we have never visited his Castletown. How many times have Ulli and Brian invited us with that grace and constant generosity we all know, but time and again incidental bad luck intervened.

Anne as a girl had known this lovely house where, two centuries ago, the Bishop Cox conceived his Orange Pippin. Latterly it had fallen into a kind of prosperous decline from which it was ultimately rescued by Brian and Ulli and I well know, superbly restored to us.

I say *to us* advisedly, for clearly every building in the land of Ireland – from megalithic Knowth to the Casino at Marino – is part of our national heritage, the architectural expression of our age-old, complex, composite social experience. That might seem obvious enough, yet since our independence we in Ireland have strangely underestimated and even ignored our own *manifold* heritage.

Our historic buildings – and in particular those great houses which survived the social order that conceived them – have frequently suffered destruction or ruin, sometimes with a vestigial hostility which Soviet revolutionaries would have found incomprehensible either from a sociological or from an economic point of view, preferring to regard their princely houses as their own invaluable and historic inheritance.

It would seem that we in Ireland tend to lack, or have somehow lost a continuing awareness of the depth and variety of our cultural inheritance. And if the world repeatedly reminds us of W.B. Yeats and the splendour of our literature, it overlooked Coole Park as we did until it was too late. Yet what would we not give today, or in eleven years' time, to have Coole back in Ireland?

In his succession of invaluable books, as in all he has done to persuade us to know and preserve what remains to us, few I think have done more than Brian de Breffny to make Ireland aware of the variety and extent of her architectural patrimony and of the threat of ruin and obliteration in which some of it still stands.

It was in addition to all this and to his other cultural commitments that, with the indefatigable support of Ann Reihill and a small band of distinguished editorial advisors, Brian devotedly edited the *Irish Arts Review,* a marvel of professional quality, providing an indispensable insight into cultural activity in Ireland.

For that alone, as for so much else, he will long be remembered with admiration, gratitude and affection.

LOUIS LE BROCQUY

In 1939, One Momentous Event Almost Went Unnoticed.

There was no shortage of big news stories in 1939. It was the year Kilkenny held off Cork to take the All-Ireland Hurling Final by a point. When the Kingdom took the laurels in the football. The year of "Gone With The Wind", "Finnegans Wake" and the lovable Morris Eight. Memories of Tommy Dorsey, a sixpenny fish n'chips...and imminent War.
One small, but significant story from that unforgettable year was almost lost amongst the headlines - the formation of The Irish Life Assurance Company.
A small story then, but one which was to have a great impact on the lives of Irish people and the face of Irish business in the years that followed.
Irish Life is a top Life, Pensions and Investment Company, with a strong base here in Ireland and thriving interests in Britain and the U.S. To date, Irish Life has over 500,000 policyholders and assets of over £3 Billion. And we're still growing, working for Ireland, benefitting our policyholders.
Needless to say, our appetite for success is as great today as it was fifty years ago.

50 YEARS IRISH LIFE
1989

If dinner hadn't already existed it would have been necessary to invent it.

EUROPEAN FINE ARTS

OLD MASTER PAINTINGS AND DRAWINGS

MARTINUS NELLIUS Active 1670–1706 in the Hague
Still-Life with roemer, oysters, a Lobster and Fruit
Signed and dated 1671, oil on canvas 71 × 89.5 cm.
Expertise: Ingvar Bergström.

Director: Dr. Marie-Theres Schmitz.

6 LOWER MERRION STREET · DUBLIN 2 · TELEPHONE 762506

THE ADAM SALEROOMS

IRELAND'S LEADING FINE ART AUCTIONEERS AND VALUERS SINCE 1887.

JACK B. YEATS RHA (1871 – 1957)
Misty Morning 1943, oil on panel 9 × 14 ins signed
Sold at The Adam Salerooms in March 1989 for the record price of £95,000.

SPECIALIST AUCTION SALES OF IMPORTANT IRISH ART
FINE PERIOD FURNITURE · SILVER AND PLATED WARE · PORCELAIN AND GLASS · VICTORIANA
BRITISH AND CONTINENTAL PAINTINGS · VINTAGE WINES AND PORT

JAMES ADAM & SONS

A NATIONAL INSTITUTION WITH AN INTERNATIONAL CLIENTELE
ST. STEPHEN'S GREEN · DUBLIN 2 · TELEPHONE 760261

THE NATIONAL GALLERY OF IRELAND
Merrion Square West, Dublin 2

National Gallery of Ireland
DIARY 1990

Contains thirty-six full colour reproductions of works in the Gallery's collection which show different aspects of Country Life. With a clear spacious format, the diary includes information on Gallery activities and international holidays and is spiral bound for ease of use. Price: **IR£7.95** (plus p&p £2.50).

National Gallery of Ireland
CALENDAR 1990

Ranging from a Russian Icon of the fifteenth century to a twentieth century masterpiece by Juan Gris, the twelve full colour reproductions in the 1990 calendar reflect the wide variety of splendid works in the Gallery's collection.
Price: **IR£5.95** (plus p&p £2.50).

Malton's VIEWS OF DUBLIN

The National Gallery of Ireland presents a specially commissioned range of twelve large (16″ × 20″) colour prints of James Malton's celebrated 'Views of Dublin'. The prints are reproductions of watercolours in the Gallery's collection.
Price: **IR£5.95** (plus p&p £2.00).

1. Trinity College
2. The Tholsel
3. St. Catherine's
4. St. Patrick's
5. Bank of Ireland
6. Casino, Marino
7. The Marine School
8. Custom House
9. King's Hospital
10. Powerscourt House
11. Four Courts
12. St. Patrick's

ORDERS (enclosing payment) should be addressed to:
The Publications Department, The National Gallery of Ireland, Merrion Square West, Dublin 2, Ireland

Mail order prices inclusive of p&p are as follows:
North America: Calendar US$25; Diary US$30; Malton Print US$20
All E.E.C. Countries: Calendar £8.45 stg.; Diary £10.45 stg.; Malton Print £7.95 stg.
We welcome Access, Diners and Visa cards.

WEXFORD FESTIVAL *Opera* 1989

*The 1989 Festival dates are as follows:
Thursday, October 26th — Sunday
November 12th. Opera performances
every night except Tuesday 7th,
Wednesday 8th and Thursday 9th.*

The three operas to be performed are

HEINRICH MARSCHNER (1795–1861)
"Der Templer und die Judin"
*A romantic opera in three acts after the
novel "Ivanhoe" by Sir Walter Scott.
First performed Leipzig December
22nd, 1829.
German text.*

WOLFGANG AMADEUS MOZART
(1756–1791) **"Mitridate, re di Ponto"**
*Opera seria in three acts after the play by
Racine. First performed December 26th
1770 in Milan (La Scala).
Italian text by Cigna-Scanti.*

SERGEI PROKOFIEV (1891–1953)
Betrothal in a Monastery (The Duenna)
*Comic opera in four acts after "The
Duenna" by Sheridan. First performed in
Leningrad, November 3rd, 1946.
Russian text by composer and Mira
Mendelssohn.
To be sung in English.*

TICKET PRICES
*Gala Night and weekends £30 each
Mid-week   £24 each*

We look forward to seeing you in '89!
Wexford Festival Opera, Wexford, Ireland.
Tel. 053-22240

Pyms Gallery, London

FINE PAINTINGS

Specializing in Nineteenth and Twentieth Century Irish paintings also British post-Impressionist and French Nineteenth Century works of Art.

BELOW:
Nathaniel Hone R.H.A. (1831–1917)
b. Dublin
Off the Kish
Oils on canvas 25½ × 36½ inches

RIGHT:
Sir William Orpen R.A., R.H.A. (1878–1931)
b. Stillorgan, Co. Dublin
A Summer Afternoon
Oils on canvas 38 × 36 inches

Pyms Gallery, London

FINE PAINTINGS

"After he had married, I spent some delightful holidays with him at *The Cliffs*, Howth, which he rented for several summers, a place of great charm, looking out south over the sparkling waters of Dublin Bay, long, lovely, never-to-be-forgotten summer days, with frequent visits to the sea and the little enclosure called Bellingham's Harbour, where we bathed and sunned ourselves on the hot rocks. Bill was always at work and painted many pictures here."

Quote by Orpen's brother Richard from *Sir William Orpen, Artist and Man* by Konody and Dark, pub. London, 1932, page 35.

THE HUGH LANE MUNICIPAL GALLERY OF MODERN ART

Azaleas by Albert Moore.
Oil on Panel; 78″ × 40″.
Lane Gift, 1912.

19th and 20th Century Irish and Continental works including the Lane Collection

Lectures or musical events
Sundays at 12 noon.

Children's Hour, Saturdays 11.30 a.m.

Guided Tours by arrangement.

Admission free to all events.

Restaurant closes 30 minutes before
gallery closing time.

GALLERY HOURS
Tuesday–Saturday 9.30 a.m.–6 p.m.;
Sunday 11 a.m.–5 p.m.
Closed Mondays.

CHARLEMONT HOUSE · PARNELL SQUARE · DUBLIN 1 · TELEPHONE (01) 741903/788761

Meeting Place
Bronze and Granite
Jakki McKenna 1988

SCULPTORS SOCIETY OF IRELAND

The Society offers a consultative service for clients wishing to commission any kind of sculpture for a public or private place.

The Society can point out sites suitable for commissions to amenity bodies, educational and local authorities, architects, private developers, private companies and others.

The Society can provide information on a variety of existing schemes around the country and help plan strategies for commissioning.

The Society can identify artists for specific projects and acts as an intermediary in the organisation and implementation of these projects.

The Society can advise on publicity for projects.

▲   ◆ ◆ ◆ ◆ ◆   ▲

For further information we recommend:

Meitheal - a photographic documentary of 70 contemporary outdoor sculptures in a variety of materials placed throughout the country. Price £6.50

'A Users Guide on how to purchase or commission sculpture'
- a comprehensive and instructive manual with case histories on sculpture commissions. Price £5.00

'Conference Report on the International Conference on Sculpture' held in Dublin in August 1988. Extensive range of essays dealing with public sculpture and the role of sculpture by distinguished writers, critics, artists, administrators and historians from many countries. Pirce £5.00

Send a postal order or cheque to:
Sculptors Society of Ireland,
23/25 Moss Street, Dublin 2.
Telephone: (01) 718746.

▼

THE BOOK OF KELLS

ONE OF THE GREATEST AND MOST MYSTERIOUS WORKS OF ART

Fine Art Facsimile Edition: Presentation box, Fine Art Facsimile and commentary volume

Re-creation of an invaluable medieval manuscript

After 1200 years the BOOK OF KELLS is so fragile that even variations in humidity can be harmful. For this reason, it is probably the best protected illuminated manuscript in the world, and very few people are ever allowed access to this treasure. It was, therefore, an honour for Fine Art Facsimile Publishers (Faksimile-Verlag Luzern) of Switzerland to be entrusted by Trinity College Dublin with the creation of the first unique and complete Fine Art Facsimile Edition of the BOOK OF KELLS, glorifying the life of Christ in the four gospels.

The Fine Art Facsimile Edition will be published in a numbered edition, strictly limited to 1480 copies world-wide, with only 740 copies reserved for English speaking countries.

A unique art collection between two book covers

The BOOK OF KELLS contains some of the most beautiful examples of book illumination ever created. All but two of its 680 pages are decorated in full colour with an indescribable wealth of symbolic painting and mystical illustrations. The work literally teems with forms representing human figures, animals and plants, some depicted in paintings covering entire pages, some as ornamentation between the lines of text.

The Fine Art Facsimile Edition – a work of art and lasting value

A high standard is required to achieve a facsimile – an exact image of the original. The 680 illuminated pages (9½ × 13 inches) are recreated down to the smallest detail, using up to ten colours on special paper, resembling exactly the original parchment. Every single page is cut according to the irregularity of the original. The facsimile volume will be fully hand-bound in white, finest leather, with gathering sewn onto double-cords – just as it was centuries ago. Each will be numbered by hand and encased in a medieval-style presentation box with uniquely crafted mountings and embossed surfaces.

An authoritative commentary volume will accompany each edition. The volume will be written by the renowned medieval art scholar Prof. Dr. Jonathan J. Alexander of the Fine Art Institute of New York, together with other eminent scholars. The volume will be edited by Peter Fox, Librarian of Trinity College Dublin. The subscription price is US$ 14 800.— until the whole edition will be published in 1990. After that, the price will be at least US$ 16 000.—. We also offer extended and individual payment terms.

For a better understanding of the BOOK OF KELLS and the Fine Art Facsimile Edition ask for the presentation kit, including two Fine Art Facsimile Pages, a 16-page information brochure and a detailed subscription offer. In addition to the presentation kit you may order the 15-minute VHS (NTSC or PAL) video film about the BOOK OF KELLS – both at the price of US$ 116.— for a trial period of 30 days.

Free 6-page information folder available.

Fine Art Facsimile Publishers of Switzerland
Faksimile-Verlag Luzern
Alpenstrasse 5, 6000 Lucerne 6, Switzerland
Tel. 041 - 51 15 71, Tlx. 868 103, Fax 041 - 51 69 02

or: The Librarian, Trinity College Library, Dublin 2, Ireland.

MICHAEL ASHUR

RECENT PAINTINGS
19th April – 12th May 1990
RIVERRUN GALLERY · DUBLIN

Riverrun Gallery
82 DAME STREET · DUBLIN 2.
TELEPHONE 01-798606

Time Vortex 183 × 183 cms, acrylic on canvas

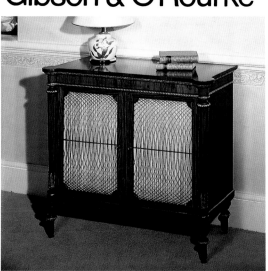

ASSOCIATION OF ART HISTORIANS

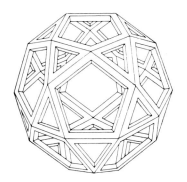

16th Annual Conference

with the support of the
Association of Irish Art Historians

will be held at Trinity College, Dublin
23rd to 25th March 1990

Theme – Regionalism: Challenging the Canon

Academic sessions will include: **Insular Art, Creating a History of
North American Art; The Reformation in the Regions: image and
discord; Popular Imagery and Critical Regionalism; Modernism and
the City: Joyce's Dublin and Beyond** and many more.

The weekend will also include an Art History Book Fair, organised visits
and receptions.

Enquiries: Fintan Cullen, Dept. History of Art, Trinity College, Dublin 2.
Tel: 772941, ex. 1012/1995; home: 887240.

Celtic Art
From its Beginnings to the Book of Kells
Ruth and Vincent Megaw

This is the first single volume to provide a
full survey of Celtic arts and crafts from
700 BC to 700 AD. It includes a detailed
examination of Celtic art in Britain and
Ireland, its determined survival under
Roman occupation and its new flowering
in the Early Christian period. With a
wealth of illustrations – many of objects
never before reproduced, this will be the
standard work in the field for many
years to come.
With 452 illustrations, 24 in colour £28.00 stg

Thames and Hudson

In the Nouveau Style
Malcolm Haslam

Here is the first book ever to trace the
progress through the whole century of a
style popularly supposed to be limited to
the years of the *Belle Epoque*. Malcolm
Haslam examines and celebrates the
diversity and brilliance of Art Nouveau
from its origins, through its flowering at
the turn of the century, and the survival of
its characteristics in the years when Art
Deco and Modernism took precedence to
its full-blown revival in the 1960s, and
right up to the present day.
*With 315 illustrations, 160 in colour
£20.00 stg Autumn 1989*

New British Art
in the Saatchi Collection
Alistair Hicks

The Saatchi Collection is unique. Perhaps
best known for its American and European
art, in recent years it has expanded to focus
on the extraordinarily creative works of art
produced by British, and British-based,
artists, and now offers a kaleidoscopic
view of recent British painting and
sculpture. With 150 reproductions –
almost all in colour – *New British Art* offers
an unrivalled opportunity to examine in
depth the achievement of more than twenty
of the most significant artists of our time.
*With 150 illustrations, most in colour
Paperback £14.95 stg Autumn 1989*

World of Art
Two new additions to this world famous
series, superbly illustrated, and
astonishing value at just £5.95 stg
(paperback).

Van Gogh
Melissa McQuillan
With 168 illustrations, 25 in colour

Abstract Art
Anna Moszynska
*With 175 illustrations, 25 in colour
Autumn 1989*

Lucian Freud paintings
Robert Hughes
Now available in paperback

'There is bonus, a benefaction even, in
Robert Hughes's introductory essay to the
book . . . a great piece of writing . . . ornate,
subtle, truthful and funny' – *The Spectator*
Lucian Freud has almost single-handedly
redefined the figurative painting of our
time. His distinctive portraits have a
haunting quality that makes them
impossible to forget. Here is a magnificent
range of Freud's work, reproduced in
superb colour, from his earliest paintings
to some of the most recent.
*With 112 illustrations, 105 in colour
Paperback £14.95 stg Autumn 1989*

For a complete catalogue and details of new and forthcoming publications, please write to Dept IARY, 30 Bloomsbury Street, London WC1B 3QP

BOOK REVIEWS

PIERRE BONNARD: ILLUSTRATOR

ANTOINE TERRASSE,
translated from French by Jean-Marie Clarke
London, Thames and Hudson, 1989, Stg£38.

This is a beautifully-produced book, as we expect of Thames and Hudson's art-books, with hundreds of reproductions, many in colour, of Bonnard's work as book-illustrator from 1891 to 1947, the year of his death. Also included are exhibition-invitations, birth-announcements and advertisements by Bonnard. This book is a sequel to Francis Bouvet's *Bonnard: The Complete Graphic Works*, a catalogue of the lithographs and etchings done by the artist himself on copper or stone.

Bonnard was one of a circle of painters, writers and musicians, and undoubtedly gained from the stimulus of their company. His illustrations are notable for his close and sympathetic reading of the text, enabling him to achieve "brilliant conjunctions of type and image". It may be that his work has contributed to maintaining interest in books which might otherwise be forgotten. Birds and animals were a particular interest of his, but his range was very wide. His drawings for a French translation of Peter Nansen's novel, *Marie*, were admired by Renoir, who found them "absolutely exquisite"; however, these are markedly different from the marginal drawings for "La 628–E8", so full of life and fun, yet clearly he found himself in total sympathy with both subjects. And remarkably, he worked very hard to achieve the apparent spontaneity of all his illustrations, as is testified by the numerous preparatory drafts and sketches done, many of which are also illustrated in this book.

HENRY MOORE DRAWINGS

ANN GARROULD
London, Thames and Hudson, 1988, Stg£45.00.
with 336 illustrations, 168 in colour

This comprehensive survey of Moore's drawing career which spanned about sixty years, is another fine book from Thames and Hudson and shows the artist's obsession with the human figure. Both figurative and abstract drawing are shown here, in a variety of media.

PRINTS OF THE TWENTIETH CENTURY– A HISTORY

RIVA CASTLEMAN
World of Art series
London, Thames and Hudson, Stg£5.95.

Until the advent of printmaking, the painter produced something unique; an exact copy was not possible. He may well at times have envied the writer, whose work can be multiplied ad lib, accurately and almost effortlessly. No wonder printmaking has attracted some of the greatest twentieth-century artists. This book deals with all of these and with the full range of techniques. There are chapters on Expressionism, Cubism, Surrealism and Pop Art, among other related subjects. Picasso dominates, but all the other expected names are here including Bonnard, Munch, Matisse, Klee, Braque, Rouault, Chagall, Miro and Dali, and the Museum of Modern Art in New York has provided all the illustrations, of which there are 195, with 33 in colour. There is also a glossary of printmaking terms and bibliography.

This book is a model of how well a paperback can look, on good paper, a firm binding and illustrations of high quality, all at very reasonable cost. As the introductory chapter points out, the fact that almost every major artist of the twentieth century created prints allows a more complete review of the history of art of this period through prints than is possible for any previous century.

DAVID HOCKNEY BY DAVID HOCKNEY MY EARLY YEARS

NIKOS STANGOS (Editor)
Thames and Hudson, 1988, Stg£12.95.

This book results from twenty-five hours of taped conversations between Hockney and Stangos in London in 1975; the text is interspersed with many black and white illustrations and some colour of works dating between 1960 and 1975, which show his competent draughtsmanship.

Among Thames and Hudson's many titles on art to be published during 1989 are *Abstract Art, The World of the Impress-* *ionists, In the Nouveau Style, Modern Art– Impressionism to Post-Modernism, Lucian Freud paintings* (paperback), *and Celtic Art from its beginnings to the Book of Kells*, as well as a host of books on other subjects including architecture and archaeology. Available again is the widely acclaimed *Celtic Heritage*, by Alwyn and Brinley Rees.

THE DUBLIN PICTORIAL GUIDE & DIRECTORY OF 1850

HENRY SHAW
with an Introduction by Kevin B. Nowlan
Belfast, Friar's Bush Press, 1988,
Stg£9.95 pb, 424 pages
including contemporary engravings.

This facsimile reprint was made from two copies of Shaw's *New City Pictorial Directory 1850*, one owned by Kevin B. Nowlan, President of An Taisce, the other by the Irish Architectural Archive, each copy faulty but, according to the publishers, "each compensating for the worst faults of the other". This book is more legible and on better paper than the first edition, which is now a collector's item. Friar's Bush Press has done us a service, and done it with style. There is high-quality paper and an attractive colourful cover and the binding is strong and serviceable, as it needs to be for a paperback its size. The unique feature of this directory is that it illustrates every street in central Dublin, and the engravings must be of great value to anyone interested in architectural history. For the social historian there is abundant material in the lists of the names and occupations of the people of Dublin. Nowlan, in his introduction, regrets that there are no illustrations of the more purely residential areas such as Merrion Square or the Liberties. The reason for this is of course that Shaw was engaged in a commercial venture and so chose the streets where he found firms willing to advertise in his directory. It did not become an annual publication, as its originator had hoped, but this is not surprising when we consider the vast amount of painstaking work that went into this one year's production.

Rosemary Ryan

ICONS/COSTAKIS

Last year the Russians of the Orthodox Church celebrated the Christianization of Russia and, to honour the event, Sarah Smyth and Stanford Kingston organized a splendid exhibition of icons from Irish collections at the National Gallery of Ireland. Seventy icons were selected from more than two hundred found at the Gallery itself, the Ulster Museum, the Chester Beatty Library, as well as in private ownership. Most were small, and used for private devotion; the majority were painted during the eighteenth and nineteenth centuries.

Because of this, the exhibition had a character of its own. While the death knell of traditional icon painting was believed to have been sounded by Peter the Great, with his reforming zeal, and there was a waning of creative energy during the eighteenth century, history has shown that good painters were still to be found, and the exhibition included both exciting and mediocre, but well-crafted, work. Grouped under headings such as *Icons of the Mother of God*, and *Icons of the Feasts of the Church*, the organizers drew attention to specifically Russian aspects of devotion, and to the Russian emphasis on personalities such as St. John the Baptist, or St. Nicholas. There was a particularly moving Muscovite representation, from the Chester Beatty Library, of Zossima giving communion on a spoon to St. Mary of Egypt, the prostitute. Contrasts in styles of painting, even in this most rigid of traditions, were apparent in images of the 'Pantocrator', or the 'Christ not created with hands'. Some artists were more faithful to Russian traditions. Others were studying Western religious prototypes, particularly from the beginning of the nineteenth century.

The exhibition catalogue, edited by Sarah Smyth and Stanford Kingston, was intended for publication as a book at a later stage, with some extra articles but regrettably this has not yet happened. However, the catalogue as it stands, provides a satisfying survey of areas not generally covered in histories of the icon. Dr. James White, who as Director of the National Gallery of Ireland was responsible for acquiring the collection of Greek and Russian icons now on display in Merrion Square, contributes an introductory history of Russian icons, concluding with a note about the Tretiakov Centre in Moscow, where Rublev's 'Old

Hilary Pyle reviews the Icons Exhibition and the George Costakis Collection Exhibition which were simultaneously shown during 1988 in Dublin.

St. John the Baptist, ascribed to the School of Rublev, 16th century, tempera, 29.5 × 68 cm. Private Collection. Photograph John Kellett.

Testament Trinity' may be seen, and the Rublev Museum in the former Spas Andronievski Monastery, where he worked with Theophanes. Alan Falconer devotes himself to an analysis of Rublev's 'Trinity' on three levels of symbolism. All of the articles are concerned with the practical function of icons, and their meaning for today, and their place in the art of recent periods.

Perhaps most interesting are R. Milner-Gulland's remarks on the revival of interest in icons from 1880 onwards, which led to the first cleaning and reassessment of Rublev's 'Old Testament Trinity'. The revival coincided with the modern symbolist movement, and so must have had its effect on Kandinsky's *On the spiritual in art*. Yet he observes that Kandinsky, deeply committed to the spiritual in art, and a member of the Orthodox Church, shows no obvious sign of icon influence in his painting, whereas Chagall, a Jew, is full of iconic references, particularly around 1910.

The contributions of Lindsay Hughes and David Jackson on icons in seventeenth and nineteenth century Russia are also excellent. During the nineteenth century, a strong nationalistic spirit gave strength to the craft, which later led to the foundation of factories, where traditional painters might make a living

despite the invasion of western ways. But the real encouragement to appreciation of icon painting dates from when Diaghilev brought an exhibition of icons to Paris, and the exhibition of Russian medieval art which was later organized in Moscow in 1913.

Seen in the context of the icon exhibition, the selection of paintings from the George Costakis collection, which formed the historical section of Rosc at the Royal Hospital, Kilmainham, was particularly interesting. George Costakis, the son of Greek parents born in Moscow, amassed his unique collection of Russian early twentieth century art when such painting was out of fashion with the new socialist regime. When he retired to Athens in 1977, he presented the major part of his collection to the Tretiakov Museum in Moscow. The remainder is now housed in New York, but parts have been exhibited in other countries, and now in Ireland for the first time.

The symbolist paintings of Malevich and Kluin, from the first decade of this century, echoed the fervent vision of the icon painters in intensity and in sublimation of imagery. Malevich's landscape, of trees on a shadowed hillside, shows the branches transfigured where they have stretched up to meet the sunlight and Kluin's miniature view of a city is spiritualized through his handling of form and colour.

Nearly twenty years later, Chasnik's 'Supremalist cross', like a huge tragic flag, white on black, is as compelling an image for meditation as the traditional figured symbol. While the small and completely abstract 'Black quadrilateral' by Malevich has progressed even further in profundity, without being a Christian image though, as Milner-Gulland points out in his catalogue essay, while Malevich regarded such abstraction as the 'zero of form', his first image of the cross was not only for the suffering of mankind, but also for the intersection of human with more than human. One fascinating aspect of the exhibition was that the designs Kudriashev made for the first theatre in Orenburg in 1920 have much in common with the first colour essays of Evie Hone and Mainie Jellett under Gleizes, in their search for an imagery that was spiritual and yet at the same time modern.

Hilary Pyle

THE DECORATION OF CORK CATHEDRAL

Neither you as Bishop and Founder of the Cathedral nor I as Architect can afford to hand down to posterity indifferent Art or badly executed work,

William Burges wrote to John Gregg in January 1877.

Fifty years hence the whole affair will be on its trial and the elements of time and cost being forgotten the result only will be looked at . . .
I am quite certain that you yourself wish all things in your Cathedral to be as beautifull (sic) as this somewhat inartistic age can make them . . . If therefore funds should not be forthcoming for the immediate execution of all the furniture, the present book will enable those who come after you, to carry on the work you have so well begun. That you should see the whole cathedral finished and that both this book and that containing the glass designs, may become useless by the realization of their contents is the earnest wish of Your faithful Servant, William Burges.

Burges was presenting his book of designs[1] to Gregg when his remarkable cathedral in Cork − which was to cost more than six times the originally planned expenditure−was half finished. The bishop already knew that, before even one stone had been laid, Burges had seen the completed whole in his mind.[2] Yet Burges, who persisted in seeing his role as that of the medieval architect, approached the bishop as such an artist would approach his patron.

Gregg had only recently been consecrated Bishop of Cork when Burges won the competition for the new building which was to replace Peter Browne's small, undistinguished eighteenth century cathedral. The approach of Disestablishment was forcing the Church of Ireland to look seriously at the state of its fabric, and Gregg happily accepted the role of patron when in 1863, Burges's ambitious project for the new cathedral was chosen courageously−or with daring− by the original committee.

Though in his nineteenth-century capacity, Gregg would have to call on the wealthy and the generous-minded of Cork to meet the repeated demands for more and more money, he regularly set the pattern by dipping into his own pocket first. So it is not surprising−again part of Burges's medieval scheme−to find the prominent points of the church interior−such as altar, sedilia and throne− dedicated to the man he regarded as patron.

A close collaboration between a bishop and an English architect resulted in the fine cathedral of St. Fin Barre's in Cork, and its remarkable interior decoration. Here, the design and progress of the project are recounted by **Hilary Pyle.**

Back choir stall, misericord carving
Frog shaving frog, with tadpoles, *1878,*
walnut carved by Walden.

Bishop's throne, *1878, oak, 46 ft.*
Detail of entrance door.

Centre choir-stall: Bird and mouse
in foliated design above the Sacrifice of
Isaac, *1878, walnut, carved by Walden.*

Even the beams above the choir-stalls honour the patron for the painted arms of the See of Cork are impaled with the arms of Gregg himself. Burges wanted a living portrait of the bishop on the throne,[3] among the succession of heads of bishops dating from the time of Fin Barre, acquiring a photograph for his sculptor so as to get an accurate likeness, and there is no doubt the speed with which the building was raised and completed in most details of architecture and appurtenances, was due to the co-operation of the nineteenth-century patron with his architect.

Burges's book of designs, presented to the Bishop, is a work of art. There are forty-six pages of plans and designs for the decoration and furnishings of choir, chancel, ambulatory, transepts and nave, meticulously laid out (with an analysis of estimated cost where possible). The drawing reflects the clarity and innocence of line he had long admired in the thirteenth-century sketchbook of Wilars de Honecort in the *Bibliotheque National* in Paris.[4] Another book of designs−for the stained glass, and prepared as early as 1868, though the windows were not approved and started on until the mid-seventies−includes drawings by his trusted colleague, H.W. Lonsdale, which are stylistically a replica of his own. To embellish the plastic rotundity of his architecture, with its Ruskinian 'decoration by shadow in the triforium arches,[5] Burges provided in both books what would be described as a multi-coloured fantasy.[6]

Despite his firm belief in the French Gothic style as the basis for his total concept, the actuality of Burges's masterpiece has little place for Gothic mystery, or medieval-inspired searching. The exterior is solid, earthed, certain; the interior glows with an unquivering faith. Burges's contemporary, Robert Kerr, declared that "Butterfield was High Church, Scott Low Church and Burges no church".[7] If Burges was a committed Christian, he betrayed no wonderings or doubts or any religious aspirations in his work. He certainly had faith in Art, Art which can enjoy metaphors taken from Christian dogma. His total spiritual concern seems to have been with architectural beauty and, whether secular or ecclesiastical, this was his sole aim in life, the one thing he searched for. In sculpture and meticulous decoration he found a means for expressing this faith.

However, his working career was short, commencing with the St. Fin Barre's commission in 1863, when he was thirty-five, and finishing eighteen years later, when the cathedral was nearly completed, together with a number of other commissions. The cathedral may be seen as his artistic testimony, using a perfection of theological symbolism to complement its artistic totality.

It is perhaps of significance that Burges started to design the furnishings for the cathedral at about the same time as he was completing his own house in London and the church of Studley Royal in Yorkshire, and disengaging himself from a commission at Knightshayes in Devon. The same zoomorphic symbolism appears in all – frogs, fish, monkeys, birds. In his house at Melbury Road in Kensington, butterflies, representing the resurrected soul, adorn the bedroom; in the cathedral they flutter in the sanctuary. The whole of the decoration in St. Mary's, Studley Royal and St. Fin Barre's Cathedral is arranged so as to reach a splendid climax in the choir and sanctuary. He fell out of favour with Sir John Heathcote Amory about the time that Knightshayes was structurally complete because Sir John thought the decoration was too lavish. But by then the house had the same crocketed capitals in the hall as may be seen as forming the principal architectural decoration of St. Fin Barre's, and representatives of humankind – stone mason, bishop, chained prisoner – similar to those in the mosaic pavement in the cathedral, and in the soffits of the arches of the entrance porches, had been carved under the Knightshayes' stairs.

Such subject matter had become Burges's recognizable hall-mark. He had always interested himself in interior design. In the first commission which he won with his partner, Henry Clutton, for the Lille Cathedral competition, it is generally thought that, while Clutton planned the exterior, Burges looked after almost the entire interior furnishings.[8] He had been at school with the Rossettis, and had his first architectural apprenticeship with Edward Blore, who designed Gothic country houses, after which he had travelled widely in northern and southern Europe, in a pilgrimage for beauty. Working on Cardiff Castle at the beginning of the 1870s for the Marquess of Bute, he developed a consistency of

West pinnacle of sedilia:
angel with harp.

West arch of sedilia:
angel with drum.

iconography which relished Islamic and pagan possibilities in Gothic[9] in a secular setting, and he now applied his individual style to the interior of St. Fin Barre's, his triumph in the ecclesiastical field.

Writing from his London office, Burges had communicated with Dr. Richard Caulfield about the spires, which were under way in 1876,[10] and he was to refer to the Dean about the furniture, but he complained to Caulfield,[11] who remained his principal correspondent, that the Dean never answered letters, and so most of the information about the dating of the furnishings and decoration comes from his letters to Caulfield. Another irritant was McLeod, the local man, a fine stone carver, to whom he referred as "M'Cloud" when exasperated. He was always writing letters and requiring answers, and threatening to give up unless he received a cheque.

Nevertheless, relations with McLeod improved, and plans for the interior progressed rapidly. On October 16 1876, shortly after he had suggested putting an additional choir organ in the little gallery over the bas-relief of David with his harp, because of the impracticality of siting the organ in the gallery at the west end, Burges wrote to Caulfield, "I am getting on well with the furniture but it is a dreadfully long affair it requires so much consideration & care". A month later he was able to say that they were nearly through – "such a Bishop's Throne – how Mr. Usborne will stare": and on January 13 the Bishop could present the book of designs to the building committee.[12]

By March 1877, estimates for the carving of the choir-stalls had been received. Mr. Walden and his men were engaged to do the carving at the beginning of April, with Burges's own sculptor, Thomas Nicholls, doing the figures, and in February 1878, Burges reported that stalls and throne would be ready in three months, and were already well advanced. On May 23, he told Caulfield that Nicholls had done an excellent portrait of the Bishop for the throne; three days later the aged Gregg passed away, too soon to use the throne himself, but probably happily aware that it would shortly be on exhibition at the Royal Academy, and at the Paris Exhibition in 1878. It is as magnificent as Burges promised, carved in solid oak, with an intricate spire rising forty-six feet into the air, which is

Burges memorial window in the ambulatory: Seven candlesticks, *1881*,
made by Saunders & Co. from cartoon by Lonsdale.

THE DECORATION OF CORK CATHEDRAL

supported at two levels by small flying buttresses. Coloured figures of St. Fin Barre, and of kneeling angels holding the episcopal coat-of-arms, appear under the top arch, and on the table. Symbols of the evangelists are carved below the gable on the altar and choir sides, and a pelican and phoenix, for redemption and resurrection, on the nave side. Beneath all is the chair of the reigning bishop, surrounded on the outside by carved heads of twenty of his predecessors. It speaks much for Burges's architectural sense, which is evident in all his decorative designs, that this controlled complicated seat, based on a plinth of red Cork marble, and soaring to almost meet the choir clerestory, is in spirit a miniature of the whole building.

The choir-stalls appear restrained beside it, yet every opportunity has been taken to employ meaningful symbolism in the strong definitive carving. There are profiles of the apostles, and images of Adam, Abraham, Ruth and David on the finials, while the *misereres*, under their hinged seats, have a frog, as an attribute of death (nevertheless one has time enough to have his beard attended to), and a grasshopper, emblematic of carelessness, as the most common symbolic devices.

In September 1877, Burges wrote to Caulfield about the mosaic pavement for the chancel, referring him to *Matthew* XIII, 47, "the kingdom of Heaven is like unto a net that was cast into the sea and gathered of every kind." "In the meshes", he wrote, "are the various conditions of human life. Outside are the (Cork?) floats and weights". He enjoyed the pun, and attached the stylized net which holds the design together to corks, placed beyond some stylized waves, between the pillars of the sanctuary, and to weights laid between the posts of the communion rail. The links of the net encase reek crosses in circles, and diamond shapes trap individual fish – including an eel and a lobster – which leap and squirm. In his marvellous drawing, with its miniature detail, the mellow water-colour picks up the rose and green colours of the chancel marble and, because Burges's artistic purpose was complete in these architectural drawings, he added a wash of shadow beneath the altar, pillar and steps to give the final effect. The design was reproduced exactly, in Paris, by a team of artists from Udine, working for the firm of

Mosaic floor, sanctuary: detail of fish.

Burke & Co., using marbles from the Pyrenees. In the hexagonal spaces, apart from two stylish gratings, are the figures of men in various professions, from king and doctor to woodcutter and slave, and the notion of the kingdom of heaven is concluded at the lower chancel step with a border of birds and butterflies, signifying the ephemerality of human life, in a flowing pattern of vine leaves, with a pelican feeding its young (for Christ's sacrifice) at the centre, and parables – of the Sower and the Good Shepherd – at each end.

While there are drawings in the Book of Furniture of the magnificent lectern, Burges was in fact using a design he had offered for the Lille competition twenty years before, executed in solid brass, and over nine feet high, standing on four lion's paws. The glass jewels, in clusters, are repeated in the elaborate chased and bejewelled boss of the stem, and catch the light of the five candlesticks set above. Still true to the proper symbolism, Burges inserted the heads of Moses and David, one the holder of divine law, the other the ancestor and precursor of Christ. Its glorious thrust, which reflects the colour and splendour of the windows in a good light, balances the squatness of the pulpit on the opposite side of the church, already *in situ* when the lectern was complete.

Contemporary critics were harsh on the circular pulpit, standing on a stumpy central column of the same kind as holds the font, and which Mordaunt Crook, Burges's biographer describes as "reduced by compression almost to the status of symbolic supports".[13]

"Vigilans"[14] dismissed the pulpit as a "large vat". He failed to appreciate the way its green marble column and the square pillars of red marble surrounding it, echo the pillars and polished columns of the sanctuary. And this was before the relaxed relief figures of the evangelists and Paul had been painted in their rich narrative colours on the body of the pulpit. Certainly the additional paint emphasizes the iconographic pattern of the whole building, by making it clear that the brilliant figures are the major protagonists of the gospel. Burges saw it only in his mind at this time because, like the sanctuary ceiling, the pulpit was not completed until after his death, but "Vigilans" could not.

The integration of building and decoration is a striking feature of St. Fin Barre's Cathedral. Solid stone, marbles and alabaster harmonize with the solidly carved oak and walnut. The scintillating geometric shapes in the chancel grille and the coquettish choir caps and responds have their dialogue with the serene Sienese colour of marbles and paint. Burges would have decorated the roofs of the nave transepts in more muted figuration to finish his design, but this was never done.

But the binding thread of the total concept is Burges's understanding of the ecclesiastical iconography as worked out by the French medieval mind. In Cork he encountered Irish puritanism.[15] His nude figures of Adam and Eve on the west front and in the first of the north aisle nave windows were not approved by the committee, and, while the latter were retained, it was only on condition that they were properly clothed in the attractive leaf garments Burges later provided. He met similar difficulties when designing the altar carvings, and had to settle for a decorative abstract instead of the symbolic figuration he had planned.

After the amended drawings for the sculpture of the west front, with its theme of Fall and Resurrection, were passed by the vestry, Burges was impatient to proceed, because the Bishop was dying, the Dean had died, and he was conscious of the uncertainty and brevity of life, perhaps anticipating his own demise three years later. McLeod began on the west gable in November 1878, preparing the ground for the gold mosaic of the tympanum. A year later, Nicholls, Burges's sculptor, advised him that eight of the

THE DECORATION OF CORK CATHEDRAL

figures in the side portals, apostles and saints, were being worked in Ballinasloe stone, which became dark when wetted. He wanted to do the wise and foolish virgins of the central portal in the lighter Ardbraccan stone–"the figures all female, the effect will be more agreeable, and the work finer".

Both stones, he said, were equally durable and while his decision about the slight contrast in colour was successful, minimally high-lighting the central portion of the strongly figurated entrances, modern pollution has proved more powerful than the durable stone, and both wise and foolish virgins have been a prey to its rotting. Fortunately the windows must look much as they did when they were being added gradually to the whole design from the early '70s until some twenty years later. The message, expressed in conjunction with the sculpture, is one of redemption and revelation.

In the nave, after the glorious wheel window of the creation designed by Burges himself, the images from the Old Testament–in single panels centred on grisaille-patterned glass–were provided by Lonsdale, who worked with him and whose figurative style was indistinguishable from his own. All of these pale images are on deep blue or red grounds while the figures of the transept windows–showing incidents from the Book of the Prophets–capture all the rich colour, and the backgrounds glow like mother-of-pearl, their sweeping curves and twists seeming to play their part in the drama of the stories. The ambulatory windows stand aside, grouping themselves in complementary association, each with their triple panels of warm coloured figures against dark grounds, illustrating the life of Christ. The Crucifixion at the centre of the ambulatory apse, is framed above the altar. Above it, in the sanctuary, is the majestic awful figure of Christ as King Crucified, for which Burges provided three drawings,

David's door (the doorway from the ambulatory to the tower stair), *carved by McLeod and Nicholls, 1879, the bronze door executed by Hatfield with silver inlay by Barkentin, 1889.*

and for which the final figure, robed in rich amber and deep blue, with other jewelled colours, was executed by another of Burges's regular assistants, Fred Weekes, in memory of Dean Arthur Edwards, who died in March 1874.

Ironically, the window Burges had set aside to be a memorial to his father, became his own memorial, because he died first, in May 1881. It is one of the climactic windows of the Revelation, showing the seven candlesticks and the four beasts, and framed on either side by St. John of Patmos and twelve elders.

Without Burges and Gregg, its architect and patron, St. Fin Barre's continued its rapid course towards completion. John Chapple, Burges's assistant, felt it "a sacred duty" to carry out his master's wishes. Burges's brother-in-law, Richard Popplecock Pullan, took over Burges's role, with Chapple's aid, and saw the west front sculptures finished in 1883,

and the painting of the pulpit. It was not until 1935 that Professor Tristram painted the angels and the pantocrator which complete the glory of the sanctuary. Burges had rightly seen his book of designs carrying on the work "so well begun", and the trial of time has shown the quality and beauty of the noble fantasy of founder and architect to have become a living reality.

Hilary Pyle

NOTES

1. *Designs for the furniture of St. Fin Barr's Cathedral, Cork–W. Burges: Architect*, 1876 (introductory letter from William Burges to the Bishop). [Manuscript volume in the possession of the Dean and Chapter, St. Fin Barre's Cathedral, Cork.]
2. Undated newscutting in *Correspondence of Cork Cathedral* (St. Fin Barre's Cathedral).
3. William Burges to Richard Caulfield, December 21 1877, *Correspondence of Cork Cathedral*.
4. See J. Mordaunt Crook in *The Strange Genius of William Burges 'Art-Architect', 1827–1881. A catalogue to a centenary exhibition organized jointly by the National Museum of Wales, Cardiff, and the Victoria and Albert Museum*, London, 1981, p. 10.
5. A.C. Robinson, *St. Fin Barre's Cathedral, Cork: historical and descriptive*, 1897, p. 25.
6. *The Strange Genius*, p. 88.
7. *Ib.*, p. 12.
8. *Ib.*, p. 89.
9. *Ib.*, p. 10.
10. The foundation stone of the Cathedral was laid on January 12 1865, it was consecrated on St. Andrew's Day in 1870, and the structure, apart from the three spires, was almost complete when the furniture and decoration were embarked upon in 1877.
11. July 10 1877, *Correspondence of Cork Cathedral*.
12. R. Caulfield, *Hand-book of the Cathedral Church of St Fin Barre, Cork*, 1881, p. 7.
13. J. Mordaunt Crook, *William Burges and the High Victorian Dream*, 1981, p. 206.
14. William Burges to Richard Caulfield, June 14, 1878, mentions the criticism in the *Limerick Chronicle* by "an idiot" "who signs himself "Vigilans" ".
15. See also *William Burges and the High Victorian Dream*, p. 384, note 28.

THE LIFE AND WORK OF OISÍN KELLY

Oisín Kelly is undoubtedly best known to Dubliners for his large bronze sculptures, the 'Children of Lir' at the Garden of Remembrance, the 'Chariot of Life' at the Irish Life Centre, and 'Jim Larkin' in O'Connell Street. Cork people will be familiar with another large bronze, the 'Two Working Men' outside the County Hall, Cork. But Oisín's output was by no means confined to bronze, and during his thirty-five year career as a sculptor, he also worked in wood, stone, pottery, cement, enamel, silver, cast iron and mosaic. He even spread his talents into textile design, and produced a very successful series of dishcloths for Kilkenny Design Workshops.

He was born on May 17th 1915, and was christened Austin Ernest William Kelly. He did not acquire the name 'Oisín' until his schooldays, when a teacher mistakenly gaelicized 'Austin' as 'Oisín' rather than 'Oistín'. To the older generation of his own family, he always remained 'Austin'. His father was William Kelly, principal of James's Street National School in Dublin, and his mother was Elizabeth McLean. Their only other child, Doreen, was born in 1917.

There was no particular artistic tradition in the family of either parent, but his father – originally from Clonmellon, Co. Westmeath – was exceptionally skilful with his hands. His skills included carpentry, plumbing, shoe-making and photography (with his own dark-room). Some of Oisín's clothes were tailored by his father, which not surprisingly made him the butt of much teasing from his school-mates. His parents encouraged his early efforts to draw and paint, but – as he himself commented later – his juvenilia showed no special promise.

He was a rather delicate child, and throughout his life was subject to heavy colds and other illnesses. Consequently, a good deal of his childhood was spent in bed, where he acquired an enduring taste for reading. He first attended his father's school in James's Street, and then went on in 1926 to Mountjoy School, where he did well at English and Irish. With the intention of winning an Irish sizarship to Trinity College, Dublin, he spent some time near *An Spidéal* in the *Conamara Gaeltacht*. His introduction to the *Gaeltacht* was one of the formative experiences of his life, and he always retained a deep affection for the people and

Oisín Kelly is best known for his large public sculptures but his actual output was far greater and his activities were far more varied. His son, **Dr. Fergus Kelly,** of the Institute of Advanced Studies, Dublin, documents the life of this modest, talented and hard-working man.

Mrs Peabody, 7 ins. high, wood.

landscape of the West. In a radio interview towards the end of his life, he described how his first visit to *Conamara* brought him in contact with what was for him a new and different civilization.

Entering Trinity College in 1933, he studied French and Irish, and started to attend night classes at the National College of Art. At this stage his main interest was in drawing, painting and woodcuts, but he also did some modelling in clay. One of his earliest surviving works is a small brightly painted *terra-cotta* group showing his grandparents with their six sons and two daughters, entitled 'The Peeler's Family'.

He emerged from Trinity College with a B.A. (Moderatorship) in French and Irish, and went on a travelling scholarship to Frankfurt-am-Main. From an academic point of view he felt that he gained little from his stay in Germany, but he derived great benefit from his attendance at the Frankfurt School of Art. He developed a particular interest in twentieth century German sculpture, and was greatly influenced by the wood-carving of Barlach. An attack of kidney-stones forced his premature return to Ireland, and to the problem of earning a living. In later years, he sometimes wondered at his automatic choice of school-teaching as a career – following in his father's footsteps – and expressed regret that he had not studied architecture, a profession with which he had much contact when working as a sculptor.

His first full-time teaching job was at Clones High School in Co. Monaghan, where he stayed for two years. In 1942 he married Ruth Gwynn, daughter of the Irish scholar, E.J. Gwynn, Provost of Trinity College from 1927 to 1937. She was a veterinary surgeon by profession. The couple moved to Waterford, where Oisín obtained employment in Bishop Foy School. In 1946 they returned to Dublin to live with Ruth's widowed mother in a large rambling house near Tallaght, Co. Dublin. The outbuildings in the yard provided ample space for Oisín's artistic activities, and he subsequently erected a wooden workshop in the garden which enabled him to work in greater comfort.

In the same year, Oisín joined the staff of St. Columba's College, Rathfarnham, where he stayed for eighteen contented years. At this school he taught Art, French and Irish, and became increasingly involved in the teaching of English, though he was without academic qualifications in this subject. As a teacher he was lively, conscientious and iconoclastic, and had a profound influence on many of his pupils. He had a particular knack of arousing interest in boys of lesser ability, and derived more satisfaction from teaching B classes than A classes. Strangely, as an art teacher he was somewhat less successful than he was when teaching other subjects, and could be testy and impatient. Nonetheless a number of his pupils went on to make their names in this field, including Patrick Pye, the stained-glass artist, Michael Biggs, the stone-engraver, and Brett McEntaggart, the painter.

Oisín's career as a sculptor can be said

THE LIFE AND WORK OF OISÍN KELLY

to start in the School of Art in Waterford, where he received lessons in wood-carving from Robert Burke. My impression is that he was happier to work in wood than in any other material; certainly much of his best work consists of small wooden items, often lovingly smoothed and polished. One of his earliest wooden figures was an abstract entitled 'Mrs. Peabody' (1944).

During his first years at St. Columba's College, he continued to carve and model, and he produced some fine heads of pupils and staff-members in wood, plaster and *terra-cotta*. In 1947–'48 he got two terms off to go to London to study under Henry Moore at the Chelsea Polytechnic. In spite of Moore's reputation as an abstract sculptor, it is interesting to record that in his classes he taught absolute fidelity to life and concentrated on anatomy and the realistic representation of the human form.

On his return to Ireland, Oisín's interests seem to have become more traditional, and in particular moved towards Irish themes. Many of his works from this period derive their inspiration from early Irish art. He did a fine *terrazzo* version of a seventh century crucifixion plaque from Rinnagan, Co. Westmeath, and his figurines for the Catholic Stage Guild are unmistakably in the style of the early Irish metal-workers. He also did a dramatic representation of 'Mad Sweeney' (1949), taking this theme from the twelfth century Irish tale *Buile Shuibhne*. Another aspect of Irish culture to which he returned again and again in the '40s and '50s was traditional dancing. He completed dozens of studies of Irish dancers – singly or in groups – in wood, pottery or bronze. Many critics have praised these works, but I must confess to finding them for the most part disappointingly immobile, when compared, for example, to his later studies of hurlers and footballers.

School life also provided him with themes. A characteristically humorous work entitled 'Masters in Chapel' shows Oisín and two other begowned masters slouched in their pew as if listening to a long and uninspiring sermon. Another plaster relief shows the school orchestra; Oisín can be seen playing the violin in the foreground.

In the late '40s a very encouraging development took place – Oisín's sculptures started to sell. His note-books record

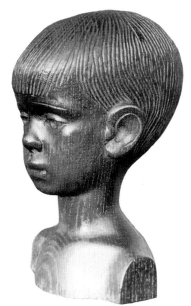

Daniel, *10 ins. high, oak.*

the purchase of various of his works, at first mainly by other artists such as Evie Hone, Betty Rivers and Tom Nisbet. He reached a wider market by exhibiting in the Irish Exhibition of Living Art, of which he was elected a committee member in 1951. His colleagues in the Living Art group included the painters Nano Reid, Anne Yeats, Norah McGuinness, Gerard Dillon, George Campbell, Fr. Jack Hanlon, and the sculptress, Hilary Heron, whose work he particularly admired. He also exhibited in the

Kilcorban Madonna, *24 ins. high, pottery.*

Royal Hibernian Academy (Associate 1958–'65, Member 1965–'81, Professor of Sculpture 1975–'81) and in the *Oireachtas*.

It was also at about this time that he began to get church commissions. Prominent among his early clerical patrons was the Society of Jesus, and his stained wooden statues of 'St. Aloysius Gonzaga' and 'St. Joseph and Child' (1951) can be seen in St. Francis Xavier's Church in Gardiner Street, Dublin. For the Church of St. Ignatius in Salthill, Co. Galway, he carved a 'Virgin and Child', and a 'Sacred Heart of Jesus'.

In a short article such as this it would be impossible to give a full account of the religious art which he produced at this period. At first, most of the larger works were in wood, such as 'Our Lady of Fatima' (1949) in the Holy Rosary Church, Ennis Road, Limerick, or 'St. Brigid' (1957) in the Church of St. Brigid, Curragh Camp, Co. Kildare. However, the difficulty of finding suitable well-seasoned tree-trunks to work with, forced him to turn to other media. He did a 'Last Supper' in pottery for the Chapel of St. Patrick's Training College, Drumcondra, and another for Zion Church, Rathgar. For the Church of St. Teresa, Sion Mills, Co. Tyrone, he executed a massive 'Last Supper' (1963) in incised slate, which looks very well above the main entrance. (Up the road from this church, a secular work of his – an enormous grasshopper (1977) – can be seen in the playground of St. Mary's Girls' Primary School, Strabane.)

Perhaps the most dramatic of all his religious statuary is the crucifixion in copper tubing which stands on the roof of the Church of the Redeemer, near Dundalk; it can be seen clearly from the Dublin-Belfast train.

He did many studies of the Blessed Virgin Mary, and avoided the sentimental treatment to which she is so often subjected. Among them there is a particularly sensitive and tender pottery figure of Mary suckling the infant Jesus. Another version of the 'Blessed Virgin with Child' was adapted by him from the medieval Kilcorban Madonna, and produced in both wood and pottery.

Oisín and Ruth had a family of seven: Fergus, Benjamin (died in 1962), Daniel, Piccola, Siobhán, Caitríona and David. Not surprisingly, his children provided the subject for some of his early works.

THE LIFE AND WORK OF OISÍN KELLY

One of the few sculptures which he executed in stone is a delightful limestone carving of his daughter Piccola as a baby (1952). Another very fine sculpture of a child is his 'Head of Daniel' (1953) in wood.

With considerable regret he resigned from St. Columba's College in 1964, and was appointed to the part-time post of artist-in-residence at the recently founded Kilkenny Design Workshops. The contract required that he should spend two days each week in Kilkenny, an arrangement which continued until his death. His activities at the Design Workshops were very varied, and he relished the opportunity to learn about the technical processes peculiar to each craft. Much of his work in Kilkenny was done in co-operation with other craftsmen. For example, the silver statuette 'Saint Patrick's Breastplate', presented by the *Taoiseach*, Jack Lynch, to his Holiness Pope John Paul II in 1979, was made by the silversmith, Desmond Byrne, to Oisín's design.

He was always very keen on the production of works which would be accessible to a wide public. He was particularly proud of a series of dishcloths which he designed while at Kilkenny. Each was based on an Irish proverb or saying; for example, the proverb *aithníonn ciaróg ciaróg eile* 'one beetle recognizes another beetle' was illustrated with two large beetles side by side. To illustrate the proverb *Ní thagann ciall roimh aois* 'sense does not come before age', he portrayed his own bald head, with the words of the proverb forming his beard and moustache. That design was chosen for the first page of the catalogue of his 1978 Retrospective Exhibition (The Ulster Museum, Belfast,

Cormorants on a Rock, *12 ins. high, pottery.*

the Douglas Hyde Gallery, Dublin, and the Crawford Municipal Art Gallery, Cork).

Another successful series consisted of reasonably priced ceramic birds, a selection from which has recently been reissued by Kilkenny Design Workshops. The series included a fine perching hawk, a raven, a snowy owl, and an owl in flight. The latter was adapted from a medieval stone carving at Holycross Abbey, Co. Tipperary. Other popular items were a male and female mallard, a teal and a wren—all hand-painted by Marie Hennesy.

As well as individual birds, Oisín became interested in doing groups of birds. He used to say that the representation of a single figure—whether man, bird or whatever—was relatively straight-

forward, but that the artist's problems really started when he tried to place two or more figures near each other. In spite of the difficulties, some of these groups were highly successful, such as a splendid group of cormorants on a rock in both pottery and bronze. Another successful group was of cattle. For the John A. Wood Memorial Trophy, he did a bronze herd of cattle with a drover, and there is also a version in wood with no drover. In 1969, a year of protest marches at home and abroad, he carved in wood a placard-holding group entitled 'The Marchers'.

He also experimented with shoals of fish and devoted much thought to the problem of how to represent movement through water. None of these shoals were wholly satisfactory, and many were left unfinished. I particularly treasure an experimental version in which the water is represented by lengths of wavy steel wire to which wooden fish are attached at intervals.

Though traditional in his general artistic outlook, Oisín was never satisfied to stick to the well-tried formula, and was constantly grappling with new ideas, some of them exceedingly difficult to bring off. A good example of the exploratory side of his art is his 'Clouds on Nephin' (cast in bronze from polystyrene, 1969) in which he tries to portray a heavy bank of clouds covering a mountain-top. Another experiment, using the same technical process, is his 'Mountain Stream', an ingenious representation of rocks and running water.

One of the effects of the Second Vatican Council was a decreased demand for religious statuary, so in the late '60s and '70s Oisín found that he was getting fewer Church commissions. To some ex-

Piccola as a Baby, *11 ins. long, limestone.*

Raven, *6 ins. high, pottery.*

THE LIFE AND WORK OF OISÍN KELLY

tent this gap was filled by State commissions. The largest of these was for the centrepiece of the Garden of Remembrance in Parnell Square. For this Oisín chose the Children of Lir changing into swans as a symbol of the painful but dramatic birth of the Irish State. This group was cast in the Minelli Foundry in Florence, and unveiled in 1971.

Subsequent bronzes were cast in Ireland at the Dublin Art Foundry. The first of these was 'Roger Casement' in handcuffs, completed in 1971 but not erected at Banna Strand, Co. Kerry, until 1984. Another statue, which dominated his workshop for a long time in its preliminary plaster form, was 'Jim Larkin' (1977), now in O'Connell Street, Dublin. He is depicted in an impassioned oratorical pose, taken from the famous photograph.

Oisín's favourite among his large bronzes was the 'Two Working Men', now in Cork. This statue has had a chequered history. Originally it was commissioned by the Irish Transport and General Workers' Union to stand outside Liberty Hall in Dublin. However, the Paving Department of Dublin Corporation refused permission for its erection on the grounds that it would constitute an obstruction. After a number of years in storage, it was loaned to Cork, where the exiled Dublin pair now gaze up—with a delightful blend of cynicism and respect—at the towering County Hall.

Though Oisín gave the appearance of being a calm, even serene person, he actually drove himself very hard indeed. His method of work seemed leisurely, and the day was punctuated by snacks and coffee-breaks, as well as a nap after lunch. But apart from these respites, he worked all day, every day, often continuing until late at night. And even when at rest, he would usually be turning over in his mind some new idea for a job—he despised day-dreaming as the lowest form of human activity.

His almost obsessional commitment to his work explains his remarkably large and varied output, but it also took its toll on his health. In his sixty-first year he suffered a severe heart-attack during a crucial stage in the construction of the full-size plaster model for the 'Chariot of Life', destined for the Irish Life Centre, Lower Abbey Street, Dublin. He made a fair recovery, and managed to get the plaster ready to be handed over to the

Oisín Kelly and the Taoiseach, Jack Lynch, with the silver St Patrick's Breastplate which was presented to his Holiness Pope John Paul II on his visit to Ireland. Photograph Lensmen, Dublin.

foundry. He also started work on two further large commissions. One of these was a turf-cutter for the Bord na Móna headquarters in Baggot Street. Unfortunately, the construction engineer found that a full-scale version of this design would be top-heavy, so Oisín had to return to the drawing-board. Before he had prepared another design, he suffered a stroke. This caused him to relinquish the commission, which was subsequently taken up by John Behan, whose fine turf-cutter can be seen outside the Bord na Móna headquarters today.

Turf-cutter, *14 ins. high, bronze.*

Oisín never completely recovered from his stroke, but he continued to work, mainly at a statue of the harpist, Carolan, for Mohill, Co. Leitrim. In this undertaking he was assisted by the young sculptress Lorna Skrine. He died at the age of sixty-five in October 1981, four months after the death of his wife, Ruth. His 'Chariot of Life' was unveiled the following summer.

His statue of Carolan was unfinished at his death, but Lorna Skrine accomplished with great skill and sensitivity the difficult task of completing the full-scale plaster model and supervising its casting into bronze. It was unveiled by President Hillery on August 10th 1986.

Oisín was particularly concerned to demythologize the artistic experience. In his view, it is false to make a distinction between 'art' and 'craft', and he frequently said that he regarded himself simply as a craftsman. In an unpublished lecture he expressed this idea in characteristically forceful terms, "any woman who knits a pullover for her husband has the same kind of experience as Michelangelo painting the ceiling of the Sistine Chapel. She knows essentially all there is to know about art". He was suspicious of the concept of artistic inspiration, and attached more importance to technical expertise. He also stressed the necessity of careful preparation for every job. In relation to his own work, this meant that for every finished article there were dozens—even hundreds—of rejected models and preliminary sketches.

He liked to work from commission—he preferred that the desire for a work of art should precede its manufacture, and paid great attention to the requirements of his customers. It was obvious that he derived great pleasure from his work, though naturally some jobs aroused his enthusiasm more than others. He was never totally satisfied with the end product. In his own words, 'the created object is for the creator always less than the image after which it was made".

Fergus Kelly

ACKNOWLEDGMENTS

I am very grateful to the following for assisting me in various ways in the preparation of this article: Daniel Kelly, Nora Godwin, John O'Leary, Piccola Dowd, Elizabeth Kelly, Doreen Healy, Dorothy Walker, and Mary Hayes (for Kilkenny Design Workshops).

UNCATALOGUED DRAWINGS IN THE KING'S INNS LIBRARY

King John signing the Magna Carta. *Water-colour, 15.5 × 41 cms.*

The King's Inns Library, Dublin, possesses a portfolio of interesting drawings predominantly relating to Dublin sculpture. No details of its provenance are available but the collection of fifteen sketches may be divided into three categories: those relating to the Four Courts, to the Custom House, and others. There is a variety of drawing styles evident within the portfolio, ranging from a heavy-handed ink sketch to delicate wash drawings, indicating that more than one draughtsman was involved.

There is a definite connection between many of the drawings and Edward Smyth, whose versatile work is the best known of any Irish craftsman in the eighteenth century. The drawings are invaluable records of his plasterwork destroyed in the Four Courts in 1922 and hitherto visualized only from descriptions and poor photographs.

According to Strickland's *Dictionary*, Edward Smyth was born in Co. Meath in 1749, the son of a stone-cutter who moved to Dublin in 1750. Smyth studied at the Dublin Society Schools, where drawing and modelling were taught, in preparation for apprenticeship to a craftsman in a chosen field. The two best sculptors in Ireland at this time were John van Nost the younger, and Simon Vierpyl, both of whom were trained in England. Smyth was apprenticed to Vierpyl whose work is

A group of drawings in the King's Inns Library, Dublin, includes sketches of the sculpture of the Four Courts and of the Custom House, Dublin. **Anne Walsh** has studied the drawings and now describes them and their importance.

characterized by its exquisite finish and his understanding of the relationship of decorative sculpture to architecture. Smyth was subsequently employed as an ornament-carver for the contractor, Henry Darley, who introduced him to Gandon. Smyth was the principal sculptor employed by Gandon and it was the commission given to undertake sculptural decoration on the Custom House shortly after 1781 that brought Smyth to prominence. Recognizing the quality of Smyth's work, Gandon continued to use him to decorate his subsequent work.

The seven drawings in the King's Inns relating to the Four Courts reveal aspects of the original internal ornamental plasterwork. One drawing, displaying the mace and staff, fasces, axe and scales of Justice, depicts the piece of original detail which has survived today in two plaques over the north and south doors of the vestibule immediately north of the main portico. The remaining six draw-

ings relate to the decoration of the rotunda before its destruction in 1922. There are four designs for the bas-relief panels in the attic above the entrances to the courts illustrating the following subjects: William the Conqueror establishing Courts of Justice; King John signing Magna Carta; Henry II, having received the Irish chieftains, granting the charter to Dublin; and James I abolishing the Brehon Laws and publishing the Act of Oblivion.

William, centre, holds an upright sword in one hand and supports the Domesday Book in the other from which drops a scroll reading "Danegilt (*sic*), Norman Laws, feudal law 1066." Behind him stands a banner-bearer accompanied by relaxed soldiers carrying shields and bows. Facing the book are clergymen, uninterested warriors and one distraught man evidently mourning the loss of the old laws.

King John sits in an unusually awkward position on his throne as he signs the Magna Carta with a quill. A man on bended knee presents him with a book while a group of people gather to either side in front of tents, their gestures directing attention towards the monarch.

Henry, holding an upright sword, is seated on a royal throne and presents a scroll inscribed "charter to Dublin 1172" to Irish chieftains who, in turn, prepare

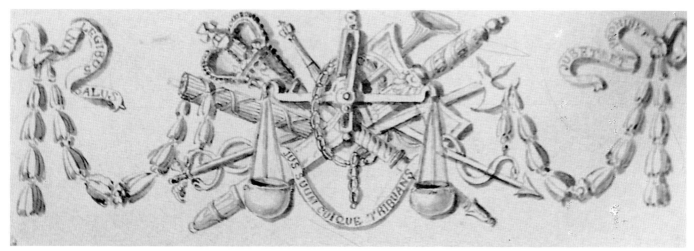

Panel "over the door in the vestibule of the Dublin Four Courts." *Water-colour, 7.5 × 21 cms.*

to present him with keys. Among them stands a bishop with the Dublin coat of arms by his feet. The King's entourage include men carrying a variety of weapons and a royal banner.

James I, holding a mace, hands scrolls inscribed "Act of Oblivion" and "Commission of Grace" to three Irishmen with outstretched arms, one of whom is genuflecting and supports a harp over two books. The King is accompanied by a line of courtly attendants.

The drawings relate very closely to the photographs taken by Constantine Curran before the destruction of the rotunda in 1922, each comprising a group of from seventeen to nineteen figures. Contemporary opinion regarded these panels as "elegantly designed and executed with a strict adherence to costume, in the habits, arms, and decorations of the times."[1] However, Curran's own reminiscences of this decoration are less complimentary, regarding their loss as the least to be regetted. "Their subjects were more than faintly absurd and their execution showed the weaker side of Smyth's genius . . . he here attempted a composition of numerous figures but only exhibited a mediocre ability."[2]

Curran singled out two criticisms: the isolation of the figures lacking in unity and rhythm, and their curious costume anachronisms. Curran points out that the Normans are depicted wearing plate armour instead of the conventional chain-mail. In assessing a comment which like his criticisms, is debatable, it must be borne in mind that the scale and

nature of the work was restrictive and consequently, detail would not necessarily be essential or work effectively. Smyth displayed a grandeur of conception rare in Irish art in eight large whole-length figures in relief, emblematic of Justice, Eloquence, Wisdom, Liberty, Mercy, Prudence, Law and Punishment, between the windows of the dome. Unfortunately only two drawings survive for these emblematic figures, representing Mercy and Justice. They are unfinished sketches with the consoles outlined in pencil and identified by their inscriptions. At this date modern dress was out of fashion in favour of classical costume and contemporary opinion admired the bold, masterly execution of the emblematic figures in "true style of the antique grotesque."

'Mercy' extends her right arm and carries an olive branch in her left. She stands on a console, obviously unfinished, drawn in pencil and containing the inscription "Mercy Thou bright resemblance of the Poor Divine." 'Justice' is personified as a blindfolded woman robed in flowing drapery. She holds a pair of scales over her head signifying her impartiality, as does her blindfolding. In her left hand she supports an upright sword emblematic of her power.

From the drawings it is difficult to ascertain the media envisaged for the construction of the sculptures – stucco or stone could have been intended. However, the use of stucco is likely if we are to believe the *Life of Gandon* according to which the work had been cast two years

earlier and then modelled *in situ*. Further, the contemporary *Dublin Evening Post*, and C.P. Curran, who saw the work before its destruction, described it as stucco-work.

Smyth's vigorous style, combined with a feeling for silhouette and for scale, is seen at its best on the Custom House. The strength of his work is evident from the Royal Arms set above the terminal pavilions of the two principal fronts. A water-colour sketch of superb quality and finish survives for the coat of arms with the words 'a duplicate' faintly written in pencil on the bottom left-hand side. A shield containing the harp of Ireland and surmounted by the crown separates the royal lion and unicorn. A contemporary observer criticized the beasts, "like a book whose preface is larger than its text, (they) may be said to be all head, and no body."[3]

However the sense of scale can be justified and the composition is highly effective when seen from below. Gandon appreciated Smyth's skills as an architectural sculptor and admitted that Smyth's proposals for the Royal Arms were better than Carlini's.

Carlini was also involved in making designs for the north front statuary of the Custom House in competition with the English sculptor, Thomas Banks (1735–1805). Paul Sandby in a letter to Gandon dated 2 February 1783 relates:

I had the pleasure of seeing the models [Note: four for the North and four for the South front of the Custom House] which Carlini has made for you, and think they

possess great merit, and with the four figures of Banks's which I also much approve of. I have taken the liberty of sending over some coloured aquatints, which will accompany the models for the statues . . .
I very much regret that it will not be in my power to send you in the case containing Banks's models my Encampments, as they are not yet printed . . ."[4]

Again, Carlini failed to secure the commission and the four statues representing the Quarters of the Globe – from east to west Europe, Asia, Africa and America – were executed by Banks and set against the attic of the north front. Four drawings from the King's Inns portfolio relate closely to these Custom House statues, representing parts of the world personified as female figures. Asia, Africa and America, depicted as full-length figures, were designed with competent draughtsmanship. There is no surviving evidence that Banks produced comparable drawings for any other commissions: it would be rash, therefore, to attribute these beautiful drawings to him.

Following the death of Thomas Banks,

Drawing for the Royal Arms, Custom House, Dublin. *Water-colour, 24.5 × 37.5 cms.*

the London *Times* of 22 May 1805 reported that the contents of the artist's studio at 5 Newman Street, London, were sold by auction. According to Christie's catalogue of Thomas Banks's sale, lot 63, containing "the four Quarters of the Globe, small whole length figures, for the Custom House at Dublin (two in clay and two in plaster)" was purchased by "Delville" at a price of £1.7s.0d.

It is possible that these three drawings were the work of Paul Sandby, who was assisting Gandon in accumulating proposals for the Custom House statues. Furthermore, Sandby's letter documents that Carlini forwarded representations of his plans for these figures.

'Asia' dons an oriental costume; her head-dress is the turban, and she holds a censer sketched in pencil. 'Africa' clasps a bow in her right hand and holds a cornucopia outlined in pencil in her left. Her head-dress is the head of an elephant and her attribute, the lion, lies behind her. 'America' carries a long bow in one hand and an inverted tomahawk in the other. She wears a head-dress of feathers and supports a short knife in her belt. A quiver full of arrows lies at her feet. Unfortunately, a representation of 'Europe' does not exist in this series. The fourth drawing differs in style and is clearly from the hand of another artist. 'Africa' on the left and 'America' to the right are depicted heavy-handedly in ink in contrast to the previous delicate wash drawings. Notes describing the standard symbolism concerning the two figures are included on the sheet:

North front statuary of the Dublin Custom House: pen and wash; pencil; 29.5 × 16 cms. Asia, Africa, America.

UNCATALOGUED DRAWINGS IN THE KING'S INNS LIBRARY

" 'Africa' is always understood by the elephant's trunk upon her head and lyon by her side. The iconologia gives her also a cornucopia in her hand filled with wheat. The common symbols of America have hitherto been the bow and arrows and feathers upon her head and about her middle to which I have added the tomahawk and scalping knife."

On 25 May 1921 the Custom House was set on fire and according to a contemporary newspaper report: "the statue of Plenty facing the river was blackened beyond all recognition, and the statue of Europe over the Northern entrance was similarly defaced and darkened."

A week later the *Irish Times* explains that the Northern facade suffered severely, though by no means irreparably. With regard to the statues as executed, the earliest useful representation is from the Lawrence photographic Collection in the National Library. Other sources to establish the original appearance of the roofline statuary of the North front of the Dublin Custom House are extremely limited. Very little attention was directed by topographical artists, draughtsmen or photographers towards the North front as opposed to the popular views of the river front.

Gandon's own drawings dated 1780[5] include part of the North front elevation with four statues set against the attic. However, the drawing is sketchy and incomplete and of little relevance to the statues as executed. Two later watercolour drawings in the Civic Museum, Dublin, represent proposed elevations for the Custom House, in which it is possible to discern the statues. However, the collection of the uncatalogued draw-

ings in the King's Inns Library provides invaluable sketches which relate very closely to the actual Custom House statues.

The three remaining drawings from the portfolio comprise a ground plan; 'a plan of the harbour of Dunlary'; and 'a draft of a light house and block house to stand below the piles near the barr of Dublin.' The ground plan is an odd one with a wide expanse of space separating two short parallel ranges. The plan may relate to an early proposal for a hall and library in the King's Inns by their treasurer William Caldbeck. According to Duhigg this amateur plan was subsequently rejected.

". . . the Treasurer's passion for architecture began to display itself in a singular manner. That extraordinary man formed the eccentric design of planning, superintending, and completing the hall and library, with the projected square."[6]

The plan of the harbour of Dunlary is drawn to scale and shows the position of the new pier high-lighted in red watercolour. The new pier projects about 400 feet. A report by Sir John Rennie in the National Library[7] concerning Kingstown Harbour contains a diagram illustrating three different modes proposed for completing the entrance. The plan proposed by Mr Cubitt relates somewhat to the King's Inns drawing, with a similar curved shape to either side of the entrance.

The draft of a light house and block house includes a ground plan and elevation drawn to scale accompanied by a detailed estimate of the charge. This structure is six storeys high on a hexagonal base with 1,135 cubic yards of

rough stone between the piles. The total cost involved to complete the project amounts to £6,271 11s.11d.

It is indeed rare in Ireland to have such an extensive collection of impressive eighteenth century drawings. The portfolio is in excellent condition and particularly proves invaluable as original sources for the history of Dublin sculpture. It is fortunate that the King's Inns Library has carefully preserved the unique collection, and I would like to acknowledge my thanks to Mr. Armstrong, Librarian of the King's Inns, for granting me access to the drawings and for his continued interest and assistance.

Anne Walsh

NOTES

1. *Dublin Evening Post*, Saturday 19 November 1796.
2. *C.P. Curran Notebook*, Vol. 9, Irish Architectural Archive.
3. *Dublin Evening Post*, 26 September 1786.
4. Letter from Paul Sandby R.A. to James Gandon Feb 2, 1783, printed in *The Life of James Gandon*, from materials selected for publication by Thomas J. Mulvany (Dublin, 1846), pp. 66-9.
5. National Gallery of Ireland, Nos. 6230-33.
6. B. Duhigg, *History of the King's Inns*, Dublin, 1806, p. 475.
7. Ms. 5217. Sir John Rennie's report respecting Kingstown Harbour 1835.

ACKNOWLEDGMENTS

Dr. E. McParland, History of Art Department, Trinity College, Dublin.
Mr. J. Armstrong, Librarian, King's Inns, Dublin.
Mr. D. Slattery, and Mr. A. Lindsay, Office of Public Works, Dublin.

LIST OF DRAWINGS

List of drawings from King's Inns portfolio with approximate measurements in centimetres.

Panel "over the door in the vestibule of the [Dublin] Four Courts." Water-colour 7.5 x 21.

Bas-relief panels in the Dublin Four Courts: William the Conqueror establishing Courts of Justice. Water-colour, 15 x 41. King John signing Magna Carta. Water-colour, 15.5 x 42. Henry II receiving the Irish chieftains, grants the charter to Dublin. Water-colour 13.5 x 41. James I abolishing the Brehon Laws and publishing the

Act of Oblivion. Water-colour, 13 x 42.

Statues in relief between the windows of the Dublin Four Courts dome: Mercy. Water-colour; pencil, 19 x 12.5. Justice. Water-colour; pencil, 20 x 18.

The Dublin Custom House Royal Arms. Water-colour, 24.5 x 37.5.

North front statuary of the Dublin Custom House: Africa. Pen & wash; pencil, 29.5 x 16. Asia. Pen & wash; pencil, 29.5 x 16.

America. Pen & wash; pencil, 29.5 x 16. Africa and America. Pen & ink, 21.5 x 36.

Ground plan. Pen & water-colour, 54.5 x 37.5.

A plan of 'the harbour of Dunlary' Dublin. Water-colour; pen & ink, 57 x 33.5.

'Draft of a light house and block house to stand below the piles near the barr of Dublin'. Water-colour; pen & ink, 47 x 30.

PAUL HENRY: AN IRISH PORTRAIT

Paul Henry (1876–1958) was one of the most influential artists to work in Ireland during the first decades of this century. Along with Walter Osborne, Jack B. Yeats and Sean Keating in the South and John Lavery and William Conor in the North, his is one of the few 'household' names among the list of Irish painters. To a considerable extent he founded single-handedly what one might call the Irish school of landscape painting. Certainly, he largely fostered the popular view of the Irish landscape, a view which fitted well with the social aspirations of the times. Moreover, as with the work of many influential artists–Constable in Suffolk, Cézanne in Provence, for example–once one has seen a 'Paul Henry' it is difficult to visit the west of Ireland and not to see it through his eyes. But, paradoxically, perhaps in part due to his early popularity and because his is a type of painting until recently out of fashion, it is only now that we have begun seriously to consider the importance and nature of his influence on Irish art.

Henry's principal contribution to Irish art was twofold: first, and most important, by the example of his early work he encouraged an interest in *avant-garde* painting, in Modernism, at a time when it was frowned upon. Second, through the Society of Dublin Painters, which he helped to found in 1920, he created, for the first time in Ireland, a forum where the more experimental artists, who were usually ignored by the Royal Hibernian Academy and other exhibiting bodies, could show their work. Reflecting on attitudes in Ireland towards *avant-garde* painting at that time, Henry later commented: "The French Impressionist movement," and, we might add, its aftermath, "which had left such a mark upon the whole of European Painting, had passed without leaving a ripple . . . upon the complacent self satisfaction of this country".[1] The expressions 'Modernism' and 'Modern Movement' are omnibus terms used to embrace those *avant-garde* tendencies, prevalent in the visual arts in the first half of this century, to which most of those artists subscribed. Generally speaking, the terms are regarded as representing the main stream of development in Western art from the time of Manet and include Impressionism, Post-Impressionism, Symbolism, Expressionism, Cubism, Surrealism and their der-

While it is sixteen years since a retrospective exhibition was held in Ireland of the paintings of Paul Henry, the prices of his pictures have increased dramatically and his work is widely known. Here, **Dr. Brian Kennedy,** who is preparing a biography of Henry, describes the artist's career and the influences upon him, and evaluates his contribution to Irish art.

ivatives. Essentially, Modernism marked an abrupt break with tradition and those artists who embraced it eschewed established forms of representational painting and concerned themselves with a more ideological and reflexive approach, in particular emphasizing qualities of the medium, of process and technique. Modernism represented the main thrust of development in the arts until about the late 1960s. It is therefore only now that we are able to view it as a historical phenomenon.

Ireland is usually regarded as having been late in encountering the Modern Movement; but this in fact was not so and for a time, at the end of the last century and the beginning of this one, a number of Irish men and women were in the vanguard of the new art. George Moore, for example, who was in Paris during the 1870s, knew several of the leading painters of the time and was one of their first champions;[2] Edward Martyn brought works by Degas and Monet[3] to Ireland in the 1880s, and Sarah Purser, who had studied at the Académie Julian in the late 1870s numbered Degas and Forain amongst her acquaintances. Also, *avant-garde* paintings were widely exhibited in Dublin earlier than in many larger centres, including either London or New York. Indeed, so much was the case that we might note here the main exhibitions of such works in Ireland during what were Paul Henry's formative years. In 1884, the year of the first *Salon des Indépendants* in Paris, James McNeill Whistler exhibited twenty-six works, including several of his then notorious 'Nocturnes', at the annual exhibition of the Dublin Sketching Club,[4] and in 1899 George Russell (AE), in the hope of stimulating the development of a genuinely Irish school of painting–significantly, Irish art was little affected by either

the rise of Irish nationalism in the nineteenth century or the Literary Revival at the turn of this century–organized an exhibition of modern paintings in Dublin which included works by Daumier, Degas, Manet, Monet, Whistler and others.[5] Russell hoped to do for the visual arts what the writers of the Revival had done for the literary arts. He felt that to achieve his purpose, rather than encourage the exhibition of works by only the foremost Irish artists, which would have been chauvinistic, one should exhibit the best of contemporary painting from outside Ireland, particularly from France, so as to provide a yardstick by which the native artists could measure themselves. Alas, his objective, at least as he envisaged it, was never reached and the whole business of the 'Irishness of Irish Art' has been an issue of debate amongst artists and historians ever since. In 1904 Hugh Lane, also in an attempt to stimulate a genuinely Irish school of painting, brought to the Royal Hibernian Academy many pictures from the celebrated collection of James Staats Forbes (1823–1904), an English railway manager and connoisseur, and thus set in motion the well-known events which led to the foundation in 1908 of the Dublin Municipal Gallery of Modern Art. Forbes's collection was particularly rich in paintings of the French Barbizon School and included numerous Corots. Lane obtained favourable terms for the purchase of many of the works exhibited provided that they went to a public gallery.[6] In 1906 Lane brought French Impressionist pictures, including several of his disputed Continental pictures, to Belfast's Municipal Art Gallery,[7] while in 1911 Ellen Duncan organized a show of works by contemporary French painters at the United Arts Club in Dublin,[8] and the following year she brought to the same venue the first Cubist pictures to be seen in Ireland. Unfortunately neither the catalogue nor reviews of the exhibition enable us to identify the works shown on this occasion;[9] all we know is that they included works by Picasso, Gris, Marchand and Herbin. The first two names especially, however, suggest that they included some of the latest innovations. By comparison, London had to wait until Roger Fry's exhibitions, 'Manet and the Post-Impressionists', held in 1910–11 and 'Second Post-Impressionist Exhibition',

PAUL HENRY: AN IRISH PORTRAIT

held in 1912, before it saw such works in large numbers; and the so-called 'Armory' show held in New York in 1913 was the first occasion on which modern art was seen there in quantity. Yet for all this activity on the part of a few individuals there was almost complete apathy in the Irish public for modern art and the Royal Hibernian Academy, despite Lane's efforts to help it in a number of ways, steadfastly refused to have anything to do with Modernism. Such, indeed, was to be its stance even until our own times.

For his part Paul Henry adopted an almost Post-Impressionist manner and he was the first Irish artist to do so. The main influences on him were the nineteenth century French painter of peasant life, Jean François Millet, Van Gogh and the American-born painter, James McNeill Whistler, whom he met in Paris. He first became acquainted with Millet as a boy in Belfast through Alfred Sensier's biography[10] and later saw his pictures for himself in Paris, where he also saw those of Van Gogh whose bold brush-work and strength of colour impressed him. But Whistler, through his emphasis on closely modulated tones and the more abstract qualities of the composition, had the greatest and the most lasting influence on him. Whistler's influence first dominated his early work, which comprised mainly illustrations for books and journals and occasional charcoal drawings of landscape (none of his early oils appears to have survived), done in the first decade of this century when he was living and working in London; but when he first went to Achill Island, in 1910, the life of the peasant community there recalled Millet who was his inspiration for the next ten years. Thereafter, until the late twenties, traces of Whistler predominate. These influences represent the two poles of his mature art, namely, from 1910–19, *genre* scenes of peasant life; and, from about 1920–21, landscape, increasingly devoid of figures. For the art historian the main problem in unravelling Paul Henry's career is to elucidate the development of these two aspects of his art and to chart his later treatment of landscape.

The main events in Henry's life are well-known, principally from his two published autobiographies, *An Irish Portrait* and *Further Reminiscences*.[11] Henry was born at 61 University Road, Belfast, in 1876, the third of four sons of the Rev.

Robert Mitchell Henry (d. 1891) and his wife Ann Berry (d. 1928). His eldest brother, R.M. Henry (1873–1950), was also well-known, having been a professor of Latin at Queen's University, Belfast, from 1907–38, a prominent advocate of Home Rule for Ireland and the author of *The Evolution of Sinn Fein* (Dublin, Talbot Press, n.d.). Life in the Henry household was rather severe and the Rev. Henry's strictly observed Protestant fundamentalism ensured a rigorous code of discipline which was maintained even after his death. Writing towards the end of his life in *Further Reminiscences*, Paul recalled that as children he and his brothers were 'held together' by a kind of parental despotism. They were not allowed to mix with or even to speak to other children. 'We "were not as other children" . . . we were like four "infant Samuels"', he said. In no other way could he explain the efforts that were made by his parents to keep them 'unspotted' from the world.[12] It is not surprising, therefore, that he later rebelled against this background and, once having left Belfast 'with only a scanty handful of regrets',[13] as he puts it, never again lived there. But he admired other aspects of his father's character and in later life was grateful to him for the discipline of the 'compulsory' walks which he took with his children in the country, especially by the river Lagan, for these gave him a lasting preference for country over city life.

While still at school Paul Henry studied art for a time under Thomas Bond Walker (1861–1933), a well-known portrait painter in Belfast. He then spent a year or so at the local college of art before going to Paris about 1898, the latter visit being made possible by the generosity of his cousin (Sir) John Henry MacFarland (1851–1935), a prominent educationalist and sometime chancellor of Melbourne University, who paid his way. In Paris he studied art for two or three years, first at the Académie Julian, where sound academic draughtsmanship was emphasized in the teaching and, secondly, at Whistler's Académie Carmen, where he learned to modulate tones in the manner characteristic of his later work. Henry clearly impressed Whistler who, in September 1899, suggested that, of the students, he should be given the job of looking after the routine financial affairs of the academy.[14]

Whether he was in fact offered this job is unknown and it would, perhaps, have been contrary to his inclinations to accept it. Moreover, from about that time, with his funds running short, he became conscious of the need to earn his living and so about 1900–01 he moved to London and for a number of years did black and white illustrations for publication in books, magazines and newspapers. While in Paris he had met the Scottish painter, Grace Mitchell (1868–1953), and they were married in September 1903. Together the Henrys shared lodgings in London with Robert Lynd,[15] whom Paul had known at school in Belfast, until the latter's marriage to the writer, Sylvia Dryhurst (1888–1952), in 1909. Lynd and his bride spent their honeymoon on Achill Island and, on hearing their enthusiasm for the island when they returned, Paul and Grace Henry decided to go and see the place for themselves. Thus they first visited Achill probably in the summer of 1910 and they stayed there for almost a year. In 1912 they settled on Achill and, apart from painting forays and visits to Belfast and other parts of the country, it was their home until late in 1919 when they moved to Dublin. However during the mid-twenties their marriage went sour, Grace had a brief flirtation with another man and in 1924 Paul met Mabel Young who had recently come from England to work in the Shelbourne Hotel. In 1930, after protracted legal negotiations, they separated–they were never divorced–and Paul and Mabel Young settled in Enniskerry, Co. Wicklow, where they lived until the 1950s. Grace, sadly, spent the rest of the '30s wandering alone; she painted from time to time in France and Italy but on the outbreak of war in 1939 returned to Ireland to live in an assortment of hotels, guesthouses and, occasionally, with her friends. She died in August 1953 and Paul then married Mabel Young. Paul Henry died on 24 August 1958 and Mabel, his second wife, died in 1974.

While the main events in Paul Henry's life are, as we have said, well known, the difficulty for the biographer arises in trying to extend the known facts, for Henry had scant regard either for the details of his personal life or for the chronology of his paintings, which he nearly always signed but rarely dated. The task, therefore, is twofold: firstly, one must construct an accurate and detailed chrono-

PAUL HENRY: AN IRISH PORTRAIT

logy of his life and career; and, secondly, one must try to match the body of his work with that chronology. Henry was egocentric and occasionally used artistic licence with historical facts in the same way as he might have done in a painted composition. Only a small handful of dates are mentioned in his two autobiographies, and these must be treated with caution, and neither Grace Mitchell nor Mabel Young is mentioned in either book, although *An Irish Portrait* is dedicated to the latter. Moreover both books deal with his career only until about 1920 or so. Next to his years in Paris, the biggest event in Paul Henry's life undoubtedly was his first visit to Achill. In an early draft of *An Irish Portrait* he tells us that this took place in 1913, but the book itself states 1912.[16] However, in an advance notice of the exhibition 'Paintings of Irish Life: Mr. & Mrs. Paul Henry', held at Pollock's Gallery, Belfast, in March 1911, the *Northern Whig* noted that both Paul and Grace Henry had recently been on Achill "for close on a year . . . living amongst the people and getting to know them."[17] Henry, in fact, went to Achill for a fortnight's holiday which he hoped to finance with a sort of roving commission from the *Graphic* and the magazine *Black and White* to prepare drawings for illustrations of the country and its people. But, with artistic licence, he later wrote in *An Irish Portrait* that once on Achill he wanted to stay there. "I had never planned anything," he said. "I always felt the urge of life should not be impeded and frustrated, and so far I had just drifted on the currents of life . . . I made another of my quick decisions, which I never regretted and taking my return ticket to London out of my pocket tore it into small pieces and scattered the fragments into the sea."[18] The truth of this story seems dubious, even though he first told it to an *Irish Times* reporter as early as 1925 and repeated it in a BBC broadcast in 1938,[19] and in any case he retained an address in London until the autumn of 1912;[20] but no doubt it appealed to his romantic spirit! But as far as his painting is concerned, from 1912 at the latest he painted exclusively Irish subjects.

About the summer of 1908 Paul and Grace Henry and Robert Lynd went to live at Knapp Hill, near Guildford, in Surrey. There Paul was inspired by the landscape, particularly with one area of bog land which he drew and painted time and time again.[21] 'Water Meadows', c.1907–10, a charcoal drawing now in the Ulster Museum, was almost certainly done at that place and time and even for such an early work his compositional technique of dividing the picture plane into two distinct parts, the upper dominated by cloud formations, the lower given to the landscape which is rendered with little detail, the two parts being linked by the upward thrust of a tree or some other compositional device, shows features which remained characteristic of his work through his career. The mood evoked by his handling of this scene is similar to that in many of his early Achill works so that it is not surprising that he felt his arrival on the island to be a sort of homecoming.[22] Also, earlier in 1910, as the result of a meeting which he had with Hugh Lane and Dermod O'Brien, he had exhibited for the first time at the Royal Hibernian Academy and so had already renewed his ties with Ireland. When he first arrived in Achill Henry was thirty-four years old and although he had carved a niche for himself as an illustrator he was clearly drifting away from such work. Moreover, in the light of his other activities and the growing number of his early exhibitions – he had contributed regularly to group shows at the Goupil Gallery, London, from 1904, held a joint exhibition with Grace at the Ulster Arts Club, Belfast, in 1907, showed at the Belfast Art Society in 1908 and 1909, and exhibited at the Royal Academy, London, in 1910 – it is clear that he was moving towards a career as a painter. The Achill visit therefore was timely for him; the island provided the subject-matter he subconsciously sought and the peasantry reawakened his early interest in Millet.

These points are well illustrated in 'Potato Diggers', c.1910–11, one of his first Achill pictures and one of his best ever works. Here the composition is succinct – the two-part division of the picture plane which we have already noted, the upward thrust of the figures linking these two parts – and the ruggedly dressed figures bent in toil express concisely the wordly lot of such people. The influence of Millet is clear, the pose of the figures owes much to 'The Spaders', which he knew from the illustration in Sensier's *Life*, and to the two figures who work in unison in 'The Gleaners', which he had seen in the Louvre. As in Millet, too, Henry's landscape has a certain monumentality and inspires a sense of timelessness – the latter quality also is a general characteristic of his work – attributes which suggest the religious and moral beauty which is often associated with labour. Henry exhibited this and similar pictures for the first time in the exhibition with his wife in Belfast during March 1911. Reviewing that show, the *Northern Whig* admired their departure from the conventional way of interpreting the landscape. They "have flung away the accepted formulas as boldly as Synge did when he began to do in drama what they have set themselves to do in colour" it commented, and admired Paul Henry's 'Prayer for the Departed', 1910–11 (present whereabouts unknown), "which has the dignity of the closing scene in *Riders to the Sea*," and 'Old People Watching a Dance', 1910–11 (private collection), a reminder that "dignity does not depend on the subject but on the manner in which it is treated."[23] The Belfast *News Letter* concurred with these views and singled out for praise the 'Potato Diggers', which it noted had been influenced by Millet, as being particularly successful.[24] Henry's first Dublin showing of his Achill paintings was in a joint exhibition with Grace Henry, Count Casimir Dunin-Markievicz, Mrs. Frances Baker[25] and George Russell (AE) at the Leinster Hall in October 1911. Of his subsequently better-known works on that occasion he showed 'Launching the Curragh', 1910–11 (National Gallery of Ireland [NGI]), and 'Clare Island', 1910–11 (whereabouts unknown), the latter epitomizing that feeling of timelessness to which we have alluded. But the *Irish Times*, however, did not care for his work, finding the "purple and green of his crudely composed 'Bog' [this picture cannot now be identified] . . . peculiarly distasteful."[26]

His technique developed slowly in these years and in March 1913 when he showed at Pollock's Gallery in Belfast he included another version of the 'Potato Diggers', painted in 1912 (NGI), in which the figure bending to the left with one arm outstretched is obviously a quotation from Millet's 'Gleaners', and the 'Turf Carrier', c.1912–13 (private collection), where the pose of the figure can be traced to illustrations in Sensier's book. The red skirts and petticoats depicted in these

PAUL HENRY: AN IRISH PORTRAIT

works were, he tells us in *An Irish Portrait*, almost universally worn by the women of Achill at that time. Of his purely landscape paintings of these years we have already mentioned 'Clare Island' but 'Connemara Landscape', 1913 (private collection), one of his very few dated works and thus useful as a guide to his handling of the medium (oils) at the time, is also a good example and again demonstrates the sense of stillness characteristic of his landscapes. As with his figure compositions the range of colours is limited in these works. Some measure of his growing prominence at this time was the inclusion of three of his pictures – 'A Load of Turf', 'Field-Workers in Achill' and 'A Prayer for the Departed' – in the exhibition of Irish art at the Whitechapel Art Gallery, London, in summer 1913. This was the first time his work had been included in such an exhibition.[27]

It is difficult to plot the development of his work between 1913 and 1920. He seems to have sold relatively few pictures at his various exhibitions in these years and the same works – or perhaps others with similar titles – turn up again and again as do his charcoal drawings such as 'The Mountainy Man' or 'A Man of the West', both 1910–19 (NGI). But several press reports do mention the continued freshness, breadth and simplicity of his work. In 1917 the *Irish Times* thought he was developing a decorative treatment of the landscape whereby his imagery was not realistic but was symbolically Irish and it singled out the 'Fairy Thorn' "where," it said, "the artist seems to have learned something from Japan without giving a foreign character to the landscape, which could only be Irish."[28] Indeed, as here, the tendency to flatten the picture plane and to emphasize the abstract nature of the various forms, influences from Whistler and Japanese prints, we shall see extended in his pictures of the early '20s.

In those works done on Achill, Paul Henry developed a style perfectly in harmony with his surroundings. In his treatment of figures, as well as his landscapes, he produced archetypes of the west of Ireland, much as Millet had done with the peasants in France. Yet, unlike Millet and the other French Realist painters, Henry's work has no social conscience, there is nothing didactic in it; it is the work only of an observer. In this respect he might be compared with Jack B. Yeats, his associate from 1920 in the Dublin Painters' Society and who had visited the West with Synge in 1905, who also was strictly an observer. But whereas Yeats worked from what he called 'a pool of memories' distilled through his sketchbooks, Henry merely recorded, never interpreted. Thomas MacGreevy, an important critic, however, did not admire what he called Henry's habit of 'overdramatising' the Irish peasants. "He sees them through the eyes of a Post-Impres-

Potato Diggers, c. 1910–11, oil on canvas, 71 × 81 cms. Private collection, Co. Cork.

PAUL HENRY: AN IRISH PORTRAIT

sionist Frenchman" he said. "Those hideous elementals set standing on a hilltop against a stormy sky are not Irish peasants. They are wanderers from that world of Neo-Romanticism, of unreal Realism, to which the characters of, say, Strindberg's plays belong."[29] MacGreevy would have felt happier with the Socialrealist manner of Sean Keating or Maurice MacGonigal, both of whom were more literary in suggestion, and who are often thought of as the true guardians of the west.

Although the years in Achill were happy and fruitful for Paul Henry, his wife, Grace, was less content there and from that time one can trace the restlessness which, sadly, became part of her later life. Grace had been brought up to a more comfortable existence than could be provided on Achill – her parents came from well-to-do families and money was plentiful at home – and no doubt, being by then in her forties, she missed her com-

forts. Also, she had a different outlook on life to Paul and sought brighter lights. Writing to Robert Lynd in March 1915, Jimmy Good, a fellow-Belfastman then working as a journalist in Dublin, commented after seeing the Henrys who were visiting the city: "Mrs. Paul is very sick at the idea of having to go back to Achill & failing Paris her thoughts turn longingly to St. Ives." And the following year he told Lynd: "Mrs. Henry . . . needs to be cheered up; Achill is for her I think a near approach to purgatory", while in March 1917 he wrote, again to Lynd: "Mrs. H. has come to Dublin for the winter . . . Henry, of course, declines to stir from Achill."[30] Such comments, unfortunately, chart the deterioration in their relationship from that time until they separated in the late twenties. It seems likely, however, that it was largely due to Grace's insistence that they moved to Dublin late in 1919 and they were for a time happy there.

On their arrival in Dublin the Henrys took a flat at 19 Lincoln Chambers but early in 1920 moved to a studio at 13A Merrion Row[31] which they occupied for the next ten years. This transfer to the city coincided with a new phase in Paul's work in which the figure compositions of his Achill period gave way to landscapes devoid of people, a phase which lasted for the rest of his career as a painter and in the first five or six years of which he produced some of his best remembered pictures. But of more immediate interest to us is his involvement from the summer of 1920 with the Society of Dublin Painters.

When he lived in London Henry frequented some 'at homes' organized by the English painter, Walter Sickert – another pupil of Whistler – at his studio in Fitzroy Street.[32] In 1907 from these gatherings emerged the Fitzroy Street Group which, revolving around Sickert, Spencer Gore, Harold Gilman, Robert Bevan and Charles Ginner – all Post-

Water Meadows, c. 1907–10, charcoal and white on paper, 34 × 46.5 cms. Collection Ulster Museum.

PAUL HENRY: AN IRISH PORTRAIT

Impressionists–was for a number of years the centre of the English *avant-garde*. Between them the members of the Group shared the expenses of running the Fitzroy Street studio. Out of this company was formed in 1908 the Allied Artists' Association–with which Paul Henry was also associated–which, guided by the critic Frank Rutter (b.1876), was a non-jury exhibiting body determined to counteract the exclusiveness of the New English Art Club and to be a sort of English version of the *Salon des Indépendants*.[33] With these models in mind, Paul and Grace Henry, in association with E.M. O'R. Dickey (another Belfast painter), Letitia Hamilton, Clare Marsh, James Sleator, Mary Swanzy and Jack B. Yeats, formed the Society of Dublin Painters in about June 1920 to circumvent the hostility of the Dublin art establishment towards modern painting. The Society took rooms on the top floor at 7 St. Stephen's Green and there held its first exhibition in August 1920. As well as regular group shows, each member was entitled to hold a one-man exhibition once a year. It is important here to remember that in those days art exhibitions in Ireland, especially small and one-man shows, were not frequent events and the latter were almost unknown. Apart from the annual exhibitions of the Academy, the Dublin Sketching Club and the Water Colour Society of Ireland, few commercial galleries or other venues existed where artists could exhibit their work independently. Before its occupation by the Dublin Painters, the St. Stephen's Green premises had been used as a studio by a number of artists, including an Italian painter called Catanio, who worked there around the 1850s, Augustus Burke (d.1891), Colles Watkins (1833–91), John Butler Yeats (1839–1922) and Walter Osborne (1859–1903). On Osborne's death Yeats again took it.[34] Following Yeats, the Gaelic League used the studio for its meetings. Rooms adjacent to this studio also had over the years an artistic clientele, being variously occupied by the Dublin Art Club, the portrait painter Sarah Cecilia Harrison (1863–1941), the Royal Society of Antiquaries, Patrick Tuohy (1894–1930), the Royal Hibernian Academy School (c.1918–39) and Sean O'Sullivan (1906–64).

The Society of Dublin Painters was inaugurated in unpropitious times politically and culturally. The events which culminated in the Anglo-Irish Treaty of 1921 were of immediate consequence; but the new Irish state, when it came into being in 1922, craved an identity for which it turned to the west, in particular to those areas where the traditions of Gaelic or 'Irish' Ireland were intact. Consequently as the '20s wore on, the political and cultural climate was increasingly coloured by government-inspired policies of isolationism. To a considerable extent this espousal of heritage centred on the culture of the Gaelic Renaissance, itself largely the creation of John Synge, W.B. Yeats, George Russell (AE), Edward Martyn and Augusta Gregory, that is, ironically, of the Anglo-Irish of thirty or so years earlier. As far as the visual arts were concerned the main characteristic required in the period was Symbolism; that works should not only arouse national and patriotic sentiment but, in Cyril Barrett's words, they should also *define* it; they should give some glimpse of what the people were striving for, of the values which they wished to preserve, and of the kind of life they intended to bring into being.[35] The full energy of the state was devoted to this purpose, notably after Mr. de Valera's victory in the election of 1932, and he and his party remained in power until 1948, the longest period of unbroken government in the history of the state. In the words of the historian Terence Brown:

> *"cultural life in the new state was dominated by a vision of Ireland . . . as a rural Gaelic civilization that retained an ancient pastoral distinctiveness. This vision was projected by artists, poets and polemicists despite the fact that social reality showed distinct signs that the country was adapting to the social forms of the English-speaking world and that conditions in rural Ireland were hardly idyllic . . . this imaginative interpretation of Irish rural life . . . served as an integrative symbol of national identity . . . .It helped to confirm people in a belief in Irish distinctiveness, justifying that political separatism which a revolutionary movement had made a lynch-pin of political life in the state."[36]*

And if the sceptic wanted proof of the distinctive genius of the Irish people he would be reminded of such works as the Cross of Cong, the Ardagh Chalice, the Books of Kells and Durrow: Ireland, in short, had a glorious past in the arts and could have an equally glorious future.

This was the volatile climate in which the Society of Dublin Painters established themselves. They, however, were not particularly concerned with nationality nor did they yearn for a distinctively Irish School and, as Bruce Arnold has remarked of their generation, many of them felt a strain and a self-consciousness at what 'being Irish' meant,[37] a predicament aggravated by the times and, no doubt for several of them, by a background in the protestant ascendancy. But they were the first innovators in Ireland to disregard the intransigence of the art establishment and their gallery, small as it was, became an important venue for exhibitions before other commercial galleries began to flourish.

From the outset the press generally were enthusiastic about the new Society. In 1923, for example, the *Freeman's Journal* thought it was producing some of the best painting in the country and a decade later the *Irish Times* in an editorial thought it had become "an institution of Ireland", putting the country "upon the map" of art. By 1942 Stephen Rynne felt able to write in *The Leader*: "If a person wanted to make an annual check-up of Irish art and had few opportunities for seeing exhibitions then he would best achieve his end by attending the Dublin Painters. Here are the liveliest of the living painters, the explorers and experimentalists . . . . They paint what they will, for the most part their touch is light, airy, deft."[38] In passing we might note some of the more *avant-garde* artists and works sponsored by the Dublin Painters: Paul Henry showed a version of his 'Potato Diggers' in 1920; E.M.O'R. Dickey, who studied art under Harold Gilman, a member of Sickert's Fitzroy Street Group, exhibited Post-Impressionist landscapes which were refreshing in comparison with the more sentimental work of most Irish artists. At the autumn exhibition in 1923 Mainie Jellett showed two Cubist compositions,[39] the first time that such pictures by an Irish artist were seen in Dublin; Cecil Salkeld, who studied art in Germany, showed works done in the manner of the *Neue Sachlichkeit* movement, which dominated European painting in the '20s. In the early '40s Ralph Cusack (1912–65), a painter now almost forgotten,[40] exhibited some of the first mildly Surrealist pictures to be seen in Ireland.

As well as promoting the cause of

Lakeside Cottages, c. 1923–30, oil on canvas, 40 × 60 cms. Collection Hugh Lane Municipal Gallery of Modern Art, Dublin.

The Fairy Thorn, c. 1917, oil on canvas, 35 × 81 cms. Private collection, Dublin.

PAUL HENRY: AN IRISH PORTRAIT

avant-garde painting through the Society of Dublin Painters Paul Henry, along with Arthur Power (d.1984), organized the exhibition 'Some Modern Paintings', held in Mills' Hall, Merrion Row, in January 1922 as part of Dublin Civic Week. In all about thirty works were shown on that occasion including some by the Continental artists Maillol, Marchand, Modigliani and Vlaminck, but the majority were by the younger British painters, many of whom Henry had known in London. Although the press spoke well of the show, Henry wrote later that "It is difficult to realise . . .how deep rooted was the ignorance and prejudice which existed at that time against any form of art which savoured, even remotely of modernism."[41]

Although he had founded the Dublin Painters Society, Paul Henry last exhibited there in 1926, but in those few years he produced, as we have said, some of his best compositions. By the early '20s his manner was mature and his subject-matter—landscape devoid of figures—firmly established. Increasingly his pictures assume a sense of stillness and timelessness rendered through a few bold shapes, a limited palette, simplicity of tone and, especially in the early '20s, an emphasis on the abstract qualities of the composition, characteristics unmistakably Whistlerian. These features are evident in 'Dawn, Killary Harbour', c.1922–23, perhaps his best ever work. However, if we compare this picture with the almost identical view in 'Leenane', 1913 (Ulster Museum), one of his few dated works, it is clear that he had a bold approach to landscape even at that early stage although his brushwork was then much more prominent and less assured. As in the Killary Harbour picture, in these years Henry often observed the landscape at dawn, savouring the stillness and purity of the air at that hour and in an interview with an *Irish Times* reporter in 1941 said he had always been struck by what he called the 'other-worldliness' and the 'sense of mystery' in the Irish landscape.[42] The absence in his work of literary references, characteristic of so many Irish painters, perhaps contributed to the underlying feeling for abstraction in his pictures. But, as Brian O'Doherty remarked, this duality of abstraction underpinning an apparently representational landscape, makes the best of Paul Henry's work important, for

it differentiates that which is regional and parochial in outlook from that which has more universal implications. "Without it," said O'Doherty, "he could be placed with his imitators, regional sentiment, playing for sentiment."[43] Yet, despite these abstract qualities, one senses also in him an intuitive reaction to the landscape—for Henry was no theorist—and an omnipresent awareness of human significance in the eternal conflict between man and the unpitying forces of nature.

From this time onwards he retained the compositional formula of boldly juxtaposed shapes, usually with the sky occupying at least half of the composition, and often, as in 'A Connemara Village', c.1923–30, picked out a few elements—a cottage, turf stacks, the play of light on water—which he highlighted in greater detail than the rest of the composition. Along with the latter picture, 'Lakeside Cottages', c.1923-30, is one of his best works of the time and represents the quintessential Paul Henry. Such pictures helped to foster the popular view of the Irish landscape and fitted well with the social aspirations of the times. His successes in these years also included a drawing of Arthur Griffith which was bought by the British signatories to the Anglo-Irish treaty and subsequently presented to the Irish government; and in 1922 the French government purchased from the exhibition of Irish art then in Paris his 'West of Ireland Village' for the Luxembourg Gallery,[44] a signal honour for an Irish painter at that time.

About 1925 two of Henry's paintings, 'Connemara' and a 'View of Lough Erne' (whereabouts of both unknown) were reproduced as posters for the London Midland and Scottish Railway Company and distributed to tourist bureaux in Europe and North America. The former picture was also reproduced on the cover of the LMS booklet *Travel in Ireland*. His lucid style was well suited to contemporary reproduction techniques which demanded simplified shapes and the use of only three or four colours. These posters perhaps fixed the archetypal 'Paul Henry' in the public mind but, in the long run, being displayed in literally thousands of sites, they debased his memory more than it deserves. This, perhaps, was the period of his greatest esteem by the public in his lifetime, but, despite these successes, from the mid to

late '20s, at a time when his domestic affairs were in disarray and his financial difficulties were mounting, his work began to fall in quality and became ever more hackneyed. Jimmy Good described his situation at the time in a letter to Sylvia Lynd: "Paul and Grace are having a very thin time, as the picture market in Dublin is dead." But they had spirit, for he continued: "As you would expect they have decided to celebrate the run of ill-luck by taking a furnished flat in Fitzwilliam Square at £3.10 shillings a week with 10/- to 15/- extra for a cook. I admire their nerve but shudder at the reaction that is going to follow in the near future." And some months later he wrote to her again saying that Paul was "desperately hard up and I don't see much chance of him making money in Dublin at present or indeed for a long time to come . . . Grace is talking of another trip to Paris and I don't suppose the question of how it will be done troubles her in the slightest."[45] Perhaps, with these problems, it is not surprising that his enthusiasm for Modernism waned at the same time—despite having recently organized the Dublin Civic Week exhibition—and he was to remain to the end, as his friend Arthur Power observed, guided by the constructional theories he had learned in the Paris of 1900. Power also recounted that some time later he suggested to Henry that he should visit Paris again to see what the Dadaists, the Surrealists and others were doing, but in reply he shrugged his shoulders, asking "What would I get out of it?"[46] In the late twenties, too, there disappeared the sometimes vibrant colours of his earlier work and the landscape, both literally and metaphorically, seems to have subdued him.

In 1930, after he finally separated from Grace, Paul Henry left Dublin and settled in Carrigoona Cottage, near Enniskerry in Co. Wicklow. There he and Mabel Young remained until a year or so before he died. He had rarely visited the west after his move to Dublin in 1919 and from now on he painted mostly in Co. Wicklow with only occasional forays elsewhere. In 1929 his 'Customs House, Dublin', c.1929 (private collection), was used as a poster for Dublin Civic Week and even at this date, in the thrust and counter thrust of line and the simplicity of the underlying forms, one can still sense the abstract nature of the composition. But as his domestic life grew more

PAUL HENRY: AN IRISH PORTRAIT

stable, his art became less adventurous and often in his pictures painted in these years the composition devolved to a *cliché* and his brushwork and handling of the medium were at times insensitive, although 'Kinsale, Co. Cork', 1939 and 'Ballintoy, Co. Antrim', 1941 (both private collections), are more assured even if a little repetitive. By the '30s, however, he had fallen prey to his own imagery and popularity. Reviewing the Royal Hibernian Academy show in 1937 the *Irish Builder* commented: "To say that in No. 117 ['The Village on a Hill'] is a typical Paul Henry is nothing to his discredit. Paul Henry would, no doubt, paint other things besides mountains if his public would let him. Seeing how well he does these mountains, one cannot blame his public for continually demanding more. One can only hope that it does not become a vicious circle."[47]

Henry painted few portraits and was less at ease in this *genre* than with landscapes. His best examples undoubtedly are all charcoal drawings and include his 'Connemara Peasant', 1910–19, done on Achill–in works such as this we can see the influence of Van Gogh and Daumier, especially in his characterization of the sitter–and 'President Cosgrave', c.1922–3 (private collection), the latter in retrospect arousing a certain pathos. Of his portraits in oils that of his brother, 'Pro-

fessor R.M. Henry', painted in 1933 for The Queen's University, Belfast, is perhaps the best. As in his drawings, here the character of the sitter is conveyed with assurance but the hands and the articulation of the arms are weak. Unfortunately this picture was destroyed in a fire in the Great Hall at The Queen's University some years ago. There are, however, a number of photographs of it. Also, an exact copy in oils was made from one of these photographs by T.E. Spence and that copy now hangs in the special collections reading room of the library at the university. Another copy of the original portrait, painted by James Sleator, P.R.H.A. (1889–1950), in 1948, hangs in St. Salvator's Hall at the University of St. Andrews where the sitter taught for a time after retiring from Belfast.

About 1945 or '46, as the result of an illness, Paul Henry became virtually blind and ceased painting; he then turned to writing and produced the two autobiographies to which we have referred. Despite the repetitiveness of his later work, he never became an academic painter, and while the landscape at times subdued him it never humbled him. Regardless of the obvious influence of his work, Henry was a lone figure in Irish art because none of his landscape contemporaries–Charles Lamb (1893–1964),

James Humbert Craig (1878–1944) or Frank McKelvey (1895–1974), for example–showed a rigour comparable to the work of his years in Achill or the early Dublin period and, by comparison, at best they remained *raconteurs* of the landscape and at worst they turned his vision into a formula. Lamb, Craig and McKelvey were often grouped together by critics when reviewing the Royal Hibernian Academy exhibitions where their works were easily compared one with another. In 1925 the *Irish Times* thought they and some of their fellow-Northerners virtually formed a 'Belfast school' of painting which, it said, "surpasses the Southern painters."[48] Indeed, it is interesting to note that that school of landscape painting–which is perhaps the nearest thing which has emerged this century by way of a distinctly Irish school, Sean Keating and Maurice MacGonigal notwithstanding, at least as popular imagination would have it–which we have described as descending from Paul Henry through Lamb, Craig and McKelvey and which was continued in the fifties and later by Maurice Wilks (1910–84) and numerous others, was an almost entirely Northern-inspired affair. That is the legacy of Paul Henry's work.

Brian Kennedy

NOTES

(The author is currently preparing a biography of Paul Henry and would be grateful to hear from any reader who may have information about or pictures by the artist.)

1. Paul Henry, *Further Reminiscences*, Belfast, Blackstaff Press, 1973, p. 68.
2. He was one of the first to write about Degas ('Degas: The Painter of Modern Life', *Magazine of Art*, November 1890, pp. 416-25) and Manet painted three portraits of him (these are the oils painted in 1878 and 1879, now in the Metropolitan Museum of Art, New York, and the Paul Mellon Collection, Virginia, respectively, and the pastel of 1879, also in the Metropolitan Museum. For details of these works see Phoebe Poole and Sandra Orienti, *The Complete Paintings of Manet*, Penguin Books, 1985, Cat. Nos. 251, 278A and 278B.) Moore was a *habitué* of the Nouvelle Athènes, a café on the Place Pigalle. During the 1870s and later, it was frequented by many of the leading writers and artists. It was there that he met Manet, Degas, Renoir, Pissarro, Monet and Sisley.
3. Martyn owned two pastel drawings by Degas, 'Two Ballet Dancers in the Dressing Room',

c.1880 and 'Two Harlequins', c.1885, and an oil by Monet, 'A River Scene, Autumn'. All of these works are now in the National Gallery of Ireland, Nos. 2740, 2741 and 852 respectively. They were bequeathed to the Gallery by Martyn along with a Corot, 'Willows', No. 853.
4. It was one of Whistler's 'Nocturnes' that caused Ruskin to accuse him in 1877 of 'flinging a pot of paint in the public's face', a remark which led to their celebrated libel case. The 1884 exhibition also included his 'Portrait of the Painter's Mother' (1871), now in the Louvre, 'Portrait of Thomas Carlyle' (1872-3), Glasgow Art Gallery and 'Portrait of Lady Meux' (1881-2), Frick Collection, New York. Whistler intended to give the first ever reading of his 'Ten O'Clock' lecture–in which he set down his aesthetic stance–at the exhibition but that did not materialize. See Ronald Anderson, 'Whistler in Dublin, 1884', *Irish Arts Review*, Vol. 3 No. 3, pp. 45-51.
5. The exhibition was held at the Leinster Hall and included, amongst other works, Edward Martyn's two pastels by Degas and his oil by Monet (see note 3 above), a Manet, 'Portrait

of a Lady', lent by George Moore, and six Whistlers, including 'Miss Cicely Alexander', the latter now in the National Gallery, London.
6. The background to the exhibition of the Staats Forbes pictures, the subsequent events which led to the opening of the (Hugh Lane) Municipal Gallery of Modern Art and the issue of Lane's so-called 'Continental Pictures' are set down in Thomas Bodkin, *Hugh Lane and His Pictures*, Dublin, Stationery Office, 1932 and later editions.
7. 'Exhibition of Modern Paintings', Municipal Art Gallery, Belfast, 20 April-26 May 1906. As honorary director of this exhibition, which was arranged by a joint committee of the Ulster Arts Club, the Belfast Art Society and the Ulster Society of Architects, Lane hoped to encourage in Belfast an interest in modern painting, as he was doing in Dublin. Indeed, in his introduction to the catalogue of the exhibition he wrote (p. ix) "It seems as if it were ordained that Belfast should have the honour of founding the first distinct 'School' in Ireland."

NOTES CONTINUED ON PAGE 54

Connemara Landscape, *1913, oil on canvas, 67 × 79 cms. Private collection, Belfast.*

Dawn, Killary Harbour, c. 1922–3, oil on canvas, 69.1 × 83.3 cms. Collection Ulster Museum.

PAUL HENRY: AN IRISH PORTRAIT

8. 'Works by Post-Impressionist Painters', United Arts Club, Dublin, 25 January–14 February 1911. Many of the forty-seven works shown on this occasion were borrowed from the exhibition 'Manet and the Post-Impressionists' held at the Grafton Galleries, London, the previous November. The best known artists included were Cézanne, Denis, Derain, Gauguin, Van Gogh, Maillol, Marquet, Matisse, Rouault, Picasso, Signac and Vlaminck. Ellen Duncan (c.1850–1937), born in Dublin, was a founder member of the United Arts Club in 1907. In October 1914 Lane appointed her curator of the Dublin Municipal Gallery of Modern Art.

9. See 'Modern French Pictures at the United Arts Club', *Irish Review* 11, May 1912, pp. 164–6; 'Post Impressionists and Cubeists' (sic), *Irish Times*, 29 March 1912.

10. Alfred Sensier, *Jean-François Millet: Peasant and Painter*, translated by Helena De Kay, London, Macmillan & Co., 1881.

11. Paul Henry, *An Irish Portrait*, London, Batsford, 1951; Henry, *Further Reminiscences*, op. cit., the latter published posthumously at the time of the retrospective exhibition of his work held at Trinity College, Dublin and the Ulster Museum, Belfast, in 1973. Brian O'Doherty, 'Paul Henry–The Early Years', *University Review* 11, 1960, is the first writer to assess the influences on and the development of Henry's work.

12. Henry, *Further Reminiscences*, op. cit., pp. 15, 20.

13. Henry, *An Irish Portrait*, op. cit., p. 8.

14. The suggestion was made in a letter to the teacher in charge of the Académie Carmen. Whistler's phrase was "why should not . . . the little Irishman be run for Massier . . . " As Henry was the only Irishman to attend the Académie Carmen this phrase clearly refers to him (Whistler Papers in the Library, Glasgow University, ref: Whistler A29). I am grateful to the University Court of the University of Glasgow for permission to quote from this letter. My thanks are also due to Mr. Ronnie Anderson of the department of Art History at the University of St. Andrews for drawing my attention to it.

15. Robert Wilson Lynd (1879–1949), educated at the Royal Belfast Academical Institution (RBAI) and at The Queen's University, he went to Manchester to work on the *Daily Dispatch* before going to London as a freelance journalist. He later became well-known, and is best remembered as an essayist, his finest work appearing under the pseudonym 'Y.Y.' which he used in the *New Statesman* from 1913–45. His essays were collected in book form at intervals. Of his other books, *Home Life in Ireland*, London, Mills & Boon, 1909, *Rambles in Ireland*, London, Mills & Boon, 1912 and *Ireland a Nation*, London, Grant Richards, 1919, are, perhaps, the best known. His wife, Sylvia, was a novelist and poet.

16. Paul Henry Papers, Trinity College, Dublin (TCD), MS 7415; *An Irish Portrait*, op. cit., p. 48, respectively.

17. 'Pictures of Irish Life', *Northern Whig*, Belfast, 11 March 1911.

18. Henry, *An Irish Portrait*, op. cit., pp. 5-6.

19. 'Connemara for the Artist: Mr. Paul Henry's Experience', *Irish Times*, 4 August 1925 and 'As I See It', BBC radio, 29 March 1938, respectively.

20. The catalogue of the annual exhibition of Belfast Art Society, held in the Municipal Art Gallery, Belfast, during October-November of that year gives his address, as for the previous year, as 13 Pembridge Crescent, London, W.

21. Henry, *An Irish Portrait*, op. cit., p. 2.

22. Henry Papers, op. cit., TCD, MS 7415.

23. 'Paintings of Irish Life', *Northern Whig*, 13 March 1911. Henry had met Synge and W.B. Yeats casually in Paris in about 1898–9. Later, in London, he read *Riders to the Sea*. "There was something in Synge that appealed to me very deeply," he wrote. "He touched some chord which resounded as no other music ever had done" (*An Irish Portrait*, op. cit., p. 48). Generally speaking the members of the Royal Hibernian Academy may be considered as the exponents of the more conventional approach to landscape painting which Paul Henry shunned.

24. 'Mr. & Mrs. Paul Henry's Paintings', *News Letter*, Belfast, 13 March 1911.

25. Frances Baker (1873–1944), painter mainly of landscapes with figures and occasional portraits. For a brief biographical note see Alan Denson, *Printed Writings by George W. Russell (AE): A Bibliography*, Evanston, Illinois, Northwestern University Press, 1961, p. 222.

26. 'The Five Artists: Pictures at Leinster Hall', *Irish Times*, 16 October 1911.

27. 'Irish Art', Whitechapel Art Gallery, London, 21 May–29 June 1913. Henry's works were catalogued as Nos. 35, 50 and 158 respectively. As Hugh Lane and Dermod O'Brien were members of the exhibition committee, they almost certainly were responsible for his selection.

28. *Irish Times*, 16 April 1917.

29. Thomas MacGreevy, draft for an article, 'The Rise of a National School of Painting', MacGreevy Papers, TCD, MS 8002-19.

30. Letters of 21 March 1915, 11 July 1916 and 12 March 1917 respectively (private collection; hereinafter referred to as Lynd correspondence). James Winder Good (1872–1930), educated at RBAI (where he met Paul Henry) and Queen's College, Belfast, had a distinguished career as a journalist. He worked on the Belfast *News Letter* and the *Northern Whig* before going for a time to Liverpool. From 1918 until its closure in the early twenties he was a leader writer on the *Freeman's Journal*. He was associated with Sir Horace Plunkett and George Russell (AE) in founding the *Irish Statesman* and became its assistant editor before leaving to join the Irish Independent. He was also for a time the Irish correspondent for the *New Statesman* and was a founder member of the Ulster Literary Theatre (obituary, *Belfast Telegraph*, 3 May 1930).

31. The rooms in Lincoln Chambers had previously been the studio of the Dublin Arts Club (Good to Sylvia Lynd, letter of 11 December 1919, Lynd correspondence); the Merrion Row studio had previously been occupied by, amongst others, Nathaniel Hone, RHA (1831–1917) and Walter Osborne, RHA (1859–1903) (Henry, *Further Reminiscences*, op. cit., p. 66).

32. Henry, *Further Reminiscences*, op. cit. p. 67. Sickert in these years was the most sympathetic advocate in England of *avant-garde* painting. In his studio he gathered around him many of the young and progressive painters of his day. For a note on his 'at homes' see Robert Emmons, *The Life and Opinions of Walter Richard Sickert*, London, Faber & Faber, 1941, pp. 133-4. Hugh Lane also attended these meetings (Wendy Baron, *The Camden Town Group*, London, Scolar Press, 1979, p. 13).

33. For a note on the Fitzroy Street Group and the Allied Artists' Association see Wendy Baron, *Sickert*, London, Phaidon, 1973, pp. 104-5. Although he frequented its meetings, Henry was not a full member of the former.

34. Katherine Tynan gives a vivid description of the studio during Yeats's occupancy in her *Twenty-five Years: Reminiscences*, Dublin, 1913, p.187.

35. Cyril Barrett, 'Irish Nationalism and Art 1800–1921', *Studies*, winter 1975, p. 398.

36. Terence Brown, *Ireland: A Social and Cultural History 1922–79*, London, Fontana, 1981, p. 98.

37. Bruce Arnold, *A Concise History of Irish Art*, revised ed., London, Thames & Hudson, 1977, p. 139.

38. 'Modern Artists', *Freeman's Journal*, 20 October 1923; 'The Dublin Painters', *Irish Times*, 3 February 1933; *The Leader*, 21 February 1942, respectively.

39. One of these may have been 'Abstract', 1922, now in the Ulster Museum (No. 2296).

40. In 1958 he published *Cadenza: An Excursion*, London, Hamish Hamilton, a sort of autobiographical novel, but in it made no mention of his painting.

41. Henry, *Further Reminiscences*, op. cit., p. 65.

42. H.L. Morrow, 'The Art of Paul Henry', *Irish Times*, 1 November 1941.

43. Brian O'Doherty, op. cit., p. 26.

44. As the collection at the Luxembourg Gallery has long since been dispersed to other French museums this picture is now in the Musée National d'Art Moderne, Paris. It was bought from the exhibition 'World Congress of the Irish Race', held at the Galeries Barbazanges, Paris, during January-February 1922.

45. Letters of 5 October 1923 and 15 April 1924 respectively (Lynd correspondence).

46. Arthur Power, 'Reassessments–17: Paul Henry', *Irish Times*, 29 June 1971.

47. 'Wisbeach', *Irish Builder*, 1937, p. 480.

48. 'Royal Hibernian Academy', *Irish Times*, 6 April 1925.

THE WHITE CITY – SIR JOHN LAVERY IN TANGIER

*. . . the chief note of Tangier is its
whiteness. White houses, sands like snow,
and, above all, a dazzling white
atmosphere.[1]*

These words were written by the Scottish laird-adventurer, R. B. Cunninghame Graham, in an article entitled 'The Atmosphere of Morocco', which was illustrated with twelve paintings by John Lavery. Despite its general title, the essay concentrates for the most part on Tangier, a city which, by the time of publication in 1909, had already received numerous eulogies. Graham's article appeared in *Sketching Grounds*, a special number of *The Studio*, a magazine in whose columns Frank Brangwyn and Norman Garstin had already recorded their impressions of the 'white city'.[2] After his visit to Tangier in 1893, Brangwyn exhibited pictures which portrayed similar motifs to those of Lavery.[3] These contacts and coincidences are part of a much larger phenomenon in the nineteenth century.[4] From the 1830s North Africa and the Middle East became places of artistic pilgrimage, but while painters such as Lewis, Lear, Gérôme and Holman Hunt preferred the eastern Mediterranean, in Lavery's era an instant Orient was to be found by simply crossing the Straits of Gibraltar. Where Orientalist painters concentrated upon narrating the Eastern way of life, the rituals of the Mosque and the Harem, Lavery's generation looked to this environment for its colour. Describing this to a fellow painter in 1897, Norman Garstin wrote,

> *. . . that wall in front of you is homely
> whitewash, and steeped for a moment in
> violet shade; a door opens and a rectangular
> slab of yellow light from the opposite wall
> of the patio makes you blink, and deepens
> the violet of the near wall; purple patches
> of shade stain the patio's red tiles with
> silhouetted pictures of fig leaves . . .[5]*

It has been claimed that for Lavery the strong light, cloudless sky, white walls and bright colour of Arab dress helped to cleanse his eye after sustained periods of studio portraiture.[6] This was certainly the case with the first visit to Morocco which took place in the early weeks of 1891.[7] Up to that point the artist had been preoccupied with the completion of the large commemorative group portrait of the 'State Visit of Queen Victoria to the International Exhibition, Glasgow,

For much of his life, Sir John Lavery regularly stayed in Morocco where he produced many fine paintings. **Kenneth McConkey**, Head of the Department of Historical and Critical Studies at Newcastle upon Tyne Polytechnic, assesses the importance of the Moroccan visits and places them in the context of their time.

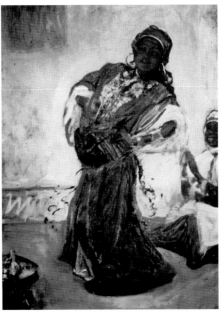

*Sir John Lavery, A Moorish Dance, 1893–1911,
oil on canvas, cut-down, 50 × 30 ins.
Private collection.*

1888'.[8] Since he had a vested interest in ensuring the success of this work, Lavery remained on hand for its showing in Glasgow in December 1890.[9] Some time soon after this event, he set sail for North Africa. Even for someone who was already well practised at painting *en plein air*, Morocco must have been as much a culture shock to him as it had been to Delacroix sixty years earlier. The streets of Tangier may not have been full of colour, but their white buildings and the clear blue sky overhead, enabled colour to be perceived afresh. The experience encouraged the painter to draw on canvas with a loaded brush and almost immediately his work began to develop in a painterly way. Within a few years, the light sable sketching of his Glasgow period gave way to a richer and more sensuous application. This development

parallels the first three trips to Morocco. Thereafter, in the early years of the century, Lavery returned regularly to Tangier, although it is difficult to date his sojourns precisely.[10] It can be assumed that after the purchase of his house, Dar el Midfah, around 1904, he went to Tangier more regularly, probably every year until 1914. There were no further visits until 1919 and in 1920 Sir John and Lady Lavery attended the wedding in Tangier of his former model, Mary Auras, to Nigel d'Albini Black-Hawkins. In later years, having become friendly with the Churchills, the Laverys found themselves more often on the Riviera than in North Africa. Lavery's North African canvases appeared principally in five London exhibitions during the thirty years when he made Tangier a regular winter base.[11]

The diversity of this work is staggering. It is often the case that in Tangier he produced his most technically advanced work. As an artist-reporter, his visual intelligence was continually challenged. However, although his painting changed stylistically during this central period of his productive life, the features of the Tangier *oeuvre* cannot easily be disassociated from the general autographic quality of his work at a particular time.[12] In a sense, the intrinsic character of the Moroccan scenes can more immediately be confronted if the work is sub-divided by categories of subject matter. The following notes may suggest a typology, a series of sub-*genres*, under which this varied production can be classified and discussed. There are, for instance, works which relate to well known exhibition-pieces, such as 'A Moorish Dance'. There are works which record specific and therefore datable events such as 'The Wreck of the *Delhi*' and the 'Funeral of Kaid MacLean', with their studies. In addition to these, there are numerous small landscapes and cityscapes which record expeditions such as the journey to Fez in the spring of 1906. Often in these incidences, Lavery's documentarist's instinct would lead him to specially inscribe groups of related pictures, a practice which owed its origins to the portrait studies of the Glasgow International suite. However, the majority of Lavery's Moroccan pictures were painted in Tangier and its immediate environs. They are street, market, roof-top and garden scenes, interiors and portraits, and a

The White City, 1893, oil on canvas, 22¾ x 31¼ ins.
Ewan Mundy Fine Art.

A West Wind, 1911, oil on canvas, 25 × 30 ins.
Private collection, photograph courtesy Pyms Gallery, London.

THE WHITE CITY – SIR JOHN LAVERY IN TANGIER

notable sequence of views of Tangier beach.

On the first Moroccan trip, Lavery's painting activities were confined to Tangier. Scenes of the city gates and street traders with their lush slabs of bright colour, allow the spectator to infer an artist revelling in the richness of a novel experience. 'Bab es Sek'[13] and 'Sok el Lechina'[14] reveal an evident delight in abstract pattern, equivalent to Whistler's 'pochades' or 'little games' played with Chelsea shop fronts. These general characteristics are equally clear in the roof-top picture of 'Tangier from the Hotel Continental', but there is greater premeditation in a larger work such as 'Snake Charmers'.[15] Yet for all the tawdry beauty of this more finished statement, a sense of immediacy is retained in the summary execution.

When he returned to Morocco the following year, Lavery had a quite different sense of mission. Rather than simply taking a tourist's eye view of Tangier, he wished to get inside the life of the harem. A group of pictures produced on this occasion all relate to the Royal Academy exhibit of 1893, 'A Moorish Dance'.[16] 'Habiba' is a first attempt at this composition.[17] It shows an Arab girl advancing from a group of seated musicians in order to commence her dance. In these terms, the event depicted equates with Gustave Moreau's 'Salomé', but Lavery's is much more inconsequential. The dancer's pose is static by comparison to the swaying movement of the

young woman in the final composition. Along the way to the end result, Lavery produced a series of small studies of seated figures to be used for the background and armed with this collection of notes he returned to the studio to paint 'A Moorish Dance'.[18] The exhibited picture, 72 × 30 inches, was probably painted in Glasgow. It was extraordinary because, being executed on a full-length portrait canvas, only the lower portion contained the main action. Unsold at the exhibition, it was returned to the painter's studio where it languished, until sometime around 1910 Lavery cut off the redundant upper portion and totally reworked the figure from one of his Moorish maids. The dress was repainted in searing greens and reds and all but one of the background figures were obliterated.

This conventional harem scene failed because, like those of earlier Orientalists, it was composed rather than being the product of an original perception. Lavery, in later years, held to his ambition to paint an actual harem and only on his trip to Fez was he given the opportunity. The experience was hardly scintillating.

> I spent a week in a very uncomfortable and cramped position . . . most of the time the place was empty, and at no time did I see the women do anything other than lie about talking, singing, playing the gimbri and behaving in the orthodox manner in which I had been told they spent their lives. They were not more than fifty feet from where I was hidden, a deep pool dividing us . . .[19]

The picture was, nevertheless, a genuine contemporary harem scene – most others, of necessity, being studio evocations.[20]

By the time of his visit to Fez, greater emphasis could be placed upon studies and sketches than upon elaborate finished exhibition-pieces. In a sense, the readers of Cunninghame Graham's and Selwyn Brinton's accounts were asked to accept the integrity of the total experience. The journey, in Cunninghame Graham's account, was more like a pilgrimage – " . . . close to an orange garden, from which came puffs of scented air, making one think, after a hard day's ride, that he had entered a terrestrial paradise . . ."[21] These qualities were clear from the accumulative effect of Lavery's smaller notes. Although concentrated in the Fez expeditions, they are apparent throughout Lavery's Moroccan *oeuvre* and especially in his apprehension of mood and atmosphere of Tangier. As an avid sketcher, he made frequent sorties into the by-ways of the city and small pictures such as 'A Street in Tangier' typify his fascination for the sun-bleached walls and strong shadows tinged with violet. Several small panels were painted in the gardens of friends and these reveal Lavery's intuitive grasp of pictorial geometry. 'The White Peacocks', for instance, probably a view of Walter Harris's garden, sets up an architecture of stage-flats, thinly bordered in blue sky.[22] The simple rectangles of this work contrast with the zig-zag parallelograms which

The Amazon, *1911, 106 × 119 ins.*
Courtesy Ulster Museum.

Habiba, *1892, oil on canvas, 10 × 11¼ ins.*
Allied Irish Bank Collection.

THE WHITE CITY – SIR JOHN LAVERY IN TANGIER

often characterize Lavery's roof-top pictures. In these instances, the horizontal format is punctuated by the corner of a parapet or by the slopes of distant hillsides. Two or three figures bask in the cool afterglow in 'Evening, Tangier'[23] and 'The Housetops, Evening'.[24] Numerous variants of these works were produced up until Lavery's last visit to Tangier and they recall the wider context of orientalist painting. In the heyday of North Africa, before the Great War, Lavery's work betrayed the relaxed atmosphere of its society. He and his daughter rode with the Tangier hunt and relaxed in the British Legation. Their friends included Walter Harris, *The Times* correspondent, the extraordinary Bibi Carleton, the impecunious Duke of Frias, as well as R.B. Cunninghame Graham. All these people were larger than life. Their portraits were painted along with those of servants and a number of alluring half-lengths of beautiful Moorish girls, 'Zachara and Hadeisha', 'Aida Ilhralme' and 'Fatima Farghe', painted before 1909, and 'Zachra', 1914, culminating in 'The Moorish Madonna', 1920. These were augmented by numerous family pictures, portraying the daily doings of Hazel Lavery, her daughter, Alice, and Eileen Lavery. Included in this group are works like 'The Greyhound' and 'The Grey Drawing Room', interiors of the British Legation with Sir Reginald Lister and the painter's daughter.[25] Eileen Lavery's wedding to John Dickinson was held in Tangier and it was she who posed for the

artist's monumental equestrian portrait, 'The Amazon', which was painted at Tangier for the Royal Academy of 1911.[26]

This rich diversity of images supported Lavery's central preoccupation which was with Tangier itself – the White City. It was the subject of a celebrated canvas of 1893 which showed the bay with groups of Arabs walking along the beach.[27] In the background, the city is stacked up on the headland. For all the invitation to rich colour which such a scene might provide, Lavery retained a minor key and was praised for doing so.[28] This definitive work gave rise to others of a more radically simplified kind. In subsequent years, Lavery became very familiar with Tangier beach and he painted it from many angles and at different times of the day. The endless variations provided by passing ships and the visibility – or not – of the Spanish coast continually excited his attention. A significant group of these beach scenes contain tiny foreground figures traversing the canvas. There is an obvious echo of Whistler whose 'Blue and Silver – Trouville' was shown at the International Society of Sculptors, Painters and Gravers in 1899.[29] Whistler, like Lavery, had swept bands of colour from side to side across the canvas. Monet's 'La Plage des petites Dalles', exhibited at the International Society in 1901, had gone further in placing two figures side by side walking along the shore.[30] This became a preferred Lavery motif. The implication of a peaceful stroll and confidences

exchanged, adds a slight suggestion of narrative to pictures such as 'A West Wind'. The artist delighted in the juxtaposition of these figures with the immensity of space, undefined by perspective. At night the white city was surrounded by a black sea. In Whistler's nocturnes the fugitive warehouses became *campanili* in the evening mist. For Lavery, looking out from his hillside vantage point upon the relentless ocean, the abstract planes expressed depth and immutable power – power which drove the S.S. *Delhi* aground off Cap Spartel in December 1911. The haunting imagery of Lavery's Mediterranean nocturnes spoke eloquently to A.C.R. Carter in 1908 when he referred to 'The Seashore, Moonlight' in a eulogistic way. It,

. . . does more than vindicate the strivings of Whistler. It is the finest nocturne painted since Turner's.[31]

These are difficult claims to verify.[32] They are, nevertheless, an indication of the high value placed upon Lavery's Moroccan canvases at the time of their production. Works begun as a relaxation from the demands of portraiture became highly prized by Lavery's contemporaries. More than anything, they summed up the exoticism of the near East, and caught picturesque qualities which, even as Lavery painted, were fast disappearing. In 1908, as he showed the recent crop of Tangier pictures, including the monumental 'Market Place, Tangier', one visitor to the city was reporting the "ir-

The Seashore, Moonlight, *c. 1908.*
Unlocated.

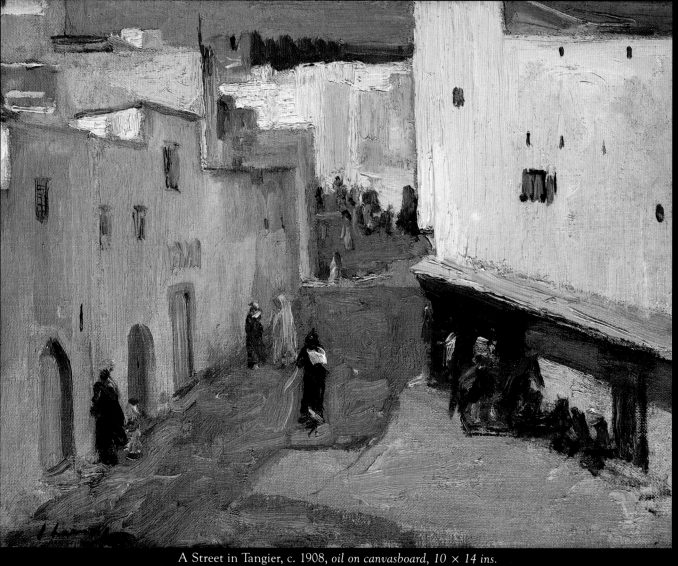

A Street in Tangier, c. 1908, *oil on canvasboard, 10 × 14 ins.*
Pyms Gallery, London.

Sok el Lechina, *1891, oil on canvas, 14 × 18 ins.*
Private collection.

THE WHITE CITY – SIR JOHN LAVERY IN TANGIER

ritation of too much that was European . . ." It was increasingly necessary to eliminate "discordant and disturbing European notes" by exercising a "discerning eye and discriminating hand . . ."[33] The influx of modern commercialism may well have led the painter to represent Tangier as a kind of fairyland suspended in moonlight. It was an image of this kind which marked him out as a "modern luminist", a quasi-symbolist painter of ghost-towns like Le Sidanier. Writing of his recent return to the Royal Academy in 1911 with a work entitled 'Tangier by Moonlight', Shaw Sparrow was moved to uncharacteristic generosity. One picture, he declared,

. . . is a moonlight scene, with white Tangier at rest in a deep mystery of greyed blue and violet and lilac, the sea beyond, vague, darkling, potent; and near at hand, across the terrace, the half-glow from an artificial light gives a dull illumination, and some natives crouch under a low wall that looks spectral . . . This nocturne is not the moonlight of Turner nor the moonlight of Whistler . . . It belongs partly to Tangier, partly to Lavery.[34]

The painter was thus the unique receiver of this vision. He alone had the trained intelligence to transmit its spectral afterglow – to see under the shroud of night the teeming life of the Grand Sok momentarily suppressed, all but for a

shaft of artificial light. By 1920 this fragrant atmosphere had evaporated and Dar el Midfah had been sold to a fellow Glasgow School painter, William Kennedy. An old man in 1933, on a cruise with his ailing wife, Lavery passed by Tangier for the last time. When he got back to London he penned a postcard to Cunninghame Graham.

We have just returned from a Mediterranean pleasure cruise passing Tangier in the twilight. I felt quite sad recalling the past. Bebe, Creeps, Frias and the rest. I suppose we ought to be grateful and believe in what you once described as that misleading statement "God is love".[35]

Kenneth McConkey

NOTES

1. R.B. Cunninghame Graham, 'The Atmosphere of Morocco' *Sketching Grounds*, special number of *The Studio*, 1909, p. 145. This article is extracted and adapted from a chapter in my forthcoming monograph, *Sir John Lavery – Portraitist and Reporter*.
2. See, for instance, Norman Garstin, 'Tangier as a Sketching Ground', *The Studio*, Vol. II, 1897, pp. 177-182.
3. Lavery's first views of the market place date from 1891, while Brangwyn's first trip of 1893 produced a notable picture of orange sellers which appeared in the Royal Academy in 1894, see *Pall Mall Gazette "Extra"* 1894, p. 56.
4. The wider cultural context of this phenomenon has been exhaustively pursued in recent years, most notably in Edward W. Said, *Orientalism*, 1978.
5. Norman Garstin, op. cit., p. 178.
6. Walter Shaw Sparrow, *John Lavery and his art*, 1911, pp. 88-89.
7. ibid., pp. 86 and 174 clearly dates Lavery's first trip to Morocco to "the autumn of 1890". Having no reason to doubt this, and recognizing that the 'State Visit of Queen Victoria . . .' was substantially completed by September 1890, I assumed that the artist must have set sail some time in October. See Ulster Museum and the Fine Art Society, *Sir John Lavery, R.A., 1856–1941*, catalogue of an exhibition by Kenneth McConkey, 1984, p. 25. A recently rediscovered appointments diary reveals that, for the most part, the artist spent the year in Glasgow. Since his first batch of Moroccan pictures was shown at the Goupil Gallery in June 1891, it is logical to suppose that Lavery visited Tangier for a shorter period than has been supposed up to now.
8. For further reference see John Lavery, *The Life of a Painter*, 1940, pp. 60-65; Ulster Museum and Fine Art Society, op. cit., 1984, pp. 24-25; fig. 7, Nos. 34-43.
9. Under the terms of the contract, Lavery retained the right to exhibit the painting for one year after its completion and he held the copyright. He also hoped to be able to sell some of the preliminary studies to their respective sitters.

10. Visits are recorded in 1892 and 1893, but there is no evidence for further trips until the early years of the century. It must be admitted, however, that since Lavery travelled extensively, it would have been possible for him to make unrecorded trips as, for instance, when he is known to have been working in Rome in the winter of 1896.
11. For a full list of these exhibitions see Ulster Museum and Fine Art Society, op. cit., 1984, p. 110.
12. Because the Moroccan works are often more sketchy than the balance of Lavery's *oeuvre* and carry seemingly uncharacteristic technical features, they attract, as a group, the greatest number of satellite paintings of dubious authenticity.
13. For a discussion of this work see Ulster Museum and Fine Art Society, op. cit., p. 42.
14. 'Sok el Lechina' was probably exhibited as 'The Little Soko – Tangier' (No. 7) in the artist's Goupil Gallery exhibition in June 1891.
15. For reference to this work see Ulster Museum and Fine Art Society, op. cit., p. 42, No. 46. At least sixteen of the thirty-five works on display in June 1891 were painted in and around Tangier.
16. R.A., 1893, No. 5.
17. This work has also been known as 'El Casbah'. For further reference see National Gallery of Ireland, *The East, Imagined, Experienced, Remembered*, catalogue of an exhibition by James Thompson, 1988. In the absence of evidence to the contrary, Thompson suggests that this work might be 'A Moorish Dance'.
18. For example, 'Study for 'A Moorish Dance', Christie's, 8 Nov. 1985, lot 217. A further study was sold in Belfast in 1984.
19. John Lavery, op. cit., 1940, p. 103.
20. 'A Moorish Harem', private collection, variously reproduced, e.g. John Lavery, op. cit., plate 14, was exhibited in the Goupil Gallery exhibition, 1908, No. 3.
21. Cunninghame Graham's account originally appeared in *The Glasgow Herald*. It is quoted here from Selwyn Brinton, 'An English artist in Morocco', *The Connoisseur*, 1907, p. 40.

Brinton states that Lavery's expedition to Fez with Cunninghame Graham and *The Times* correspondent Walter Harris, took place in the spring of 1906. Lavery (op. cit., p. 96) gives the month as February. However, his view of the city is clearly inscribed '1907' and this suggests that the artist either misdated the work – in this case unlikely – or went there on two consecutive years.
22. 'The White Peacocks', formerly Cynthia O'Connor Gallery, Dublin, appears to relate to a number of small garden scenes, one of which, 'The House of Walter Harris at Tangier' is illustrated by Selwyn Brinton, 'Some Recent Paintings by John Lavery, R.S.A., R.H.A.', *The Studio*, Vol. XLV, 1908, p. 178.
23. For reference to this work see, Ulster Museum and Fine Art Society, op. cit. 1984, pp. 65-66.
24. For reference to this work see National Gallery of Ireland, op. cit., 1988, p. 177.
25. Ulster Museum and Fine Art Society, op. cit., 1984, p. 68.
26. 'The Amazon', R.A. 1911, No. 85, Ulster Museum, Belfast. Numerous studies for this work dating from 1908 onwards, exist in private collections.
27. A study on panel for this picture was exhibited in MacMillan and Perrin Gallery, Vancouver, c. 1982.
28. A.C.R. Carter, 'John Lavery R.S.A.', *The Art Journal*, 1904, p. 10.
29. International Society of Sculptors, Painters and Gravers, 1889, No. 135.
30. International Society of Sculptors, Painters and Gravers, 1901, No. 80.
31. A.C.R. Carter, 'Recent Work by Mr. Lavery', *The Art Journal*, 1908, p. 234.
32. Both 'The Seashore, Moonlight' and 'Moonlight, Tangier' remain untraced.
33. Robert E. Groves, 'Morocco as a Winter Sketching Ground', *The Studio*, Vol. XLV, 1908, p. 25.
34. Walter Shaw Sparrow, op. cit., 1911, p. 111.
35. Card dated 8 September 1933, National Library of Scotland, Edinburgh. "Creeps" was Joseph Crawhall and Bebe was obviously a reference to Bibi Carleton.

INTERVIEW WITH ALISTAIR WILSON

How did you become a sculptor?

After school the plan was that I would take up farming, so I spent a year on the family farm, a year at agricultural college, and another at home. Whenever I had spare time I would paint, but I soon concluded that art wasn't something that you did occasionally, and that to achieve anything worthwhile you had to work at it full time. So I went to the local art school in Preston to do a foundation course. After that I moved to Bath, where I spent another three years and took a degree. I went to Bath to do a split painting/sculpture course, and at first I worked on the assumption that I wanted to follow both directions separately, but later I realized that there needn't be an absolute divide between painting and sculpture, so I started doing a series of pieces that combined the two. I think this is a philosophy that has remained with me. At that time—it was in 1972 or 1973—quite a few students at the college were beginning to be involved in Performance Art, and while the idea of Performance never seemed like a serious option from my point of view, my own work began to develop in the direction of *private* performance, because most of the pieces I was making were collections of objects, in which the ritual of *making* was important. The objects ended up as 'bundles' that were capable of being put together in a kind of ritual of distillation.

So you were conscious, even then, of an interest in distillation, which subsequently became a major theme in your work?

In an abstract sense, yes. I knew that I was condensing an activity that I felt was very important.

The Welsh sculptor, Alistair Wilson, has exhibited widely in Ireland and is represented in several public collections. Here, he talks to **John Hutchinson** about his work and the themes and methods he employs.

What happened then?

The objects that I was making were rather like tents; they were like paintings on hessian, stretched over willow or hazel branches. I suppose they owed something to Barry Flanagan—but you only consciously become aware of similarities after your own work has taken a parallel course. I'd chosen Bath specifically because it was a rural college, and I felt that it would suit my background and interests—never having lived in a city I was a little wary of urban environments—but by the end of three years at Bath I knew that London had to be faced at some point. I felt slightly apprehensive, because most of the materials I'd been using were very 'rural'. My main equipment was a paint-brush and penknife, and while that kind of approach fitted quite naturally with the environment that I was used to, to continue in the same vein in London, where those materials weren't readily available, didn't seem honest or appropriate. So I thought about this for a while, and began to realize that it wasn't those particular materials that were important; it was more significant that I'd been using materials that immediately came to hand. Having made that discovery, subsequent decisions were much easier. I

started working on reconstituted newspaper, remaking it into sheets and solid blocks. Through that activity—which was basically standing for hours on end shredding paper and reading yesterday's news—I began to think about just how transitory and ephemeral newspapers are. They last only for a short while, but they're nonetheless very specific in nature. So I would take a particular newspaper every day, reconstitute it, and the resultant objects became a kind of material diary.

Was this process of reconstitution another form of condensation, a kind of retrieval of essences?

I suppose so. With hindsight, I can look back and see that I've been making the same work for fifteen years. Then I started reconstituting parts of trees—I'd take a branch and remake it in sawdust, using a mould; and the mould would be included in the finished piece, with the original and cast. I also realized that the moulds had been an important aspect of my work in reconstituted paper. So I was beginning to become interested in the idea of containers, vessels, and casts.

That is another of your perennial interests. Can you explain it?

At that stage I was attracted by the perfection of the concept of a 'container'. The design of the container—be it the Holy Grail, a cow's horn, or a plastic cup—follows directly from the concept, and there is, in a sense, a continuum between the designs. I was also conscious of the container as a potent sexual and archetypal image. So I began to work with pots.

Shelter, *(open and closed), 1973. Hazel saplings, hessian and paint, 250 × 170 × 150 cms.*

Golden Boat, *1987, patinated copper and gold leaf on copper, 100 × 100 × 66 cms.*
Photograph Chris Hill.

Between a rock and a hard plate, *1984, granite, gold leaf and patina on copper,*
90 × 90 × 90 cms. Photograph Chris Hill.

INTERVIEW WITH ALISTAIR WILSON

What actually happened was that I would throw a certain number each day, choose one, and discard the rest. I eventually found myself in a studio where the walls were covered with images of containers of one sort or another, which became more and more abstract. I would take the images and translate them back into three dimensions, carving them into wooden moulds, and casting them in lead from the moulds. I'd end up with the mould, the cast piece, and the rejects. The next step was to grind up the pot shards, and to use the brown dust to make shapes on the floor. I made a series of copper moulds and sieves, and used them to cast the shapes directly on to the floor. That was the first time I worked with copper.

Is there any connection between the ground clay and the powdered pigment that you used so prominently in later work?

In 1975, between Bath and Chelsea, I was awarded a DAAD postgraduate scholarship, and among the things I did in Berlin were a couple of series of calligraphic drawings using ground pigments and charcoal. I later utilized this approach more sculpturally at Chelsea, and, as you suggest, picked up on it again in the pigment pieces. Looking back, one of the constant features of my work has been the process of storing images, methods, and materials, which I subsequently use when they seem appropriate.

When did you start using colour in the sculpture?

Colour, as a symbolic element in the sculpture, was introduced in the show at the Orchard Gallery, Derry, in 1979. It was also the first time I began to work with the idea of water. Water was interesting to me because comparatively little energy will transform it into ice or steam and, because the process is reversible, as it is with unfired clay, lead, and bronze. I used powder as a water symbol, and when it was cast in a mould it would gradually 'dissolve' and end up as powder on the floor. So the show was full of blues and reds. They weren't quite as vivid as the pigments I used later; the reds were rustier in hue, and the blues were pale. That was the work which gradually turned into 'Stills' about three years afterwards.

Untitled, *installation shot, 1976. lead cast from wooden mould.*

Was 'Stills' a particularly significant turning point?

With 'Stills' I began to realize what had been happening in the previous seven or eight years. I saw a pattern emerging; I could see that the work was all about order, chaos, and the ways in which those two principles keep flowing from one to the other. I saw that I was gradually working through chaos, creating order, then breaking it down again – the breakdown is very important. 'Stills' was based on that activity. I was using the distillation of water as a metaphor, and the work was really as much to do with mental as physical activity.

The symbolism was more apparent in the next series, 'A Quest for Passion', which could be approached as a kind of allegory.

Yes, and it was specifically about the connections between intellect and emotion. I wanted to evoke the notion of an inner search, and to suggest the interaction of the sensual and the rational.

Is that why the forms are so much more free and loose?

Yes. 'Stills' in many ways, was a definitive body of work. I began to feel that those

ideas, in that particular form, had run their course. I was also very conscious of the fact that many of the subtleties of 'Stills' had been missed. Reviewers, particularly, had taken the work on its most obvious level, and hadn't dealt with what I considered to be its more important aspects. I realized that I should take at least part of the blame, and on reflection concluded that I may have imposed too much order on the promptings from my sub-conscious. The metal took the form of straight pipes, cones, and other simple shapes, even though there were allusions to much freer forms. I began to use the materials more freely, and to let the activity of working with the material dictate the final form. For instance, I allowed blue colour to arise from the patination of the copper, which also brought into play the idea of *reaction* – the colour was a direct result of chemical changes. I think it is also relevant that, at this point, my working method became more integrated with the activity of drawing, so the pieces didn't need the clues that two-dimensional work had hitherto provided. In a sense I was drawing with the materials.

Has drawing always been important to you?

Yes, I've always drawn, using the word in its loosest meaning. I've found it a great catalyst to thinking – you can make great leaps with the minimum of physical effort. As a sculptor it is also very liberating because you're not tied down by gravity or scale, and that is a substantial benefit. But although it has always been integral to my work, drawing is a *parallel* activity. I very rarely draw and make objects at the same time, and almost never make preparatory drawings for the sculpture. That's why in the 'Quest', the loose handling of the materials, the modelling and the carving, seemed to make drawing redundant – for a while, anyway. I'm sure I'll start drawing again. In fact, I'm already making some prints.

Do the symbols in the 'Quest' – the vessel, flame, and water – have specific meanings?

Yes and no! They're archetypal images, and they have strong associations. One of the ideas was that both the flame and the water can be the aggressor and the victim. Neither is permanently dominant, and the balance between the two is quite precarious. The container, or boat

INTERVIEW WITH ALISTAIR WILSON

Five, seven eleven, *1989, cement fondue,*
slate and copper, 96 × 192 × 50 cms. Photograph Chris Hill.

Atoll, Atoll, *1988, copper and cement fondue,*
83 × 80 × 46 cms. Photograph Chris Hill.

After Gilbert, *1989, 68 × 65 × 17 cms.*
Photograph Chris Hill.

image, became the mediator between the two. The full title of the exhibition, 'Quest for Passion and Other Seafaring Tales', although tongue-in-cheek, was intended as a clue to the multiplicity of possible meanings.

How is your new work developing?

I'm on a twelve-month sabbatical at the moment, so for the first time in ten years I have the prospect of a long period of constant work ahead of me. A lot of things are happening. I'm working in clay again, modelling reliefs in negative and casting them. Colour, at present, seems to be taking a back seat, and most of the patinas I'm using are black – but it is a very exciting and experimental period, so I wouldn't like to predict the form that the work will take in a year's time. Scale in something that I'm rethinking, because in recent years my sculpture has tended to be quite small.

On the other hand, 'A Quest for Passion' could almost be read as an installation, so the scale of the work was ambiguous.

That's the way my work nearly always develops. My large pieces have usually been made up of a combination of smaller elements. This may have something to do with the early days, when everything I made was intended to be disassembled and packed up. I never work on a scale that doesn't suit the image, the material, and the method, so the work rarely ends up much larger than body-size. But now I'm experimenting with various scales.

How do you perceive your work in the general context of contemporary sculpture in Ireland?

I find it difficult to assess my work in that way, but I'd like to think that it compares favourably with contemporary sculpture anywhere. I've never tried to align myself with any particular artistic trend. I feel quite strongly that fashion is very transient, and I've tried to ensure that my work has its own integrity, although obviously ideas are going to touch and relate to current preoccupations, as that is in the nature of things. My work is very much geared to the long-term, and my hope is that it has the strength to transcend its own time and place.

John Hutchinson

EDWARD SMYTH, DUBLIN'S SCULPTOR

"That young man is going to become the most celebrated sculptor in Ireland,"[1] remarked a man to his companion as they spotted Edward Smyth strolling about Stephen's Green, Dublin, in the summer of 1771. The prediction was prompted by Smyth's having taken first place in a competition for a memorial to the recently deceased Dr. Charles Lucas, irritant of the Establishment and champion of the city's commercial interests.

Smyth must have felt exhilarated. Still only in his twenties, he had been awarded the commission over the famous and long established John Van Nost, and to add to the triumph Van Nost had exposed himself to ridicule by his attempts to alter his own model by lengthening its neck during the course of its exhibition. Dublin relished a whiff of indiscretion and, conversely, applauded the triumph of the "social, affable and courteous" Smyth.[2]

Edward Smyth's origins are obscure. As the two men in Stephen's Green remarked "Pity is, that this lad should not enter the world backed with a moderate fortune. Had his noble-spirited father lived how would (his reputation) blazon."[3] This remark shows he needed to earn his living, which is apparent from other sources, and also that he was probably one who, to say the least, lacked a consuming passion to get on in the world, and that, while his father had provided well for him during his lifetime, he had bequeathed him no capital. This father was reputedly either a stone-cutter or an Army captain, as cited in Strickland's account:

"Edward Smyth was born in the county of Meath in 1749. According to Warburton, Whitelaw and Walshe's History of Dublin *he was the son of a captain in the army and was born in 1749; but the* Dictionary of National Biography *gives the date of his birth as 1749 and says that his father was a stone-cutter who settled in Dublin about 1750."[4]*

The register of St. Thomas's parish, Dublin, may throw some light on his age as it lists an "Edward Smyth" as aged 67 at the date of his death:[5] presuming it was our Edward, this would make him born in 1745. The year is important, not least because of the Lucas competition. If he was born in 1749, he would have been about twenty-two in 1771, if it was nearer 1745, though he was no less talented, he

Patrick Lenehan presents a comprehensive survey of the sculpture and plaster-work of Edward Smyth which can still be admired on many of Dublin's most notable buildings.

River Liffey, *Custom House.*

Atlantic Ocean, *Custom House.*

was not quite such a youthful prodigy.

Though a world of opportunity should have opened before him after his success, Smyth seems to have gained no more commissions of note; he was in the employment of Simon Vierpyle, to whom he had been apprenticed, presumably after basic training at the Dublin Society.[6] Vierpyle, a Dutchman born in London in 1725, had come to Ireland to copy antique statues for the Earl of Charlemont, and settled in Dublin, where his most celebrated work was at the Casino. It is interesting to note a four-sided relationship. Sir William Chambers (the Casino's architect) taught James Gandon; Simon Vierpyle taught Edward Smyth. Chambers employed Vierpyle (on the Casino) and Gandon employed Smyth.

Shortly after completing his Lucas memorial, Smyth left Vierpyle to work for Henry Darley,[7] an eminent builder based in Abbey Street. Here his main work was carving panels and ornaments for chimneypieces as well as plasterwork. Since it was for his plaster-work that he was recommended to Gandon, a great deal of this must have existed in Dublin – and probably still does. From this anonymity he emerged in 1780 when the people of Lisburn commissioned him to produce a memorial to Lieutenant William Dobbs, who was killed in the battle in Belfast Lough between the Royal Navy's ship, *Drake,* and the American sloop, *Ranger,* in 1778. The monument stands on the south side of the altar in Lisburn Cathedral, a pyramid of dark marble with four separate carvings; at the very top the Dobbs coat of arms, next a medallion with a profile of the deceased young man with a trumpet-bearing angel reclining upon it, beneath a sarcophagus with a vigorous representation in relief of the sea battle, and at the base an inscription.[8]

Smyth did other memorials but, as Homan Potterton has remarked, considering how outstandingly good were his architectural sculptures, "it is somewhat of a surprise to discover his church memorials are often extremely poor in design and execution." He also observes that "it is possible to characterize his style of tomb design and to recognize his script . . . the most striking feature of (his) design . . . is the medallion portrait; and it is of note that Smyth was a friend of the medallist William Mossop the elder, and assisted him in the design of

EDWARD SMYTH, DUBLIN'S SCULPTOR

some of his medals."[9]

In 1781 James Gandon, a well-known English architect, arrived in Dublin to build a new Custom House for the Revenue Commissioners. He engaged the local firm of Thomas Darley for the stone masonry, but knew nothing of local craftsmen and indeed had been led to believe that no worthy artist whatsoever worked in Ireland. Therefore, before leaving London he had made agreements with some of the sculptors who had worked on London's Custom House, Somerset House (recently built by Sir William Chambers), commissioning Thomas Banks to do the Four Quarters for the north front in Dublin, and Augostino Carlini to do two of the four allegorical statues for the south front and also the Arms. He enquired of Darley (who employed many marble sculptors) whether he knew of a local artist capable of producing the remaining sculptural decorations. "Mr Darley instantly recommended to his notice Mr Edward Smyth, an excellent modeller and an artist of high capability; and, as a confirmatory proof of his powers as a sculptor, referred him to the statue of Dr Lucas, then in the Royal Exchange, executed by Smyth." Gandon, impressed by this, gave Smyth "drawings of ornaments intended for the interior of the cupola, requesting him to make models," and was well pleased with the results, despite the fact that Smyth was described as being at this time "a humble, retiring modest man, subsisting on very slender means in a back-room in Mecklenburgh Street." A little later, when Carlini sent over his design model for the Arms, Gandon asked Smyth to produce a design model, without showing him Carlini's version. Smyth "produced a composition so noble, and so pre-eminently superior, both as to grouping and execution to that which Carlini had sent, that Mr Gandon turning to Darley said, 'This will do: this is the artist I require; he must go alone and quit your employment.' He instantly wrote to his patron to say that there was no further necessity to send to London for models or sculptors, as he had then found in Dublin an artist capable of the highest works of art, either as a modeller or sculptor."

The building of the Custom House created a variety of opportunities for local artists and craftsmen. It is probable that Smyth did the fine plaster decoration that embellished the interior, as implied by the account of his introduction to Gandon. All this work has been destroyed. Externally, he did two of the allegorical figures above the south portico, his 'Plenty' and 'Industry' being placed alongside Carlini's 'Neptune' and 'Mercury.' These four were ruined in the War of Independence, but some surviving fragments have been assembled in the garden at the north-west corner. Mercury's hat is clearly on the head of the figure on the right, but as there is no sign of Neptune's trident or any possibility that the other two heads could be male, we may conclude that Neptune has disintegrated and the two remaining figures are Smyth's 'Plenty' and 'Industry'. His 'Commerce', crowning the dome and criticized by at least one visitor to the city as "too massive in its proportions," has been familiar to Dubliners for generations.

Set at the roof-line on the ends of the north and south fronts are the four armorial arrangements whose design had originally so pleased Gandon. The shield shows the Arms of the Kingdom of Ireland, not, as might perhaps be expected, those of the reigning sovereign, and the supporters are full of animation, showing the still surviving influence of baroque and rococo. Twenty years later, after the Union, Smyth sculpted a more restrained armorial, showing the Arms of George III, to place over the gateway to Gandon's King's Inns, a mute testimony to changed political circumstances. The only other of Smyth's works which can be described—even remotely—as political is the allegorical study in the tympanum of the river-front portico of the Custom House. After a design by Carlini, it is entitled "The friendly union of Great Britain and Ireland with Neptune driving away Famine and Despair."

Smyth's riverine heads almost unbelievably escaped damage, and they are regarded as not only his finest works but indeed as the finest Irish sculptures of the eighteenth century. Architecturally, they function as keystones above dominant windows and entrances, and the modern viewer, encountering them for the first times, is often overwhelmed by puzzlement: fourteen heads with fourteen expressions and a great variety of natural objects borne upon or about each head. To put it at its simplest, one sees plenty of "form" but little enough "meaning." Meaning, however, there is in plenty. Edward Smyth was well acquainted with the art of iconography, and these heads are distinctly iconographical, their individual forms deliberately chosen to tell a story, a sort of 'picture-writing.'

The sculptures are sometimes called river-god heads, an attractive name that conjures up the image of a god dwelling in his river, controlling its course and flow, its cataracts and eddies, its turbulence and its peaceful reaches. Not only is he at one with its waters but he also knows its banks, being constantly aware of the country through which he directs its course. It is this association that Smyth brings to life in his sculptures: they are sentient with living thought.

Smyth was hard at work in 1784 when a list of the rivers was published in the *Dublin Evening Post* on May 1st.

> *The building of the new Custom House is carried on with the greatest spirit, and when completed will undoubtedly be the first edifice of its kind in Europe. Among the variety of elegant with which this sumptuous pile is embellished are 13 (recte 14 in all) colossal heads, emblematic of principal rivers in this island, with singular descriptive ornaments, in a style of sculpture admirably executed.*
>
> *The idea of colossal heads over several doors of the new Custom House is by no means a new one. It is copied from Somerset House in England, where colossal heads are placed in the same manner, and by their ornaments denote the productions of the several rivers of England.*
>
> *It must be confessed that the execution of the heads of the new Custom House is vastly superior to that of Somerset House. One of them is emblematic of the Atlantic and the others of the following rivers: Boyne, Lee, Suir, Lagan, Lough Erne, Blackwater, Nore, Shannon, Barrow, Mourne (i.e. Foyle), Bann, Liffey, Slaney.*

This report did not locate the river heads on the Custom House but in the early 1940s Dr H.G. Leask attempted to do so. One head bears a date and another a date and its own name. Liffey was easy to identify and Leask felt that the three next most important rivers would have been allocated places of importance secondary only to Liffey. In this way he was able to make a useful start. Thereafter, his job was two-fold; firstly, to name all the fruits, cereals, fish and animal life, etc. with which the heads are embellished; secondly to match them to his

EDWARD SMYTH, DUBLIN'S SCULPTOR

River Boyne

River Foyle

River Barrow (or Nore)

River Blackwater

River Bann

River Suir

River Slaney

River Shannon

River Erne

River-god heads, Custom House. Courtesy Office of Public Works.

EDWARD SMYTH, DUBLIN'S SCULPTOR

Plaque above dining-hall entrance, King's Inns.

knowledge of eighteenth century topography, a subject that must have taken an immense amount of research.

There is only one female head among the fourteen and since it is in the central position, overlooking the river itself, it must be Liffey or "Anna Livia." Smyth has put a great wealth of detail about the head, including flowers, fruits, ferns, berries, peas and pine-cones, but most notable is the trident, symbolizing the "rights of Admiralty possessed by the city of Dublin over the waters of the port and Bay of Dublin." The face "approaches the ideal of Greek beauty" and is clearly intended to be classical and supreme among the other riverine heads.

The sculpture to the left – a mighty head of sullen aspect, teeming with fishy wealth – is Erne, though no single feature enables one to be completely certain. Salmon, pike, eel, shells and bulrushes are present, all of which might be claimed by other rivers. However, Lough Erne was famous for the sheer variety of fish found in its waters, which seems to indicate that river.

The next head is a fierce, pugnacious one, surmounted by the prow of a ship breaking a chain connected on either side to a castellated tower; the head-band carries the date '1689'. The river Foyle, on which Londonderry is situated, is obviously represented here, and the details on top are intended to recall the relief of the besieged city.

To Liffey's right is a finely modelled head, clearly marked '1690'. It has sheaves of wheat above and is regal in its features

and expression, clearly suggesting the 'Royal County of Meath', while the date recalls the Battle of the Boyne. Something in its expression is a little sad.

Further east is a river-god's head representing either Barrow or Nore. The top of the head is covered by the fell of a sheep, a leg at each side, the facial expression is sullen and from the wide, flat mouth issue a large quantity of fish. A slow-moving river, rich in fish, is suggested here. Both Nore and Barrow fit this classification, but while Nore was particularly well known for its net fisheries, there is evidence that the Barrow had many sheep-walks on its banks.

Around the corner, on the east pavilion, are, first, Blackwater and then, towards the north end, Atlantic. Blackwater, bearing a basket of apples above temples teeming with fish, is a straightforward identification, because "no part of Ireland was so notable for apple culture in the eighteenth century as the upper valley of the Munster Blackwater."

Atlantic is a rugged face with deep-set eyes and dolphins visible in the heavy beard; it bears a trident and crescent moon above, with a pinnacle on the left (the word 'Atlantic' is legible) and a compass card to the right.

On the north front, the first riverine head is a genial face "adorned by a rich vein of poetical fancy", the moustache and beard droop in silky folds, a turban of linen-like folds envelops the head which is crowned by what looks like flax. All this suggests an association with

linen manufacture while the clusters of berries may be an exaggeration of the hops essential to brewing. The conclusion must be Bann. Across the turban are loops of pearls and this river claimed the fresh-water pearl.

Under the portico of the north front – a location secondary only to the south river front – are three heads. The three ports next in importance to Dublin must be represented here: they were Limerick, Cork and Belfast.

The head on the left bears a trident, flanked by cornucopiae filled with grains and fruits, hair and beard are covered with oak leaves and acorns, the face is dignified and calm. The trident, symbolizing a connection with the mighty Atlantic ocean, and other characteristics reinforce the conclusion that this is Shannon.

The centre head is noble, vigorous and mature. It bears an anchor flanked by the bows of two cargo-laden ships. In the eighteenth century Cork was a long-established and busy port, second only to Dublin in importance. This head represents Lee.

The third head must be Lagan. In 1780 Belfast was a comparatively new city and this face is lightly bearded and youthful; moreover it was a centre for linen and about this face hang ample folds of a cloth which might be linen.

To the right, at the western end, is a rugged, staring face with, on top, raw wool enveloping weavers' bobbins which stand on the broad creases of a heavy woollen cloak. A river famous for its

EDWARD SMYTH, DUBLIN'S SCULPTOR

Plaque above old Prerogative Court entrance, King's Inns.

woollen industry is indicated and experts agree that it is Suir.

Around the corner is Nore or Barrow, again the identification is uncertain. It is a sleepy face but displays great strength of character. On top is a net complete with ropes and floats and on the cheek are some dripping fish.

Slaney is at the far end. One can pick out a crab and, at the side, some oysters as well as ears of corn. The wavy lines of the beard suggest a river of rapid flow. As the Slaney at Wexford harbour provides an abundance of shell fish and runs for some of its lively length through lands noted for corn crops, experts conclude that it is this river.

The riverine heads were very well received. When Derry Corporation decided to erect a memorial to William III on the occasion of the hundredth anniversary celebrations in 1789, they commissioned Gandon's pupil and friend, Henry Aaron Baker, to design and build a triumphal arch at Bishop's Gate. Smyth was asked to do the keystone heads for it, one for each side. They are clearly direct copies of two of the Custom House heads, Boyne and Foyle. Boyne has survived well; Foyle has weathered a great deal, yet is quite recognizably pugnacious though perhaps not as fierce as his Custom House prototype.

While the Custom House was being built, Gandon was asked to submit plans for alterations to the House of Lords (now the Bank of Ireland on College Green, Dublin). The Lords favoured more spacious accommodation and a

better entrance because their function as Court of Final Appeal had been restored to them in 1782. Gandon employed Smyth to produce three allegorical statues for the pediment, representing qualities with which the Lords would wish to be associated–Justice, Wisdom and Liberty.

The sculptor, now about forty, had become, in the few short years since meeting Gandon, a busy and successful artist. Indeed, during the years between the beginning of his Custom House work (1782–3) and the completion of the Four Courts (1796) he gained virtually all the best commissions in the city and earned a large income. On 10th April 1787 the *Dublin Evening Post* reported that he was at work in the yard of the Parliament House and commented enthusiastically that the emerging statues would be the finest executed in Europe in forty years. These statues are iconographical but, unlike the naturalistic river-god heads on the Custom House, draw upon classical sources for their symbolism. One of the greatest of such classical sources for artists was the Italian Cesare Ripa's *Iconologia*, written in 1593 and translated into many languages. In 1778–9 an illustrated English edition was published, and amongst the hundred and fifty or so subscribers listed are "Mr James Gandon" and, intriguingly, "Mr Smith, Dublin."[10] In the year of publication Edward Smyth had only his Lucas monument behind him and one cannot conclude that this reference is to him, though it is clear from his works that he

had studied Ripa's volume. An edition published in Augsburg between 1758 and 1760 by J.G. Hertel was lavishly illustrated and is a most useful guide to Ripa's iconography.[11]

Of these roof statues, Smyth's 'Justice' is obviously quite different to that in Hertel, and relies simply upon sword and scales to express its meaning. The figure itself has deteriorated badly during the many years it has stood upon the portico, but even so retains its character from a sympathetic distance.

Smyth's 'Wisdom'–also a different interpretation from Hertel's–was re-worked in the 1940s by his great-grandson, George Smyth, and thus is the only one of the three with a fresh head. She has several of the attributes of the Greek Athene–the helmet, the shield with the head of Medusa, the owl and the staff. The strong grasp of her left hand holds what seems to be a serpent and, balancing Athene's owl, is a dove which, according to Ripa "signifies the heavenly influence of truth." This statue was raised to the pediment on 4th September 1787, according to Faulkner's *Dublin Journal*, "amidst the acclamations of a number of spectators."

Hertel's version of 'Liberty' illustrates the main accessories associated with the allegory as depicted by Smyth–the cat and the Phyrgian cap, which was presented to newly-freed slaves of ancient Rome as a symbol of emancipation. This particular cap disappeared some time between 1803, when a drawing of this part of the Bank of Ireland clearly shows cap

EDWARD SMYTH, DUBLIN'S SCULPTOR

and staff, and 1813 when, in another drawing, they are missing. Possibly somebody had wished to make a political point! The cap was replaced in 1946 by George Smyth, on the Bank's instructions.

Edward Smyth returned to this building after the Act of Union (1801) which made the Irish Parliament Houses redundant and allowed their purchase by the Bank of Ireland. Gandon had retired to Lucan and Francis Johnston was engaged as architect for the necessary alterations. A secret condition of the sale was that the purchasers should subdivide and alter the chambers so as to destroy their old appearance. It was also suggested "that they should render the outside uniform and . . . reconcile the citizens to it . . . by making the edifice more ornamental." Three roof-line statues to match the three around the corner on the old House of Lords entrance were decided upon and, in January, 1807, Johnston wrote to the Directors of the Bank that "if this work can be accomplished by natives, I am sure, gentlemen, you would give them preference. My wish is (and I trust you will not object to it) that you will allow me to employ Mr. Edward Smyth who has abilities if he would exert them . . ." It seems that the Directors were "profoundly ignorant of Smyth's merits as a sculptor." They found him a nervous, unpretending man and were unimpressed. In a further letter Johnston wrote to them asking for permission to employ Smyth "to make models . . . and also to allow me to pay him a sum not exceeding twenty guineas for doing the same. We have a design model by Kirk, a young man of abilities who does the stone carving at the Bank, but I should wish another for consideration done by Smyth."

After an interval, Johnston had in hand two sets of models, Kirk's and Smyth's. Yet he seemed dissatisfied for, having made enquiries in London, he wrote inviting the Directors to "judge whether it might not be advisable to get a design from Mr Flaxman or some other eminent statuary in London . . . which we could execute here with our own artists and I suppose the expense of getting such designs on a sufficiently large scale would not exceed fifty pounds." When Flaxman sent over his designs, Thomas J. Mulvany, then a young artist, was employed to copy them. Strickland terse-

Charles Lucas, *City Hall (Royal Exchange).*

EDWARD SMYTH, DUBLIN'S SCULPTOR

The Marquis of Buckingham, *St. Patrick's Cathedral.*

ly summed up the affair: "Flaxman sent over three small pencil sketches from which copies were made by Mulvany and handed to Smyth." Put this way, it sounds like a deliberate insult.

Nevertheless, Smyth made models from these drawings, and it was these designs by Flaxman that the Directors selected. Two of them stand today in the Bank's new headquarters in Baggot Street while the third has been currently mislaid – perhaps lying concealed in the College Green premises.

Flaxman also features in the correspondence between Johnston and the Directors over the question of price. He intimated that he would require £1,137 10s. to execute the works. Once again Smyth was pressed forward by Johnston, who wrote "Mr Smyth has proposed to do them and find the stone for £450 . . . see the difference, £687 10s." He continued winningly, "Suppose you gave Smyth, in case his work met your full approbation, £50 or £100 more, still there would be a saving of £587 10s." (Smyth actually got a bonus of £50.) It shows just how hard Johnston had to work to convince the Directors that Smyth should do the job.

It is a pity that the designs chosen were Flaxman's as it would have been particularly interesting to have seen how Smyth, in his full maturity, would have treated the iconographical statues, of 'Fidelity', 'Hibernia' and 'Commerce'. The version of 'Hibernia', which he had made for the Society was then only six or seven years old. 'Fidelity' was a new subject to him and surely his design would have been different from this smooth, Neo-classical and rather characterless androgyne. His designs would have had 'force and animation' with his usual effects of light and shade.

'Hibernia' sits in the centre of this group, to the left is 'Fidelity', arms crossed on her breast, to the right 'Commerce' holding in her right hand a ship's tiller with a *cadduceus* engraved upon it, this being in classical times the badge of a sacred person who was to pass unmolested. The heads have all been replaced in accordance with the models done by Smyth for Johnston.

Soon after completing his work for Gandon at the Parliament House, Smyth set about the lengthy task of decorating Gandon's new Four Courts. The site beside the Liffey had long been chosen

EDWARD SMYTH, DUBLIN'S SCULPTOR

Royal Arms, King's Inns (Henrietta Street entrance).

for this purpose; Thomas Cooley, who died prematurely, left some work which Gandon incorporated into his own, designing another building at the far end of the site to match Cooley's and putting the domed Courts in the centre so that the whole complex took the shape of the letter "E", opening on to the river quay. He screened each opening with an arcade flanked by arches and on each arcade Smyth set a Trophy containing a variety of iconographic accessories, all appropriate to Law. Clockwise, from the bottom left are a roll of parchment, lictors' rods, more parchment, a sword, part of a scales and a key. Originally there was a crown on top, but it must have been damaged during the siege in 1922, for on restoration it was replaced by the ball to be seen today. Beneath the harp are the words *Saorstat Eireann*, the Irish Free State, which was the correct designation at the time of restoration. At the top right, derived from an Egyptian hieroglyph, is an eye upon an oval finial, representing the prudent eye of Justice penetrating men's actions. Beneath is the axe within the lictors' rods, more parchment and finally what may be a sceptre. Under the harp is a serpent with a bridle in its mouth, implying evil controlled by temperance.

Just below and to each side of the centre portico are set decorative panels with more iconographic accessories, while high above the portico is a group of five statues in a beautifully harmonious arrangement. The standing figures are eight feet tall. In the centre is Moses, the law-giver of the Hebrews, undoubtedly the most dramatic of any of Smyth's roof-line statues. The figure's pose gives an impression of tremendous strength and authority, exactly what the sculptor intended. Moses is accompanied by four allegorical figures: 'Authority', who reclines in an elegant, regal pose upon a throne, cradling a sceptre in her left arm; 'Justice', who, over the years, has lost her forearms, though one of the pans of her scales is clearly visible; 'Mercy', who is barely identifiable, her left arm is missing and the right seems intended to bear something—perhaps an olive branch, sniped off by a passing bullet; and 'Wisdom', with her shield tucked under her arm and her hand clasping a serpent, in a similar manner to the figure on the House of Lords. All these five statues are in very poor condition, yet from street level they retain something of their original success, still decorating the building in a handsome way.

Gandon's Four Courts met a sorry fate, which is described by Maurice Craig as follows:

"In the closing days of June, 1922, the Four Courts was held by Republican forces under Rory O'Connor and bombarded by field artillery, fired by Free State forces on the southern quays. The garrison mined the building before evacuating it and in the resulting explosions, both the inner and outer domes were destroyed, the south-east and south-west wings and the south-west portion of the arcaded screen were badly ruined. The entire building was also burnt."[12]

All Smyth's interior work save for two little plaques in the ante-hall were reduced to rubble. These two examples of his extensive interior plaster-work contain a jumble of iconographical items—scales, cadduceus, mace, chain, fasces, axe, sword, spear, all allegorical paraphernalia of Law. For over a century a profusion of his plaster-work had adorned the high domed Great Hall. The *Dublin Evening Post* of 19th November, 1796 reported:

Round the inside of the Dome is a continued frieze of foliage, festoons of oak leaves etc., and on the centre over each window, united with their ornaments are eight medallions of the ancient legislators much larger than life. These include Solon, Confucius, Numa, Lycurgus, Alfred, Moses, Manco Capac and the Irish lawgiver Ollamh Fodhla. In the piers between the windows are executed in stucco eight colossal statues in basso-relievo emblematic of Justice, Eloquence, Wisdom, Liberty, Mercy, Prudence, Law and Punishment, all executed to the bold masterly fine style of the antique grotesque but the eye is particularly attracted by the

EDWARD SMYTH, DUBLIN'S SCULPTOR

Trophy, Four Courts.

statue of Punishment who stands on the fasces, the axe surrounded with rods, the strings of which are unbound as letting them loose to execute judgement, while the statue had its head averted and the hand before the eyes as loth to behold the punishment that justice obliges Law to put into force.'

In *Dublin Decorative Plasterwork*, C.P. Curran gives drawings of four of these figures made from photographs he had taken many years previously.[13] Two other photographs are in the Office of Public Works, Dublin. A study of all six illustrations with the account just quoted leads to the undoubted conclusion that Curran has misnamed his figures. His 'Justice' is certainly 'Punishment,' and his 'Punishment' probably 'Eloquence.'

After the Four Courts came the King's Inns, Gandon's last public work. As mentioned earlier, Smyth carved the Royal Arms for the Henrietta Street gateway, but most of his sculpture is on the great west front of the building, where there are two storeys of windows and a third level expressed externally by alternating medallions and plaques. This facade has three sculptural themes emphasizing the functions of the building: the entrance to the Dining Hall, on the left, and the entrance to the old Prerogative Court (now the Registry of Deeds), on the right, are both embellished by a plaque and car-

yatids, while the central section, which has an archway leading to the yard behind, bears an elaborate plaque.

The plaque above the Dining Hall entrance contains eleven figures each of which is iconographical in the classical tradition, unlike the natural iconography of the river-god heads on the Custom House. The central figures are involved in a marriage ceremony. The male on the left is Dionysus, god of the senses and of wine, carrying in his left hand a thyrsus, and behind him are women engaged in a ritual. He married Ariadne ('most pure' or 'high fruitful mother of the barley'), and in Smyth's plaque the lady to his right fits this image, because she bears a cornucopia over her shoulder. Her companion to the right holds a garland and both her posture and the flowers suggest a festive dance or bacchanal. Beside her another girl carries a winged vase, representing the wine for which Dionysus was famous, its wings implying the light-headedness and flights of fancy which result from its indulgence. Next is a female figure with what looks like a crown, probably the crown of Hephaestus, the *Corona Borealis*, presented by Dionysus to Ariadne. On Dionysus's right is a male figure standing behind a tripod vessel whose feet are cloven like a satyr's. He is playing upon a twin flute, the attribute of the Muse, Euterpe. Then comes Ariadne

herself with her overflowing cornucopia, and to her right a figure representing the abundance of harvest, carrying in addition to cereals, the twisted rod often associated with Asclepius, god of medicine, with the implication that a healthy life emerges from the harvest of the fields. To her right is a figure bearing a basket full of the fruits of the earth, and holding a vase as if spilling the contents: she provides a neat foil to the girl with the winged urn since she clearly favours moderation in alcohol, for the vase pouring out its contents is an iconograph for Temperance. Lastly there are two female figures associated with each other, the young one blowing blasts of music against the old one, huddled over a fire, driving her away, so to speak. Smyth's message is, 'Abundance is here, but Winter follows – keep her away as long as possible.'

The entire plaque, with its eleven separate figures, is thus a detailed picture-story. It tells that some of the richest moments of a man's life come from the fun, merriment and festiveness of enjoying the fruits of the abundant earth, that food, wine, music and dance mix wonderfully together, but remember that temperance should be present and, finally, that, winter-like, Death waits always in the wings. It was good advice to those about to enter the Dining Hall, but lest it depress the mind unduly, there is a

EDWARD SMYTH, DUBLIN'S SCULPTOR

liberating wink from the two bacchantes at the doorway. On the left is 'Plenty', and on the right 'Wine'. This pair, and their sober cousins on the other door, are believed to be the only stone caryatids in Dublin.

There is dispute as to the meaning of the plaque over the centre archway. One school holds it depicts Elizabeth I receiving gifts; on the left the Barons present a copy of Magna Carta and on the right the Bishops proffer a Bible. Elizabeth, long since dead, was an archetype of the monarchy, yet had to recognize the will of the people and of the church. The rival school, led by C.P. Curran, claims that no event justifies such an explanation, but that the panel represented "the restoration of the Society of the King's Inns in 1607 and the chief figure is either James I or the Deputy – Chichester – who brought about the changes."

The plaque above the right-hand entrance to the old Prerogative Court is no bacchanalian revel but concerned with the business of the law. The first figure on the left is an old man with a scythe, obviously a representation of Time. He is winged to suggest Time's fleetness and his right hand clasps a mortar, the tool to grind the dust to which we all come. Beside him is a female with book and pen who represents History, her foot resting upon a footstool as an emblem of superiority. The next female figure seems to be present solely to balance the group. Beside her is another with a trumpet and an open book in her hands; these and her proclamatory stance tell us that she is Fame, announcing the heroic deeds of history. Beside her is a beautiful young woman holding a mirror, the accepted emblem of virtue, enabling Prudence to look backwards and forwards. The female with scales and sword is immediately identifiable as Justice. The brazier's flames suggest the welding of Prudence and her partner in union or perhaps the love between them. The helmeted central figure to the right is clearly Wisdom, with her spear and shield. At her feet are Athene's owl and a cock which was also associated with her. To her right is a female with a key, and it should be noted that had the cock accompanied her, it might have altered her identification to Vigilance, but the key is sufficient to endorse the conclusion that she is actually Security. The next male figure simply suggests Law and

on his right two men, one with a book under his arm ready for consultation, are engaged in discussion; one may assume they represent Disputation or Discourse. This plaque's iconography was designed as a statement that justice was ultimately and reliably available from the judicial system: Time, History and Fame are witnesses; Security, Law and Discourse are the system's servants and when Prudence unites with Wisdom, Justice is supreme. The caryatids provide a final reminder that security and law are the pillars of justice. These mature, benevolent figures radiate confidence: with such supporters, who could fear?

Standing in front of King's Inns is a large statue of Themis which previously stood in the centre of the Great Hall of the Four Courts, bearing aloft a gas-jet (she was piped up her back for the purpose). No signature is visible but the work is probably Smyth's as it seems to have been part of the original decoration for the Courts.

Smyth's sculpture also adorned the inside of the King's Inns. In the Benchers' Chamber, just above the entrance to the Dining Hall, are two small identical heads of Justice. They are remarkably simple compared to the florid plasterwork all about the room, a difference suggesting that justice must be devoid of worldly frivolity, be blind to it in fact, a pure spirituality further implied by the sexless appearance of these heads which are neither male nor female.

The immense, lofty rectangular Dining Hall contains two pairs of allegorical figures: 'Justice' and 'Wisdom' are high above the Benchers' dais, with 'Temperance' and 'Prudence' at the far end "where they may be profitably considered from the tables where the law students sit." This 'Justice' reclines upon a globe; the balance wherein she weighs the good and evil of men's actions is suspended from her right hand while her left arm cradles the sword wherewith to carry out her judgements. 'Wisdom' rests upon three large volumes, one of which is marked "Solomon", and the shield in her left hand displays the Paraclete and sunrays, instead of Medusa's head as in the House of Lords figure. This is Divine Wisdom, whom lawyers are not shy of claiming; her sovereignty is proclaimed by her spear and her eyes are directed upwards, her attention on the supernatural.

At the far end are 'Temperance' and

'Prudence', 'Temperance' holding a restraining bridle and emptying a vase of wine: "moderation in all things." 'Prudence' holds both her mirror and an arrow which is entwined with an eel: circumspection is her characteristic.

Like Gandon, Smyth has suffered from damage to his major works; loss by fire or bombardment as in the case of the Custom House and the Fourt Courts, or by alteration as at King's Inns. His finest surviving exterior carvings are the baroque riverine heads on the Custom House, while the figures in the King's Inns Dining Hall are the only extant examples of his stucco-work based on classical allegory.

After King's Inns, some other commissions followed – including the return to the former Parliament House – and extensive plaster-work in the Chapel Royal (now St. Patrick's, Dublin Castle). Before the Chapel was finished, he died suddenly on 2nd August, 1812, "deeply lamented by all who had the happiness of a personal acquaintance with him." We are told he had been a man "of the most amiable and engaging private qualities," but today he can only be known through his works. His river-god heads have a unique place in the history of Irish art, while his roof-line statues – particularly Moses on the Four Courts – which stand above traffic-thronged streets so entirely different from his own time, are such a part of the city today that Smyth is still "Dublin's Sculptor".

Patrick Lenehan

NOTES

1. *Public Monitor*, 22–24 July 1773.
2. *Ibid.*
3. *Ibid.*
4. Walter G. Strickland, *A Dictionary of Irish Artists*, Dublin and London, 1913.
5. Viola B.M. Barrow, 'Edward Smyth', *Old Dublin Society*, 24 Jan. 1979.
6. C.P. Curran, 'Mr Edward Smyth', *Architectural Review*, 1947
7. Strickland, op. cit.
8. Homan Potterton, *Irish Church Monuments 1570–1880*, Ulster Architectural Heritage Society, 1975.
9. *Ibid.*
10. Copy in the British Museum. Trinity College, Dublin, has an earlier version in French.
11. A recent publication, *Cesare Ripa: Baroque and Rococo Pictorial Imagery*, faithfully reproduces these illustrations.
12. Maurice Craig, *Dublin 1660–1860*, London, 1952.
13. C.P. Curran, *Dublin Decorative Plasterwork*, London, 1967. Ill. No. 113 shows drawings entitled Justice, Wisdom, Punishment and Mercy.

THE 'BUDDHA BUCKET' FROM THE OSEBERG FIND

Of the great quantity of Irish metal-work recovered from Viking tombs in Norway, one of the most intriguing finds is the so-called 'Buddha Bucket'. It comes from what is probably the finest remaining tomb, the great ship burial of Oseberg which dates from the ninth century. Its name is derived from the pair of cross-legged or 'Buddhist' schematic figures which form the mounts or 'ears' to its handle. It undoubtedly represents loot, as do the other antiquities found, being mostly plunder from the raids on Irish monasteries which began in the late eighth century. Many of these raids were launched from the fjords of west Norway, and, of all the Scandinavian countries, it was probably Norway which had the closest connections with Ireland during the Viking period.

Irish craftsmanship seems to have been highly prized, and Viking tombs have yielded many important and valuable examples of Irish metal-work, including the only known eighth-century crozier.[1] By far the largest group of items recovered are personal ornaments, mainly mountings of varous shapes and sizes, detached from saints' shrines or holy books, and then refashioned into brooches.[2] Used in addition to the twin-tortoise type of brooch, they completed the full set of dress ornament in Viking Norway.[3]

The Oseberg bucket belongs to the second largest group recovered – bronze vessels.[4] It is notable that it was discovered within a great tomb, like the Miklebostad hanging bowl, which is decorated with very similar escutcheons very similar to those on the bucket, was also found in an aristocratic tomb.

The Viking dead were furnished with every possible requirement and luxury for their journey into the next life, from jewellery to domestic vessels. That this journey was envisaged as a voyage is evident from the widespread practice of ship burial, reflecting the enormous importance of seafaring in that society. This custom, and the grand scale of burial, was unparalleled in the rest of Europe at the time, least of all in Ireland, since the Irish, being Christian, did not, as a general rule, bury precious objects with their dead.[5] The Oseberg Find is the epitome of a Viking ship burial from the highest stratum of society, and perhaps the most valuable and lavish of all Viking Age discoveries. The 'Buddha Bucket', one of a vast array of grave goods, was found

Margaret Mac Namidhe is a graduate of the National College of Art and Design, where she now lectures. During 1988 she attended a course on Art in Norway and here discusses some Irish art objects of the early Christian period.

The Buddha Bucket, *overall view, bronze mounted yew bucket probably from around the late seventh century H. 36 cm D. 32 cm. (bottom), 26 cm (rim). Courtesy Universitetets Oldsaksamlingen, Oslo.*

among a collection of household objects and textiles, including another bucket,[6] within the burial chamber itself, which contained the cremated remains of two women.

The bucket is in the same remarkable state of preservation as the rest of the find, which takes the name Oseberg from the farm in Vestfold, on the western side of the Oslo fjord, where it was excavated in 1904. The exceptional 'blue clay' of the subsoil of this area preserved the contents of the burial mound intact for centuries, although it was plundered in the early medieval period. Probably because it is a domestic object, albeit a highly refined one that shows no evidence of use, the bucket was one of the few items of metal-work that escaped the attentions of the grave robbers.[7] The chief glory of the find is the magnificent wood carving which is seen not only on the ship itself, but on most of the other important objects including a cart, sleighs, sleigh shafts and strange, animal-head

posts. There is a variety of different styles but animal motifs predominate, from the frieze of gripping beasts on the prow and stern posts, which rise majestically above the body of the ship, to the fabulous interlaced creatures of the animal-head posts which, with their curved necks, bared teeth and predatory expressions, may have served some ritual or ceremonial function.[8]

The small squat geometric escutcheons, with their impassive expressions, on the otherwise unadorned pail, could not be in greater contrast to objects such as these. Made of yew, and encircled by three equidistant bronze hoops, the bucket measures thirty-six centimetres high, thirty-two centimetres in diameter, at the bottom, and twenty-six at the rim. The bodies of the escutcheons are embedded between the first bronze band and the rim, with the handle attached to the back of the protruding heads. Thus they appear as integral, functional parts of the vessel rather than as purely decorative fixtures, and their square and compact shape complements its sturdy character. Beautifully cast in bronze, in high relief, the head is flat topped, lined by semi-circular grooves radiating from a small indentation in the middle of the forehead and divided by a central line. Huge oval eyes, convex and blank, dominate the clean-shaven face, emphasized by jutting brows joining the long narrow nose. A down-turned segment defines the mouth, and the cheeks are rather Slavic, high, wide and well-modelled. The body combines four interlocking compartments of red and yellow *champlevé* enamel in T-shaped cells, with a central Greek cross of blue and white *millefiori*. Long schematic arms flank the body, with small knobs for 'shoulders' ending in diminutive hands grasping the clasped feet. The equally diminutive legs are bent sharply at the knees and crossed again in the middle. The bucket's popular name results from this yoga-like posture and from the inscrutable mask-like face and frozen, stylized appearance. Any suggestion of actual Oriental or eastern influence would be misleading as it is undoubtedly of Irish provenance. Nevertheless, it displays a curious blend of different features which derive from both Christian and Celtic sources. The schematic figure style and enamel technique are characteristic of the early Christian period, but are usually found in ecclesiastical contexts. The cross-legged posture, on the other hand, probably stems from a Celtic cult, one that was particularly potent and liable to incur ecclesiastical disapproval in the Christian period. It is this strange mixture of contrasting elements, the persistence of an ancient pagan feature along with the emergence of an early Christian style, that is, perhaps, the most fascinating aspect of the figure.

The 'family' of bronze vessels to which the Oseberg bucket belongs also includes hanging bowls, cauldrons and handled saucepans, with buckets the smallest section and hanging bowls the largest. The bronze used contains a high proportion of tin, a fine alloy not found in native Norwegian bronzes. The yew of the bucket is also found in the caskets of the small house-shaped shrines, such as the one at Melhus.[9] Many of the other vessels are also decorated, particularly the hanging bowls, usually on the escutcheons, but sometimes on the base and rim as well. The escutcheons on that vessel are partly anthropomorphic: two human masks arranged on either side of an enamelled square. There are also three human-shaped escutcheons on a hanging bowl discovered in the river Maas in Holland, probably brought there by the Vikings.[10] The bowl is complete, of the same shape as the Miklebostad bowl, but badly worn. There is no evidence of *millefiori* and the red and yellow enamel arranged in small squares has changed colour, due to oxidation. Although extremely weathered, the modelling of the head is clearly very different to and much smaller than the Norwegian escutcheons. The lowest compartment contains a simple X-shaped design, which Françoise Henry describes as a conventional rendering of crossed legs, but it is much coarser than the finely articulated hands and legs of the Oseberg escutcheon and cannot compare with it technically.[11]

Although the sequence and dating of Irish metal-work of the seventh, eighth and ninth centuries is difficult, with little information remaining about the organization and distribution of the craft, the quality of the enamelling on the Oseberg figure indicates a late seventh century date.[12] The distinctive use of polychrome *champlevé* and *millefiori*, bounded by thin lines of bronze in a striking geometric pattern, reflects the experimentation and development of this

Figure of St. Matthew from the Book of Durrow, *Vellum, from around the mid seventh century. Reprinted with permission from the Library, Trinity College, Dublin.*

THE 'BUDDHA BUCKET' FROM THE OSEBERG FIND

Anthropomorphic escutcheon, *details from the Miklebostad hanging bowl.*
Bronze, enamelled in polychrome champlevé with millefiori, probably from around
the late seventh century. Courtesy the Historisk Museum, Bergen, Norway.

period, a time of growing sophistication and abundant production. Red, the easiest colour to produce even under primitive conditions, is also the first colour to be used first when *champlevé* was introduced by the La Tène Celts around the first century A.D. While there is evidence for the production of *millefiori* in Ireland from the fifth century, it was probably introduced from the Continent.[13] This style, broadly speaking, replaced the older spiral and triskel patterns. The mix of *millefiori* floating in red enamel (such as the enamel inlay on the Melhus shrine or the beautiful disc on the bottom of the Miklebostad bowl) disappeared, as did reserved spaces of bronze. This development may be due to a number of factors, for example, the demands of the panels of *millefiori*, which require a square or rectangular frame; or through the influence of *cloisonné* work in Anglo Saxon jewellery, and the geometric patterns in late Romano-British mosaic pavements.[14]

The escutcheons on the Miklebostad hanging bowl are so similar to those on the Oseberg bucket that the same factory may have been responsible for both. This bowl was found containing cremated bones, mingled with charcoal, in a specially protected artificial hollow in the large ship burial of a chieftain in western Norway. There are three escutcheons altogether on the rim. They are functional, attaching the vessel to the chains from which it was once presumably suspended, although no hanging bowl has ever been found complete with chains. This late version of a hanging bowl, of the type found in Viking tombs, was probably originally an ecclesiastical vessel, either a reflecting bowl for a sanctuary lamp[15] or a container for church water.[16] The head of the escutcheon is more domed and oval, and larger in proportion to the body than the Oseberg figure, but has the same arrangement of facial features with the addition of what appears to be a stylized beard. Bereft of arms and lacking the cross-legged posture, the body is more abbreviated, with simple legs and out-turned feet, and the enamelling is more elaborate. Green is used in addition to red and yellow, and the Greek cross is formed of four compartments of L-shaped cells of enamel with a central panel of enamel and *millefiori*, with four chequered corners.

THE 'BUDDHA BUCKET' FROM THE OSEBERG FIND

The manuscript version of this style is found in the St. Matthew figure from the Book of Durrow, from about the same period. His splendid chequered cloak, combining red and yellow and *quasi-millefiori* squares in a chess-board effect, shows the obvious influence of the enamel style. The figure is again schematic, again lacking arms, and with short legs protruding beneath the cloak, and feet turning to the right. The head is more in proportion, more rounded, sinking into the shoulders but with the same impassive expression. The medium allows for more detail and he has been given a beard, (a herring-bone pattern from chin to ears), and hair arranged in a distinctive wig-like tonsure parted in the middle. Without the embellishment of colour or pattern available to the scribe or the metal-worker, the most radically abstracted version of the figure style appears in stone. Carved in unyielding granite, the Apostles on the base of the High Cross of Moone in Co. Kildare are reduced to large pear-shaped heads with huge round eyes and long narrow noses, dominating small, square, block-like bodies and simple out-turned legs and feet. Arranged in three groups of four, their collective impact is forceful in its simplicity and repetition.[17]

Although stylistically part of the same

Cernunnos, *lower panel, south face of the North Cross, Clonmacnoise, Co. Offaly. possibly of the eighth century. Courtesy Office of Public Works, Dublin.*

'family' of figures discussed above, the Oseberg escutcheon is remarkable for the position of the legs. The most likely explanation of this posture is that it derives from the important Celtic deity, Cernunnos, who was usually depicted squatting, and whose widespread and complex cult was second only in importance to the

great cult of the head. His cross-legged position was probably based on the typical sitting position of the Celts as a whole. According to classical writers, they did not use chairs but preferred to squat on the ground. The name 'Cernunnos' is known from a fragmentary relief from Gaul, whence his cult, with roots as far back as the Bronze Age and proto-Celtic period, probably spread. He was particularly associated with fertility, both animal and human; and so his cult, subject to regional variation, was particularly potent.[18]

Probably the most magnificent representation of Cernunnos is found, appropriately enough, in metal-work, on a great Celtic vessel, the silver cauldron of Gundestrup in Denmark, dating from the late second century or early first century B.C.[19] The god is depicted at his most regal and powerful, complete with all his attributes. He sits, cross-legged as 'Lord of the Animals', with ascendancy over the various creatures which surround him, most notably the stag, his cult animal, who has identical antlers. A torc, symbol of divinity, is around his neck; he holds another in his right hand and grasps a ram-headed serpent in his left. The face of the Gundestrup Cernunnos shares the same inscrutable intensity of the Oseberg figure, and the emphatic

Cernunnos as 'Lord of the Animals', *plate from the Gundestrup Cauldron, great silver bowl, from the late second or early first century B.C. Courtesy the National Museum, Copenhagen.*

Anthropomorphic escutcheon in squatting posture, *detail from the 'Buddha Bucket'.*
Bronze enamelled in polychrome champlevé with millefiori, probably from around the late seventh century.
Courtesy Universitetets Oldsaksamlingen, Oslo, Norway.

THE 'BUDDHA BUCKET' FROM THE OSEBERG FIND

jutting brows found in both is a feature typical of Celtic cult heads.

As a late manifestation of a squatting figure originating in Ireland, moreover one in metal-work, the Oseberg escutcheon is extremely unusual. Cernunnos, or Cernunnos-type figures, became particularly potent symbols in the Christian period. In addition to the antiquity of the cult and its association with fertility, the figure and attributes of the god himself were transformed. Cernunnos, so splendidly depicted on the Gundestrup Cauldron, became debased into the squatting, horned, ram-headed, serpent-bearing figure of Satan. In Ireland, a scattered collection of images of this type have escaped the vicissitudes of time but, unlike the metal-work version in exile, they all seem to be carved in stone.

A stone figure from Boa Island, Lough Erne, in Fermanagh, which was part of a particularly active cult region in pre-Christian times, has a large pear-shaped head, janiform in this case, with diminutive legs crossed underneath a small body. The evidence from the Christian period includes a horned figure carved on one of the pillars accompanying the Carndonagh Cross in Donegal. Although badly worn it appears to be cross-legged and may be clasping its knees. Also of note is an upright, but antlered, figure flanked by wolves, 'Lord of the Animals', on the north shaft of the Market Cross of Kells. Of particular relevance to the Oseberg figure is

The Twelve Apostles, *detail of base of the high Cross of Moone, Co. Kildare, possibly of the ninth century.*
Courtesy Office of Public Works, Dublin.

the carving on the lower panel of the south face of the North Cross at Clonmacnoise. Although Carola Hicks has disagreed with Anne Ross's identification of this figure as Cernunnos,[20] it adopts an unmistakeable position, evident despite the elaborate and now rather weathered interlace entwining the body. The legs are bent sharply at the knees and crossed again in the middle, exactly the same arrangement as on the escutcheon. In the wide oval eyes, there

is also a certain facial resemblance.

Fragmentary and elusive though they are, these scattered and varied images show that a deeply rooted and ancient pagan concept persisted, leaving indelible traces in the Christian period. The Oseberg figures belong to this sparse evidence but are also, as apparently the only extant examples in metal-work, remarkable and rare specimens. While they derive their ancestry from Celtic roots, they belong stylistically to a family of figures from the early Christian period. The squat, schematic shape and bold, geometric enamel-work are characteristic of the late seventh century, typical of the emerging stage before the full development of the mature early Christian style that was to dominate the eighth century. As a product of this period, the 'Buddha Bucket' is indeed an intriguing object with perhaps a unique variety of features. The escutcheons on its rim display an early style, usually found in an ecclesiastical setting, but here show a squatting posture associated with a particularly potent Celtic deity, now surrounded by the fierce animal ornament of the magnificent carved objects of the great Oseberg Find.

Margaret Mac Namidhe

I would like to acknowledge the assistance of Dr. Susanne McNab, whose generous advice and immense knowledge were invaluable in writing this article.

NOTES

1. Françoise Henry, *Studies in Early Christian and Medieval Irish Art, Vol. 1, Enamels and Metalwork*, London, 1983, p. 135.
2. Jan Petersen, *Irish Antiquities found in Norway*, Vol. V of *Viking Antiquities found in the British Isles*, Ed. Haakon Shetelig, Oslo, 1940, pp. 7-11.
3. At one particular grave in Oronsay, even the tortoise brooches were replaced by Irish bronze mounts originally meant as book clasps. Haakon Shetelig, Ed., *Civilization of the Viking Settlers in relation to their Old and New Countries*. Vol. VI of *Viking Antiquities*, Oslo, 1940, p. 98.
4. Jan Petersen, op. cit., pp. 10-11.
5. Françoise Henry, op. cit., p. 117.
6. This bucket is also made of yew and has rich brass mountings but has four simple iron carrying rings. Thorleif Sjøvold, *The Viking Ships in Oslo*, Oslo, 1985, p. 44.
7. There is also a bronze object in a truncated pyramid shape, also of Irish provenance, with

red and yellow enamel and *millefiori* in angular compartments found at Oseberg. Françoise Henry, op. cit., p. 108.
8. David M. Wilson and Ole Klindt Jensen, *Viking Art*, London, Second Edition 1980, pp. 49-66.
9. Jan Petersen, op. cit., fig. 82.b. p. 73. Also Françoise Henry, op. cit., plate XXXV, p. 158.
10. *Ibid.*, pp. 172-174.
11. *Ibid.*
12. Michael Ryan, 'Some Aspects of Sequence and Style in the Metalwork of Eighth and Ninth Century Ireland', *Ireland and Insular Art, 500-1200 A.D.*, Royal Irish Academy, Dublin, 1987, p. 66.
13. There is particular evidence from Garranes Fort in Cork. Françoise Henry, op. cit., pp. 98-99.
14. *Ibid.*, pp. 107-110, also T.D. Kendrick, *Anglo Saxon Art*, London, 1938, pp. 100-101.
15. Françoise Henry, op. cit., p. 118.

16. Rupert Bruce Mitford, 'Ireland and the Hanging Bowls: A Review', *Ireland and Insular Art, 500-1200 A.D.*, op. cit., p. 66.
17. This schematic type has been identified and classified as the A2 style of figure by Dr. Susanne McNab, *Irish Figure Sculpture in the 12th Century*, unpublished thesis, Trinity College, Dublin, 1989, pp. 90-105.
18. Anne Ross, *Pagan Celtic Britain*, London, 1967, pp. 127-166.
19. Ruth and Vincent Megaw, *Celtic Art from its Beginnings to the Book of Kells*, London 1989, pp. 174-177.
20. Carole Hicks maintains that the "antlered god" described by Ross, the "tendrilled head and the ornamental treatment of the limbs" derive from the manuscript tradition rather than from "an underlying pagan element". Carola Hicks, 'A Clonmacnois Workshop in Stone', *Journal of the Royal Society of Antiquaries of Ireland*, Vol. 110, Dublin, 1980, pp. 20-22, 30. Anne Ross, op. cit., p. 147.

CASTLE COOLE, CO. FERMANAGH

Castle Coole, Co. Fermanagh, entrance facade.

If the name Castle Coole arouses expectations of a remote and haughty mansion, James Wyatt's chaste Neo-Classical temple does not disappoint. When first sighted across its lovely undulating demesne, it makes an unforgettable impression. Built between 1789 and 1795 for the 1st Earl of Belmore, its perfection is all the more extraordinary for having been based on earlier plans of Richard Johnston (the foundations of whose design had already been laid).

In his *History of the Two Ulster Manors of Coole and Fenagh* (London and Dublin, 1881), Somerset Lowry-Corry, 4th Earl of Belmore, gives the following history and description of the house:

"... the house was roughly estimated to cost about £30,000. By the time that it was finished, it had cost about £54,000, and taken about double the time to build that was expected ...

The restoration of Castle Coole posed many problems, the resolution of which, inevitably, will not be to everyone's taste. George Mott describes the completed work on this late eighteenth-century house.

The house is faced with Portland stone. This was sent to Ireland in the brig Martha, chartered for the purpose, and which seems ultimately to have been lost. The stone was landed at Ballyshannon, in Donegal Bay. It was then carted with oxen for about ten miles to Lough Erne. From thence it was conveyed to Enniskillen in lighters, and finally carted to Castlecoole. The entire cost of procuring, quarrying, and sawing the stone at Portland, as well as at Castlecoole, was about £12,000 Irish. The stone for the basement part of the house and the interior walls seems to have been quarried in the deer-park at Castlecoole, and to be a sort of quartz. The walls were pretty well up, by the end of 1793. The joiner's and carpenter's work took a long time, and was not finished till November, 1798. The house, however, was inhabited by the family before all was completed; in fact the old house was accidentally burnt down, in 1797, it is said, through an ashpan having been left upon the staircase ... The house, which is about 280 feet in length, is a Grecian one, and consists of a centre, and two wings with colonnades. The wings consist only of a basement, and one story of family rooms. The centre of the house has, above the basement on the ground floor, five reception rooms—one of them (the saloon) an oval room. The other four, the drawing-room, dining-room, library and billiard room, are thirty-six feet long by twenty-four feet wide and eighteen high. The principal hall is to the front: the staircase hall is on the west side, between the library and drawing-room.

Sitting-room

Staircase

CASTLE COOLE, CO. FERMANAGH

Up-stairs there are bedrooms and dressing-rooms, and a large bow-windowed sitting room. A large lobby in the centre of this part of the house is lighted by a skylight. Round this is a gallery with pillars, lighted with two additional skylights, and into this gallery a number of rooms open. These, though called attics, were mostly intended for visitors; and several of them are very good rooms, were it not that their windows are too high up, so as to suit the exterior architecture of the house, which has a stone balustrade, running nearly all round, behind which are these windows . . .

The mouldings, cornices and some of the ceilings are very well executed, and were by a Mr. Rose, of London. There are two scagliola pillars in the front hall, and two pilasters on the front staircase, by Mr. Bartoli. In each of the four principal reception rooms, and in the front hall (where are two fireplaces), there are very handsome marble chimneypieces, sculptured in London, by Westmacott."

It would appear that the 1st Earl of Belmore, who died in 1802, ran out of money before the house was finished. The furnishing and decoration were carried out by his son, the 2nd Earl. To this end, the 2nd Earl hired the prominent Dublin upholsterer, John Preston. Preston's accounts of the work carried out between 1807 and 1825 at Castle Coole survive and represent a meticulous chronicle of the decorative agenda. As so many of the actual objects and textiles provided by Preston remain in the house, Castle Coole is as important for its regency decoration as for its Neo-Classical architecture.

The restoration of Castle Coole by the National Trust (begun in 1980) is a saga almost as interesting and eventful as the story of the house itself. Over the years since the house was sold to the Trust by the present Earl's father, the façade was increasingly damaged by splintering due to the infiltration of water behind the finely cut blocks of Portland stone and the rusting of the iron cramps used for fastening the stone cladding to the rubble structural wall behind. Half-measures or patchwork solutions were impractical and the results would probably have been unsightly so it was decided to dismantle the exterior cladding of the entire building, remove all the cramps and replace them with stainless steel.

The radical de-construction of Castle Coole entailed by the replacement of the

Bow room

Bow room

CASTLE COOLE, CO. FERMANAGH

Lobby

Lobby

exterior stone shell led to the decision to redecorate the interior as well. Inevitably this presented some complex stylistic decisions as to the temporal focus of the restoration: the chaste classicism of Wyatt's original interior design or the sumptuous Regency of Preston's later work for the 2nd Earl. The National Trust's excellent new Guide to Castle Coole argues that "...the balance between these periods in the house's grandeur has been struck primarily through the existing furniture in the rooms. Where Wyatt's cool classicism and perfection of line predominates, such as in the dining-room, no attempt has been made to return to a Preston scheme. Where Preston's Regency style is manifest, such as in the saloon and drawing-room in which the furniture is dominant, a return to the Regency fabrics and curtain design will enhance the decorative scheme. And in such rooms as the library, where the family have continued to adapt and accumulate furnishings and contents, a flavour of Victorian, Edwardian and present day interests will be maintained." The guide also comments that "A certain amount of schizophrenia within a house is of interest and inevitable, given the way that houses, like families, grow and change over time. This policy will ensure that each room is integral while the whole reflects the development of Castle Coole for almost 200 years."

The National Trust's restoration of Castle Coole is a magnificent achievement. James Wyatt's scrupulously detailed exterior looks much as it did when the house was first built – the side pavilions especially, so reminiscent of Sir William Chambers's Marino Casino in Dublin, can be enjoyed for the intricate play of volumes and detail that Wyatt lavished on them.

The hall, empty and stately, as Wyatt expressly wanted it, is sparsely furnished with pieces designed by Wyatt for the house: painted wooden tripod candle-stands and superb hall chairs with the Belmore crest from the Dublin firm of Kidd. The statues in the niches are later additions. The wall colour, which continues out in the staircase and up into the bedroom lobby has been the subject of debate. The National Trust made their choice on the basis of a scrape of the colour specified by Preston shortly before 1816 because "it enhances the architect-

Saloon (looking through to dining room)

CASTLE COOLE, CO. FERMANAGH

ural features of the room, brings the scagliola columns into relationship with the rest of the room, and warms the space visually." Some have argued, however, that the choice of a colour so close to the porphyry red of the scagliola columns has the opposite effect – the columnar screen seems more dramatic in photographs of the room taken before the restoration. Perhaps judgement should be deferred until the whole scheme for the hall can be completed and the colour of the walls is seen in relation to Preston's elaborate scarlet and black draped entrance-wall.

Preston provided the continuous running drapery with its splendidly deep valance for the warm and welcoming library. The 1857 'figured Crimson Silk Poplin' is still at the windows. The chimneypiece, like the others on the main floor, was carved by Richard Westmacott of London in 1795 with naturalistic drapery and must have seemed *avant garde* in the newly finished house.

The *enfilade* of drawing-room, saloon and dining-room forms a series of gracefully contrasting spaces. The diningroom, the plainest of the three, is substantially as Wyatt intended. The furniture was designed by Wyatt and made by the joiners working on the house. The oval saloon, used for grand occasions, is appropriately gorgeous with scagliola pilasters, an elaborate plaster ceiling and splendid inlaid mahogany doors that are curved to fit the bow of the walls. The gilt furniture in this room was all supplied by Preston. It is interesting to note the high prices paid for the pier-glasses with gilt frames (£880), an indication of the elevated cost of large sheets of glass. The four elaborate lampstands represented the biggest outlay in the room (£944) possibly because of their complicated gilding.

The drawing-room had been left unfurnished at the 1st Earl of Belmore's death in 1802. In 1816 the 2nd Earl commissioned John Preston to supply the furniture and hangings for this most important room. Preston provided '2 Very Superb Grecian Couches' (at the then enormous price of £490), thirteen armchairs, twelve side chairs, pier tables, a 'Large & Singularly beautiful Table Circular top, broad behul border . . . supported by 4 richly carved & gilt standards upon a shaped Porphyry plinth, elevated by 4 finely carved paw feet, all double gilt.' Preston's description of this import-

Library

Entrance Hall

Lobby (Stove)

ant furniture is no mere hyperbole. The 'Grecian' couches especially are fascinating objects that seem caught in the process of metamorphosis from Classical objectivity to Romantic languor.

The lobby is probably the most interesting architectural space in the house. The device of a top-lit landing is not unusual in Ireland (Bellamont Forest, the Provost's House, Trinity College, Dublin, and Castle Ward are earlier examples). Wyatt's masterly solution at Castle Coole is particularly well worked-out in that both monumentality and mystery are achieved with disarmingly simple means.

After the exhilarating experience of the lofty lobby, the two rooms to which it leads are somewhat anticlimactic. Preston supplied the state bed in 1820 (George IV visited Ireland in 1821, perhaps Lord Belmore anticipated a royal visit); he also supplied the red flock wallpaper.

Opposite the State Bedroom is the Bow Room which formerly served as a ladies' sitting room or 'work' (or needlework) room (as it was described in 1816). It was restored and redecorated under the supervision of David Mlinaric in 1979–80. The original Chinese-style wallpaper, supplied by Robert Dynas of Dublin in 1807, was found intact behind the pier glasses and copied. The original curtains were still hanging in the 1870s and these were copied and re-hung in their idiosyncratic way with the pattern in the central panel running vertically. The curtains are edged with an elaborate beaded fringe which adds both richness and frivolity to the design. The bamboo chairs were in the room in 1816 but were not supplied by Preston. The harp and some of the more comfortable furniture was added later in Victorian times.

The vast amount of money, time, and expertise spent on the restoration of this most splendid of Irish houses is more than justified by the result. Only the news that dry rot has been discovered on the external wall of the State Bedroom casts a shadow on this satisfying achievement. It is a chilling reminder of the vulnerability of Ireland's architectural heritage.

George Mott

Photographs by George Mott

INTRUSIONS AND REPRESENTATIONS: THE LANDSCAPE OF WICKLOW

Though the land from Dublin to Arklow is comparatively fertile, cut off from the west by hills and dissected by rivers that flow eastwards to the sea, the terrain in central and western Wicklow, composed mainly of granite covered by bog, is one of the most sterile in Leinster. In its earliest history, the region was inhabited by tribes who played little part in the general affairs of the province, and it was referred to as the territory of the *fortuatha* or aliens. Some areas never appear to have been settled, either by prehistoric tribes or by the Celts, although ancient cairns and passage graves exist on mountain peaks, and the Sugar Loaf – possibly one of the three 'heights' of Celtic Ireland and probably the *Oe Cualann* of old Irish documents, was topped, according to legend, by a *Sid* or fairy palace![1] It was a desolate place, though there may have been reasonably substantial settlements near what are now the towns of Wicklow and Arklow. A deteriorating climate, with increased rainfall, was probably the reason for a rapid spread of the peat cover, which eventually drove the population down from the upper and middle reaches of the mountains.

It is clear from the 'Life' of St. Kevin of Glendalough that in pre-Norman times vast areas of the Wicklow hills were covered in forest. A northern portion of this woodland survived into the Middle Ages, while in the south the forest on the Wicklow/Wexford border was still extant in the seventeenth century. Missionaries such as Palladius and possibly St. Patrick, are reputed to have landed in Wicklow, but there were few monastic sites of any importance. St. Kevin's monastery at Glendalough, however, rapidly became a centre of learning, commercial wealth and political influence, despite being founded far from other major settlements. It was, however, close to several local communication routes leading from west to east across the mountains. St. Kevin himself is reputed to have come from Kildare along one such route – through the Wicklow Gap and down the so-called 'Madman's Road.'

Glendalough was the first significant development in the region. The monks fled temporarily when it was attacked by the Vikings, supposedly leaving their treasure in Borenacrow, the high pass between Glendalough and Glenmalure, but they returned and the monastery

John Hutchinson, who lives in County Wicklow, discusses here the depiction of that county, its landscape, history and people, and analyzes the relationship between reality and image.

flourished until the thirteenth century. After the Vikings came the Normans, who drove the O'Tooles and O'Byrnes from Kildare into the Wicklow hills. It remained their territory for four centuries until the Elizabethan era. Only in 1606, some twenty years after the Battle of Glenmalure, did Wicklow become a county under English law, the last part of Ireland to be so designated, the Normans and English being loath to venture into the hills and wooded valleys, from whence the Irish chieftains launched their attacks on the Pale. Eventually, in 1655, Wicklow was symbolically appropriated by Sir William Petty's 'Down Survey,' which mapped the area for the English government. The result was a visual image of control and order, an emblem of domination.

While the Down Survey map of Wicklow does not reveal very much about the landscape (the mountains are represented as hillocks, in profile), it is probably the most important early visual image of the new county. It was, of course, a foreigner's view of the land; the Irish, in contrast, preferred to define the landscape in narrative or historical terms. That attitude, still prevalent, is reflected in an article entitled 'Kings in Wicklow',[2] in which Aodh de Blacam writes, "Splendid scenery lacks a soul if it is in country without history". In Wicklow, he says, "the chief retreat is a valley of the saints", and "every lovely view has some heroic story". The essay, while introduced by a paragraph praising the beauties of the county, concerns itself mainly with the *Leabhar Branach* (the Book of the O'Byrnes), a volume of Gaelic ceremonial verse. The ballads tell of the exploits and achievements of Irish warriors and scholars who found shelter at Ballinacor, near Glenmalure, the seat of Fiach MacHugh O'Byrne. De Blacam's approach echoes that of the balladeers, because the *Leabhar Branach* apparently contains few, if any, direct descriptions of the landscape. This was typical for, as De Blacam observes rhetorically, "How often writers of Irish history lament that

they have to go to foreign records for the homely things!"

It is telling, too, that J.B. Malone, in his classic book of rambles called *Walking in Wicklow*[3], always draws attention to the historical associations of the locations he is describing. "Keep straight ahead at the crossroads to go up Glenmalure, the grandest and most historic glen in Wicklow", he says; "where every square yard has its proud, defiant memories of the long stern struggle of the dispossessed to regain their own". And there is a certain irony in the re-appropriation of the map by Malone and his fellow walkers, for it is a sign for the democratization of the landscape. Nor is it accidental that *Walking in Wicklow* opens as follows, "It is said, on very doubtful authority, that some rock-climbers once repaired to a quarry in the foothills of the Wicklow Mountains, and solemnly advanced to the foot of the crag, bearing the apparatus of their craft and mystery, coils of the best Alpine rope, and boots benailed on a Himalayan scale. Suddenly the voice of an urchin, perched upon a nearby rock, broke the silence: 'Eh, Mister! What are all them ropes for? Jemser here can get up without them!'".

As the English and Anglo-Irish grip on the county strengthened, so the landscape began to undergo some major changes. In 1610 Sir John Davies observed that "The Native Irish" had not exploited the land, "therefore it stands neither with Christian policy nor conscience to suffer so good and fruitful country to lie waste like a wilderness."[4] With such ideas in the backs of their minds, the English took it upon themselves to subjugate and cultivate the countryside. Concurrently, visual images of Co. Wicklow began to proliferate. An anonymous painting of the Kilruddery Hunt,[5] dated about 1730, unambiguously represents the transformations. Although dwarfed by the Sugar Loaf behind it, Kilruddery is at the centre of the image, with formal gardens extending to the left, while huntsmen and hounds, their large scale completely at variance with physical reality, overwhelm the hillside. The Knight of Glin and Edward Malins have described this picture as "charmingly naive",[6] but in his very innocence the artist has baldly reproduced the ethos of the eighteenth-century aristocracy.

Some years later, George Barret paint-

James Arthur O'Connor, A View of the Devil's Glen.
Courtesy National Gallery of Ireland, No. 825.

George Barret, A View of Powerscourt Waterfall.
Courtesy National Gallery of Ireland, No. 174.

ed Powerscourt House,[7] which stands a few miles away to the west, also beneath the Sugar Loaf. (The Palladian mansion, positioned on the site of an earlier house and castle, was designed by Richard Castle between 1731 and 1741). Like Kilruddery, it is located at the centre of the painting, and in the foreground, two horsemen survey the scene. The high vantage point, conspicuous in this picture and in the 'Kilruddery Hunt', is a characteristic of many eighteenth-century 'house portraits', precisely because it suggests a sense of control. But here, that convention is modified, and we are presented with the new Palladian house as an enviable property, at once near and inaccessible. At a glance we can vicariously own the house, because through an unconscious identification with the horsemen, we can imagine ourselves as being able to enjoy, with the appropriate seignorial attitude, the mansion in its paradisaical setting. The setting is, in more than one respect, the obverse of that of 'Kilruddery Hunt', where 'nature' is aggresively dominated by the landowner and his culture. The view of Powerscourt, which nestles comfortably in a hollow, surrounded by deciduous trees and backed by an exaggeratedly lofty Sugar Loaf, reflects the attempt by the wealthy classes to disguise the hierarchies of society by 'naturalizing' the signs of their authority. The house is shown as part of the landscape, as an improvement to the wilderness; the significance of the Sugar Loaf is reduced to that of a grand back-drop. And Barret's horsemen, instead of hectically galloping all over the mountain, regard it from a position of detached equanimity.

The wish to naturalize signs of wealth and prestige is also expressed in an engraving of 'Mount Kennedy' (another Co. Wicklow mansion), by Thomas Milton, after a painting by William Ashford, in which a gentleman and his wife rise up on their horses, as if in admiration, as they come upon the house at the end of a rutted lane. A labourer with a pitchfork on his shoulder stands in a shaded hollow in front of his master and mistress, and is 'contentedly' setting about his business. As Ann Bermingham has noted,[8] the 'natural' landscape, suggested here by the mature trees and rutted lane, allows "for a conveniently ambiguous signification, so that nature was the sign of property, and property the

sign of nature". The formal garden, of the kind that can be seen in the painting of Kilruddery, stood somewhere *between* art and nature, but the landscaped garden "tended to collapse the distinction". As Bermingham notes, "by conflating nature with the fashionable taste of a new social order, it redefined the natural in terms of that order, and *vice versa*."

Roland Barthes once observed that the ideological power of trees as symbols resides in their particular compound of the 'natural' and the 'political', as trees and woodland can be used either to politicize social relations, or to neutralize them.[9] The symbolic associations of trees help to explain their preponderance in eighteenth and early nineteenth century British and Irish landscapes. Another print of the same period, 'Glanmore' (after John Carr), shows the castellated house, situated near the entrance to the 'sublime' Devil's Glen. (Another castellated house, Castle Howard, was admired by a contemporary because "The adoption of the ancient English style of architecture is peculiarly judicious in a mountainous and romantic country, like Wicklow.")[10] Glanmore's estate was particularly admired for its trees, which are prominently featured in the engraving.

Enthusiasm for trees is a comparatively modern phenomenon. Until the middle of the eighteenth century, dense woodland was regarded as wilderness, and only by moving away from the forest could a man become civilized. (The word 'savage' derives from the Latin *silva*, or wood.) Thus Edmund Burke could say that the "ancient Hindus" had developed a civilization possessing "all the arts of polished life, whilst we were yet in the woods"[11] and also urge George Barret to pursue his artistic muse in the wooded valleys of the Dargle near Powerscourt.

The planting of trees accentuated an impression of naturalized power, with devices such as avenues, clearings, rides, belts, clumps, and screens creating particular visual and ideological effects. For instance, the cutting of a vista through existing trees, or the creation of a long tree-lined avenue, indicated the subjection of the countryside to the authority of the grand house. The result, as Andrew Marvell once put it, was that "like a guard on either side, the trees before their lord divide."[12]

Most forms of aristocratic tree-planting were deliberate, if unconscious, assertions of ownership. The view from a house, according to picturesque theory, should be open only if all the land in sight belonged to the householder, in which case the vista would gratify his "love of possession". But if someone else's property obtruded, then a screen of trees should be erected to conceal it. Uvedale Price, one of the architects of picturesque theory, held that trees should conceal the extent of the property if small, and display it if large. He also argued that a more painterly style of landscaping, especially one modelled on Dutch or Flemish prototypes (as can be seen in the Milton print of Mount Kennedy), was particularly humane, for "the love of painting considers the dwelling, the inhabitants, and the marks of their intercourse, as ornaments to the landscape". Deciduous trees, if represented in the Dutch manner, "grounded" the gaze, and introduced an element of humility. In Price's opinion, wise landscape development involved the blurring of class boundaries—although, naturally, the hierarchy of aristocratic values was never seriously questioned.[13] Again, this attitude is suggested in the image of Mount Kennedy.

Pretentious planters, anxious for instant effect, liked to plant conifers (as in Glanmore), as well as limes and chestnuts. Oaks, however, were the most highly regarded of trees, followed by beech and elm. Oaks were considered to be incomparably patrician. Edmund Burke echoed this sentiment when he described the English aristocracy as "the great oaks that shade a country", and when he favourably contrasted the "*chiaroscuro*" of mature wooded English parkland to the clarity and brilliance of "experimental" landscapes like the "geometrical constitution" of revolutionary France.[14] Established deciduous trees suggested political security and a system of inheritance that ensured the transmission of property, which made it worth planting for future generations. This, of course, was an attitude that was peculiar to the ruling classes, and it came late to Ireland, for as Sir John Davies said in 1610, inheritance in this country was so uncertain that the Irish never planted orchards.[15]

Tree planting had an economic foundation as well and, because of its aristo-

INTRUSIONS AND REPRESENTATIONS: THE LANDSCAPE OF WICKLOW

cratic associations, it was one of the few aspects of agriculture that were highlighted in landscape paintings. (Most forms of labour were not considered compatible with Arcadian idylls or 'sublimity'.) One of the appealing qualities of 'picturesque' painting was precisely its exclusion of any references to work, or to the conflict and disturbance caused by social change. Landowners did not choose to think of themselves as being in business. Instead, they saw themselves as staunch pillars of a stable and traditional society, so their attention was directed at the maintenance of their status at the pinnacle of the social hierarchy. Planting woodland, perhaps especially in a county like Wicklow, which had once been perceived as a forested wilderness, was an effective way of naturalizing that aspiration. James Arthur O'Connor, who painted in the 1820s and 1830s, was one of the few artists who infused his Wicklow landscapes, be they wooded valleys or 'sublime' glens, with any semblance of individual sensibility.[16]

The 'sublime' aspects of Co. Wicklow were much relished in the eighteenth century, and Powerscourt Waterfall, which epitomized the sublimity of the landscape, was frequently depicted in paintings, most notably by George Barret.[17] The waterfall was a fixed point in the itineraries of tourists and travellers searching for the civilized thrill of awesome scenery. And as it became an attraction, so new perceptions of the place eroded its traditional associations. These latter were centred on the O'Tooles and O'Byrnes, for during the time of Felim MacHugh O'Byrne, son of Feach, the valleys near Enniskerry were in the hands of the O'Tooles (the lands were confiscated in 1589, and granted to Richard Wingfield). In a poem celebrating Felim, known as 'the raven of Leinster', the area is referred to as 'Glenn Ese', the glen of the waterfall.[18] It was not noted, however, for its beauty.

Nevertheless, the visual splendour of the waterfall was frequently extolled in print by the Anglo-Irish. In 1741, for instance, the Reverend Edward Chamberlayne wrote[19]

While Nature smiles, obsequious to your call,
Directs, assists, and recommends it all.
At last she gives (O Art how vain thy Aid)
To crown the beauteous Work – a vast Cascade

Thus in Improvements shines the Attick Taste,
Thus Eden springs where once you found a Waste.

The "Waste", "Improved" by Lord Powerscourt through the tasteful construction of walks, bridge, gazebos, and so forth, was thereby transformed in the eyes of his contemporaries – perhaps especially because it was confined within the bounds of a grand estate. Indeed, the enjoyment of the 'sublime' or 'picturesque' was almost invariably confined to the vicinity of large houses, with the result that the Rev. Mr. George Wright's *Guide to Wicklow*, published in 1822 with illustrations by George Petrie, "displays that almost pathological preoccupation with Gentlemen's Seats that was, of course, normal in his time", as J. B. Malone acidly points out.[20] The love of wilderness, or 'sublimity', is thereby revealed as an acquired cultural taste, not the 'natural' response to landscape that it pretended to be. The very term 'picturesque' makes that clear. To refer to the countryside as being like a picture (and particularly to look at it reflected in a tinted Claude Glass, so as to turn it into an image of a painting) is the corollary of the naturalization of culture. It is the culturization of nature.

Avondale, also on the tourist route (and celebrated for its trees, planted by Samuel Hayes), was described by a contemporary as "a wilderness of sweets",[21] an evocation that accords with the sentimentality of the "distressed" cottage in its woods. An idyll of poverty, like mountainous sublimity, was enjoyed as long as it was an affectation or, at least, when it was contrived within a grand social context. Those on the picturesque tour, like today's travellers who prefer to ignore the dingy reality of Wicklow's country towns and "bungalow blight", were seldom very much concerned with the reality of life for the majority of the county's inhabitants. Their attitude to the landscape was exclusively aesthetic – an attitude that is in itself blameless so long as it isn't founded on an insensitivity to needs other than one's own. But such insensitivity, of course, was often the norm, and the ruling classes' appreciation of Wicklow's 'sublimity' did nothing to hinder the imposition of a military road through the glens and around the peaks, or the construction of military barracks in scenic

areas like Glencree, Glenmalure, and Aughavannagh.

George du Noyer, a pupil of George Petrie, who worked for the Ordnance Survey in the 1830s (it is notable that when he was so employed, "he developed a love and knowledge of the ancient art and archaeology of Ireland"),[22] was one of the few artists who depicted the 'sublime' hills and mountains of Wicklow with accuracy and without exaggeration. In contrast, W. H. Bartlett's contemporary engravings of similar views are so stylized that they seem generic, rather than specific. The image of 'Glenmalure Head', for example, bears only the vaguest relation to reality, such is its visual rhetoric. Nor are there any references to the historical associations of the glen. The only sign of humanity, past or present, is a tiny shepherd and his flock, Bartlett's views are a kind of wish-fulfilment, idealized and insubstantial. It is perhaps not coincidental that he was English.

Nineteenth-century visitors to Wicklow, like most tourists, saw beauty in the reflection of their own preconceived tastes, so while their representations of the county were usually sympathetic or flattering, they were invariably selective. And in that regard, 'picturesque' views have obvious similarities with today's postcards, which nostalgically glorify a 'real' Ireland that corresponds to predetermined ideals.[23]

In the last decade or so there has been renewed interest in the 'indigenous' culture of Ireland; postcard photographs of cottages, shopfronts, and old farms have a ready market, as do portraits of elderly people with interesting faces. These subjects are presented to us as living relics of an age that is in the process of being eroded by ugly modernity. Insight Ireland, for example, publishes a card of a 'Remote Cottage in Wicklow.'[24] Its composition is not very different from Barret's view of Powerscourt. The photographer, and, by extension, the viewer, looks down from the top of a hill at a simple cottage with a red roof, which is apparently deserted. A few sparse trees surround it. Behind the cottage, deep in a valley, looms another hill, which is half-hidden by dark shadows. The cottage, like the eighteenth-century mansion, is set up as the "object of our desire" (to use psychoanalytic phraseology), and, more specifically, as the feminine object of a

Joseph Peacock, Festival of St. Kevin at the Seven Churches of Glendalough.
Courtesy the Ulster Museum.

Erskine Nicol, The Seafront at Bray, Co. Wicklow. pencil & water-colour with white highlights on paper.
Courtesy National Gallery of Ireland, No. 7587.

INTRUSIONS AND REPRESENTATIONS: THE LANDSCAPE OF WICKLOW

dominant male gaze. It is as if we are being invited to enter it, to inhabit it, which further underlines the implicit sexuality of the image. This is contemporary Wicklow, as photographed by an outsider, revealed to us as a humble but inviting feminine presence, threatened by intrusive obscurity—in other words, by incipient modernization.

What the photographer has left out of his image is the 'unaesthetic', those aspects of the environment that do not coincide with his 'insight' into the 'real' Ireland. The result is unwittingly aggressive, for it suggests a wish both to possess and to exclude. It is highly unlikely that a local Wicklow man would ever take such a photograph, because he would be more conscious of the human value of 'ugly' modern developments. And if he has not died or emigrated, the erstwhile inhabitant of the 'remote cottage' is probably now the proud owner of a dull bungalow, replete with creature comforts.

It is unusual to find an eighteenth or early nineteenth-century Wicklow landscape that shows people at work. One such picture is Thomas Sautell Roberts's engraving of men digging for gold in the hills—although the subject of the picture is really the gold mines, not the workers. (Roberts also depicted other Wicklow scenes, including 'A Rebel Retreat in the Devil's Glen; General Holt is represented as appointing his evening guards', and an 'Irish Hut, Co. Wicklow'. He also painted several portraits of the aristocracy in landscape settings.)[25] Joseph Peacock painted the extraordinary 'Festival of St. Kevin at the Seven Churches of Glendalough' in 1817,[26] an image that painstakingly represents the 'pattern', a celebrated festival-cum-fair that was held annually until 1847, when it was suppressed because of rowdiness and fighting. Despite its Romanticism, this is a rare example of a Wicklow landscape that focusses on people, as opposed to the view. Another Wicklow painting with human activity as its focus is Erskine Nichol's water-colour 'View of Bray',[27] which shows the town in its heyday as an Edwardian seaside resort. But because of its Romantic associations, Wicklow has seldom been visually represented as a place where the common man lives and works: it has more often been portrayed as a beautiful wilderness that the cultured man can subdue, and to which

Detail of Wicklow Mineshaft, Avoca. Courtesy Gene Lambert.

he can withdraw in order to admire the 'sublimity' of nature.

Some recent paintings of Wicklow have re-introduced signs of human labour while still retaining references to the county's 'sublimity' and to established conventions. Cecily Brennan's large and unstretched bird's-eye views are as dominating in their vantage point as any eighteenth century house portrait, but central to these pictures are the State Forestry plantations—regimented crops of unaesthetic trees grown for economic reasons on behalf of the people of Ireland. She has also painted Wicklow turf bogs, which similarly focus on man's labour and his interaction with the landscape.[28] Gene Lambert, who temporarily abandoned painting in favour of photography some years ago, has photographed the detritus near the defunct Avoca mines. His prints have a grim aesthetic beauty, but are essentially oblique comments on unemployment and the despoiling of the environment, and thereby bring to the fore social implications of man's abuse of the environment.

These, then, are images of Wicklow that have narrowed the gap between an outsider's and an insider's perceptions of the landscape. But they still cannot be considered as populist. To find the most widespread and commonly accepted visual images of Wicklow today, we have to turn to 'Glenroe', the popular television soap opera. Yet despite Wicklow's current *sobriquet*, 'The Garden of Ireland', the residents of this imaginary village never cast an admiring eye on their surroundings. Nor does the camera ever dwell on the beauty of the landscape. In 'Glenroe' the land is not forgotten or ignored (it is the basis of the villagers' livelihood), but is not aesthetically represented.

In a recent article entitled 'Romanticism in Ruins: developments in Irish Cinema',[29] Luke Gibbons argues that "the very features which enhanced the Irish countryside in the eyes of visitors, and which were accordingly attributed to nature—wildness, simplicity, primitivism—were seen internally as *social* conditions, part of the stresses and contradictions within a colonial society". Overturning conventional theories about Ireland's inherent Romanticism, Gibbons sought to demonstrate that in indigenous cultural terms, man was always central to the landscape.

"For the Romantic movement", he writes, "part of the attraction of ruins lay in the decay they exuded. Ruins conveyed a sense of an irretrievable past, their relapse into a state of nature underlining the transience of human achievement. In Ireland, ruins and antiquities carried with them an entirely different set of associations. Instead of being recuperated by nature, they dominate the landscape . . . the very survival of ruins meant that they had withstood the ravages of time and successive waves of invasion, thus attesting to the continuity between the past and the present, and the resiliences of Gaelic civilization". As a pertinent illustration of this attitude, which he describes as a "capacity to reclaim landscape for a political project", Gibbons points to Seamus Heaney's idea that bogland is the most characteristic feature of the Irish landscape, because of "its ability to hoard the relics of the past acting as a metaphor for Irish popular memory. The preservative powers of bogs are such that even nature is converted into an outdoor museum, forcing the eye inwards, as Heaney puts it, rather than drawing it towards the horizon".

But there is another side to this argument. Fintan O'Toole has written about the idealization of rural Ireland by Gaelic Nationalists.[30] He pays particular attention to the authors of the Irish Literary Revival, who turned to the West of Ireland in order to find the sense of community and social cohesion that they lacked in Dublin. In doing so, according to O'Toole, they "aristocratized" the peasantry, and postulated a "natural" link between peasant farmers and the land. They thus ignored the fact that rural Ireland was not a peasant paradise but a money economy riven by class divisions. These Nationalist writers, by sentimentally harping on a non-existent Golden Age, divided the nation into two opposing states: rural Ireland, innocent and unspoiled; and urban Ireland, corrupt and fallen. In O'Toole's view, this fictional division obscures changes that have taken place in the countryside, and makes rural Ireland more susceptible to insensitive processes of modernization. The continuing opposition of the country to the city, of nature to culture, he argues, has been vital to the maintenance of a conservative political tradition. 'What

has been missing, O'Toole concludes, 'is a Utopian tradition, drawing its poetry from the future'–in short, 'a myth of transformation'.

The Irish landscape tradition is thus being re-evaluated in various fields of enquiry. These new assessments plainly have their own inadequacies, and this article is no exception. Why, it might be asked, must one analyse paintings in such a way as to reduce them to ideological statements? Is Wicklow not a beautiful county, and do these pictures

not reflect its attractions? The answer to the last question is obvious enough, but it is arguable that only by subjecting such images–and one's own thinking–to a process of deconstruction will any objective beauty be perceived. Landscape, as opposed to 'the land', is not a natural phenomenon: it is a way of structuring, representing, or symbolizing our surroundings.

John Hutchinson

NOTES

1. Most of this historical information has been gleaned from Alfred P. Smyth's *Celtic Leinster*, Dublin, 1982.
2. 'The Irish Monthly', September 1944. The article was brought to my attention by Luke Gibbons.
3. J. B. Malone, *Walking in Wicklow*, Dublin, 1964.
4. Quoted in Keith Thomas, *Man and the Natural World, Changing Attitudes in England, 1500–1800*, Harmondsworth, 1984, p. 14.
5. Illustrated in Edward Malins and The Knight of Glin, *Lost Demesnes*, London, 1976, pl. 14.
6. *Ibid.*, p. 12.
7. Paul Mellon Collection, Yale Centre for British Art.
8. Ann Bermingham, *Landscape and Ideology, The English Rustic Tradition 1740–1860*, London, 1987, p. 14.

9. See 'Myth Today', in R. Barthes, *Mythologies*, London, 1972. Translated from the French edition of 1957.
10. Malins and Glin, op.cit., p. 174.
11. Quoted in Thomas, op.cit., p. 195.
12. Quoted in Thomas, op.cit., p. 207.
13. See 'The Political Ideology of Woodland', by Stephen Daniels, in *The Iconography of Landscape*, ed. D. Cosgrove and S. Daniels, Cambridge, 1986.
14. Quoted in Thomas, op.cit., p. 218.
15. Quoted in Thomas, op.cit., p. 210.
16. For further information on O'Connor's landscapes, see this writer's article on the artist in *Irish Arts Review*, Vol. 2, No. 4, Winter 1985.
17. National Gallery of Ireland, Cat. No. 174.
18. Smyth, op.cit., p. 55.
19. Quoted in Malins and Glin, op.cit., pp.174-175.

20. Malone, op.cit., p. 19.
21. Quoted in Malins and Glin, op.cit., p. 172.
22. W. J. Strickland, *Dictionary of Irish Artists*, Shannon, 1969.
23. For further information on this subject, see 'Irish Postcards and Mood Photography' by Tanya Kiang in *CIRCA* 43, Dec.–Jan. 1989.
24. Photograph by Peter Zoller for Insight Ireland postcards.
25. Strickland, op. cit.
26. Ulster Museum, Belfast.
27. National Gallery of Ireland, Cat. No. 7587.
28. For further information on Cecily Brennan's landscapes, see this writer's article on the artist in *Irish Arts Review*, Vol. 3, No. 3, Autumn 1986.
29. *The Irish Review*, No. 2, 1987.
30. 'Going West: The Country versus the City in Irish Writing', in *Crane Bag*, Vol. 9, No. 2.

THE PAINTINGS OF BRIAN BOURKE

In the mid-'60s Brian Bourke caused something of a scandal in Dublin when he exhibited a series of nude self-portraits; these showed the artist standing or seated beside his easel, wearing nothing but a top-hat, a party paper hat, or holding an umbrella. I remember the disquiet I felt as a schoolboy on being confronted by a portrait of the naked artist with a fireman's helmet (1965). Some years earlier, in 1959, Bourke had returned to Ireland from London, and criticism was made in some quarters that he was introducing a foreign degradation, the squalor and savagery of Francis Bacon, into Irish art. Not just the public, but also some critics, were outraged by the artist. He was accused of not being able to draw. One critic spoke of the "gutter colours" which he used; another referred to his "concentration camp mind".[1]

Bourke has always remained something of an outsider in Irish art. Although a founder member of the Independent Artists in 1960, he resigned from the group shortly afterwards when it introduced a policy of selection. During the 1960s and '70s, when many of his contemporaries were turning towards abstraction, or adopting international art movements, Brian Bourke steadfastly continued to work figuratively representing the traditional subjects of figure and landscape, when it was almost impossible to see such subjects at any of the advanced exhibitions. This may seem unimportant now, when portrait and landscape subjects are commonplace at most group exhibitions, but it required courage at the time.

While many of his contemporaries were looking to American Abstraction for inspiration, Bourke was studying the work of early Italian and Germany artists, and discovering the early twentieth century German Expressionists. While other artists of the time were making Paris or New York their mecca, in 1964 and 1966, Bourke slipped off quietly to southern Germany. Later, in the 1970s, he moved to the West of Ireland – not the scenic coast-line of Connemara, but the forgotten hinterland of *Iar Connacht*. With the increasing popularity of figurative art in the 1980s, Bourke was included in an important exhibition, 'Making Sense' at the Project Arts Centre, Dublin in 1983.[2] It might have seemed that he had entered the 'mainstream' at last, or that fashion had caught up

Brian Bourke's painting reflects an independent and uncompromising man. He has been very successful since he began exhibiting in the 1960s and, following a retrospective in 1989, **Dr. Julian Campbell** assesses his life and work.

Self-portrait, oil on canvas, 40 × 30 cms.

with him. But this was not the case. His paintings were almost subdued in this company; he dwelt uneasily among the Neo-Expressionist artists of the 1980s.

Bourke has never belonged to any school, is wary of an art establishment, and suspicious of teaching at art school. Through a career of thirty years, there have been many phases of his work. He has refused to stand still, often avoiding expectation, alternating between different subject matter, or experimenting with different media. Yet his position as one of the leading contemporary Irish artists has never been in doubt. He has always had his admirers, and has been generous of his time with students, or interviewers, so that the facts of his life are well-known. He has exhibited regularly. In 1982, Dr. James White and Goldsmith Press published a book, *Brian Bourke, A Catalogue of his Work*, and in 1985 David Shaw-Smith's R.T.E. film brilliantly captured the life and times of the artist. Bourke is a member of *Aosdána*, and a recipient of the prestigious *Cnuas*.[3] In summer 1988 a large retrospective of his work was organized by the Galway Arts Festival[4], and he was one of the Irish representatives at the Rosc International Art Exhibition held in Dublin in the autumn of that year. In January 1989 his

retrospective opened at the Royal Hospital, Kilmainham, Dublin.

This exhibition was principally dedicated to his paintings and drawings, although some of his sculptures were also included. He is an intensely prolific artist, and has experimented with a variety of media: oil paint and acrylic, watercolour, crayon or pencil (often within the one painting); etching; sculpture in bronze or wood (sometimes painting his sculpture). Each person may admire a different aspect of his work: his early portraits, perhaps, or his Bavarian landscapes; his self-portraits or his landscapes of Connemara; his humorous etchings of Don Quixote or Marcel Marceau, or his recent Sweeney series; his portraits of 'J', or his austere sculptural heads. He has been admired as a great 'colourist' and a brilliant draughtsman, as an original sculptor and a satirical etcher. But in whichever medium he is using, he has always tended to work in series. In some of his landscapes, for instance, he works on a number of canvases concurrently. Bourke's apparent singularity or idiosyncracy has often proved to be ahead of its time; his admiration of German painting, for example, or his interest in literary themes; his devotion to self-portraits, in different media; the painted frames around his pictures; his interest in working in series, and his early use of the diptych or triptych (which has now become a commonplace in Irish art); his painted sculptures or the poetic or quirky titles to his exhibitions such as 'Frau Stutz's Cherry Tree', which give his shows a certain enigma, the sense of an event taking place. Ignoring fashion, he is an artist who has always expressed humanist values and a sense of humour.

As Kieran Corcoran observes, "Brian Bourke's art is based upon what he has experienced directly: his own self, family, friends, lovers, places he has lived, novels, plays and poems he has enjoyed".[5]

It has been said that art begins with one's own face. The theme of the self-portrait has been a constant in the work of Brian Bourke, sometimes representational, sometimes grotesque, scrutinized or scrutinizing, sardonic or self-mocking. He often takes on different guises or personae. From the early nude self-portraits to the Sweeney series, when the artist appears to identify with the king turned outcast or madman, there is a strong

Self in Garden, *oil on canvas, 120 × 112 cms.*

THE PAINTINGS OF BRIAN BOURKE

sense of autobiography. The second picture in the retrospective (and illustrated on the cover of James White's book) was a small, exquisite self-portrait of the artist with sad, baleful eyes and a white hat, against a criss-crossed lacquered background of red, mauve and blue, and surrounded by a gold circle. There is an almost medieval, iconic feeling to this and to many of his portraits. There have been comical drawings, as in the 'Self as Don Quixote', 1980–81, or in painted masks or puppets. The artist is not afraid to represent himself naked, or ageing, grimacing into the mirror or making faces at the viewer.[6] He frequently wears different types of hat; a woolly cap or a clown's hat, a sailor's cap or a wide Spanish hat. For he believes that each type of head-gear gives a different mood or countenance to the picture.

Bourke, undoubtedly, has been influenced by two great mid-century artists, Francis Bacon and Giacometti, sharing some of their figurative and humanist concerns. Writers and critics have often claimed Bacon and Giacometti as 'existential' artists, who represent the isolation or alienation of twentieth-century man. But the two artists would claim that they are less concerned with 'the human condition' than with perception. Brian Bourke might similarly deny over-serious interpretations of his work, whether literary or psychological. Nevertheless, the continued scrutiny of his own face, of women and other friends, of figures in space, do reveal his concerns, psychological as well as perceptual. He is concerned with the emotional effect of hats and clothing and, above all, colour. But always to counterbalance the intense seriousness of his work, there is the mocking, self-irony of a twentieth-century court jester. In a recent interview with John Hutchinson, Bourke remarks, "I'm a figurative painter . . . but I'm also interested in abstract painting. I understand it, and have a great liking for it. Therefore, as far as I'm concerned, there is no competition between figuration and abstraction."[7]

Brian Bourke was born into a large and talented family in Sandymount, Dublin, in 1936. One of his brothers, Fergus, is a leading Irish photographer. Another, Eoin, opened an art gallery in Munich in the 1960s. Brian was very attached to his older sister, a delicate and somehow unwordly girl, who died when she was only

twelve. Her death had a deep effect upon him, making him aware of the fragility of the people one loves, and the transience of life, and perhaps creating in him a certain ironic defensiveness against the world.

Bourke studied for a brief period at the National College of Art in the early '50s. But his disappointment with its teaching methods led him to criticize the staff, and he left before the year was up. He moved to London in 1953, and remained there for six years, working as a barman, as an assistant in a hospital operating theatre, and in other odd jobs. He attended St. Martin's School of Art for a year (later under the sculptor, Anthony Caro, St. Martin's became the centre for abstract steel sculpture in Britain), and also took classes at Goldsmith's School of Art. But his greatest education was gained from visits to the National Gallery, the Tate Gallery, and the smaller commercial galleries around Mayfair. At the National Gallery he discovered the work of the Italian and German 'Primitives', admiring their use of colour and composition, and responding sensuously to their tactileness and smell. 'The Madonna and Child Enthroned' by Cosimo Tura, with its perspective and its extraordinary colours, (particularly its striking greens), made a particular impression upon him. He also admired an altar-piece by the Bartholomew Master, and Pollaiuolo's painting of a girl growing into a tree. Later, in the National Gallery of Ireland, he appreciated early Italian and German paintings, 'The Crucifixion' by Giovanni di Paolo, for instance, and portraits by Conrad Faber. And on his visits to Bavaria 1964–66, he discovered German masters such as Michael Pacher and Jan Pollack. The treatment of space, the purity of colour, and the imagery of these later Gothic paintings fascinated him. He studied the artists' methods of constructing pictures, working within rectangles and creating different scenes and perspectives within one painting.

At the Tate Gallery in the 1950s he admired the work of modern artists, particularly 'Northern' masters such as Van Gogh, Munch, and Ensor, for their expressive power and 'material' use of paint. In the galleries around Bond Street and Cork Street, he saw the work of contemporary artists. The gallery owners were often helpful in showing him paintings by their artists in back rooms. James

White speaks of the impact upon the young Bourke of seeing paintings by the then virtually unknown Irish artist, Roderic O'Conor (at Roland, Browse and Delbanco) for the first time in 1956 or 1957.[6] (As Bourke recalls, a critic had dismissed O'Conor's paintings at the sale of Somerset Maugham's collection, and his paintings did not sell easily.) The thought of this forgotten Irish artist, living in exile in France until his death in 1940, struck a chord in the young Bourke, and the bold and colourful French canvases of Breton peasants, landscapes and still-lives, painted in red and green, mauve and orange stripes, made a deep impression on him. The influence of O'Conor may be also seen on Francis Bacon at this period, particularly in his series in homage to Van Gogh, 'The Artist on his Way to Work', with their rich brush-strokes and unusually lyrical colours (1957). Bourke recalls visiting a Bacon exhibition, and the effect of seeing the Van Gogh series and 'Screaming Pope' pictures on a gallery above his head. Although not a particular admirer of Bacon, nevertheless he loved his sensual use of paint at this period, which Bacon lost in later paintings, and was interested in his treatment of the human figure in space. During this period in London, Bourke also saw paintings by contemporary Australian 'primitives', Sidney Nolan and Arthur Boyd. The images of ragged, sometimes masked, figures in a mythical Australian landscape, and the rough 'casual' paint surface, made an impression upon him although now he believes that Nolan's later paintings also lost the quality of this period. It is interesting to note that all these artists– O'Conor, Bacon, and Nolan–have Irish connexions.

Upon his return to Ireland in 1959, Bourke settled at Booterstown, Co. Dublin, and devoted himself to painting full time. His young wife and child and his immediate environment appear in his early paintings. He was a founder member of the Independent Artists in 1960. Although he did not remain for long with this group, he shared common figurative concerns with other Independents, such as James McKenna, John Kelly and Michael Kane. The Francis Bacon Exhibition at the Municipal Gallery in Dublin in 1963 and the Emil Nolde Exhibition at the Royal Hibernian Academy in 1964, made a considerable

THE PAINTINGS OF BRIAN BOURKE

impact upon many young Irish artists of the period, not just Bourke, but also Patrick Graham, Jack Donovan and Charles Harpur, and perhaps, Barrie Cooke and Louis le Brocquy also. Bourke's figure studies and nude self-portraits show the influence of Bacon, not so much in the figures themselves, as in certain compositional devices, such as a flat section of canvas or table, or an abstract background. However, Bacon preferred to use photographs, so as not to be distracted by the physical presence of the sitter, whereas Bourke worked directly from life, thus giving his pictures a greater directness and more personal quality.

In his series of 'Sunflower' paintings, for example the dour but strangely haunting 'Decaying Sunflowers', 1965 (Cat. No. 19), at the Hugh Lane Gallery, Dublin, there is an obvious tribute to Van Gogh and Roderic O'Conor, with the dappled background of greens and maroons. But the sombre colours, the wilting flowers and the abstract vase and foreground, give Bourke's painting a strong identity of its own. Similarly in his garden paintings of 1966–67, his garden in Booterstown is lush and wooded, with crowded sky, and sombre, expressive colours, as if painted in a Bavarian forest. In some pictures, the figure of a woman with a large umbrella stands in front of the trees. The agitated sky is as much a part of the composition as the figure or trees. The presence of a flat yellow umbrella against sombre greens and browns has a dazzling effect. But the umbrella, as the varying hats in the self-portraits, is not really a device, such as Bacon might use to hang the composition on. Rather, Bourke is interested in the effect that such objects or colours have upon the mood of the sitter, and the picture as a whole.

His series of small heads, such as the 1972 self-portrait (Cat. No. 2), almost like sculptures set in landscapes or surrounded by geometric frames, show his further investigation of the object in space, the psychological effect of distance and colour. This interest in space and the incisive 'sculptural' drawing, show Bourke's admiration for the work of Giacometti. (A large retrospective of Giacometti's sculptures and drawings was shown at The Tate Gallery in 1966.) The Swiss artist was concerned with trying to *see* correctly, whether the figure was a few

inches away or at the far end of a room.

When Bourke exhibited in the 1960s, with his curious expressive canvases, his uncompromising nudes, and his distinctive palette, he seemed to have appeared from out of the blue. There was an almost middle European Expressionist quality to his work, completely different from any other art at the time. During the 1960s he made several visits to southern Germany, responding to the different quality of its light from that of Ireland, and to the upright, rather than horizontal, form of the woodland landscapes. In his landscapes of Polling in Bavaria, the lush greenery of trees and swirling shapes of foliage fill the composition. In some pictures, the village baker is shown out for a walk (Cat. No. 67); in others the sky and roadway are dappled with complementary colours. On a subsequent visit to Germany in 1968, Bourke worked on a series of forest paintings. These have a much greater sense of movement, rich colours (greens and reds, purples, oranges and blues), piled on with wild exuberance. In the retrospective exhibition, six large Bavarian paintings were assembled together (Cat. Nos. 80-85), the colours and lines on one canvas leaping on to the next to form a powerful unified whole. Bourke's paintings have something in common with the landscapes of Austrian Expressionist, Kokoschka. Kokoschka wrote:

"When I paint a portrait I am not concerned with the externals of a person... In a face I look for the flash of the eye, the tiny swift expression which betrays an inner movement. In a landscape I seek for the trickle of water that suddenly breaks the silence."[9]

In Bourke's Bavarian paintings, one seems to be in a quiet mysterious forest. Yet at the top of each picture, a Starfighter Jet is passing overhead. This was the period of the Russian invasion of Czechoslovakia in 1968 when Western jet fighters were passing back and forth to the German border each day. Bourke included the Starfighters (as the baker at Polling), "because they were there". It would have been false to leave them out.

When exhibited at the Dawson Gallery in Dublin in 1969, Bourke's forest paintings again seemed original, with their rich yet slightly murky colours and their upright perspective. The artist explains how he uses an Oriental rather than a traditional Renaissance perspective.

Traditionally in European painting there is a vanishing point towards which all lines converge. But in Oriental perspective, Bourke believes, the vanishing point is behind the viewer. Thus the viewer is brought right into the landscape, which seems to rise up before him, giving a great sense of participation. Individual, too, is Bourke's technique, a technique not gained at art school, but through watching and questioning other artists at work, and mainly through trial and error. Technique, he believes, is not so much something that can be taught, as "that which makes the thing work". His own technique and interest in different materials is characterized by a willingness to experiment, thus he may use oil paint or acrylic on water-colour paper. Within one painting, he may use a variety of media, initially laying down a water-colour base, then a wash of acrylic. He then uses oil paint for the larger part of the picture. Melted beeswax may be mixed with the oil paint to give a denser, more workable surface. Pastel in parallel or cross-hatched strokes may be used to build up the forms of tree or sky, pencil or crayon to outline the shapes of a figure or landscape. Within one painting there is thus a tension between thick gestural brush-strokes, thin washes of paint, or precise marks in pencil. Bourke's painting methods are intuitive rather than pre-meditated, and the result is vigorous and radiant. His landscapes capture the presence of nature, with its profusion and sense of movement; in his portraits, fluid pencil lines brilliantly capture the features or hands of the sitter. Each of his pictures is characterized by this distinctive Bourke flourish. The artist has been equally adventurous as a sculptor, painting on wood and even bronze, or using materials such as *papier-mâché*. Although generally avoiding art schools, Bourke is a gifted teacher. In the late '60s he conducted excellent life classes, free of charge, at the Art Society in Trinity College, Dublin. In the early '70s he was an inspiring teacher at the Dun Laoghaire School of Art.

Visits to Switzerland in 1972 and 1974 resulted in a number of notable paintings, particularly his memorable exhibition entitled 'Frau Stutz's Cherry Tree', at the Dawson Gallery in 1975. The exhibition showed vigorous Swiss landscapes and a series of pictures in which a ladder is propped up against a wind-swept tree.

Knockalough Summer '77, oil on canvas, 126 × 116 cms.

Woman with an Umbrella, *oil on canvas, 136 × 120 cms.*

THE PAINTINGS OF BRIAN BOURKE

The artist explains how he lodged with a Hungarian widow, Frau Stutz. The other villagers hung streamers from their trees to frighten the birds away from their cherries; Frau Stutz suspended masks in her own branches. But the innocence and slight craziness of the idea also struck him, and the theme of masks, magic and theatre has surfaced several times in subsequent years: in his drawings of Marcel Marceau, for instance, or his self-portraits with masks; in his making of carnival masks for street theatre or Punch and Judy shows, or his Sweeney paintings, where the naked Sweeney crouches in a tree.[10] In a large triptych in the Frau Stutz exhibition, landscape is simplified and schematized, the wind-swept clouds rendered in long brush-strokes which break out of the oval frame, or the orchards animated by gestural flourishes of paint or crayon. The tree also provided a focal point for his four animated *gouache* paintings, 'Landscape Early Spring' in 1974 (Cat. Nos. 56-59) (Bank of Ireland Collection).

In the mid-'70s Bourke moved to Co. Galway, living in a cottage in Knockalough in the middle of a lonely landscape north of Spiddal. This was partially a need to get away from the art world of Dublin, but mainly an urge to immerse himself in unspoilt nature. During the next few years he produced numerous paintings of this open country of bog, rolling fields and hills, stone walls, scrubby woods and distant mountains, under wide, ever-changing skies. He continued the themes that he had painted on the Continent, but responded anew to the wilder, more open countryside of the West of Ireland. He focussed on one corner of the landscape, a lonely wind-swept tree in the shelter of a stone wall, painting numerous canvases of this subject through the seasons, under wind, rain and snow. The tree was shown with blossom in spring, green in summer, or bare and leafless in winter. The sky was an important part of the composition: blue and sparkling, overcast or filled with broken clouds, or revealing a rainbow that broke into the painted oval frame. In the Russian version of the film, 'War and Peace', there is a scene where Prince Andrei is wounded and falls to the ground; he looks up at the treetops and sky, seeing great clouds and skies changing and unfolding before his eyes, as if time had speeded up. There is a similar

mystical, pantheistic feeling to Bourke's Knockalough landscapes, as the artist is immersed in nature, trying to capture the change of light and the passage of time. Such work was refreshing in the '70s when few young artists were dealing with the theme of nature as a subject, especially landscape painted in the open air. Bourke's exhibition at the Taylor Gallery in 1978, 'Knockalough, Eight Seasons' was filled with vibrant, colourful paintings of the Western landscape. One large picture (Cat. No. 85) contained eight smaller paintings of the same wind-swept tree and wall.

The artist has continued to work in series. A subsequent Taylor Gallery exhibition in 1983, 'Portrait of J. with a Basque Hat', was devoted to paintings and sculptures of one woman. In each painting she was shown in a different pose, or wearing a different dress, but she always wore the same wide black hat. Here Bourke's brilliant academic skills, his fluid draughtsmanship and modelling were fully evident, combined with his free, sensuous painting style. In the 'Portrait of J. with Green and Red Striped Dress' (Cat. No. 92), the face is exquisitely modelled with almost sculptural brush-strokes, the eyes are large and pale, almost unseeing, the woman's bosom and clasped hands tenderly observed. Characteristically, the acute representation is counterbalanced by Bourke's awareness of the flat surface of the canvas: the woman without a chair as if suspended in space, the radiant red and green stripes of her dress, and the playful, floating brush-strokes in the background. The sculptures of 'J' in bronze – in some cases the head bare without hair–combine the sparseness of Giacometti with the fullness of the sitter, and his own feelings towards her.

The idea of devoting an exhibition to one sitter was novel, if not unique, in Irish art. In England, the painter, Lucian Freud, has absorbed himself with painting intense and heavily-worked pictures of friends and lovers, and a recent exhibition had been devoted exclusively to portraits of his mother. Bourke may lack the physical and psychological rawness of Freud's paintings, but possesses a greater sympathy and sense of humour. His finest work, whether portrait or landscape are those done directly from life, or when he is immersed in nature; this sense of identification gives his work its strength

and intensity. In this he is different from the Neo-Expressionists with whom he is sometimes associated. The latter often distort or generate emotion, sometimes violent, gratuitously. (Bourke, in fact, despises so-called 'Bad painting'.) His painting is based on life, on loving observation and intense draughtsmanship. While remaining his own man, and experimenting in different media, his dedication to traditional subjects such as portrait and landscape over the past thirty years has won respect and admiration from Irish painters such as Patrick Graham, Gene Lambert, Geraldine O'Reilly and Michael O'Dea, and generations of art students. The Brian Bourke retrospective revealed an astonishing body of work and an individual vision, an exuberant sense of colour linking one painting to the next, and a celebratory feeling for life.

Julian Campbell

NOTES

1. I am very grateful to the artist, Brian Bourke, for talking to me at length about his life and work, on several occasions, particularly at his home in Co. Galway in July 1988. Quotations by the artist refer to these conversations unless otherwise stated. I am also grateful to Jay Murphy for her help.
2. 'Making Sense. Ten Irish Artists, 1963–1983', Project Arts Centre, Dublin. Catalogue by Henry J. Sharpe.
3. *Aosdána* is a body or affiliation of artists, writers and musicians, established by the Arts Council of the Republic of Ireland in 1981 to honour those who make a contribution to the arts in Ireland. *Cnuas* is a grant or annuity of £5,800 to assist members of *Aosdána* to work full time at their art.
4. *Brian Bourke. Paintings and Sculptures 1963–'88*, introduction by Seamus Heaney and Kieran Corcoran, Galway Arts Festival Ltd., 1988. Catalogue numbers in my text refer to this exhibition.
5. *Ibid.*, p. 4.
6. See, in particular, Bourke's series of drawings and etchings, 'Self and Don Quixote', exhibited Taylor Galleries, Dublin, 1981.
7. 'Resisting the Written Word'. Interview with Brian Bourke by John Hutchinson, *In Dublin*, 2nd February 1989, pp. 14-15.
8. James White, op. cit.
9. Oskar Kokoschka, *My Life*, London, 1975.
10. For further information on Bourke's 'Sweeney' series, see Sarah Walker, 'Heaney, Sweeney and Brian Bourke's drawings'; *Irish Arts Review*, Vol. 4, No. 4, winter 1987, pp. 68-71. Also *Rosc '88*, Dublin, 1988, Catalogue of exhibition by Rosemarie Mulcahy, pp. 52-54.

PATRICK J. TUOHY 1894–1930

One would imagine that an artist described by Thomas MacGreevy as "the most travelled and, in the good sense, the most scholarly of our painters,"[1] singled out by critics in London and New York and who, during his brief career, portrayed many of the important personalities in the emerging new Irish state – actors, clergy, gentry, military, politicians and writers – would be widely known. Patrick J. Tuohy was one of Ireland's most gifted portrait painters. His tragic death in 1930 at the age of thirty-six and his slow method of working resulted in a relatively small output – perhaps less than two hundred paintings and drawings.[2] Few of his works are on public view and those in private hands seldom come on the market. A combination of these factors has mitigated against recognition of his rare talent except by a few enthusiasts.

Patrick Tuohy was born on 27 February 1894 into a middle-class professional Dublin environment. His father, John Joseph Tuohy, was a respected surgeon; his mother, Máire Murphy, was a native of Roundwood, Co. Wicklow. The family, which included Patrick's two sisters, Máire and Bride, lived in a plain Georgian house at 15 North Frederick Street, within sight of the elegant spire of Findlater's church, Parnell Square. At the age of fourteen, Patrick was among the first group of pupils to attend St. Enda's College, Rathfarnham, the school for boys established by Pádraic Pearse, the poet and revolutionary. The school opened in September 1908 and Dr. Tuohy was its medical officer. At St. Enda's Pearse attempted to instill in the boys a strong sense of their Irish nationality, particularly their great Celtic past embellished with legends of the mythological Cuchulainn and those super-heroes of the Fianna, Fionn and Diarmuid. Two pen and ink drawings in the Hugh Lane Municipal Gallery of Modern Art, Dublin (hereafter referred to as HLMG), dating from this period, reflect these interests.[3] The young Tuohy does not appear to have excelled in his studies with the exception of art. Reproductions of his work were published in the school magazine, *An Macaomh* – along with work by Jack Yeats, A. E. and Estella Solomons.[4] This intensely nationalistic education does not seem to have had any lasting direct effect on Tuohy, whose interests were to be more European than

The early death of Patrick Tuohy in 1930 cut short the career of that very talented painter. In this extensive article, **Dr. Rosemarie Mulcahy** assesses Tuohy's work in the context of twentieth-century art.

Séan O'Sullivan, Portrait of Patrick Tuohy, *signed lithograph, 29 × 23 cms. Photograph George Mott.*

national. Despite the physical handicap of having been born without a left hand, his talent for drawing was such that he was encouraged by the art master, the sculptor Willie Pearse (Pádraic Pearse's younger brother) to enroll for night classes at the Metropolitan School of Art.

It was a good time to be a student at the Metropolitan School of Art, where the painting school had been revitalized by the talented and forceful William Orpen. In 1902 Orpen had started teaching there part-time and by about 1906 he was making twice-yearly visits from London to his native Dublin, a pattern which continued until 1914.[5] Orpen re-introduced the Slade system which put great emphasis on life drawing and drawing from the nude. A series of sensitive time-studies after the nude dating from this period show the rapidity with which Tuohy absorbed what his master had to teach. The example of Orpen's virtuosity as a portrait painter and the glamorous aura of his success as a society painter in London inspired his more gifted pupils – Séan Keating, James Sleator, Margaret

Crilly (later Mrs. Harry Clarke), Leo Whelan and Patrick Tuohy, whom he considered to be one of the most able. In later years, however, Tuohy sometimes felt that the "towering shadow of Orpen had held back the development of his own art."[6]

Among his earliest paintings are Wicklow scenes – his uncle had a farm at Lough Dan – painted in 1906–9 when he was in his early teens. Although during his life he painted numerous small landscapes, none of these rise above the status of the Sunday painter; his talent lay in portraiture and it was to mature rapidly. Caricature postcards of frequenters of the National Library, to which in those days the Metropolitan School of Art was adjacent, done when he was a schoolboy (c. 1909) attracted the attention of Joseph Holloway, who believed that they "showed great promise and originality of outline."[7] Joseph Holloway (1861–1944), architect to the Abbey Theatre, and patron of the arts – especially theatre – and a voluminous diarist, became an enthusiastic supporter of Tuohy's work.

The vivacious 'Girl in a White Pinafore' (National Gallery of Ireland), dated 1910, painted when he was sixteen, shows by the convincing representation of anatomy, immediacy of expression and distribution of light and shade, how early he had grasped the essentials of portraiture. Painted in oils on board, the pigment is applied with broad, lively strokes and its unfinished state reveals part of the confident underdrawing. Two still-life paintings in oil, probably done c.1908, are of particular interest as they show an early exploration of modernism which was soon abandoned. Painted in the deep rich colour harmonies and the shallow spatial recession of the post-impressionists, they show an awareness of the still-life paintings of Cézanne and Gaugin. By 1910 he had mastered a more classical style in 'Still life with Eggs and Bay Leaves', though he seems to have abandoned this genre soon after. In 1911 Tuohy won two small Taylor prizes at the Royal Dublin Society and each year thereafter until 1918 – with the exception of 1917 – he was awarded a prize or a scholarship.[8] His arresting portrait of a 'Mayo Peasant Boy' (HLMG) shows that by the age of eighteen Tuohy was already an accomplished portrait painter. The boy, dressed in a brilliant red smock, is portrayed with a directness and realism

The Little Seamstress, water-colour, 72 × 52 cms. Courtesy Hugh Lane Municipal Gallery of Modern Art.

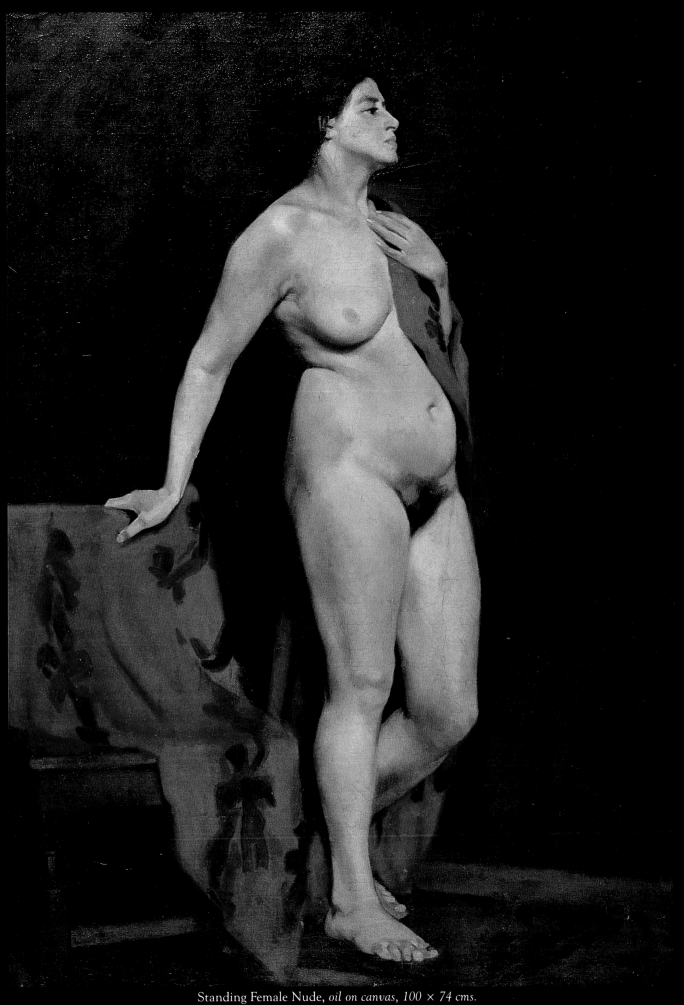

Standing Female Nude, *oil on canvas, 100 × 74 cms.*
Photograph John Searle.

PATRICK J. TUOHY 1894–1930

which were to become characteristic of his style. In this early work we can see a sensual delight in the texture and colour of the pigments, undoubtedly under Orpen's influence. There is a sense of unease and vulnerability about the sitter which is emphasized by the hands which seem impatient in their still pose. In an undated letter, c.1911 (HLMG), from Tourmakeady, Co. Mayo, where he spent that summer, written to his friend and fellow student at the MSA, James Sleator (1889–1950), he drew two small sketches of the 'Mayo Boy'. "I have done two indoor subjects, a portrait of a little boy in a red petticoat and a little girl eating potatoes and drinking milk." The vigorous brush-work is characteristic of Tuohy's early work and shows the influence of Orpen. The unfinished portrait of a 'Woman in a Black Hat' is painted with similarly vigorous stokes and probably dates from about the same time. This rare early letter gives an impression of the young Tuohy's personality. It reveals a commitment to his work and his frustrated attempts at painting landscape. "It is nearly impossible to study any piece of nature this changeable weather . . . " and "Skies are the very devil now anyhow, they go like hell, big, white and blue." Tuohy was a slow and deliberate worker, he needed subjects that stayed still. The letter reveals also that he had already decided that the British School had nothing to teach him—although Orpen advised his students to study in London. Within a few years he was to turn to the painters of Spain, France and Italy for inspiration. "I suppose there is a lot of dull heavy work in London, like if the artist had blisters on his arse for sitting at it and a sore wrist from leaning his hand across a maulstick . . . . A subject should be considered, weighed up and tried day after day to get any result. There is too much smart work going now . . . . You may say I am a cheeky youngster but I am only giving my views, without mock modesty." We also glimpse his romantic nature, "I fell in love again at the College but she went away before I spoke to her. Thank God in a way."

In 1914 he painted two of his finest pictures, 'The Little Seamstress' for which he won a Royal Dublin Society Taylor award in 1915 and 'The Model', signed and dated 1914. In the latter, Tuohy portrays a nude adolescent girl, seated against a

Woman in a Black Hat, unfinished,
oil on canvas, 64 × 59 cms.
Photograph John Searle.

patterned background, a white shawl draped across her thighs and a cloth wrapped around her head; she looks extremely vulnerable. Her fragile, pre-pubescent body is brilliantly lit and given the quality of marble sculpture. It is a haunting image. The restrained and subtle use of colour—the muted pink, grey and green of the background and the whites tinged with mauve and yellow—is unusual in such a young painter. Tuohy was yet to visit Spain but was already attracted to those qualities of dignity and sincerity expressed by the Spanish masters. In 'The Little Seamstress' (HLMG)—an unusually large water-colour—Tuohy is seen to have been a master of that medium. The girl's expression is both intense and preoccupied. As in 'The Model' a patterned background is used to good effect—the purple dress and the muted red and turquoise-striped tablecloth are complemented by the yellow-patterned wallpaper. The composition is confident and assured in spite of the difficult sideways positioning of the figure on the chair and the foreshortening of the outstretched arm. The handling of the shadows is exceptionally rich for water-colour. The sitter is Mai Power, sister of the sculptor Albert Power, whom Tuohy often used as a model. Mai remembers how she first came to sit for Tuohy. "Patrick had difficult relations with his father, who was strict and did not understand artists. On

one occasion he discovered his son at home working from a live model, whom the irate Dr. Tuohy put out of the house."[9] Given the brilliant execution of this water-colour, it is surprising that Tuohy seems to have abandoned the medium very early. 'Supper Time' (NGI) is an early example, which won him the Taylor Scholarship in 1912. This family scene is an exercise in light and reflections—the polished table, silver vessels and the window were vehicles for the young painter to show his virtuosity.[10]

Patrick Tuohy's growth to maturity as an artist was to take place against considerable odds, opposition from his father, financial insecurity and a lack-lustre and conservative art world in Dublin. The grimness of this environment is confirmed by Orpen when recalling his more gifted pupils including ". . . young Tuohy, a lad with one hand, and I was told by a good artist lately, that he is doing the best work in Dublin. But don't imagine for one moment that they could sell their works in Dublin then. No, the Dubliners preferred a £5 mock J.F. Millet any day. I hope all this is changed now, and that the people I have mentioned above are receiving some praise and money for their labours of love."[11] The years 1916–23 were the most violent and politically turbulent in the history of modern Ireland—the Easter Rebellion of 1916, the War of Independence 1919–21, the Civil War 1922–23. It has been claimed that Patrick Tuohy was a member of the Irish Citizen Army and that he fought with Pádraic Pearse in the General Post Office in Dublin in 1916 and later escaped to Spain.[12] The Irish Citizen Army was created by James Connolly and Sean O'Casey out of the remnants of the 1913 Dublin lockout. Its membership was composed of those who were prepared to arm in support of public ownership and its ideology was both nationalist and socialist. There is no evidence that Tuohy subscribed to such radical political ideals. As to the possibility that he fought in the G.P.O., with his disability he could hardly have manipulated a gun. Undoubtedly, his parents were ardent nationalists—his mother was active in women's organizations and his father attended the wounded.[13] It is possible that Patrick assisted his father on his medical rounds. However, there is no evidence that his nationalism was of the active kind. Had he been a combat-

PATRICK J. TUOHY 1894–1930

ant he would have been entitled to a state pension and a republican funeral; he received neither. Unlike Seán Keating (1889–1977), an active republican who tried to create a type of Irish painting that would express the heroism of the new Ireland, such as 'On the run–War of Independence' (Allied Irish Bank Collection), illustrated in *Irish Arts Review*, 1988, Tuohy did not refer to contemporary political events in his work.

It is more probable, if less colourful, that he went to Spain in 1916 with his Taylor Scholarship money to study painting. He stayed there for about a year, gave private tuition in painting and frequented the Prado. In the portraits of the Spanish masters he must have found confirmation of his natural inclination to portray his sitters with directness and intensity, and to pursue his interest in tonal values and the use of restrained colour harmonies. He seems to have painted little in Spain, for when in 1918 he first exhibited at the RHA, he showed only two paintings, 'The Mayo Peasant Boy' and 'The Wicklow Labourer', both of which had been painted several years earlier.[14] The year 1918 marks Tuohy's establishment as a professional artist. Apart from exhibiting at the RHA he also began teaching at the Metropolitan School of Art.[15] Hilda van Stockum, then a student of Tuohy, describes his appearance as 'small and dapper, (he) had black hair and a clipped red moustache. His left hand was missing from birth and he wore an artificial one covered with a black glove, but you did not notice it much."[16] His personality was complex. Renowned for his short temper and sharp tongue, he was also subject to fits of depression. Yet he could be a stimulating and witty companion. Thomas MacGreevy recalls "his habitual sense of tragedy illuminated by the extravagantly rueful sense of fun that was one of his most loveable characteristics."[17] Mai Power, a favourite model, found him not at all gloomy, but lively with a good singing voice–he was a member of the Palestrina choir at the Pro-Cathedral–and he sang while he painted."[18] If he did not suffer fools gladly, he was equally hard on himself. Hilda Roberts, a pupil and close friend, found him to be very unsure of himself and full of doubts.[19] This is confirmed by Hilda van Stockum's observation that "he had a perfection in his mind which he never reached, so he was

The Model, *1914*,
oil on canvas, 91.5 × 76 cms.
Photograph John-David Biggs & Co. Ltd.

often despondent."[20] Perhaps the most revealing observation is that by Phyllis Moss Stein, who knew him better than anyone, "Tortured by misgivings and doubts, insecurity and fancies not usually dominant in normal persons–he did not allow himself happiness. The stress was almost constant. He had so many friends but they seldom could give him any repose–he would not let them."[21]

His 'Standing female Nude' and 'Self-portrait with two Women' are among the finest paintings produced in Ireland in the first half of this century. The nude is rare in Irish art and this mature dark-haired woman is painted with a directness and detachment that makes this picture a superb example of the classical tradition. It has none of the sexual innuendo of Orpen's nudes; it is firmly within the French realist tradition, bringing to mind in particular the magnificent naked muse in Gustave Courbet's, 'The Painter's Studio', 1855 (Musée d'Orsay, Paris). Tuohy's nude is unselfconscious in her mature beauty and the scarlet drapery which she holds across her left breast is used to brilliant effect. The brush-work is smoother than in his earlier work and there are green skin tones in the areas of shadow. In Maurice MacGonigal's 'Dublin Studio' at the Dublin School of Art, c.1935 (Limerick City Art Gallery), reproduced in *Irish Arts Review*, 1988, we are given a view of how the model would have been

posed in the life class. This method was a legacy of Orpen's method of teaching which placed considerable emphasis on anatomy and on the life class. Prior to his time, students had had little opportunity to work from the female nude as there was difficulty in finding models willing to pose. Beatrice Glenavy relates that "As it was almost impossible to get a female model for the nude in Dublin he (Orpen) brought girl models from London. Some of them added much to the social life of the Bohemian element in the city."[22] Because Tuohy reached maturity as an artist so young, his work can be difficult to date. However, the latest possible date by which this magnificent nude could have been painted is 1922, the year it was shown in Paris in 'L'Art Irlandais' at the Galerie Barbazanges. The exhibition, which had been arranged through the efforts of Maude Gonne McBride, was a celebration of the newly created Irish state and showed the best of Irish art and craft. Tuohy was in good company, with Osborne, Nathaniel Hone, John Butler Yeats, Lavery, A.E., Leech and Keating, among others.

Possibly from the same period is the memorably atmospheric 'Self-portrait with two Women', in which the artist is seated at his easel.[23] The bare studio wall is draped with moss-green velvet and the space bathed in a diffused light. Shafts of light illuminate the faces of the painter and his models who appear to be suspended in a trance-like, timeless moment. The whole scene is reflected in a mirror–the edge of which can be seen along the bottom of the canvas–which contributes to the trance-like atmosphere. The colour harmonies are subtle yet daring in the range of greens and blues. The strategically placed glass bowl of flowers and a peacock feather fills the space between the artist and the models and the scarlet poppy ignites the centre of the composition. Orpen painted many self-portraits which show his reflected image, and the one to which Tuohy's comes closest is the 'Self-portrait with Venus' (HLMG). There are similarities in the way in which both artists are positioned to the left in three-quarter profile, with the edge of the canvas in progress just visible. Orpen shows the mirror frame while Tuohy omits it, thereby creating a more complex spatial ambiguity. However, the spirit that permeates this picture is that of 'Las Meninas' by Velázquez, which

Self-portrait with Two Women, *oil on canvas, 89 × 104 cms.*
Photograph John Searle.

PATRICK J. TUOHY 1894–1930

Tuohy must have admired and studied in the Prado. The atmosphere, light, the sense of arrested time–even the touch of scarlet is reminiscent of the rosette on the Infanta Margarita's dress–is an obvious legacy of Tuohy's visit to Spain. Surprisingly, this painting, which probably dates from about 1919–22, never seems to have been exhibited. Related to it is the unfinished half-length self-portrait which shows the artist at work on the portrait of a woman (Kneafsey Gallery, HIVE, Limerick).

With the establishment of the Irish Free State Tuohy received his share of commissions–official portraits of the late Archbishop Walsh (University College Dublin), P. O'Malley, T.D. and Deputy Speaker of Dail Eireann, General Piaras Beasley T.D. and General Richard Mulcahy, painted in 1923 when he was Commander in Chief of the Free State Army and Minister for Defence. The latter, though unfinished (no doubt in those turbulent times Mulcahy was unable to give the painter the numerous sittings that he usually required) is an excellent likeness of Mulcahy whose lean face and intense expression show the strain of his heavy responsibilities. In this portrait, for which there is an oil study in the National Gallery of Ireland (No. 4128), we can see Tuohy's method of working up the canvas in monochrome, starting with the face, and later adding colour once satisfied with the volume of the figure. It has to be said, however, with the exception of the latter, that Tuohy was not at his best in this type of commission.

About 1922 Tuohy began painting his most ambitious work, 'The Baptism of Christ' (on loan to HLMG). In this huge canvas (180 × 303 cm) he demonstrated that not only was he an accomplished portrait painter but also capable of handling a large-scale composition with a number of figures. Exhibited at the RHA in 1923 under the catch-all category of 'Decorative', the subject and its treatment place it firmly in the tradition of history painting, a *genre* which was then virtually moribund in Ireland. It is also a devout painting and, at a time when religious art was in the grips of shallow sentimentality, its dignified realism must have been startling. Tuohy captures the deep spiritual significance of the moment and, like a Renaissance artist, introduces his friends into the scene. His rival, Seán Keating, is the ruggedly visionary Baptist, Thomas MacGreevy –later to become director of the National Gallery–a devout kneeling onlooker,[24] the painter, Seán O'Sullivan, sits back on his heels in amazement and the young girl who turns her head away showing a lustrous mane of hair is Phyllis Moss, the student who was to become Tuohy's fiancée. Stylistically, the painting shows an awareness of Puvis de Chavannes in the composition, flat use of paint and generally pale colouring; undoubtedly Tuohy had studied his magnificent 'Beheading of the Baptist' which had been given to the Municipal Gallery by Hugh Lane (now in the National Gallery, London).

'The Baptism' was to bring Tuohy to the attention of a wider audience. Frank Rutter, critic for the *Sunday Times*, singled the painting out for special praise in his review (3 May 1925) of the Royal Academy Exhibition in London. "The

The Baptism of Christ, *oil on canvas, 180 × 303 cms. On loan to The Hugh Lane Municipal Gallery of Modern Art.*
Photograph courtesy National Gallery of Ireland.

great and delightful surprise of this room is the truly decorative and reverently expressive 'Baptism of Christ' (No. 291) by a hitherto unknown Irish artist, P.J. Tuohy. Mr. Tuohy, who has been able to understand Puvis de Chavannes without imitating him, is at the Dublin School of Art. So was Orpen. To prophesy is hazardous, but Tuohy is an artist I shall keep my eye on." MacGreevy also observed the debt to Puvis de Chavannes, and believed "the artist was feeling towards a mature statement on the subject of the greatest drama of human history." While lavish in his praise, he had reservations, "The John the Baptist has true visionary quality but the Christ, though grave and dignified, seems less than an ideal conception of the Incarnate Word."[25] Here, the usually perceptive MacGreevy failed to appreciate that Tuohy's greatest strength as an artist was his refusal to idealize. He uncompromisingly portrays a haggard, very human Christ, resigned to the suffering ahead.[26]

When given the opportunity, Tuohy showed himself capable of handling religious subjects with distinction. The reredos he painted for the church of Loreto Convent, though rejected by the sisters, was highly praised by connoisseurs. Holloway recalls Tuohy's pride in an article written by Edward Martyn in praise of the reredos.[27] 'The Agony in the Garden' is now in the Church of Christ the King, Cabra. According to Thomas MacGreevy it was painted when Tuohy was about twenty-five, and in his view is "the crowning work of his first youth."[28] His earliest known religious commission is a series of ten ceiling canvases, representing scenes from the life of Christ, painted in 1913–15, for the Jesuits at Rathfarnham Castle (Office of Public Works). Other religious paintings by Tuohy include 'St. Brendan' c.1924, 'St. Lawrence O'Toole' c.1925, 'St. Patrick' c.1926, and Stations of the Cross at Culmullen.

Tuohy spent the summer of 1923 on a study tour in Italy, in the company of Phyllis Moss, an intelligent and attractive young woman of independent spirit. They visited Florence and Rome and it was an enriching experience; he was surrounded by the works of the great masters and he was in love. It was probably the happiest time of his life and it was followed by a period of sustained creative activity. At the RHA exhibition

John Stanislaus Joyce, 1923–24, oil on canvas, 99 × 79 cms. Courtesy The Poetry/Rare Books Collection. State University of New York at Buffalo, print supplied by James Joyce Cultural Centre, Dublin.

in Spring 1924, Tuohy made an impressive showing and his portraits of John Stanislaus Joyce (father of James Joyce), James Stephens and Lord Fingall were enthusiastically reviewed by the critics. "Visitors will be caught by the artist's great power of character and interpretation" wrote The Irish Times critic.[29] For A.E. (George Russell), editor and art critic of The Irish Statesman, the exhibition was "dominated by Patrick Tuohy, whose portrait of 'Simon (sic) Joyce' is, in my opinion, the best picture on view. The nervous hunched-up figure with taut hands and puckered face is full of vitality, and it is more remarkable – this fixing of an expression of transient querulous irritability – when we consider the slow elaboration of the method adopted and the artist's determination to be unhurried, whether his sitter was raging or not."[30] James Joyce wrote to Sylvia Beach, "Did I tell you that in giving his award in Dublin Sir John Lavery passed over the portrait of my father (second prize) and gave the first prize to Mr. Keating. The press says the award was "keenly criticised."[31] A.E. concludes, "the exhibition has revealed the real talent of Mr. Tuohy, and I will remember it for that if nothing else . . . in the midst of much sloppy work it is a delight to find a painter who can labour and delight in taking pains."[32]

Tuohy's students at the MSA included

Seán O'Sullivan, Hilda Roberts, Norah McGuinness, Christopher Campbell, Hilda van Stockum, Nano Reid, Phyllis Moss and Stella Steyn. About this time, Tuohy defined his approach to the art of portraiture in a letter to an aspiring student.[33] He emphasized the importance of what he called, "the right environment" and expressed a preference for the art school over the private studio ". . . because you meet students of one's own age . . . and one learns much from watching the mistakes and successes of one's fellow students." He stressed the need to learn to paint and draw from life, alternating working from the paid model with painting "ordinary sitters", as too much of the former leads to slowness. There is perhaps an implied criticism of Orpen in the warning, "You will want to guard against letting your artistic interest be dominated by technique . . ." and he goes on to suggest as a remedy regular visits to good collections and the private studios of the best artists. For Tuohy the key to good portraiture was in observation, "Do not expect over much to be imparted from them to you directly, you must depend mostly on your own continuous observation." He also warned against too much book illustration as being "not good for a portrait painter."

Although Tuohy shone, it was in a very lack-lustre setting. The artistic climate in Dublin was uninspiring for a young man of his talent. Ireland was untouched by modern 'isms'; it was as though post-impressionism, fauvism, cubism, futurism had never happened. There was little encouragement to experiment and the RHA was in the doldrums. Thomas Bodkin complained of "the retrogression which has marked all their exhibitions in recent years. The exhibits are few in number and poor in quality."[34] Independence had been won in 1921 only to be followed by a bitter civil war (1922–23) and national identity was, understandably, an obsession. There was hunger for an art that could be seen as essentially Irish. Seán Keating, Jack B. Yeats, Paul Henry, and a few others attempted to address this need, but The Irish Times critic, for one, found "very little that can be described as Irish in feeling and in atmosphere."[35] A.E. analyzed the situation succinctly, "Ireland is a country where the painter has yet to create high national tradition."[36] He also expressed the opinion that art teaching

PATRICK J. TUOHY 1894–1930

at home was inadequate and the situation would not be remedied unless financial support was forthcoming to help artists pursue their studies. "Too many because of poverty get no other training than they can get in Ireland and their talent remains stunted. They continue to paint somewhat as they did as art students, their facility increasing, but with no real technical advance. I hope when the art schools come under the Ministry of Education that some provision will be made so that artists of the calibre of Keating, Tuohy or Whelan could get scholarships which would enable them to study in London, in Madrid, in Rome . . . Too often forced to remain here in an anaemic art atmosphere, they lose heart and their art lacks vitality."[37]

Perhaps encouraged by A.E.'s stirring words, Tuohy set out again for Italy. On the return journey, in early May, he stopped off in Paris, where Phyllis Moss was then studying art; he also met up with his friend, Thomas MacGreevy, who recalled his insatiable appetite for art. "The treasures of Italy had not left him satiated. We careered through Paris, seeking out everything in the way of art that we thought might be worth looking at together."[38] When they visited together the Caillebotte collection at the Luxembourg, the quality that Tuohy admired most in these painters was "their sincerity . . .'tis the sincerity of 'em", and he returned again and again to Manet's 'Balcony'. Later they talked of the possibility of having a native school of Irish painters and agreed that they "should have to study not what South Kensington had been imposing on the Dublin School of Art for half a century, but the European painters themselves, and at the fountain-head in their own countries."[39]

On that visit to Paris—no doubt encouraged by the success of his 'John Joyce'—and with a commission from a client, Tuohy approached James Joyce with the request that he sit for a portrait. Phyllis Moss accompanied him to the Joyces's apartment near the Champs de Mars.

"Mr. Tuohy came to Paris to make a drawing of me, if I consented, on the commission of a friend. He pressed me very hard for me to pose for my portrait. I argued with him for a long time. I have refused scores of requests to sit to painters and sculptors, having a very profound objection to my own image needlessly repeated in a picture or bust. In fact years

James Joyce, 1924, oil on canvas, 61 × 48.5 cms. Courtesy The Poetry/Rare Books Collection. State University of New York at Buffalo, print supplied by James Joyce Cultural Centre, Dublin.

ago casual glimpses of it in shop mirrors etc used to send me speeding away from it. I think I was right. For underfed, overworked, ill-dressed, with septic poisoning gradually undermining my health and unable to attend to it for sheer want of time and want of money I must have been a dreadful spectacle. It is not so bad now, of course, but still I think an artist could employ his brush better. I asked Mr. Tuohy if he wished to paint me or my name. He said he wanted to paint me. I heaved a sigh and consented. I have given him fifteen sittings, very tiresome. It will be finished in a week. It will be in the Paris Salon of 1925 with the portrait of my father."[40]

The twenty-eight sittings in all took place almost daily for a month. According to Arthur Power, the portrait was painted at 2 Square Robiac. "He was always there in the middle of the floor with his jam jars and his brushes around him."[41] Phyllis Moss recalls, "They got on each other's nerves during the sittings, and Patrick had a hard time of it for he admired Joyce very much."[42] Joyce was not an easy sitter, though in fairness it must be said that he was under enormous stress due to the eye operations he had to undergo about this time—on one occasion even postponing an operation in order to facilitate Tuohy.[43] Tuohy tried to enliven the sittings by making conversation, even daring on one occasion to philosophize about the importance to an artist of capturing his subject's soul. "Never mind my soul. Just

be sure you have my tie right," Joyce replied.[44] During these sessions he used Tuohy as a source of information on his native city. "Joyce listened avidly to all that he said, everything that concerned Dublin was food and drink to Joyce. He plied Patrick with intimate questions about the streets, the houses, the people. He remembered everything, he was insatiable . . ."[45] All of this was delivered by Tuohy in a Dublin accent which must have strongly evoked the city of Joyce's imagination.[46] In return, the painter was inserted in *Finnegan's Wake* as "Ratatuohy" and remembered in a Limerick.

*There's a funny facepainter dubbed Tuohy
Whose bleaklook is roseybud bluey
For when he feels strong
He feels your daub's all wrong
But when he feels weak, he feels wooey.[47]*

When the portrait was finished, Joyce wrote to Harriet Weaver, "I am glad you like the portrait. I like the folds of the jacket and the tie. He did not tell you all about the ownership because he is going to have a little game with a person in Dublin first. As you may have seen by his eyes he is very malicious—in the good sense of the word if it has one."[48]

Although the portrait was not entirely to the sitter's liking, this probably related more to Joyce's aversion to seeing his visage reproduced rather than any serious criticism of the painter. Joyce is portrayed half-length, against a patterned background, in the white jacket he habitually wore while working in order to maximize reflected light. Tuohy conveys a sense of the writer's total absorption in his interior world. The long head, with its slightly protruding jaw, expresses the sadness and boredom which Phyllis Moss observed to be characteristic of him.[49] The following year Joyce commissioned a sketch of his mother from a photograph—May Joyce had died in 1903—and sat for a second portrait, which was to be a failure.[50] Evidently, Joyce attached importance to Tuohy's portraits, for in 1927 he wrote to Harriet Weaver, "It is rather singular that for the last three years I have been carrying three photographs of Tuohy's portraits in my pocket—those of my father, myself and James Stephens."[51]

Between 1922 and 1926 Tuohy did a series of brilliant pencil portraits of distinguished personalities in the contemporary Irish theatre, which show him to have been the most talented of his gener-

PATRICK J. TUOHY 1894–1930

ation in this medium. The powerful, large drawing of the actress, Ria Mooney, dated 1922, has an extraordinary immediacy. The head is fully modelled with a subtle play of light and shade while the rest of the figure is drawn with a lighter, more sketchy touch – a characteristic of Tuohy's drawing style. The actress, shown half-length, is dressed in Spanish costume for her part as Doña Sol in *Blood and Sand* (1908) by Vincente Blasco Ibáñez.[52] We are struck by the total honesty with which Tuohy portrays his sitter, confirming that he was the only artist of the period who did not resort to flattery when faced by a female subject; one has only to look at Lavery and Orpen to see the different criteria they applied to male and female portraiture. As to technique, in his portrait of the poet and playwright, Pádraic Colum (1881–1972), dated 1924, the lead is rubbed into the textured surface of the paper to achieve a *chiaroscuro* effect. The portrait of Sean O'Casey (HLMG), done two years later, shows a lightening in technique, with a greater use of line and the application of fine hatching to create the shadows.

In 1927 Tuohy emigrated to the United States of America – he had become despondent about his career in Ireland. According to Thomas McGreevy, "He did not feel that his income from teaching and from portrait-painting in Dublin was sufficient to enable him to marry."[53] He first went to South Carolina and later settled in New York. Financial difficulties continued to be a source of anxiety, although his loyal brother-in-law, Pat O'Brien, did what he could to help. Among his contacts were the writer, Pádraic Colum, who had moved to America in 1914 and the actor, Dudley Digges who, with his wife the actress, Maire Quinn, had emigrated and made a successful career in New York and Hollywood. By 1929 Tuohy was living at 145 W. 85 Street and had a studio at 440 Riverside Drive. Helen Byrne Hackett, a gallery owner of Irish descent, was impressed by his work and when she organized the first American exhibition of contemporary Irish art, Tuohy was its star. Tuohy helped her to organize the exhibition. He made only one trip back to Ireland, which may have been for this purpose. "Tuohy stands out as a Portrait Painter" ran a headline in *The New York Sun*, 30 March 1929, "Mr. Tuohy paints very well. I fear he paints portraits

Ria Mooney, *1922, pencil on paper, 61 × 44.5 cms. Photograph George Mott.*

Pádraic Colum, *1924, pencil and crayon on paper, 39 × 30 cms. Photograph John Searle.*

Seán O'Casey, *1926, pencil on paper, 42.5 × 35.5 cms. Courtesy Hugh Lane Municipal Gallery of Modern Art. Photograph John Searle.*

better than any one we have at present in America . . . His people are alive and his affectionate interest in them gives the canvases a sparkle all over."

A year later, in February 1930, he wrote to an American cousin, "You must come along some time soon and see my work. We are having another Irish exhibition of pictures this month at Hackett Galleries, 9 E. 57. I am working very hard for me considering I am in my studio at ten in the morning and work till five. I am painting some lovely ladies including Claudette Colbert (Film Actress) and also Walter Hampden, Actor, the others you would not know, they are just citizens." Research needs to be done on these "American" paintings.[54] Before the second exhibition Helen Hackett came to Ireland and in advance Tuohy wrote to Patrick O'Brien on Gallery notepaper. "This is to introduce Mrs. Hackett who made such a great success of the Irish Exhibition here. She would like to talk to you about my Decoration in the Harcourt St. Municipal Gallery and to see any pictures of mine you have . . . P.S. I want Mrs. Hackett to arrange with you to have the 'Baptism of Christ' brought over here for exhibition."

At this time Tuohy was also actively involved in founding a club for Irish graduates in New York. At a time when, on the surface, his career seemed to be going well, his life came to a tragic end, by his own hand. In August 1930, at the age of thirty-six, Patrick Tuohy was found asphyxiated by gas in his studio on Riverside Drive. The sad news was cabled to Dr. Tuohy by Pádraic Colum. After a Requiem Mass at the church of St. Paul the Apostle, the body, in a massive oak and leaden coffin, was returned to Ireland by ship to Galway, by train to Broadstone station and thence to the Pro-Cathedral for burial in Glasnevin on 16 September. *The Irish Times*, 17 September 1930, described the attendance as "large and representative including many of the best known figures in Irish literary and artistic circles."[55]

In a recent article the late Edward Maguire, himself a distinguished portrait painter, acknowledged his debt to Tuohy and wrote, "I feel there has been little progress in portraiture since Patrick Tuohy died in 1930."[56] We must await a retrospective exhibition before a fuller assessment can be made.

Rosemarie Mulcahy

PATRICK J. TUOHY 1894-1930

NOTES

Unless stated to the contrary, all paintings and drawings mentioned in the text are in private collections. The main public repositories of Patrick Tuohy's work are The National Gallery of Ireland the The Hugh Lane Municipal Gallery of Modern Art, Dublin:

NGI: 'James Stephens', 'Frank Fahy', 'Biddy Campbell', 'A Landscape in the West of Ireland', 'A Portrait of a Young Girl', 'General Richard Mulcahy', Supper Time' (water-colour).

HLMG: 'Mayo Peasant Boy', 'Baptism of Christ' (on loan), 'The Little Seamstress' (water-colour), 'St. Brigid', 'The Shelbourne Hotel from St. Stephen's Green', 'Study of a Girl' (water-colour), 'Seán O'Casey' (drawing), 'F. R. Higgins' (drawing), 'Domenic Bowe, sculptor' (lithograph), 'Roddy the Rover' (pen and ink), 'The Flight of Cuchulainn' (pen and ink), 'Entry into Battle' (pen and ink).

Copies of all the letters from which I have quoted have been deposited in the archive of the National Gallery of Ireland. I wish to take this opportunity to thank the relatives of Patrick Tuohy–Mr. Tim O'Brien, Misses Nancy and Pauline O'Brien, Mr. P. J. O'Brien, Dr. John O'Brien, Dr. Martin O'Brien and Dr. Margaret Lenehan for their generosity in providing me with material. I am grateful to the many owners who allowed me to see and photograph paintings and drawings and to Phyllis Moss Stein and Hilda van Stockum for their informative and interesting letters about Patrick Tuohy. Patrick J. Murphy has made a study of Tuohy's life and work (as yet unpublished). The principal published sources on Patrick Tuohy are Hilary Pyle, *Irish Art 1900–1950*, in association with *Rosc*, Crawford Municipal Art Gallery, Cork, 1975, pp. 68-69; Alan Denson, *John Hughes 1865–1941*, Kendal, 1970; Anne Crookshank and the Knight of Glin, *The Painters of Ireland c.1660–1920*, London, 1978, pp. 273–74. Edward Maguire, 'The Art of Portraiture', *Martello*, Summer 1983, pp. 31-34. Gearailt Mac Eoin-Johnston, 'Patrick J. Tuohy R.H.A.', *Martello*, Spring 1985, pp. 42-44.

1. Thomas MacGreevy, 'Patrick Tuohy R.H.A. (1894–1930)', *Father Matthew Record*, No. 7, July 1943, p. 5
2. Patrick J. Murphy has catalogued just under two hundred pieces. The catalogue for the 'Memorial Exhibition Patrick Tuohy R.H.A.: Paintings, Drawings, Sketches, 1911–1930', Mills Hall, Dublin, 1931 (preface by Thomas Bodkin), lists fifty-seven works. The exhibition was organized by the artist's sister, Bride Tuohy, and paid for by Phyllis Moss Stein.
3. 'The Flight of Cuchulainn' and 'Entry into Battle'. A third pen and ink drawing, 'Roddy the Rover', was done as an illustration for a book by Standish O'Grady.
4. These included a sheet of six profile drawings, 'Faces at Sgoil Eanna' (Vol. 1, Summer 1909, p. 69), which show an as yet untrained hand but an interest in character; 'In Co. Wicklow' (Vol. 1, No. 2, Christmas 1909, facing p. 28) and 'Faces', in the same volume facing p. 38. *An Macaomh* (The Youth) ran to only four issues in all from Summer 1909–December 1910. For St. Enda's, see Ruth Dudley Edwards, *Patrick Pearse, the Triumph of Failure*, London, 1977.
5. See John Turpin, 'The Metropolitan School of Art 1900–23', Part I, *Dublin Historical Record*, Vol. XXVII, March 1984; Part 2, Vol. XXVIII, March 1985; Part 3, Vol. XXVIII, June 1985.
6. Bruce Arnold, *Orpen. Mirror to an Age*, London, 1981, p. 163. Phyllis Moss Stein observed in a letter to the author, 5 January 1979, "Patrick was a good painter before he was taught at all . . . I doubt that Orpen's influence was really good for him. Orpen probably never developed his potential talent."
7. Joseph Holloway, 'Loss to Irish Art. An Appreciation of Patrick Tuohy', from a press-cutting with neither source nor date.
8. For scholarships and prizes (titles of winning works not always recorded) see the *Reports and Proceedings of the Royal Dublin Society*. 1911 : No. 4, £5 and No. 18, £5; 1912 : Taylor Scholarship of £50 for 'Suppertime', No. 2; 1913: No. 5, £30; 1914 : Taylor Scholarship of £50 and £10 for No. 2; 1915: Taylor Scholarship of £30 for 'Bad News', No. 5 and £10 for 'The Little Seamstress'; 1916: £10 for 'The Legend' (water-colour), No. 20; 1918 : £20, No. 9 and £5, No. 30.
9. Mai Power in conversation with the author in 1978.
10. Other water-colours by Tuohy include the 'Study of a Girl' (HLMG), 'The Rehearsal', 'Peasant Woman' and 'The Legend'. Phyllis Moss Stein, who knew Tuohy during the last ten years of his life, does not recall him using water-colour. Letter to the author, 4 March 1979.
11. William Orpen, *Stories of Old Ireland and Myself*, London, 1924, p. 69.
12. Murphy, Pyle, Crookshank and Glin, Mac Eoin-Johnston and Turpin all hold that Tuohy was a combatant in the Rising and fled to Spain. Maurice MacGonigal, a friend, and one of the few art students to join the Irish Republican Army (he was imprisoned for his republican activities), has stated that Tuohy was not a combatant. (Verbal communication with Ciarán MacGonigal.) According to Phyllis Moss Stein, "he usually avoided all political turmoil. When he and I watched the Custom House in flames he made no comment one way or the other." (4 March 1979.)
13. Mary Tuohy was active in Cumann na mBan and one of the founder members of *Aonach na Nodlag* (a Christmas fair to promote Irish goods), along with Arthur Griffith, Seán MacDermot, Countess Markievicz and Mrs. Wyse Power. Mrs. Tuohy was also active in raising funds ". . . to tide Arthur Griffith over this crisis." (Letter from Mary Tuohy to Joseph Holloway requesting a subscription, National Library, Holloway Papers, M.S.22, 410, March 1915.) John Joseph Tuohy died 16 August 1936. There was a large and distinguished attendance at his funeral, which included President and Mrs. de Valera, Seán T. O'Kelly, Vice-President of the Executive Council, J.M. O'Connor, S.J., Rector of Belvedere College, Miss M. Pearse, T.D., P.T. McGinley, President of the Gaelic League and representatives of the 1916 G.P.O. garrison.
14. 'La Española', exhibited at the RHA in 1919 (No. 159) may have been painted in Spain.

The present whereabouts of the 'Wicklow Labourer' is unknown. Reproduced in the *Irish Independent*, 15 September 1930, it shows a man, half-length, with a moustache, wearing a cap and collarless shirt and is described as being on exhibition, along with the 'Baptism of Christ', at the Municipal Gallery, Harcourt St. (No. 175) 23½ × 19½ ins., loaned by Mr. John L. Burke. Joseph Holloway, op. cit., refers to having purchased 'An Arklow Man' and the 'Aran Boy', "perhaps the two most noted of his subject paintings", at an exhibition in the Rotunda. *The Freeman's Journal* (9 December 1911, p. 4) art critic described Tuohy's canvases (three) as "remarkable, as coming from the brush of a boy artist."
15. See Ann Stewart, *Royal Hibernian Academy of Arts. Index of Exhibitors 1826–1979*, Vol. III, Dublin, 1987.
16. Hilda van Stockum, 'Dublin Art School in the 1920s', *The Irish Times*, 6 March 1985 and continued on 30 March 1985.
17. MacGreevy, op. cit.
18. In conversation with the author, 1978.
19. In conversation with the author, 1978.
20. Van Stockum, op. cit. "He was much less self-confident than the others–like Keating, for instance. He needed encouragement which I don't think he got."–Hilda van Stockum in a letter to the author, 27 January 1989.
21. Phyllis Moss Stein in a letter to the author, 5 January 1979.
22. Arnold, op. cit., p. 166. This is possibly the work for which Tuohy won a silver medal at South Kensington for painting the nude. See Alan Denson, *John Hughes*, Kendal, 1969, p. 500.
23. According to Mai Power the two women were sisters of a fellow student of Tuohy's called Rigney. Verbal communication, 1978. Tuohy mentions the painting in a letter dated 636 N. Main Street, Greenville, South Carolina, 13 August 1927, to his brother-in-law, Pat O'Brien. "Tell Bride I saw Rigney in New York, he is the same two and nine pence. His sister Maggy is married in N.Y., the one that posed for the picture of myself at a mirror, with two girls behind. Bride has the picture herself, I think."
24. "The yearning absorption of the second figure on the right in the ceremony was an expression imposed by the artist, for I was myself the model and I had nothing to yearn over or to be absorbed in, as I posed, kneeling, in profile to the painter, except the drab grey-green of a wall in a studio at the School of Art." MacGreevy, op. cit.
25. *Ibid*.
26. In 1924 Tuohy was awarded the Tailteann Silver Medal for this painting. In a description of the Municipal Gallery, P. Browner singled out 'The Baptism'. "This large canvas claiming the major part of one wall, draws all eyes. How many who have stood to admire have recognized in its groupings some Dublin residents now eminent in the professional life of the city?" *Irish Independent*, 13 June 1939. Regrettably, this important work has deteriorated and is in urgent need of restoration.

27. Holloway, op. cit.

28. MacGreevy, op. cit.

29. *The Irish Times*, 7 April 1924, p. 4.

30. *The Irish Statesman*, 19 April 1924, p. 166.

31. James Joyce to Sylvia Beach, 17 August 1924, in Richard Ellmann, *Letters of James Joyce*, New York, 1966, Vol. III, p. 107.

32. *The Irish Statesman*, loc. cit.

33. Patrick Tuohy to Wanda Porter, Clogher, Co. Tyrone. Probably written about 1923–24 when he was painting a portrait of Lord Fingall. Tuohy had met Wanda Porter's sister at Lady Fingall's.

34. *The Studio*, Vol. 87, Jan.–June 1924, p. 284.

35. *The Irish Times*, 7 April 1924, p. 4.

36. *The Irish Statesman*, loc. cit.

37. *The Irish Statesman*, 17 May 1924, p. 296.

38. MacGreevy, op. cit.

39. *Ibid.*

40. Joyce to Harriet Shaw Weaver, Paris, 24 May 1924, Stuart Gilbert, *Letters of James Joyce*, London, 1947, pp. 214-15. "This is to introduce Mr. Patrick Tuohy who has painted my father. He will show the photograph. I like it and would like to have your opinion of it." To Myron C. Nutting, Paris, 30 May 1924, Ellmann, op. cit., p. 96. "The same paper that speaks of your eye trouble amongst the social events, says that Tuohy has done your portrait. Very quickly, it seems. I am glad you have let him. His portrait of Pappie is a wonderful study of the little old Milesian. I am especially glad that Tuohy is not that irritating kind of clever painter that sees in his sitter only a type. The likeness is striking. The face, the pose, the hands especially I recognise and looking at them I feel that I know how they have come to be so. Compared with this portrait, Augustus John's of Hardy (which I used to like) now seems to me wooden." Stanislaus Joyce to James Joyce, Trieste, 7 August 1924, *ibid.*, p. 101.

41. Patricia Hutchins, *James Joyce's World*, London, 1957, p. 155.

42. *Ibid.*

43. "Mr. Tuohy has added still another complication by insisting on remaining another week. I have now given him twenty-six sittings, he was to have left today but last night he begged for two more and as he is forfeiting his salary as professor at the Dublin school of art I consented. He will telegraph to you when he arrives in London and bring you the portrait. He has to get a special cage made as the paint will not be dry." In a postscript: "The operation, Dr. Borsch says, ought to be done. He cannot do it on Wednesday as Mr. Tuohy wants that day. It will be made on Saturday." James Joyce to Harriet Shaw Weaver, Paris, 2 June 1924, Ellmann, op. cit., pp. 96-97.

44. James Joyce to Harriet Shaw Weaver, 27 June 1924, Ellmann, *James Joyce*, New York, 1982, p. 566.

45. Phyllis Moss quoted in Hutchins, op. cit. p. 149.

46. "May I introduce a friend of mine, Mr. Patrick Tuohy, an Irish painter who did a portrait of my father and is finishing one of me. You may find him interesting. His accent, which is very Dublin, may be perhaps a little difficult to understand." James Joyce to Robert McAlmon, Paris, 30 May 1924, Ellmann, *Letters of James Joyce*, op. cit., pp. 95-96. Ellmann's account of Tuohy is curiously derogatory. "Joyce put up with Irishmen gladly, but he found Tuohy's conversation boring and did not greatly like the portrait." p. 95, note 5.

47. See *Finnegan's Wake*, p. 432. I am grateful to Robert Nicholson, curator of Joyce's Tower, for bringing this to my attention and for his friendly assistance in my research. A copy of the Limerick was given by Joyce to Phyllis Moss on St. Valentine's Day 1927. The original is in the Lockwood Memorial Library, New York State University at Buffalo. Quoted by Crookshank and Glin, op. cit., p. 273.

48. 27 June 1924, Gilbert, op. cit., pp. 216-17.

49. Hutchins, op. cit., p. 149.

50. "Tuohy'a portrait of Pappie is touring USA. I asked him to try to do a sketch of mother from photographs. He managed to get two faded ones. Has Eileen any? If so it would be advisable to send copies of any or all at once to him (Prof. P. J. Tuohy, Metropolitan School of Art, Kildare Street, Dublin) as he is thinking of going to Spain." James Joyce to Stanislaus, Paris, 28 September 1925. Ellmann, *Letters of James Joyce*, op. cit., pp. 127-28. The photograph on which the drawing is based is reproduced in Stan Gébler Davies, *James Joyce. A Portrait of the Artist*, London, 1975, between pp. 64-65, it shows three generations –Joyce with his father and mother and maternal grandfather. Of the second portrait of himself Joyce wrote, "He wants to come here to paint me. He certainly wants me to pose myself and he certainly wants himself to pose me for himself and certainly he does now be wanting to paint me posed by himself, himself for myself. (With apologies to Miss Gertrude Stein)." Joyce to Shaw Weaver, 13 June 1925. Gilbert, op. cit., p. 228. "Tuohy's portrait is a failure. The Colum article is also." Joyce to Shaw Weaver, Zurich, 22 July 1932, Ellmann, *Letters*, op. cit., p. 250.

51. 31 May 1927, Gilbert, op. cit., p. 254.

52. I am grateful to Aidan Grennell for identifying the sitter. Other portraits of theatre personalities include 'Pádraic Colum', 'F.R. Higgins', 'Sarah Allgood', 'Brinsley MacNamara' and F.J. MacCormack'.

53. MacGreevy, op. cit.

54. According to Mai Power the New York paintings are lighter in colour than the earlier work. Among the portraits painted during that period are 'Master David Challoner' (illustrated in MacGreevy, op. cit.), 'Dr. Robert E. Siebels', 'Mr. Jocelyn H. de Grasse Evans', and of the actor Dudley Digges, whose unfinished portrait was found in Tuohy's studio after his death.

55. In a letter to Harriet Shaw Weaver, Etretat, 6 September, 1930, Joyce wrote, "Tuohy, who painted my father and me has just committed suicide in New York." Ellmann, *Letters*, op. cit., p. 202.

56. Edward Maguire, 'The Art of Portraiture', op. cit.

PATRICK OSBORNE, AN IRISH STUCCODORE

In the fifth volume of *The Georgian Society Records* the authors enthusiastically revealed the discovery of a bill for the plaster-work at Davis Duckart's Palladian masterpiece, Castletown Cox, Co. Kilkenny.[1] "It is of unique value," they noted, "both in demonstrating our contention that the plaster-work was carried out by Irishmen, and in informing us of the cost of this type of ornament."[2] The bill, now in the collection of Baroness Ulli de Breffny, was dated 19 August 1774 and was signed by the plasterer, Patrick Osborne, and by the Clerk of Works, John Nowlan. It costed the plaster-work at Castletown at £696 10s. 5d. and, of even greater interest, specified the cost of the decorative elements. These ranged from the four Corinthian capitals in the

While very little has been discovered about the presumably Irish stuccodore, Patrick Osborne, his association with work on two buildings is documented.
Seán O'Reilly, Research Assistant at the Irish Architectural Archive, summarizes the literature on Osborne and discusses in detail his known *oeuvre* and what may be attributed to him.

hall (£11 7s. 6d.)[3] to the dining-room ceiling (£34 2s. 6d.), and the 1,591 feet of plain cornices (£33 2s. 11d.). The Castletown plaster-work, described as being "in the best tradition of rococo

plaster-work",[4] is of the highest quality. Its ornamental motifs of scrolls, festoons, garlands, birds and so forth, are richly modelled in high relief, carefully finished and disposed with a restraint hardly common in Irish rococo plaster-work. Considering a document of such significance, correctly reprinted here,[5] and the quality of Osborne's work, an assessment of this Irish artist and designer is clearly long overdue.

There are only two historical sources documenting Osborne's work, the aforementioned bill, and the records of Cork City Corporation.[6] The latter conclusively link Osborne with the plastering, from 1768, of the newly constructed Cork Mayoralty House, now part of the Mercy Hospital. Here, as at Castletown,

The rich yet controlled decoration of the Entrance Hall at Castletown Cox.
Photograph W. Garner. Courtesy of the Irish Architectural Archive.

PATRICK OSBORNE, AN IRISH STUCCODORE

*Patrick Osborne's earliest documented ceiling is in the Staircase Hall of the former Mayoralty House, now the Mercy Hospital, Cork.
It was carried out between January and October, 1768.*

Details of staircase ceiling, Mercy Hospital, Cork. Photograph George Mott.

PATRICK OSBORNE, AN IRISH STUCCODORE

Duckart is recorded as the architect.[7] Duckart's life is not well recorded,[8] though his twice documented collaboration with Osborne is an important factor in the determination of the latter's *oeuvre*. From this association, Osborne's name has been plausibly linked with the more rococo elements in the Franchini decoration at Duckart's Kilshannig, Co. Cork,[9] though this remains undocumented. The Cork Mayoralty House is the first recorded collaboration between Duckart and Osborne.

Cork City Corporation took its first step in providing a suitable residence for its mayors in a meeting held on 13 August 1763.[10] They then established a committee for the building of a house "for the habitation of the Mayors of this City, on the ground on Haman's Marsh",[11] recently reclaimed and prestigious land. On 6 May 1765 Duckart presented plans for the Mayoralty House and agreed to execute the work at a cost not exceeding £2,000.[12] Though Duckart's costing and supervision of the work were less than perfect,[13] the Corporation spared no ex-

The Measurement & Bill of the Stucco Work done in ye New Building at Castletown	£	s.	d.
294 ft. of Corinthan Entablature in the Great Hall and Drawing Room @ 5s. ft.	73	10	0
96 ft. of ornament Entablature in ye Saloon @ 5s. per ft.	24	0	0
104 ft. of Ionic Entablature in ye dining parl @ 4s. 6d. ft.	23	8	0
279 ft. of Entablature with dentiles in ye back parlour breakfast room & bed chamb over the saloon @ 1s. 3d. ft.	17	8	9
138 ft. of ornamented cornice in the Corridores each side of the Great Hall	20	14	0
55 ft. of Scrole ornament on the Great Stairs @ 2s. 6d. ft.	6	17	6
74 ft. of Doric Entablature in the Great Stairs @ 5s.	18	10	0
24 ft. of Cornice enrich under ye gallary of ye Great Stairs @ 2s.	2	0	0
85 ft. of Archatraves round ye Wind @ Do @ 8d. ft.	2	16	6
446 ft. of Astragal moulding in the Staircase & Hall @ 3d. ft.	5	11	6
32 ft. of bedmould under the Strings of the Stairs @ 1s. ft.	1	12	0
15 ft. of Cornice moulding on the Gallary of ye Stairs @ 1s. ft.	0	15	0
181 ft. of Moulding in pannell in the Staircase Wind and circular head door @ 3d.	2	5	3
53 ft. of Stop moulding round ye wind of ye Stairs @ 2d.	0	8	10
1806 ft. of Moulding on pannells of the Staircase @ 4d. ft.	30	2	0
15½ ft. of circular archatrave round ye staircase door @ 1s. ft.	0	15	6
79½ ft. of plain Entablature in ye bedroom over ye back parl @ 11d.	3	13	6
1591 ft. of plain cornices @ 5d. ft.	33	2	11
760 ft. of plain mouldings in the uper Story @ 3d.	9	10	0
102 ft. of Staff moulding in the uper Story @ 1½d.	0	12	9
758 yds. of plain coated ceilings @ 6d. p. yd.	18	19	0
1906 yds. of coated walls @ 5d. p. yd.	39	14	2
173 yds. of cove ceiling @ 9d. p. yd.	6	9	9
707 yds. of wall plaistering for Paper @ 3d. p. yd.	8	16	9
Breakfast Room Ceiling ornamented and 3 in ye cornice	18	0	0
Dining Parlour Ceiling ornamented	34	2	6
Walls of the Dining Parlour pannell and ornament	55	0	0
Drawingroom Ceiling ornament	45	10	0
Saloon Ceiling ornament	45	0	0
Hall and Staircase Ceilings ornamented	60	0	0
4 Corinthian Capitols in the Hall	11	7	6
4 Circular Head Wind in the Hall & Saloon @ £2 5s. 6d.	9	2	0
43 Festoons in the pannell of the Great Hall @ 16s. 3d.	34	18	9
56 Festoons in the Great Stairs @ 11s. 4½d.	31	17	0
	£696	10	5

Rec'd from His Grace the Lord Arch Bishop of Cashell the sun of One hundred & Sixty-two Pounds, five shill and ninepence, which with severall sums rec'd before makes the sum of Six hundred and ninety-six Pounds ten shill and five pence being the Contents of the within bill and in full of all Acc'ts this nineteenth day of Aug't 1774.

per ser't
Jno Nowlan

Pat'k Osborne

Corrected transcript of the bill for the plaster-work at Castletown Cox, Co. Kilkenny, dated 19 August 1774, and signed by Patrick Osborne and John Nowlan.

pense in decorating their rather curious new building.[14]

On 22 January 1768 the overseers of the Mayoralty House engaged "Patrick Osburne (*sic*) for stuccoing the staircase lobby and drawing-room of said house".[15] In October a balance of £60 13s. 3d. was paid to Osborne for his work on the lobby and staircase hall.[16] It was not until 28 November 1769 that the final payment of £82 1s. 0½d. was paid to Osborne for the plastering of the drawing-room.[17]

Though its detail has been marred by over-painting, Osborne's work is well executed, if traditional in design. The staircase ceiling, framed by a Doric entablature, has its abundant decoration controlled by a determined symmetry. Masks, urns and bouquets mark the diagonal axes, while baskets of fruit are centred along the walls between the corner designs. All are framed with intertwining, broadly symmetrical foliated scrolls. The modelling is in high relief and, for fruit and floral motifs, is distinctly naturalistic. A niche on the staircase is

Detail of the corinthian entablature and ceiling of the Drawing Room *in Castletown Cox.*
Note the crisp detailing and the masks in the upper moulding of the cornice.

PATRICK OSBORNE, AN IRISH STUCCODORE

surmounted by cornucopia, branches and a bird, and is again essentially symmetrical in composition. The motifs are repeated in the two-storey drawing-room or ballroom at the top of the house. Here birds replace masks as framing motifs in the ceiling, and the rich Corinthian cornice, uncomfortably broken by the square windows, is enlivened by cornucopia. Osborne's detailing was originally of a much higher quality than it might now seem. This may be confirmed by a comparison with Castletown Cox where the fine preservation demonstrates the crispness of Osborne's execution.

Castletown Cox was built from about 1767 by Michael Cox, Archbishop of Cashel.[18] Davis Duckart was the architect[19] and in Castletown he designed his finest country house. The double-pile plan with a spinal corridor, screened entrance hall and lateral staircase belonged to a tradition in Ireland that returned

to the Kildare Castletown. Its elevation, however, was of more ambiguous origins. The three-bay unpedimented frontispiece with fluted pilasters recalled both the by then, old-fashioned William Winde design for the Duke of Sheffield's house in St. James's Park,[20] and Ange-Jacques Gabriel's very à la mode Petit Trianon of 1762.[21] The detailing and wings were, however, as much Duckart's and personal, as the interior plasterwork was Osborne's and Irish.

The entrance and staircase halls, the two finest rooms in the house, were both panelled and decorated with festoons. The entablatures were perfectly scaled, both with respect to the rooms and to their details, while in the ceilings Osborne gave full rein to his powerfully fluid modelling. In both ceilings central roses were framed by flowing borders of leaves and flowers, which seemed to hold back the exuberant rococo foliated

scrolls bursting from the corners and sides of the rooms. The drawing and dining-rooms, flanking the central saloon at the rear of the house, had their plaster-work supplemented with birds and cornucopia. In the drawing-room, with its birds carrying garlands, cornucopia and a centrepiece of musical instruments, Osborne used motifs more commonly associated with his Dublin contemporary, Robert West,[22] while the panelled dining-room had birds reappearing in the frieze. The crisp precision of Osborne's execution in all these rooms was clearly the work of a master of rococo plaster-work.

It is, however, the saloon decoration, described as "transitional" by *The Georgian Society Records*,[23] which is of the greatest importance in understanding the evolution of Osborne's work. Its restrained geometrical design signifies a new awareness of the then fashionable

The Staircase Hall at Neptune derives from Duckart's hall at Castletown Cox. The plasterwork is pure Osborne.
Photograph W. Garner. Courtesy of the Irish Architectural Archive.

PATRICK OSBORNE, AN IRISH STUCCODORE

The Staircase Hall at Castletown Cox.
Photograph W. Garner. Courtesy of the Irish Architectural Archive.

PATRICK OSBORNE, AN IRISH STUCCODORE

Neo-classical decoration. Furthermore, it provides an incontestable link between Osborne's work and a house near Dublin, Neptune[24] (later Temple Hill House and, since 1930, St. Patrick's Infant Hospital in Blackrock).[25]

In 1767 James Dennis, later Baron Tracton, purchased the land on which Neptune was soon built.[26] Dennis was a native of Cork – his remains were removed to the old St. Fin Barre's after his sudden demise in 1782[27] – and it was possibly through his contacts there that he became acquainted with Patrick Osborne and, very probably, Davis Duckart. The exterior of Dennis's new house bore little relationship to Duckart's other, typically personal work. However, the interiors were singular, if

Entrance Hall of The Chamber of Commerce, Waterford. *Photograph George Mott.*

somewhat debased, versions of the Kilkenny mansion.

Neptune's saloon ceiling provides the most secure connection with Osborne through its simple, if unsatisfactory, elaboration of the Castletown saloon. The nearly square plan of the latter is adapted to the rectangular design required at Neptune through only two simple adjustments. The circular centrepiece of Castletown is elongated into an oval and is then extended further through the addition of octagonal motifs at either end. Apart from minor details in the frame mouldings[28] and the division of the centrepiece, the ceiling designs are virtually identical; even the leaf borders are repeated, though their inter-twining varies to accommodate the rectangular

The ceiling of the Saloon at Castletown Cox. A 'transitional' ceiling showing Osborne's move towards the neo-classical style. Photograph W. Garner. Courtesy of the Irish Architectural Archive.

design. Even the mantel plaque, as if boasting its pedigree, repeats that in the dining room at Castletown, a ploughman with his two horses and his dog.[29]

The staircase hall is a simplified, almost debased, version of its Castletown parent. Windows, panels, festoons and particularly the foliated Vitruvian scroll recall Castletown Cox both in general form and in detail. The plaster-work as executed possesses the typically rich character of Osborne's technique. However the extent of Duckart's involvement in this building must remain in doubt. The awkward relationship between windows and ceiling, evident in the present state of the hall, may derive from its original design. This finds no echo in Castletown.[30]

Detail of Staircase at The Chamber of Commerce, Waterford.

What is now the chapel repeats Castletown in a less direct manner. The panelling and entablature recall details of the hall and dining-room, while the modelling displays Osborne's naturalism at its best. The hall is less clear in its origins, though the suspended drapes over the doors echo the hall at Florence Court, Co. Fermanagh, where Duckart may[31] or may not[32] have been involved. Certainly the Neptune design is more tastefully decorative than the heavier Florence Court work.

While the saloon at Neptune signifies Osborne's move into late eighteenth-century decoration, the traditional association of Osborne with the Chamber of Commerce in Waterford[33] appears unfounded. The house was built by William

The ceiling of the Saloon at Neptune, now St. Patrick's Infant Hospital, Dublin. *It is a simple elongation of the Castletown design.*
Photograph W. Garner. Courtesy of the Irish Architectural Archive.

PATRICK OSBORNE, AN IRISH STUCCODORE

Morris about 1795. The attribution of its essentially Neo-classical interiors to Osborne may derive from the high quality of the work and the unusual birds in high relief in the magnificent oval staircase hall. If Osborne's connection with the Morris residence could be proved, a body of work might be stylistically associated with it, including Waterford's Christchurch Cathedral.[34]

A tentatively suggested stylistic association between the plaster-work in the now lost Dunsandle, Co. Galway, and Castletown Cox[35] is hardly likely. It is based on a similarity between garlands in the two houses. The Dunsandle saloon, though echoing details of the Castletown dining-room, is more clearly related to a room in Robert West's 86 St. Stephen's Green, and a now destroyed ground-floor room in Charlemont House, Parnell Square.

Osborne, despite some particularly interesting documentation, remains a mysterious figure. With the first publication of his bill, he is described by *The Georgian Society Records* as "probably a Waterford plasterer.[36] In contrast, Curran lists him as a Dublin plasterer[37] though no primary source for this has been recovered. He does not appear as a grantor in the Registry of Deeds, suggesting that he never expanded his trade into the domain of building, as did several of his Dublin contemporaries.[38]

Osborne's origins, like his later work, are uncertain. Curran, considering the then unknown origins of the Franchini, suggested a Franco-Italian background as "a pure guess".[39] He was recently proved incorrect, as was his spelling of their name.[40] However, it is in that spirited tradition of "guesswork" that a possible background for this less renowned Irish artist might be suggested.

While there were numerous Osbornes in Cork, Limerick and Waterford, if one uses the relatively uncommon combination of Patrick and Osborne[41] as a guide to the plasterer's origins,[42] (which it well might not be), two important sources direct attention to the area around Ardee, Co. Louth. Arthur Vicars's *Index to the Prerogative Wills* names a Patrick Osborne as a tobacconist in Ardee before 1786.[43] In the nineteenth century a family of Osbornes from Mullacrew, north of Ardee, with Patrick as a common Christian name, are recorded as emigrating to America.[44] This family is known to have

A festoon in the Entrance Hall of Castletown Cox. *It cost Michael Cox, Archbishop of Cashel, 16s 3d, in August 1774.*

had another cousin in Louth also called Patrick Osborne.[45] There is no particular problem in considering a Louth origin for an essentially southern stuccodore. If Osborne's apprenticeship at Kilshannig is to be accepted, the Franchini, or indeed Duckart himself may have lured him south from Dublin. The journeys of the peripatetic Franchini themselves indicate the willingness of eighteenth-century plasterers to travel.

To recapitulate, Osborne can be seen as a rococo plasterer of unknown origins who may have been apprenticed to the

Franchini at Kilshannig. His first documented work was in the Cork Mayoralty House and this was soon succeeded by his work at Castletown Cox, completed in 1774. Before the completion of this commission he became acquainted with Neo-classical interior decoration and adapted his trade to its new requirements. Very soon after Castletown—perhaps even during his work there—he was involved in some manner with the decoration of Neptune in Dublin. In his later years, he may have established a business in Waterford working as a plasterer in the Neo-classical style. However, this putative activity is very uncertain, being datable to some fifteen years after his last known work.

Despite the unusual detail provided by the historical documents, the information relating to Osborne encourages many more questions than it answers. Why, for example, was Archbishop Cox prepared to pay so much more, half as much again as for either of the halls, for the Neo-classical saloon ceiling? Was Osborne's move towards Neo-classicism dictated solely by business? What were the causes of the dramatic change?

Osborne himself remains a mysterious figure. His origins are obscure. His link with Neptune, though stylistically valid, cannot be clearly specified and his move towards Neo-classicism in the saloon there is distinctly uncomfortable. His later life is also uncertain. Could he, a rococo plasterer of the highest order, have mastered the problems of Neo-classical decoration and produced the superb interiors of Morris's town house in his later years?

Above all these questions and uncertainties lie the beauty and craftsmanship of his work at Castletown Cox. Here Patrick Osborne's artistry establishes him as one of Ireland's finest eighteenth-century plasterers.

Seán O Reilly

ACKNOWLEDGMENTS

I would like to thank the following people and institutions for their assistance in the preparation of this article—David Griffin, Ann Simmons, Rose Dunne, Ian Lumley, Dr. Edward McParland, Baron Brian de Breffny, Waterford Harbour Commission, Waterford Chamber of Commerce, Mercy Hospital, Cork, The Royal Society of Antiquaries of Ireland and The Irish Architectural Archive.

PATRICK OSBORNE, AN IRISH STUCCODORE

NOTES

1. T.U. Sadleir, ed., *The Georgian Society Records of 18th Century Domestic Architecture and Decoration in Ireland*, Dublin, 1913, Vol. 5, Appendix. I have retained the more usual spelling of Duckart's name.
2. *Idem.*
3. So called in the bill. Actually they were two capitals and two half-capitals.
4. Sadleir, op. cit., p. 73.
5. In reprinting the bill, both Sadleir, op. cit., and Brian de Breffny in 'Stucco Work by Patrick Osborne at Castletown Cox', *Irish Ancestor*, Vol. 13, No. 1, 1981, pp. 15-17, mistakenly record that Osborne did "1,591 ft. of plain cornices in ye bedroom over ye back parl^r."
6. Richard Caulfield, *The Council Book of the Corporation of the City of Cork from 1609 to 1643, and from 1690 to 1800*, Guildford, Surrey, 1876, pp. 774 *et seq.*
7. *Idem*, pp. 815-816 and see below, note 19.
8. Knight of Glin, 'A Baroque Palladian in Ireland, The Architecture of David Duckart–1', 'The Last Palladian in Ireland, The Architecture of Davis Duckart–2', *Country Life*, Vol. CXLII, 1967, pp. 735-739, 798-801. For Duckart's engineering see W.A. McCutcheon, *The Industrial Archaeology of Northern Ireland*, H.M.S.O., Belfast, 1980.
9. de Breffny, op. cit.
10. Caulfield, op. cit., p. 774.
11. *Idem.*
12. *Idem*, pp. 815-816 and Knight of Glin, loc. cit.
13. Caulfield, op. cit., pp. 815-816 and Knight of Glin, loc. cit.
14. Caulfield, op. cit., records the decoration and furnishing of the house in great detail.
15. *Idem*, p. 826. The "drawing-room" is here taken to mean the two-storey ballroom on the second floor of the house.
16. *Idem*, p. 833.
17. *Idem*, p. 845.
18. Sadleir, op. cit., pp. 73-76 and Appendix.

19. *Idem.* There appears to be no contemporary evidence for Duckart's involvement, though the attribution is hardly in question. Duckart's will, noted by Sadleir, may have provided further information.
20. Knight of Glin, op. cit.
21. *Idem.* The echoes are more obvious when one considers Castletown Cox in the context of the earlier Limerick Custom House.
22. C.P. Curran, *Dublin Decorative Plasterwork of the 17th and 18th Centuries*, London, 1967, pp. 57-65.
23. Sadleir, op. cit., p. 74.
24. Sister Katherine Butler RSC, 'Neptune on the Temple Hill', *Dublin Historical Record*, Vol. 39, No. 3, 1986, pp. 98-107 and F.E. Ball, *A History of County Dublin: the People, Parishes and Antiquities from the Earliest Times to the close of the eighteenth century*, 1902, Part First, pp. 18-19.
25. Katherine Butler, op. cit., pp. 104-105.
26. F.E. Ball, op. cit.
27. *Idem*, also *The Irish Builder*, 1894, p. 173, 260.
28. The Castletown inner frame has flowers inside the guilloche which are absent from Neptune's, and the Castletown outer frame has a bead-and-reel moulding on its inner edge which is simplified in the Neptune moulding. The detail is more crisp in Castletown while the lines of the frames are more acute in Neptune.
29. Such a detail by no means confirms the link. This plaque design recurs again at Mount Juliet, Co. Kilkenny, with only minor modifications.
30. The original character of the hall is, of course, uncertain. However, Duckart was equally casual about the windows inside the ballroom in the Mayoralty House where the entablature is crudely broken by their heavy frames.
31. Knight of Glin, op. cit.
32. Maurice Craig, *The Architecture of Ireland*

from the earliest times to 1880, London and Dublin, 1982, pp. 195-196.
33. Brian de Breffny and Rosemary ffolliott, *The Houses of Ireland, Domestic architecture from the medieval castle to the Edwardian villa*, London, 1975, p. 155.
34. I am indebted to Mr. Ian Lumley for this suggestion. Though damaged and restored, some of the original plaster-work still remains.
35. Knight of Glin, op. cit.
36. Sadleir, op. cit., Appendix. The inclusion of the Waterford Morris house, the Chamber of Commerce, in the illustrations may have promoted its attribution to Osborne.
37. Curran, op. cit., p. 110.
38. It is easy to mis-read the passage in Caulfield, op. cit., p. 826–"Ordered that the overseers . . . agree with Patrick Osborne for stuccoing . . . , and also with a proper person for erecting four marble chimney-pieces . . . also for erecting a portico . . ."–as indicating Osborne's involvement in all these activities.
39. Curran, op. cit., p. 31.
40. Brian de Breffny, 'The Lafranchini Brothers, Biographical notes on the stuccodores from Switzerland', *The GPA Irish Arts Review Yearbook*, 1988, pp. 212-221.
41. "Osborne" is taken as embodying variant spellings such as Osburn, etc. No Patrick Osborne is listed in the Index to Grantors at the Registry of Deeds in the 18th and early 19th centuries. No Osborne family in the upper classes seems to have had a Patrick in its family.
42. See Rosemary ffolliott, 'Irish Naming Practices Before the Famine', *The Irish Ancestor*, Vol. XVIII, No. 1, pp. 1-4.
43. Sir Arthur Vicars, ed., *Index to the Prerogative Wills of Ireland 1536-1810*, Dublin, 1897.
44. Josephine Osborne, *The Osbornes of County Louth Ireland and Nicollet County, Minnesota USA*, private printing, USA, 1978.
45. *Idem*, p. 193.

INTERVIEW WITH RICHARD GORMAN

You were born and reared in Ireland, you say you feel Irish and that what you do is Irish. But now you live in Milan and regard yourself as a citizen of the world. However, primarily, you are an individual and an artist. How did your artistic career begin?

At the Dun Laoghaire School of Art and Design, where I became a student at the age of thirty. After that I did a year of classes, two evenings plus Saturday mornings; it was quite intense, ten hours a week. By that time I was working in the family business but at the end of it all, I came to the conclusion that I wanted to do painting full time.

At the age of thirty you were already mature, How did you decide to become an artist in the first place?

When I was very young, I was interested in art but because I was the eldest son in a family that owned a garage, to become an artist was not an easy thing to do. I was scribbling and drawing ever since I can remember but I was neither convinced nor yet committed. Then at the age of seventeen, I showed my work to a gallery in Dublin and was told that I was no good. I believed them because I thought that they knew what they were doing whereas I did not, and I forgot about it. After that experience I did a degree in Business Studies which was not a total disappointment because, although it was hard work, I enjoyed college. I went to Trinity College, Dublin, and that was fine. After that I worked for Ford in England. I was a buyer of racing cars for our competitors, and I was travelling a lot in Europe. After a short stay in America I returned to work for the family business in Dublin. Initially it was awful but gradually I began to enjoy it. I was never interested in just making money but the organizational problems involved interested me.

But I was already thirty years old and began to realize that before you click your fingers you are sixty and I felt that I had not done anything in my life. At the same time I had started art school and that was going brilliantly. I was working with Margaret West and Trevor Scott and everybody was so open-minded that I was really provoked into thinking about becoming a painter. I was at that time desperately unhappy so I made my decision to become a painter in an irrational

The Irish painter, Richard Gorman, has continued to participate in many of the major exhibitions in Ireland while extending his career in Europe from his home base in Milan. **Sanda Miller** interviewed him in London where he was staying briefly between Tokyo and Milan.

Black Clac, *lithograph, 64.7 × 50 cms. Photograph courtesy Benjamin Rhodes Gallery, London.*

way perhaps. I worked incredibly hard in art school because I was so miserable in the beginning. I am now extremely happy but I know that there is something behind me so that whatever may happen, I have got my work and it will always save me.

How were you painting after you emerged from your academic training?

I was still involved in ideas which I am not now, what I thought at that time were clever ideas – and illustrating them in a way. My paintings ended up as illustrations of ideas and the same was true of my sculpture: I would have an idea and I would make something I thought expressed it. This was in 1980. In 1982 I had an exhibition in the Project Gallery in Dublin. I showed paintings, lithographs and etchings as well as welded steel and wooden sculptures, pieces that went on

the wall and were in a way rather jokey. I don't think it was awful but there might have been a touch of cynicism about Conceptual Art in my work. I was also guarding myself, not wanting to give myself away. That is why I was trying to make things which were ideas that did not give me away very much. In a way I was also cynical about the art world. But it was not enough and after that opening I spent the entire summer thinking about it because I found it difficult to get going again. To go to art school had been a dramatic decision and it worked and what I needed now was another dramatic decision because I am ambitious and I wanted to be good.

During that period I had been to Paris and worked with Jacques de Champfleury who made lithographs on stone. Michael Farrell had all his work done by Champfleury, and introduced me to him. I decided to sell the house in Ireland and work in Paris for a year. I was lucky to have had financial assistance because I owned shares in the family business which was still going when I left Ireland but subsequently collapsed. In Paris I just printed and made lithographs. Lithographs are fascinating and beautiful to make. It was also a beautiful workshop and ambience and I had a good working relation with Jacques de Champfleury. I had two exhibitions of drawings and prints in Paris, at the Atelier Champfleury and the James Mayor Gallery respectively. These prints helped me work out something I discovered during that time. When I was passing through London I saw an exhibition of the collection of George Costakis at the Royal Academy which, in fact, came to Dublin in 1988. That was extraordinary because I find the Russian Constructivists so emotional and yet so controlled in their geometric renderings. There were a lot of things I wrote down. I loved the show but particularly the covers of the little booklets the Constructivists were printing. The titles too were extraordinary: there was one called 'A Tango with Cows', another 'Conversation with the Tax Inspector about Poetry' and yet another 'Baby Camels in the Sky'. I made lithographs using some of the titles.

What kind of visual language did you invent for yourself?

In 'Baby Camels in the Sky', you see two

INTERVIEW WITH RICHARD GORMAN

camels sort of stamped and the sky just drawn lines, so in a way they were childish, innocent-looking, conceptual images.

Living in Paris and using prints made me focus on one medium and one city but I also learnt to laugh. Perhaps this was something to do with the concept of 'displacement activity' in which I was interested at that time. For example, if you lose your keys you should not look for them; you should do something else and you will find the keys, but if you make the finding of the keys into an issue you will not find them. I found it interesting that I was able to solve harsh problems by accident when I thought I was just solving technical problems of printing. In printing, everything is back to front and black and white, when you are thinking in colour. The point is that by not confronting the problems of 'Art' with capital 'a' and instead concentrating on the technical problems of making, the 'harsh' looked after itself.

When I began to paint, I remembered again the 'displacement activity' when I saw a beautiful show by Howard Hodgkin in London. In the catalogue, he said that he wanted to make things *alla prima* but that was never enough because the paintings lacked something and although they seemed right, it was too facile; they had no history behind them. So he would keep going beyond that to try to finish with the same energy as that with which he started. It was Howard Hodgkin's catalogue that put me on to the right way to painting. Before that I used to confront a painting and take it on like a fight and really lose my temper with it. That is not a good idea. It is a good idea to get upset but not to get into that high nervous energy state when you just do damage. I don't mean that you should not destroy, at times, but you should do it in an involved way. I am constantly in doubt about painting. Usually I have a system which I worked out for myself. I tend to work on several paintings at the same time and I get to the point when I do not know what to do with them any more and become very aware of it. Everything becomes slippery and I turn them against the wall just before I completely lose my temper and I leave them like that. So I would have, at any time, about twelve or twenty or more paintings turned against the wall and maybe three out on which I would work simultaneously. I find this good because painting is a mixture of

destruction and making. Every time you have made a decision that such and such a thing should be such and such a colour, tone, weight etc., you then have to take it out if you are going to change something. It is not a process of attrition like a carving where you are taking something away again and again; it is the opposite. You are building but you are destroying at the same time because if I decide that that corner is not working, I have to paint over a valid decision.

Why do you call painting a process of destruction? Do you completely obliterate something or do you let it work for you by allowing colour, let us say, appear through the new layer which covers it?

Sometimes you really have to block out the colour because the most dangerous thing is when you think that you have to hold on to really beautiful bits here and there. Very often these are the very bits you have to destroy to try and make the painting work coherently.

When you start a painting, do you know which way you are going?

No! I don't know with what colours it will end up; I don't know anything.

How do you start your first mark on the canvas?

The canvas is never white and the first thing I do is to gesso it and then put a little oil paint just to 'dirty' it – then I begin, usually with people, animals or objects.

But where are they? I can not see any in the paintings before me.

They come and go. There is a guy in bed in one of the canvases in front of you and the one next to it is a chair and a crocodile. But I should not be saying to you what it is, because they are the most obvious ones. In some of my other paintings the people may have gone altogether.

Don't you know if they've gone?

No. I can not even see them but I don't look for them any more. They don't seem relevant; they were starting points which at times reappear: faces or bits of landscape for instance.

Obviously colour is very important in your work. Does it connect with you moving to Milan?

Yes, Milan was very important. I don't know why I chose Milan but the logic was this: I thought Italy! but I did not want to go somewhere too beautiful and romantic which eliminated Rome, Florence, Siena in one go. I thought of Milan, a hard-nosed city, or so it seems, so I went there and settled straight away. That was four years ago.

Let's be analytical about your work because this is when it becomes interesting. How would you describe your paintings at the point when you arrived in Milan?

I had acquired more control of line with etchings and lithography. I also learnt with lithography that there was a right time in the day to attack which, at that time, was at about seven in the evening when I actually wanted to do the painting on the stone. There would be jazz on the radio, people finished up work, there was a nice feeling. It was darkish, winter, and I would just get the feeling right and do it. I was using colours, but very muted ones, partly for financial reasons. When I started painting in Milan, I had a tendency to make a single object or follow a single idea or in sculpture, a single totem or icon; the same held true of etchings.

Were you ever interested in Abstract Expressionism?

Yes, very much. One of the painters I was really interested in was Willem de Kooning. I find his series of 'Women' really beautiful. That kind of freedom still with control – he was going so fast at the end and you can see that there is no tidying up – became my ambition: to be able to make fluid, non-cerebral paintings. I am trying to get as close to this as I can all the time but tend to destroy everything at the end. I try not to be precious.

I also like Bonnard and have been influenced by his wonderful colours. But colour is such a dangerous thing because the usual battle I have is to try not to make something which looks too pretty. If you stay in greys you are not going to look pretty whatever you do; it will be serious. When you get into colour you can look frivolous without meaning to look frivolous and even if what you are

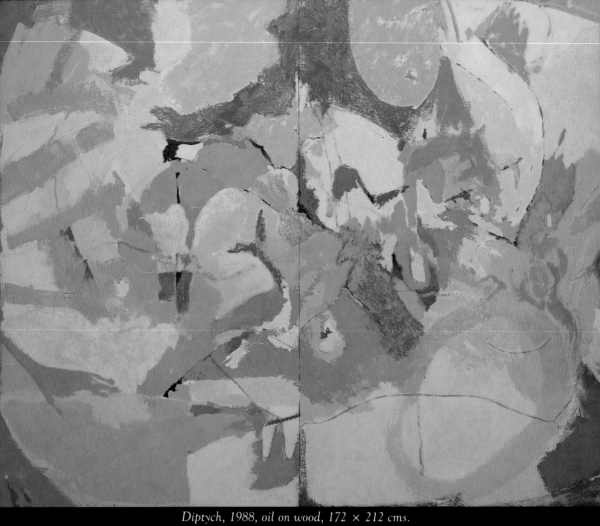

Diptych, 1988, oil on wood, 172 × 212 cms.

Triptych, 1988, oil on wood, 252 × 375 cms.

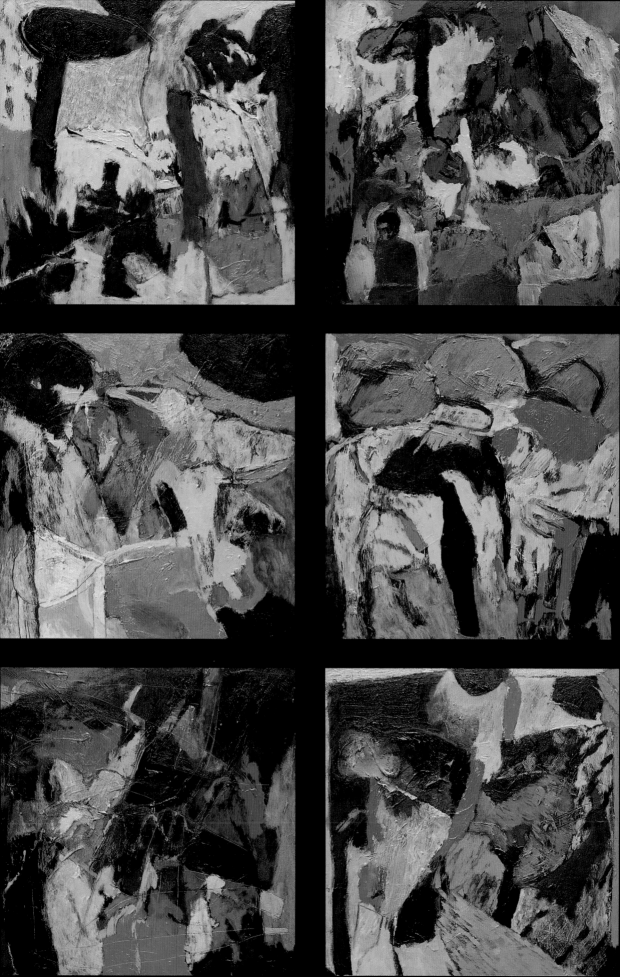

Le Grand Meaulnes 1–6, *oil on wood, 39.4 × 39.4 cms.*

INTERVIEW WITH RICHARD GORMAN

doing does not feel frivolous. The works I paint at the moment have all very bright colours. The ones in front of you constitute a triptych I call 'Mare' (sea). They are 'Piccolo Mare'; 'Mare' and 'Piombo' for lead, because a lot of the grey in it is lead glued on.

That is most unusual, something I never heard of before.

I make all my frames of lead and glue them on round the corners. I have not heard of anyone else doing that but lead has a nice, sensual feeling.

For me lead is the most dead of all metals. Lead for me is death.

For me it has an attractive feel and it makes a nice border for my paintings because its sheen feels a little like oil painting.

Did Italy contribute to this dramatic change in your palette?

It did but it was not to do with the bright sunlight and all that, because Milan is sombre, filthy dirty and foggy so you cannot say that it was the light. I think it came with confidence because I dared more. I was getting little bits of success. Everybody needs a little success, not a lot, just a few good things to happen because at times it is difficult to make yourself believe that what you do is serious and worthwhile; that what you are doing isn't just complete masturbation. You need this kind of encouragement!

Large Rocker, *lithograph, 65.4 × 48.8 cms. Photograph courtesy Benjamin Rhodes Gallery, London.*

In my most recent paintings the colour is darker again. I painted them in September last but I am not sure why the palette changed. Perhaps because it struck me that I ought to take care about colour because I did not want to make things that were too delicious going down Bonnard way, when I am not Bonnard. I was making abstract paintings and I wanted them to have a great punch in them as well as be good graphic.

I am going to ask you a difficult question. You travel a lot but you are Irish. I want to know about your 'Irishness', that Celtic sensibility which I presume should be sombre.

I suppose it should be sombre but then look at James Joyce, he was not sombre at all. He was full of joy and laughter. *Ulysses* is full of laughter! It is like *Monty Python's Flying Circus*. Joyce even said that there isn't a single serious word in the whole book. It is serious, of course, because it is art and Joyce had an amazing perception in the way people think. I always think of myself more as European. I feel Irish, that is sure, but not in any political nationalistic kind of way.

Do you think that the feeling is reflected in your art in any sense?

I don't know. If you look at my colours you might say that it is not there! What I do has to be Irish because I am Irish and I was brought up, educated and lived in Ireland, so what I do is Irish in that sense, but not consciously Irish. I am not interested in my Celtic roots, for example, any more than in most other things. I am not fascinated by Newgrange and that kind of Irishness. I am more interested in the whole swim of the vegetable markets of life, just colour and things happening and looks passing between people at parties and just being alive. I don't seek to capture anything when I paint – it is just a thing between me and it; but I suppose if it is anything, it would be a coloured vegetable market.

Sanda Miller

SYMBOLISM IN TURN-OF-THE-CENTURY IRISH ART

It is curious that with the current interest in all aspects of Symbolism, witnessed by an ever increasing number of books, journals, exhibitions and catalogues exploring the subject, references to manifestations in Ireland are still confined to Oscar Wilde and W.B. Yeats. The visual arts tend to be overlooked.[1]

The diverse and widespread influence of the two eloquent high priests of Byzantium is duly acknowledged. They were as well versed in the esoteric French literature, which bred the international movement defined as Symbolism,[2] as in the subsequently equally influential English Romantic and Utopian visions of Pre-Raphaelitism. Although nurtured by the ideological preoccupations of the *fin-de-siècle* Symbolists, embracing Synthetism, Mysticism, Occultism and Decadence, Yeats's complex and richly evocative images were inspired by Celtic mythology. He "found in Ireland mythology, unfamiliar even to Irish readers, and in itself rather cloudy and vague, a treasury of symbols ready to his hand . . . In taking Symbolism to Ireland, he fed it with new resources and gave it a special accent which leads us to think of his poetry from the point of view of its national qualities rather than from the point of view of its relation to the rest of European literature."[3] Similarly, the thwarted philosophical quest of the hyperaesthetic adolescent, Stephen Daedalus, "a bat-like soul waking to the consciousness of itself in darkness and secrecy and loneliness", a soul "swooning into some new world, fantastic, dim, uncertain as under sea, traversed by cloudy shapes and beings"[4] begins in cloistral, unmistakeably Irish, corridors, alternatively redolent of incense and stale food, heaven and hell. Joyce's prose casts the familiar images of Decadence in a Dublin vernacular.

It is ironic that Yeats's poems *The Wanderings of Oisin* (1889) were partly responsible for triggering off the idiosyncratic Celtic Revival of the Glasgow Four, about 1894[5] rather than a similarly synthetic expression of European Symbolism in Dublin. That year, Althea Gyles (1868–1949), "very tall with dusky red-gold hair and a voice of commanding music",[6] who had met Yeats through their shared interest in the Hermetic Order of the Golden Dawn, drew her first designs – a cover and spine – for his *Poems* (1895). Her subsequent illustrations for

In this detailed article, **Dr. Nicola Gordon Bowe**, whose book on Harry Clarke is being published in 1989, deals with the neglected subject of Symbolism in Irish visual art.

The Secret Rose (1897), *Poems* (1899) and *The Wind among the Reeds* (1899), fusing gnostic symbolism, a flattened Celtic brand of *Art Nouveau* and the influences of Rossetti, Ricketts, Beardsley and Behrens, led to his eulogy of her art as "the personification of the beauty which cannot be seen with the bodily eyes, or pictured otherwise than by symbols".[7] Oscar Wilde (whose ballad 'The Harlot's House' she illustrated with hedonistically "silhouetted shadows on a blind"[8] for a privately circulated volume under the imprint of Leonard Smithers' Mathurin Press), referred to her as "an artist of great ability" shortly before his death in 1900.

There are certain analogies between her careful, dream-like, small-scale studies and those of the equally unconventional American-born Pamela Coleman-Smith (c. 1877–1950), whose nickname 'Pixie' reflects the nature of her work. Similarly drawn to Hermeticism and the Occult, as well as to Irish folklore and the expression of music through painting, she collaborated with both W.B. and Jack Yeats on an assortment of ventures between 1900–1905, but these were principally in England and America. The importance of pioneering new dramatic concepts and theatrical masques which attempted a pared-down synthesis of all the arts in representations of a fundamentally symbolist character, can only be alluded to here. Both she and Jack Yeats (1871–1957) reflect the influence of Gordon Craig in their set designs for W.B. Yeats; Jack Yeats's mountain backcloth design for his brother's *The King's Threshold* (1913) is also redolent of the stark, brooding landscapes of the Swiss Symbolist, Ferdinand Hodler.[9]

In Dublin, 1894 was marked by the foundation of the Arts and Crafts Society of Ireland whose exhibitions between 1895 and 1925 would feature the work of those artist/craftsmen and women who best represent what may be seen as the Irish expression of a multi-faceted international movement. In art, symbolism by definition must involve the visual expression of ideas; as Wilde has said, "All Art is

at once surface and symbol".[10] By 1891, when Albert Aurier attempted a definition of the current trend in France, illustrated by the art of Gauguin,[11] an ideological structure, opposed to the myth of progress, to positivism, realism, naturalism and historical materialism, had emerged. A rich vocabulary of dreamed images, deliberately ambiguous, enigmatic, fatalistic, sensual or erotic, escapist or obscure and interpreted in what became recognizable forms[12] was established, closely related to contemporary literary, poetic and musical ideas. These often varied according to national romantic tendencies. Mythical consciousness was bound to respond to political, social and economic upheavals; thus there are parallels between French reactions to the Franco-Prussian war, the revolutionary Commune and ensuing Republic, and Ireland's struggle for Home Rule, culminating in the 1916 Insurrection and the establishment of a Free State in 1921.[13] The subversive side of Symbolism, rejecting "Bastien-Lepage's clownish peasant staring with vacant eyes at her great boots"[14] in favour of a more evocative reality, yearned for a seemingly contradictory synthesis of what Xavier Mellery called "the dense presence of the past" with an apposite modernist iconography.

It is interesting but beyond the scope of this article to note that none of those Irish artists who lived in France and Belgium c. 1880–1914[15] espoused the cult of Symbolism. Only the moody, melancholy studies of the short-lived Frank O'Meara (1853–1888),[16] reminiscent of Millais, Puvis and Corot, or an exceptional painting like the poundingly mysterious 'Bull by Moonlight' (c. 1895)[17] by the expressionist Roderic O'Conor (1860–1940) or Paul Henry's youthful drawings after Rossetti can be seen as such; Mary Swanzy's (1882–1978) later paintings, post-1940, display a disquietingly expressive symbolism shared with Wilhelmina Geddes (1887–1955), too late to be considered as Symbolist.[18] It was the artists who lived and worked in Ireland and were caught up in the romantic nationalist climate during the key period of 1890–1920 who found expression in Symbolism. Of those who had studied in France or Belgium, Kathleen Fox (1880–1963), Beatrice Elvery (1883–1968) and Harry Clarke (1889–1931)

AE Russell, "Is This Not Great Babylon That I have Built?"
Courtesy Hugh Lane Municipal Gallery, Dublin, No. 87.

AE Russell, The Winged Horse, 1904. Courtesy Hugh Lane Municipal Gallery, Dublin.

Harry Clarke, Illustration of Oscar Wilde's *De Profundis*, 1913.
Photograph courtesy of Sotheby's, Belgravia, London.

SYMBOLISM IN TURN-OF-THE-CENTURY IRISH ART

Maud Wynne and Percy Gethin, detail from the Lake Isle of Inisfree embroidered panel, 1900–10.
Courtesy of National Museum of Ireland

stand out, while their older contemporary, Constance Markievicz, the Rebel Countess ("simply not a real painter"[19]) produced exhorting images to further the cause of independence. The latter's cousin by marriage, Maud Wynne (1868–1957), embroidered four panels (1900–1910)[20] illustrating Yeats's *The Lake Isle of Inisfree,* following *cloisonné*-like designs by the Sligo painter, Percy Gethin (1874–1916), akin to those of the Nabis and Van de Velde in their flat horizontal rhythms and rich colours.

W.B. Yeats's visionary role in kindling Irish aspirations tends to eclipse that of his contemporary, George 'AE' Russell (1867–1935). The dipthong AE, by which Russell became known from 1888, is the first syllable derived from 'Aeon', "the name the Gnostics gave to the earliest beings separated from the Deity",[21] appeared to him in a waking dream at the beginning of his spiritual journey through life. Writer, painter, philosopher and mystic poet of vision, Theosophist and enlightened agriculturist, he was a key figure in the Irish Revival, particularly as the influential editor of *The Irish Homestead* (from 1905) and *The Irish Statesman* (from 1923).[22] His most lasting legacies are his ethereal paintings and critical writings. In these he became the most prophetic and accessible spokesman of the artistic aspects of the Revival.

"The Celtic Renaissance in Ireland" as he conceived it,

> "has . . . come about . . . through the almost simultaneous awakening of a number of Irishmen to a higher ideal of beauty and perfection in their art than hitherto; and just because they have a more perfect means of expression the Celtic spirit is much more apparent, for that is something which cannot be analyzed, or gained by thought, or by making use of any particular set of symbols. It already exists

Ethel Rhind and the Dun Emer Guild, Smuainteac (Reverie), c. 1912.
Courtesy of National Museum of Ireland.

and is the heritage of all, and whenever the mind is subtle and plastic enough to yield to its protean influence, it shapes the human imaginings into a harmony with its own ideals so that they express the dreams long hoarded in the Celtic fancy . . .".[23]

Yeats records that when they were art students in Dublin c. 1884, "he did not paint the model as we tried to for some other image rose always before his eyes . . . and already he spoke to us of his visions",[24] although his "early admir-

ation for the works of Gustave Moreau", William Blake and Rossetti and training in "academic Graeco-Roman forms" seemed to aid these.[25] He frequently "felt with great intensity the presence of . . . supernatural beings and heard their music passing into the earth."[26] These luminous, crested, androgynous images of an indeterminate cosmology recur in most of his best paintings, usually in smoky colours in oil or on paper. Apart from notable oil paintings in the Hugh Lane Municipal Art Gallery in Dublin such as ' "Is This Not Great Babylon That I Have Built?" ' and 'The Winged Horse',[27] presented by Lane to the gallery in 1908 as part of his collection and in the Armagh County Museum, the National Gallery's collection includes fifteen murals rescued from the walls of his editorial office in the Irish Agricultural Organization Society at 84 Merrion Square. Dreamy, heroic idylls representing the journey of the pilgrim soul, painted and repainted in spare moments on brown wallpaper, these are vaguely redolent of Moreau, Redon and Puvis; whereas his earliest murals of 1892/3, painted during his seven year residency at the Dublin Lodge of the Theosophical Society at 3 Upper Ely Place depict a richly detailed universe of elemental spirits, heavenly bodies and human and divine figures on a variety of scales. Their profound significance can only be surmised[28] but their visionary integrity is impressive and in keeping with the Rosicrucian doctrine of the Sâr Peladan (1892), extolling mystical painting of "a mural-like character". He subsequently painted the brown wallpaper of his drawing room in Rathgar with fairies and gods and decorated Elizabeth Yeats's printing room at Dun Emer in Dundrum with a decorative scheme of plumed

SYMBOLISM IN TURN-OF-THE-CENTURY IRISH ART

angelic beings in pastels. Either he or Yeats may have provided the inspiration for a poppy-bordered tapestry panel, 'Smuainteac' (or 'Reverie'), woven at the Dun Emer Guild to the evocative design of Ethel Rhind (c. 1878–1952), an artist of the Tower of Glass stained glass studio. AE was a valued mentor and adviser to both these craft workshops.[29]

Between 1904 and 1915 he turned increasingly to landscape settings. His careless technique, short-sightedness and the daunting task of depicting his mystic visions rendered his output variable. Although he greatly admired the sculpture of his older contemporary, John Hughes, not least for its technical accomplishment, there are several pieces by Hughes's exact contemporary, Oliver Sheppard (1865–1941), and his student, Beatrice Elvery, which can be termed Symbolist. Sheppard's marble sculpted head (c. 1908) of 'Roisin Dua', the poet's Dark Rosaleen, set into the plinth of his Clarence Mangan Memorial in St. Stephen's Green, personifies the Spirit of Poetry, Ireland and the poet's own "loneliness, darkness, suffering and despair";[30] in proud reverie and softly outlined, her rose-strewn hair fosters small symbolic figures in relief. His 'Inisfail' (1906) and 'Death of Cuchulain' (1911) became potent figurative symbols of the 1916 Rising. Little of the versatile Elvery's early sculpture has survived, nor have the idealistic graphics and paintings she did for Patrick Pearse's school, St. Enda's, its publication, An Macaomh or her illustrations for The Heroes of the Dawn (1913) by AE's wife, Violet. Her most Symbolist extant work, embodying the impassioned aspirations of her more nationalist friends, is the small plaster head, 'Glendalough' (1904), modelled to evoke the silence of the upper lake, "the extraordinary sense of something brooding over"[31] the ancient monastic valley where she had spent the night. The treatment of the little naked figures, symbolizing the Seven Churches, who shelter in the tresses of the hollow-eyed muse recall Rodin–"All is idea, all is symbol. So the form and the attitude of a human being reveal the emotions of its soul . . . When a good sculptor models a statue . . . he must clearly conceive the general idea; then he must keep this idea of the whole in his mind in order to subordinate and ally to it every smallest detail of his work".[32]

Oliver Sheppard, Roisin Dua, *c. 1908, from the James Clarence Mangan Memorial, St. Stephen's Green, Dublin. Photograph Pieterse Davison International.*

Beatrice Elvery, Glendalough, *1904. Courtesy Hugh Lane Municipal Gallery, Dublin.*

Kathleen Fox, Music, *enamelled panel, 1909. Private collection.*

Elvery's various interpretations of the favoured Symbolist Mother-and-Child theme link her with her aunt, Phoebe Traquair (1852–1936), Dublin born and trained, who left for Edinburgh in 1873. They both exhibited with the Arts and Crafts Society of Ireland; in 1895, Traquair's silk and gold thread embroidered panels symbolizing 'The Salvation of Mankind' (1887–93), reflected her synthetist philosophy–"that tireless seeking . . . for the exact line or colour, which will embody the feeling or thought received by the artist, this is what all art comes to in the end"[33] – and were acclaimed in Dublin. At the Society's third exhibition in 1904, her enamelled casket, illustrating scenes from the 'Life of the Madonna', and triptych, 'The Kiss', were shown beside P. Oswald Reeves's similarly Symbolist panel, 'A Falling Star'. Both were inevitably influenced by Rossetti and Alexander Fisher, the English master craftsman with whom Reeves (1870–1967)[34] had worked in London, before moving to Dublin in 1903 to inaugurate highly successful enamelling and metal-work classes at the Metropolitan School of Art. Reeves's own and his students' work parallel the Birmingham School's late flowering of Pre-Raphaelitism in their predilection for spiritual themes of questing souls, draped and ethereal, in rich or aqueous colours. The commanding angelic matriarch on the presentation album which Reeves made for Sir Horace Plunkett in 1908 (tragically destroyed at Kilteragh in 1922) reappears in his imposing Grangegorman War Memorial of 1920.

Several artists found youthful expression in his classes. One was Dora Allen (1885–1981),[35] whose 'Excalibur' panel of 1909 illustrates the submarine vision of a disdainful siren and her dragon, guardians of the magic sword. The thick, golden mane of hair undulating above her in the watery depths, her rapt features and glistening mythical setting place her in the realms of Symbolism. Kathleen Fox, subsequently a more conventional painter, produced an allusive 'Music' panel and silver zodiacal mirror that year, after her outstanding *basse-taille* enamelled goblet, 'Going to the Feast' of 1908, which showed a procession of figures robed in deep, jewelled colours. Ernest Corr's horizontal plaque, 'A Heroic Tale' (c. 1906) is similarly evoc-

DEEP·IN·CLEAR·STILL·WATERS·ON·A·ROCK·EXCALIBUR·THE·HUGE·CROSS·HILTED·SWORD,
WAS·WROUGHT·WITH·MYSTIC·CHARMS·AND·SUBTLER·MAGIC·THAN·OUR·OWN.

TO·RISE·FROM·OUT·THE·BOSOM·OF·THE·LAKE·TO·WIN·FOR·RIGHT·TO·DRIVE·THE·HEATHEN·OUT,
THAT·NOBLE·CAUSE·AND·NOBLE·AIM·MIGHT·REIGN·WITH·THE·NOBLE·KING. D·R·A·1909

Dora Allen, Excalibur, 1909. Photograph Pieterse Davison International

Harry Clarke, The Colloquy of Monos and Una, *illustration to Poe's* Tales of Mystery and Imagination, *1923.*
Photograph by Pieterse Davison International.

SYMBOLISM IN TURN-OF-THE-CENTURY IRISH ART

ative, if reminiscent of Burne-Jones. Another metal-worker, Mia Cranwill (1880–1972), Dublin born but Manchester trained, specialized in designing jewellery and enamelled metals on symbolic and Celtic themes, illustrating poems like Yeats's *Inspiration*, AE's *Babylon*, lines from his *National Being* and Bardic incantations. Most of the major figures of the Celtic Revival and their spouses commissioned or wore her creations.

By 1917, when the Fifth Arts and Crafts exhibition was held, an artist had emerged whose "mastery of technique" and "application of it to the ends of exceeding beauty, significance and wondrousness" was unprecedented. "The sustained magnificence of colour, the beautiful and most intricate drawing, the lavish and mysterious symbolism"[36] of his eleven stained glass windows (1915–17) in the Honan Chapel at Cork University revealed Harry Clarke as a latter-day Symbolist. Like James Joyce, educated by the Jesuits at Belvedere College in that peculiarly Irish preserve of Catholic sensibility, his empathy for Symbolist literature, art, music and theatre was manifest as early as 1907 in a drawing of 'Salomé' adapted from Gustave Moreau. (That year, the Fine Art section of the Irish International Exhibition in Dublin included the work of Beardsley, Burne-Jones, Simeon Solomon, Watts, Khnopff and Ricketts.) It reappears in a potent illustration of Heine's possessed fiddler 'Paganini' (1912), in a rainbow-coloured interpretation of Oscar Wilde's 'De Pro-

P. Oswald Reeves, A Falling Star, *1904. Courtesy of the Cecil Higgins Art Gallery, Bedford.*

fundis' (1913), filled with etiolated spirits and severed heads, and in three Beardsleyish illustrations to Yeats's 'Song of Wandering Aengus' (1913). Always a voracious reader (of Baudelaire, Poë, Nietzsche, Keats, Coleridge, Dante, Goethe, Maeterlinck, Flaubert, Pater etc.), his earliest student panels and illustrations demonstrate the depth of research he devoted to illustrating each subject. His love of enigmatic, symbolic and dramatic details and attitudes and a mediaeval delight in juxtaposing the grotesque with the sublimely beautiful became apparent early in his career. These culminate in his haunting, saffron-robed 'Judas' panel of 1913, adapted from a mediaeval window in Chartres Cathedral. The influence of the Vienna Secessionists, notably Klimt, is first apparent in his illustrations to Coleridge's nightmare 'Rime of the Ancient Mariner' (1913–15). The Byzantine element in Klimt and Clarke's detailed study of mediaeval glass in France and England are developed in the Cork windows, each portraying "an ecstatic figure segregated from a human tower"[37] sumptuously orchestrated in a series of key colours. The climax of this device is seen in his Terenure 'Coronation of the Virgin' window (1923), with its cringing base figures and thickly studded figurative tapestry of Old Testament characters. They encapsulate what is termed Synaesthesia,[38] a stylized interrelationship of abstraction and symbol, and lure us into their bemused trances through enigmatic expression and hieratic stance.

Phoebe Traquair, Despair, *1899, embroidered panel. Courtesy National Galleries of Scotland, Cat. No. NGS 1865.*

SYMBOLISM IN TURN-OF-THE-CENTURY IRISH ART

Clarke's hypersensitive graphic skills, idiosyncratic vision and religious sensibility, synthesis of a wide range of literary and art historical references, with his incomparable manipulation of the jewelled qualities of glass, gave his work a dimension usually only dreamed of by the Symbolists. His sinister, 'flesh-creeping' illustrations to that testament of Symbolism, Poë's *Tales of Mystery and Imagination*, begun in 1914, were published in 1919 and 1923, although some of his Hans Andersen illustrations (published 1916) had already revealed that taste for the macabre and unwordly which would mark his illustrated *Faust* and Swinburne, causing one reviewer to remark, "Here is the world of the psychoanalyst made visible".[39] In 1917 he made the first of a series of magical miniature panels, illustrating scenes from literature in richly glowing ruby and blue glass, intricate detail and unprecedented technical achievement. The most Symbolist of these depict Heinrich Heine's ominous ballad (1918) of 'A Meeting' between a bewitching Mermaid and Merman[40] and Flaubert's *S. Julien* (1919) whose legend the novelist had fancifully based on a thirteenth century stained glass window in Rouen Cathedral. A decadent high priest of Byzantium, lofty, of a sepulchral "paleness almost radiant"[41] and "remote and unaccustomed beauty, somnambulistic, frail, androgynous",[42] his "blue mind steeped in the roses of dead essences",[43] he is "draped in the blind cold fire of precious stones"[44] in "an agony of trance".[45] Clarke portrays him reflecting with foreboding on his past life of unquenchable sadism, symbolized by "Amelekite slings . . . Garamantian javelins . . . Saracen broad swords and Norman coats of mail"[46] visible above his crusading banner in the inlaid recesses of the Imperial Palace of Occitania. Clarke made this and its companion panel, 'Gideon' immediately after seeing Diaghilev's exotic Russian ballet, 'Schéhérazade' in London. By then he had evolved an idealized androgynous archetype:[47] heavy-lidded, ascetic, lost in reverie, a deathly pallor, red-gold hair and tapering fingers contrasting with elaborately stylized apparel. Such creatures are discernible in his windows in Killiney ('The Angel of Hope', 1919), Phibsborough ('The Adoration of the Sacred Heart', 1919), Terenure (Lady Chapel window, 1922–3), Balbriggan

Harry Clarke, illustration of James Elroy Flecker's poem, The Dying Patriot, *1920.*

Harry Clarke, stained glass panel illustrating Synge's poem, Queens, *1917. Private collection.*

('The Visitation' and 'The Raising of Lazarus', 1923–4), all in Co. Dublin, Wexford ('Adoration of the Virgin', 1919) and Castletownshend ('Nativity', 1918 and 'St. Martin', 1920).

Like many of his older contemporaries, he worked in a variety of media, crossing the boundaries of an Arts and Crafts, Symbolist or *Art Nouveau* definition, but invariably focussing on unexpected correspondences; these include his illustrations to the 'Vivace Scherzando' of Lizst's Valse Impromptu in A Flat Minor, James Elroy Flecker's poem 'The Dying Patriot', Pöe's poignant 'Colloquy of Monos and Una' in praise of music for the soul, the spectral frontispiece to the ill-fated Dublin New Town Plan and his fantastic staircase windows illustrating Keats's 'Eve of St. Agnes' in moonlit tones of blue and gold-pink and another, the Geneva window, depicting fifteen excerpts from Anglo-Irish literature.[48] Sadly, proposals to illustrate J.K. Huysmans's *A Rebours* and Baudelaire's *Fleurs du Mal*, to which Clarke's imagination would have been ideally suited, were curtailed in 1930 by his galloping consumption.

AE was in no doubt that "Harry Clarke has a genius which manifests itself at its highest in stained glass", that "the full soul of the artist" was not "manifested until he can let light pour through his design . . . I imagine that if one scraped a little the subconscious mind of the artist you would let in a flood of rich colour out of some inner luminous aether, where the fire is more brilliant than the eye can see, and the only way he could recreate that colour for us was by the art he practises . . . From jewelled crowns to shoe buckles there is endless invention. The glass glitters like the breastplate of jewels made for Aaron the High Priest . . . Here is ruby smitten with gold and emerald twinkling with silver lights. Starry points of colours break through everywhere. But one has to *see* the colour. It cannot be imagined from any description".[49] Because most of his work is in churches and books, Clarke's reputation as Ireland's foremost Symbolist artist has, on the hundredth anniversary of his birth, been eclipsed too long.

Nicola Gordon Bowe

ILLUSTRATIONS OVERLEAF
NOTES ON PAGE 144

Harry Clarke, St. Julien, *stained glass panel, 1919.*

Harry Clarke, detail of Angel of Peace, Holy Trinity Church, Killiney, 1919.

SYMBOLISM IN TURN-OF-THE-CENTURY IRISH ART

NOTES

1. However, in the exhibition, 'The last Romantics' at the Barbican Art Gallery in London from February 9–April 9, 1989 John Christian has included paintings from Ireland by AE and Harry Clarke.

2. See Edmund Wilson, *Axel's Castle*, New York, 1931 (reissued Glasgow, 1976); Mario Praz, *The Romantic Agony*, Oxford, 1931, for a symbolist vocabulary; Philippe Jullian, *Dreamers of Decadence*, London, 1971 and *The Symbolists*, Oxford, 1973; Robert L. Delevoy, *Symbolists and Symbolism*, London, 1978 and Robert Goldwater, *Symbolism*, London, 1979.

3. Edmund Wilson, op. cit., essay on W.B. Yeats, pp. 28 and 30; also Richard Ellmann, *The Identity of Yeats*, London, 1964.

4. James Joyce, *A Portrait of the Artist as a Young Man*, 1916.

5. See Holbrook Jackson, 'The Discovery of the Celt', *The Eighteen-Nineties*, London, 1913, pp. 178-89.

6. Born into an old Anglo-Irish family from Kilmurry, Co. Waterford, she studied art in Dublin and London, at Pedders and the Slade. See Ian Fletcher, 'Poet and Designer; W.B. Yeats and Althea Gyles', *Yeats Studies*, No. 1, 1971, pp. 42-86, who writes (p. 42), "What tenuous fame Miss Gyles possesses she owes to Yeats".

7. W.B. Yeats, 'A Symbolic Artist and the Coming of Symbolic Art', *The Dome*, I, October 1989, pp. 233-5.

8. Ian Fletcher, op. cit., p. 73.

9. Hilary Pyle, *Jack Yeats in the National Gallery of Ireland*, exhibition catalogue, Dublin, 1986, pp. 34-5 notes that "W.B. Yeats wanted 'impressions' of the world his characters lived in, rather than 'exact pictures of any moment in a play'." Here "he reached a level of abstraction that is uncharacteristic, and unlike any of his miniature drama designs".

10. Philippe Jullian, 1971, op. cit., p. 258.

11. Albert Aurier, 'Symbolism in Painting: Paul Gauguin', *Mercure de France*, Paris, March, 1891, quoted Robert L. Delevoy, op. cit., p. 82.

12. See Mircea Eliade, 'The Myths of the Modern World' in *Myths, Dreams and Mysteries*, London and Glasgow, 1968, p. 32.

13. Such parallels, of which there are many in the tumultuous years of the first two decades of this century in Europe, will be considered in my forthcoming publication, *Design and Nationalism: The Arts and Crafts Movement in Ireland 1886–1925*.

14. W.B. Yeats, 'Four Years: 1887–1891', Book I of *The Trembling of the Veil* (1922), republished in *The Autobiography of William Butler Yeats*, New York, 1965, p. 83.

15. See Julian Campbell, *The Irish Impressionists – Irish Artists in France and Belgium 1850–1914*, exhibition catalogue, National Gallery of Ireland, Dublin, 1985.

16. Ibid, p. 48.

17. See Jonathan Benington, *Roderic O'Conor 1860–1940*, M.A. thesis, Courtauld Institute, London, 1982, pp. 15-16.

18. See Julian Campbell, *An Exhibition of Paintings by Mary Swanzy, HRHA (1882–1978)*, Pyms Gallery, exhibition catalogue, London, 1986 and the author's 'Wilhelmina Geddes', *Irish Arts Review*, Vol. 4, No. 3, Autumn 1987, pp. 53-9.

19. Sean O'Faolain, *Constance Markievicz*, London, 1934, p. 51.

20. See the author's exhibition catalogue, *The Dublin Arts and Crafts Movement 1885–1930*, Edinburgh, 1985, No. 154.

21. Henry Summerfield, *That Myriad-Minded Man*, Gerrards Cross, Bucks., 1975, p. 14; also pp. 12 et seq. and pp. 30-1.

22. See Alan Denson, *Printed Writings by George W. Russell (AE): a Bibliography*, Evanston, Illinois, 1961.

23. AE Russell, 'An Irish Sculptor–John Hughes RHA', *Journal and Proceedings of the Arts and Crafts Society of Ireland*, Vol. I, No. 3, 1901, pp. 243-8.

24. W.B. Yeats, 'Reveries over Childhood and Youth' (1914) in *The Autobiography*, op. cit., p. 53.

25. W.B. Yeats, 'Ireland after Parnell', Book II in *The Trembling of the Veil*, in *The Autobiography*, op. cit., p. 163.

26. Henry Summerfield, op. cit., p. 13; also see Mircea Eliade, op. cit., 'Symbolisms of Ascension and "Waking Dreams"': The Magic Flight', p. 99 et seq.

27. See the *Illustrated Catalogue* of the Municipal Gallery of Modern Art, Dublin, 1908 (reprinted Dublin, 1984), Nos. 4 and 21.

28. See Summerfield, op. cit. for possible interpretations, pp. 37, 63 and 66; the murals are illustrated here and in Catherine Fahy, *W.B. Yeats and his Circle*, National Library of Ireland, Dublin, 1989 (back cover).

29. See the author, op. cit., Edinburgh, 1985, No. 135, also 'Women and the Arts and Crafts Revival in Ireland c. 1886–1930', *Irish Women Artists*, exhibition catalogue, National Gallery of Ireland, Dublin, 1987, pp. 22-7 and p. 183.

30. Beatrice Glenavy (née Elvery), *Today We will only Gossip*, London, 1964, p. 30. See also biographical entries on Sheppard and Elvery in Alan Denson, *John Hughes Sculptor, 1865–1941, A Documentary Biography*, Kendal, 1969.

31. Letter from Lady Glenavy, September 21st 1967, quoted by kind permission of the Curator, The Hugh Lane Municipal Gallery of Modern Art, Dublin; see also the author, Edinburgh, 1985, op. cit., No. 90 and *Irish Women Artists*, op. cit., p. 163.

32. Paul Gsell, *Rodin on Art*, London, 1912, quoted in Albert Albert Elsen (ed.), *The Rodin Journal*, Stanford, 1982, p. 13.

33. Letter to her nephew, December 1893, quoted from a lecture mss., Elizabeth S. Cumming, *'Little Lyrics': the applied art of Phoebe Traquair (1852–1936)*, c. 1984.

34. Reeves had trained in Birmingham before proceeding to London. See the author's 'The Arts and Crafts Society of Ireland (1894–1925)' in *Aspects of British Design*, Journal No. 9, The Decorative Arts Society, 1985, pp. 29-40 and Alan Crawford (ed.), *By Hammer and Hand*, Birmingham, 1984.

35. She married Reeves in 1913. For Reeves's students' panels mentioned below see the author's exhibition catalogue, op. cit., 1985.

36. P.O. Reeves, 'Irish Arts and Crafts', *The Studio*, Vol. 72, No. 295, October 1917, pp. 15-22. See also the author's 'Wilhelmina Geddes, Harry Clarke and their part in the Arts and Crafts Movement in Ireland', *The Journal of Decorative and Propaganda Arts*, Spring 1988, pp. 58-79, where some of the Clarke material referred to, is well illustrated.

37. Werner Hofmann, *Gustav Klimt*, Salzburg and Greenwich, Connecticut, 1971, p. 33. For a list of Clarke's windows see N. Gordon Bowe, M. Wynne and D. Caron, *Gazetteer of Irish Stained Glass*, Dublin, 1988 and *The Stained Glass of Harry Clarke 1889–1931*, The Fine Art Society, exhibition catalogue, London, 1988. Clarke's Honan Chapel windows are described in detail in the author's *The Life and Work of Harry Clarke 1889–1931*, Ph.D. thesis, University of Dublin, 1981, Vol. I, Chapter 4.

38. Werner Hofmann, *Gustav Klimt*, London, 1972, p. 36.

39. *Artwork*, Vol. II, No. 6, Jan/March 1926, p. 103. For a list of Clarke's published illustrated books and reproductions of his major unpublished illustrations, see the author's *Harry Clarke – His Graphic Art*, Mountrath and Los Angeles, 1983.

40. See the author's *Harry Clarke*, exhibition catalogue, Douglas Hyde Gallery, Dublin, 1979, No. 153, also 'The Miniature Stained Glass Panels of Harry Clarke', *Apollo*, Vol. CXV, No. 240, Feb. 1982, pp. 111-113.

41. Description of Villiers de l'Isle-Adam's hero from his drama, *Axël* (1890), quoted in Edmund Wilson, op. cit., p. 206.

42. Walter Pater, essay on Aesthetic Poetry (1868), *The Selected Works of Walter Pater*, London, 1948.

43. Maurice Maeterlinck, *Les Serres Chaudes*, quoted in Jullian, 1971, op. cit., p. 250.

44. O.W. Milosz, *Poemes de la Décadence*, ibid., p. 237.

45. W.B. Yeats, 'Byzantium' from *The Winding Stair and Other Poems* (1933), *The Collected Poems of W.B. Yeats*, London, 1939.

46. Gustave Flaubert, 'The Legend of S. Julien the Hospitalier', *Les Trois Contes* (English translation), London, 1946. The Symbolist context of this panel is fully discussed in N. Gordon Bowe, op. cit., 1981, Chapter 5, p. 319 et seq.

47. See Eliade, op. cit., 'Androgyny and Wholeness', pp. 176-7.

48. See the author's *Harry Clarke*, op. cit., 1979, Nos. 173–176 and *The Stained Glass of Harry Clarke 1889–1931*, op. cit., 1988.

49. Y.O., 'The Work of Harry Clarke', *The Irish Statesman*, August 8th 1925, p. 692.

JOHN SEMPLE AND HIS CHURCHES

John Semple (c. 1801–c. 1873) came of a long line of architects and builders. But he was a maverick and his small (known) output sets him apart from all the other architects of his time. His two best-known churches are the 'Black Church' (St. Mary's Chapel-of-Ease) just off Dorset Street in Dublin, and Monkstown, so conspicuously sited behind Longford Terrace. The Black Church is the quintessence of all that made Semple unique, while Monkstown stands apart from the rest but is almost equally remarkable.

If other architects are foxes, with a number of tricks up their sleeve, John Semple is a hedgehog who knows one big trick, and his most typical churches have something of the prickly character of that animal.

Mr. F. O'Dwyer has established that this John was almost certainly the great-grand-nephew of George Semple, whose

John Semple was responsible for many of the churches built in the Dioceses of Dublin and Kildare during the first half of the nineteenth century. Here, the architectural historian, **Dr. Maurice Craig,** who has investigated this architect's life and work, records his findings and lists the churches which he can attribute to Semple.

brother, Edward, was his great-grand-father. Our man's father, also John, of Marlborough Street, was a building-contractor, who built (and perhaps designed) the Round Room of the Mansion House in 1821.

John (of the churches) seems to have been born about 1801 and became his father's pupil and, in due course, partner.

Like his father, he was a sheriff's peer (a municipal rank just below alderman). They were in business together as John Semple and Son, Architects, and Engineers, at 13 College Green. He was City Architect from 1829 to 1842, when he seems to have fallen victim to the Municipal Corporation Act of the previous year. He had also been architect for the city prisons, the roads and the pipe-water works.

The fourteen or fifteen churches with which he can be credited were all, it seems, built within a very short space of time – hardly more than six or seven years, so that most of them must have been going up at the same time. The earliest drawings date from 1825,[1] and the dateable churches seem to have been completed in 1831. The Board of First Fruits was about to be abolished (in 1834) and this may have had something to do with the spate of building activity.

Tallaght, Co. Dublin. Courtesy of the Irish Architectural Archive.

JOHN SEMPLE AND HIS CHURCHES

Semple was the Board's architect for the province of Dublin, comprising the dioceses of Dublin, Kildare, Ossory, Ferns and Leighlin, that is to say, south Leinster.

In or near Dublin are the Black Church; Donnybrook in Anglesea Road; Rathmines (like the Black Church, on an island site); Whitechurch; Kiltiernan (Kilgobbin) and Tallaght. A little further afield is Newbridge, Co. Kildare, at the south-west end of the town, formerly on the main road but now bypassed, and still further away is Abbeyleix of which the west end only is his. To these must be added the church at Graigue (the suburb of Carlow on the west bank of the Barrow, parish name Killeshin).

Then there is a group of four, all in the Diocese of Kildare, and not much frequented. They are Feighcullen (four miles east of Rathangan, OS 16N 7321); Rathangan (south of Edenderry, OS 16N 6710); Ballykeen or Killeighy at Clonygowan (four miles north-west of Portarlington, OS 15N 4716) and Garryhinch or Clonyhurke (three miles north-east of Mountmellick, OS 15N 4911), all more or less on or near the Bog of Allen.

Finally, in the Cooley peninsula, there is a small church called Rathcor, or The Bush, which looks as though Semple might have had a hand in it.

The distribution of these churches, predominantly in the dioceses of Dublin and Kildare (at that time united though since separated) and especially in the western and emptier parts of Kildare, suggests the active participation of William Magee, who was appointed to the See of Dublin in 1822 and died in 1831. Magee was a very militant Protestant from Fermanagh and an opponent of the Emancipation Act, and though he suffered all his adult life from "blood to the head"[2] and was reputed to have been mentally unbalanced in the last two years of his life, we need not believe the legend that he refused to consecrate any church which was not capable of being used as a fortress.

The typical Semple church has narrow lancet windows between closely spaced buttresses which terminate in gablets and sometimes also in pinnacles, a slender west tower with, if the money allowed it, a needle spire and – perhaps the most constant feature of all – a west door without any impost and in place of mouldings, a series of joggled planes

Donnybrook (at Simmonscourt Road), Dublin, *by George Petrie. Courtesy of the National Gallery of Ireland, Cat. No. 6305.*

Kiltiernan (at Kilgobbin), Co. Dublin, *by George Petrie. Courtesy of the National Gallery of Ireland. Cat No. 6303.*

receding to frame an uncomfortably narrow opening. Mouldings are almost completely banished and their place taken by smooth surfaces, conoidal or plane. Not all the churches have all these features. Neither Graigue nor Rathangan have buttresses, and there are no spires at Rathangan, Ballykeen, Garryhinch or Newbridge. The tower at Newbridge is fairly convincingly finished off, but the battlements at Ballykeen are wretched and the top of the tower at Rathangan does not seem to have the Semple touch. In these cases, as at Garryhinch, it may well be that a spire was intended but never carried out. Tallaght has no tower, but the tower of the mediaeval church still stands beside it. Feighcullen is by a large margin the most accomplished and attractive of the 'bog' churches, which makes it all the sadder that it is standing derelict though still complete and sound.

Semple was a rationalist architect. It is hardly going too far to call his stripped-down gothic a kind of cubism. Rationalism reaches its apogee in the interior for which he is best known: that of the Black Church. At least two more of Semple's churches were originally vaulted, one of them (Rathmines) with a parabolic vault like that of the Black Church. The other vaulted church was Abbeyleix,[3] but the body of it, like that of Rathmines, has been rebuilt and I have found no record of the form of its vault. I have some recollection, perhaps not very reliable, of having heard long ago that Graigue (Carlow) was also originally vaulted; but this so far lacks confirmation.

The integrity of Semple's vaults is another aspect of his rationalism. Barrel-vaulted churches occur, though sparsely, down the centuries, following the Romanesque of Cormac's Chapel, Ardrass, Co. Kildare[4] and Taghmon, Co. Westmeath,[5] both of the fifteenth century, Hollywood, Co. Wicklow[6] of the late seventeenth, and Tibohine (Frenchpark), Co. Roscommon, apparently of 1742. Some of these may have been in Semple's mind, but it also possible that he was influenced by European architectural theory. Amédée François Frézier, in *La Théorie et la Pratique de la Coupe des Pierres* of 1737–9,[7] advocated an inverted catenary form for vaulting for 'perfect equilibrium'. Wilhelm Tappe (*Darstellung einer neuen, äusserst wenig Holz erfordernden und höchstfeuersicheren Bauart*, Essen, 1818–21)[8] advocated a method of

Feighcullen, Co. Kildare. *Photograph David Davison.*

building in the 'parabolic style' (really catenary) which used very little timber and was fire-resistant. Much later, W.R. Lethaby, in his famous little book, *Architecture* (1912), says "The early Eastern arch of brick was a tall semi-ellipse rising gradually from the walls and turning rapidly at the top . . . when we become accustomed to it, it is seen to be the most beautiful form of arch, for it is the most perfect and scientific." Lethaby had in mind the palace of Chosroes and the adjoining sixth-century church at Ctesiphon on the Tigris.[9]

Though catenary, parabolic and semi-elliptic curves are mathematically distinct from one another, for the present purpose they do not differ greatly. To determine which Semple used would require exact measurement and analysis,

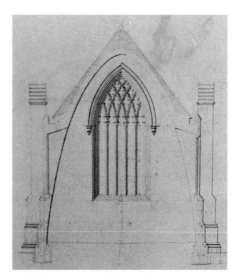

Rathmines, sectional drawing by John Semple. Courtesy of the Representative Church Body Library.

and perhaps it is not, after all, very important.

The internal effect is startling in the extreme. There are, strictly speaking, no walls, because the roof begins to curve inwards at floor level. The interiors of Rathmines and Abbeyleix must presumably have been similar. In many of the smaller churches, though not in all, the interior is spanned by a series of massive diaphragm-arches borne on corbels, all apparently of stone but in reality of timber and plaster. Semple's characteristic interior detail is also abstract in character, and, typically, somewhat overscale, as witness the quasi-Egyptian doorheads in the gallery of the Black Church, or the Monkstown interior.

Rathmines was greatly enlarged in 1886,[10] and only the west end is as Sem-

Monkstown interior. *Courtesy of the Irish Architectural Archive.*

Rathangan, Co. Kildare.

Cloneyhurke (at Garryhinch), Co. Offaly.

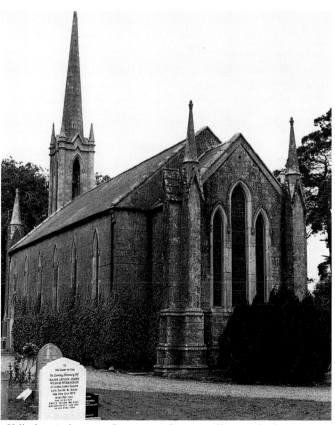

Killeshin (otherwise Graigue or Graiguecullen, in Carlow town, west of the Barrow). *Courtesy of the Irish Architectural Archive.*

Newbridge, Co. Kildare.

JOHN SEMPLE AND HIS CHURCHES

Ballykeen (Killeighy) *formerly at Cloneygowan, Co. Offaly. Now demolished. Photograph M. Craig.*

ple left it. But it seems that his north and south walls were faithfully rebuilt in their new positions, so that the church still has very much the appearance of being by him.

These churches were not expensive. Whereas the English Commissioners founded in 1818 had provided for two grades of new church, costing up to £10,000 and costing up to £20,000, the Irish Board of First Fruits gave a loan of £4,154 for Donnybrook, and a grant of £900 for Ballykeane.[11] The builders' estimate for Whitechurch was £1,845 (in 1825) and Kiltiernan is said to have cost £1,900. Tipperkevin (apparently not built) was estimated at a mere £900.

The *Dublin Penny Journal* gave these churches a mixed reception, recognizing their originality but somewhat critical of their style. It took separate notice of Donnybrook (under the name of Simmonscourt), Kiltiernan (which it mistakenly credited with a "stone roof") and Rathmines. It preferred the smaller to the larger, as having less pretension.

After his seven years of hectic activity, Semple disappears from sight for thirty years, only to have his competition entry for the rebuilding of St. Andrew's, Dublin, in 1861, reproached for being old-fashioned. The hedgehog had rolled himself up into a ball and gone into hibernation. But time had moved on.

Maurice Craig

NOTES

1. Representative Church Body Library, Dublin.
2. *Dictionary of National Biography*, s.v. 'Magee, William'.
3. S. Lewis, *Topographical Dictionary of Ireland*, 1837, s.v. 'Abbeyleix'.
4. Craig and Glin, *Ireland Observed*, 1970, p. 10.
5. H.G. Leask, *Irish Churches*, III, 1960, p. 19.
6. M. Craig, *Architecture of Ireland*, 1982, pp. 213, 217.
7. G. Germann, *Gothic Revival in Europe and Britain*, English edition 1972. Mr. F. O'Dwyer drew my attention to this book, for which I am very grateful. Plate 94 illustrates a 'parabolic' church by Tappe, in project form.
9. R. Krautheimer, *Early Christian and Byzantine Architecture*, 1965, p. 215.
10. Rathmines Vestry Books, courtesy of the Rector.
11. S. Lewis, op. cit., s.v. 'Donnybrook', 'Ballykeane'.

THE ART-CARVING SCHOOLS IN IRELAND

In the general upsurge of activity in the minor arts in Ireland in the 1880s and 1890s, one craft to become particularly widespread was wood-carving. The evidence for it is to be found, not only in numerous references in art and craft magazines and exhibition catalogues of the time, but also in a small number of surviving pieces which have been identified. Many people practised the craft, the majority of them attached to wood-carving classes or schools. As an important aspect of the arts and crafts movement in Ireland, indeed, as an important element in the Irish Revival, involving industrial as well as artistic endeavour, it surely deserves to be better known.[1]

Before examining the work of some of these Irish wood-carvers, the steps by which the rural schools came about and their art form established, should first be recounted.

In the early 1880s some rural classes for the teaching of simple arts and crafts were set up in England following the suggestion of an American, Charles G. Leland,[2] who had proposed such a move in his book, *Minor Arts*, published in 1880. These classes were held by a few individuals in different parts of the country on Saturday afternoons. The pupils were working boys and the art that was chiefly practised was wood-carving.

In an attempt to consolidate the various groups in England, the Cottage Arts Association was formed in the spring of 1884 by Mrs. E.L. Jebb. The number of classes increased rapidly and by the end of that year the organization changed its title to the more comprehensive one of the 'Home Arts and Industries Association'.[3] Its objectives were to help members to organize classes and instruct the pupils, to make designs available to the members, to hold a yearly exhibition and to publish a yearly report.

It was this English-based Home Arts and Industries Association that was reported to be setting up classes for wood-carving in Ireland in 1886.[4] Curiously enough, just as Charles Leland had earlier been the inspiration for the cottage industries movement in England, he can be seen to have pointed the way with regard to such activity in Ireland. In 1883, in an article entitled 'An Opening for the Unemployed in Ireland' published in *Longmans' Magazine*, he had proposed the development of minor art industries in Ireland.[5] In his

Dr. Paul Larmour, lecturer at Queen's University, Belfast, introduces us to some of the Irish wood-carving schools of the 1880s to early 1900s, at the same time throwing new light on the origins of the arts and crafts movement in Ireland.

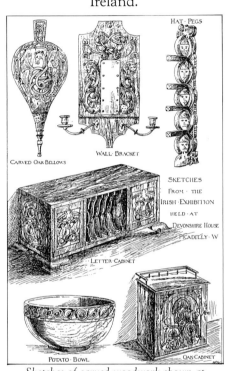

Sketches of carved woodwork shown at the Irish Exhibition at Devonshire House, London, in 1888. From The Building News, June 22, 1888.

article Leland had expressed his belief in the capacity of the Irish peasant for industrial art. He believed that if the proper education were given, the Irish could do as well in industrial art as the English and in that he saw an important element for the regeneration of Ireland:

Ireland is poor—very poor—and any kind of generally disseminated industries, so that they were barely remunerative would be a blessing to her . . . . There is a very rapidly growing demand for the products of such decorative-art industries as the Irish are capable of producing. Let them at least be tried in what they once excelled . . . . Can anyone doubt that a young person who has actually mastered several minor arts, such as modelling, carving, and inlaying, would be able to earn a living by them . . . .
Ireland is ready for industrial reform, and the experiment might be begun at once. It would not cost large grants of money; it

could be initiated in village schools and private circles, and taken up by individuals at little cost, and the teaching might be made to pay as it went''.

This is to some extent what the Home Arts and Industries Association were to do three years later when they set up their art-carving schools in Ireland, for not only were there social and artistic objectives in their work but there was a commercial element as well in the great annual sale held each year at the Royal Albert Hall in London to which Irish classes were to send their work.

At the same time there were other initiatives which were to foster cottage industries in Ireland including wood-carving. A move was made to create a more local focal point for the various scattered, and for the most part isolated, industries. In 1886 a committee consisting of some of the leading ladies in Ireland was set up to ensure that there would be a good representation of Irish industries at the Edinburgh International Exhibition that year. In the wake of the exhibition that committee, led by the Countess of Aberdeen, proposed to form a central society in Dublin akin to Mrs. Jebb's Home Arts and Industries Association and indeed proposed to amalgamate with it.[6] Although amalgamation does not appear to have been achieved, the eventual outcome was the formation of the Irish Industries Association in 1886.[7] Its main concern was with lace, which was sold through its depots in Dublin and London, but it did try to promote wood-carving too, including it, for example, in 'The Irish Village' at the Chicago World Fair in 1893.[8]

Incidentally, Irish wood-carving was represented at the Edinburgh Exhibition by some pieces exhibited by a group called the Irish Association for Promoting the Training and Employment of Women, based in Kildare Street, Dublin, where scrivenry, plan-tracing, and illumination were also pursued.[9] We hear of them again the next year when they were responsible for the 'Irishwomen's Jubilee Offering to the Queen'.[10] It took the form of a large oak chest, carved with Celtic interlaced ornament, which contained an illuminated address bearing nearly one hundred and fifty thousand signatures. We are told that the chest was carved by some Irish ladies who pursued bog-oak carving as a recreation but they are not identified.[11]

THE ART-CARVING SCHOOLS IN IRELAND

No doubt it was the Irish Industries Association which was responsible for the inclusion of carved wood-work in the exhibition of work by the Irish School of Art Needlework at Devonshire House, Piccadilly, in 1888. The critic in the *Building News* felt that the standard of wood-carving was not as high as in English 'Home Arts and Industries' work, but found the exhibits of interest nonetheless, largely on account of the Celtic ornamentation carved on most of the pieces.[12]

Independently of the Home Arts and Industries Association and of the Irish Industries Association, a successful effort to develop Irish cottage industry, including an attempt to promote wood-carving, was made by Mrs. Alice Hart. The Donegal Industrial Fund, which she founded, was one of the great successes of the Irish Revival in the 1880s in terms of regeneration of home industry, alleviation of the poor, and, in artistic terms, of the revival of Celtic ornamentation. The story of the setting up of the fund in 1883 and the development of the 'Kells Embroidery' merits recounting another

time; with regard to wood-carving the story can be taken up in the summer of 1888 when Mrs. Hart decided to make some effort to train boys in carpentry and wood-carving, having realized how greatly carpenters were needed in the congested districts of County Donegal.[13] She brought three Donegal farm boys to London. One of them returned homesick but the other two, John Alcorn and Patrick Culbert, remained to be trained over a two-year period at the Polytechnic in Regent Street, at Messrs. Howard's workshops, and under Mrs. Hart's personal direction at Donegal House learning drawing, designing, wood-carving, carpentry, building, construction and geometry. By October 1891 they were ready to return home to open a workshop in Gweedore to train apprentices and hold classes in drawing, wood-carving and carpentry. As well as making carts, barrows and cradles and taking orders for building work locally, they also had orders for carved and art-work sent on from Donegal House. The most prestigious of these was for twenty-four carved owls, from twelve to fifteen inches high,

for Lady Aberdeen. They were to be mounted as decorations on the oriel windows of a rest house built by the Countess and called the 'Owleries'. That commission was actually placed and started before the boys left London. The preparations for the job of relief carving involved sketching at the Zoological Gardens, the purchase of a live owl for the boys to live with whilst studying Morris's *British Birds*, and modelling an owl in clay under the direction of the sculptor, Conrad Dressler. Two owls were carved at Donegal House, the remainder at Gweedore. When they were all finished they were exhibited at Donegal House in the summer of 1892. The *British Architect* noticed the exhibition and illustrated sketches of an owl and other pieces which show us some of the range of things produced. There was a small letter rack with chip-carving, a large cabinet with stylized plant motifs after a design by Harrison Townsend, one of the progressive school of English architects of the '90s, panels of medieval and classical inspiration, and a table and chair after Albrecht Dürer. "There can be no doubt

Carved newel post at *Glenstal Abbey,*
Co. Limerick, by the Ahane
Wood-Carving Class, 1888.

Log Box *carved by the Ahane Wood-Carving Class.*
Private collection.

that architects and their clients in giving orders to the Gweedore carvers, would be encouraging a most benevolent intention and doing a real benefit to the rising generation", wrote the *British Architect* adding that orders could be taken, and executed at the workshop, for carved panelling, carved parts of furniture, carved work for churches, ships, saloons and the like which would "compare well with the cheapness of Italian work, and much cheaper than most similar work in London."[14] It was clearly a worthwhile experiment which promised much, but for some reason we hear little of Mrs. Hart's wood-carving venture again.

On the other hand, the classes in wood-carving set up by the Home Arts and Industries Association appeared to flourish. Among the most reported-on classes in the early years were two from County Limerick, the Ahane Class based at Lisnagry, and the Clonkeen Class at Barringtonsbridge. They seem to have been quite closely associated. We first notice the Ahane Class at work in the stairway of Glenstal Castle, the massive Norman-Revival castle that had been begun near Murroe in 1837 for Sir Matthew Barrington but was not completed until the 1880s by Sir Croker Barrington. The neo-Norman-cum-Celtic Revival bannisters erected on the stairway have carvings of interlaced knot-work and birds bearing the inscriptions "Carved by M. Minahan, P. Downey and others of Ahane Class, 1888", and "W. Bickley, Limk. 1888". We may take it that the members of the Ahane Class did the carvings while Bickley from Limerick was responsible for the construction of the wood-work. The newel post finials are particularly deserving of note, being very robust pieces of Celtic ornamental carving in the round.

There is no one full account of Ahane, Clonkeen, or this Glenstal work but from various scattered sources we can surmize that the Ahane Class was founded by the Barrington sisters, Charlotte and Maria, nieces of Sir Croker Barrington. During the 1890s, however, they were listed as teachers of the Clonkeen Class, while Miss A.E. Bourke of Thornfields, Lisnagry, was listed as teacher at Ahane. It is likely that the Barringtons, having got one class going and in safe hands, went on to found another in the area very soon after.

Both the Ahane and Clonkeen Classes

Mirror back *carved by Edward Hartigan of the Ahane Wood-Carving Class. Private collection.*

Chair *carved by Edward Hartigan of the Ahane Wood-Carving Class. Private collection.*

contributed regularly to the Royal Dublin Society and other exhibitions in the 1890s. Among the various people named in the exhibition catalogues as carvers with Ahane or Clonkeen, we might notice particularly Thomas Coghlan of Grange, Lisnagry. In 1890, as a member of the Clonkeen class, the eighteen year old Coghlan exhibited a 'window seat' at the Home Arts and Industries Exhibition at Birmingham. The piece was illustrated in *The Queen* newspaper, at the time.[15] It was carved with twisting and writhing serpents with scaled backs and crested heads, which were rather Chinese-looking in inspiration, although probably considered to be Celtic at the time.

Coghlan continued to exhibit with Clonkeen in 1891 and 1892, but from 1893 appeared in the catalogues under Ahane. As late as 1912, by which time Ahane had ceased to exhibit as a class at the Royal Dublin Society shows, Coghlan was entering on his own, in the 'amateur' category. He is remembered to the present day as having executed wood-carving for the Vatican but the details are not known.[16] Another pupil of the Ahane Class who is remembered today is Edward Hartigan (1864–1942). He carved many pieces, ranging from small gifts for his family and friends, such as a Celtic-ornamented hand-mirror, to larger items such as overmantels and fire surrounds. He was also responsible for a very remarkable piece of furniture, a chair in which the front legs and back support are like the legs of an antelope, the back legs are like horns, and the seat is carved to represent wool.

Two other pieces might be mentioned here as showing the vigorous character of Ahane ornamentation. A log box which, until recently, was among the furnishings at Thornfields (where the teacher of the class, Miss Anne Bourke lived), was carved with plant forms, whilst a croquet-stand, exhibited at the Home Arts and Industries Association Exhibiton at the Albert Hall, London, was carved with intertwining animals and Celtic interlace.[17] It was ornamented by Michael McAuliffe and adapted by Miss Bourke. Work by McAuliffe was shown at several exhibitions, such as the Royal Dublin Society shows from 1893 to 1900, and at the Arts and Crafts Society of Ireland in 1895. On that same occasion Ahane was also represented by works from Anne

THE ART-CARVING SCHOOLS IN IRELAND

Bourke and Thomas Coghlan, with a Miss Plowden and a Mr. Simpson listed as designers.

At the Clonkeen Class the designer was Madam O'Grady as we learn from *The Queen* in 1892. Reporting on the Home Arts and Industries Association Exhibition at the Royal Albert Hall they wrote

"Clonkeen sent some very good carving, and we were glad to see an effort made to revive the old Celtic patterns. At present, however, there is a tendency to overfinish in the execution. Madam O'Grady, the designer for the class, sent a most spirited grotesque semi-bat and semi-dragon holding a half-crescent mirror, which showed her not only to be a skilled designer, but a clever carver."[18]

Madam Elizabeth O'Grady from Kilballyowen was certainly a skilled carver. Three panels of plant studies which she carved in limewood in very high relief are as fine examples of the *genre* as one could hope to find. Her talents clearly extended to Celtic ornamentation also. *The Queen* in 1891 illustrated part of a panel

Crescent Mirror *by Madam Elizabeth O'Grady of the Clonkeen Wood-carving Class, Co. Limerick. From* The Queen, *June 25, 1892.*

from Clonkeen shown at the Albert Hall that year. Its ornament consisted of scaly intertwining serpentine and dragon-like zoomorphs. Of this piece, the paper remarked "Celtic designs never fail to attract the eye by their artistic quaintness. They are especially adapted for carved work, successful embossing of the same requiring matured skill and experience".[19]

Madam O'Grady herself was exhibiting wood-carvings as early as 1883, at the Irish Fine Art Society, where she showed an Irish cross and a picture frame. She also exhibited at the Royal Dublin Society in 1893, in the amateur category. As a class, Clonkeen exhibited at the Royal Dublin Society during the 1890s and into the first few years of the 1900s. Their last appearance at a major event appears to have been at the Dublin International Exhibition of 1907 when an oak hall chest constructed by W. Bickley and carved by James Moloney was among the exhibits in the Home Industries Section. The chest can be seen in the foreground of a photograph of a corner of the Arts

Limewood panels *carved by Madam Elizabeth O'Grady. Private collection.*

THE ART-CARVING SCHOOLS IN IRELAND

*Carved oak reredos in Curraclone Church of Ireland, Co. Leix,
by the Stradbally Wood-Carving Class. Completed 1913.*

and Crafts Sub-Section at that exhibition, which was published in *Irish Rural Life and Industry*.[20]

Regular exhibitors at the R.D.S. shows included the Stradbally Class from Co. Leix. It was founded by Miss Jane Perceval (1823–1895). Early pupils included three members of the Dobson family from Stradbally, Annie, William and Maud, and Kathleen Shaw (1875–1962) who later took over as teacher of the class. The group's work does not appear to have been illustrated in any of the usual publicatons of the time but examples may be seen in Curraclone Church. There is an oak bible stand, dated 1892, carved with an interlaced knot-work pattern, a Celtic-bordered oak hymn-board, and a large oak reredos which was completed in 1913. It is a very impressive piece, semi-circular headed and divided into many panels, all carved with Celtic ornament, mostly knot-work. Consisting as it does of many separate pieces, we can surmize that it was the work of a number of different hands. Indeed, 'composite works' were often carried out by the carving schools.

The impression we get of some of the schools is of good earnest endeavour, of spirited designs and vigorous workmanship, and of a worthwhile recreation that was also remunerative. The teachers in most cases appear to have been interested amateurs, hailing usually from the nearest big house, and often from the local rectory. Looking at the list of schools exhibiting at the 1897 Royal Dublin Society show, for instance, we find that the Kilfane, Bray, Inistioge, Thomastown, Kilkenny, and Strabane classes were all run by Church of Ireland clergymen's wives or daughters, and in one case by the clergyman himself.

There were, however, classes where eventually a more professional approach and a more commercially-based organization became evident. At Killarney, Lady Kenmare had formed an early class for drawing and wood-carving which had apparently succeeded well and revealed some talented individuals, but this class was then reorganized in 1896 by Viscountess Castlerosse. She renamed the class the Killarney School of Arts and Crafts and engaged a master from London to open the school and carry it on through the winter. The school's fortunes were described two years later by Lady Castlerosse:[21]

THE ART-CARVING SCHOOLS IN IRELAND

"The class was a great success, and members increased as time went by. A good deal of work was done, and sold at the sale of Irish Industries at Killarney and through private orders; the school began to be known and we saw that before another winter we must place it under a permanent manager who would live on the spot. Last year we began our winter's work by engaging a master from the Guild of Handicrafts, and giving him the management of the school. Since then it has rather changed its character, and has become a thriving industry by day, and school of instruction by night. A turning lathe and circular-saw were given to the school; and the work now includes cabinet-making, in all its branches, carving and gilding. There are now twelve men and boys regularly employed by day, while the evening class, for instruction, numbers twenty; and we are unable to keep pace with the numbers of orders received".

She referred also to some examples of the school's work – a carved bed made for the Duke of Portland, which was awarded two gold stars for general excellence at the Home Arts and Industries Association exhibition at the Albert Hall, a panel carved in walnut from a design by Aymer Vallance, the well-known English designer, which also received a high award, and a life-sized figure of a winged boy carved by another pupil who had then gone on to earn "high wages" in London.

The Killarney school was evidently capable of producing good work, and some of it was selected by the Arts and Crafts Society of Ireland to be shown at the Inaugural Art Exhibition at the People's Palace in Glasgow in 1898. Further appearances were at that society's own exhibitions – in 1889 when a writing table was shown, and in 1904 when a carved cabinet made for presentation to King Edward VII, was shown, by which time the school was known as the Killarney Furniture Industries. To the World's Fair in St Louis they sent a carved oak bedstead, two chairs and a settee, gilt candlesticks and sconces, and a fire screen and mirror. As well as carved work, the school developed cabinet-making. "As regards cabinet-making for which Dublin was once so famous, it may be said that as an art industry (save in the sense of skilful reproduction of Chippendale and Sheraton work), it hardly exists in Ireland, except in one locality – Killarney".[22] Thus wrote one commentator in 1902 who went on to write of the various articles produced: "these are all

Oak altar cross, *Christ Church, Bray*, by the Bray Art Furniture Industry.

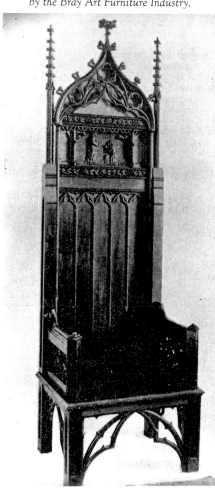

Bishop's Chair *by the Bray Art Furniture Industry. From* Irish Rural Life and Industry, *1907.*

alike marked by a peculiar tastefulness and grace of design, and they put it in the power of the visitor to Killarney to obtain a fitting memento of his visit to that enchanted region".

Another class, which eventually developed into a well-organized commercial industry, was that at Bray, Co. Wicklow. It had been founded in 1887 as a choir-boys class held in the parochial hall but was later affiliated to the Technical School. Miss Kathleen Scott, daughter of the local rector, was one of the teachers in the 1890s. By 1902 she was joined by Miss Sophia St John Whitty (1878–1924). Born in Dublin, Miss St John Whitty had studied at the South Kensington School of Art Wood-Carving before opening a studio in Dublin where she and her sister gave lessons in carving, modelling and embroidery, while attending the Dublin Metropolitan School of Art. Then, after a short period studying wood-carving at Bruges in Belgium, Miss St John Whitty was appointed teacher of wood-carving at the new Bray Technical School. Under her guidance, the Bray Wood-Carving Class soon developed into the Bray Art Furniture Industry with Miss St John Whitty as manager, designer and instructor in cabinet-making and carving. A foreman cabinet-maker worked under her, apprentices learned their trade, and in the evening carving classes there were some forty voluntary students, who followed other occupations by day.[23]

The carvers at Bray executed a considerable amount of church wood-work. Some of it can be seen in Christ Church, Bray, which contains some of Miss St John Whitty's own figure-carving. There is a Bishop's Chair of 1902, choir-stalls, a prayer desk, and a lectern of 1914. There is also an oak altar cross completely covered with carved Celtic interlace. This could well be the same piece as the 'Celtic altar cross' carved by John Burke of the Bray class and exhibited at the Royal Dublin Society show in 1905, where it was labelled "not for sale". Many other pieces of church wood-work are listed in the exhibition catalogues of the time, such as the Bishop's Chair designed by W.L. Whelan and K.A. Scott, and executed by four people, which was shown at the Arts and Crafts Society of Ireland in 1899, or the one shown at the Royal Dublin Society in 1906. Hymn boards, book-stands and prayer desks abounded, but the Bray carvers also seem to have exhibited just as many domestic furnishings, such as the writing desk, 'Scandinavian' chair, and hall chairs executed by James Bellew and shown at the R.D.S. in 1909, or his oak chest at the Arts and Crafts Society of Ireland in 1910.

The Bray wood-carvers seem to have been very prolific but their success was not to last. As Kathleen Scott recounted, "carved and inlaid work to the value of about £8,000 had been sold when the Declaration of War in August, 1914, led to the withdrawal of several important orders. There was no reserve of capital, and to save bankruptcy the industry had to close down immediately."[24]

The First World War was probably the death knell of all the old wood-carving schools, and indeed probably of other rural art industries also. Immediately on outbreak of war, the Royal Dublin Society premises at Ballsbridge were occupied by military authorities and the Art Industry Shows were abandoned for some years. After the war we find art school students and other individuals exhibiting carved wood-work but the old rural classes have gone. One such individual to carry on for a short while after the war was Alice Shaw of Terenure, Dublin. In 1892 she had been teacher of both the

Carved screen *designed by Alice Shaw, executed by the Terenure Carving Class. From the* Journal and Proceedings of the Arts and Crafts Society of Ireland, *1901.*

Greenmount and the St. Patrick's Band of Hope Classes; by the mid-'90s her group of pupils was known as the Terenure Class. One of their pieces was illustrated in the Journal of the Arts and Crafts Society of Ireland in 1901.[25] It was vigorously carved with interweaving dragons, "cunningly devised" as one experienced critic put it, and it certainly shows that Shaw was a spirited designer. Miss Shaw showed examples of her own design and execution at the big exhibitions in Glasgow in 1901, St Louis in 1904 and Dublin in 1907. Then, in 1920 at the Royal Dublin Society, exhibiting in the professional wood-carvers category, and in 1921 at the Arts and Crafts Society of Ireland, she made late appearances before she, too, left a stage that had been departed by the other late Victorian carvers some years earlier.

Paul Larmour

All photographs by the author.

ACKNOWLEDGEMENTS

I wish to thank Peter Lamb of Dublin, and Roisin De Nais of Limerick County Library, who have assisted my research in various ways.

NOTES

1. The subject has not so far been discussed in any surveys of Irish furniture although it has been mentioned, in the context of the revival of Celtic ornament, in Paul Larmour, *Celtic Ornament* (The Irish Heritage Series: 33), Dublin, Eason and Son Ltd., 1981, with examples illustrated.
2. Charles Godfrey Leland was Director of the Industrial Art School in his native Philadelphia. He spent some time in England in the 1880s and had been present at the Industrial Exhibition of Irish Arts and Manufactures in Dublin in 1871. He was author in America of a series of twelve handbooks on various crafts, including woodcarving, and in 1886 published an article 'Home Arts – No.1 Wood-Carving' in the *Art Journal*.
3. See E. L. Jebb, 'The Home Arts and Industries Association', *The Magazine of Art*, Vol. 8, 1885, pp. 284-298.
4. See *Dublin University Review*, Vol III, 1886, p. 359.
5. Charles G. Leland 'An Opening for the Unemployed in Ireland', *Longmans' Magazine*, Vol. III, No. XIII, 1883, pp. 44-51.
6. See *Edinburgh International Exhibition, 1886. Women's Industries Section. Guide to Irish Exhibits.* (Compiled by the Countess of Aberdeen), Dublin, Hodges Figgis & Co., 1886, preface pp. 7-12.
7. See Ishbel, Marchioness of Aberdeen and Temair, *The Musings of a Scottish Granny*, London, 1936 (chapter XII –'The Romance of Irish Industries', pp. 131-145).
8. Some of the carved furniture and other wood-work was illustrated in *The Queen, The Lady's Newspaper*, Jan. 7, 1893, p. 8.
9. See *Edinburgh International Exhibition, 1886. Womens Industries Section. Guide to Irish Exhibits*, p. 67.
10. See G. R. Redgrave, 'The Queen's Jubilee Presents at the Bethnal Green Museum', *The Art Journal*, 1888, pp. 140-143, where the casket is illustrated and described. It is now to be seen at Osborne House.
11. *Amateur Work*, May, 1888, p. 324.
12. *The Building News*, 1888, May 11, p. 690; June 22, p. 872 (illustration on p. 891).
13. See Alice M. Hart, 'The Story of the Donegal Wood Carvers', *The British Architect*, August 5, 1892, pp. 96 and 105 (with illustration).
14. T. Raffles Davison, 'Carved Work by the Gweedore Technical School', *The British Architect*, August 5, 1892, p. 96.
15. See *The Queen, The Lady's Newspaper*, July 3, 1890, p. 13.
16. Information from Edward Hartigan of Castleconnell, Co. Limerick, in 1980, who also provided information on his father, Edward Hartigan (1864–1942).
17. Illustrated in *The Studio*, Vol. 8, No. 40, July 1896, p. 95.
18. *The Queen, The Lady's Newspaper*, June 25, 1892, p. 1060 (illustration on p. 1061).
19. *The Queen, The Lady's Newspaper*, June 13, 1891, p. 944.
20. *Irish Rural Life and Industry* (ed. W.T.M. – F.), Dublin, 1907, p. 225.
21. The Countess[*sic*] Castlerosse, 'The Killarney School of Arts and Crafts', *Journal and Proceedings of the Arts and Crafts Society of Ireland*, Vol. 1, No. 2, 1898.
22. *Ireland Industrial and Agricultural* (ed. William P. Coyne), Department of Agriculture and Technical Instruction for Ireland; Dublin, 1902, p. 277.
23. See foreword by K. A. Scott in *The Flaming Wheel* (Nature Studies in the Counties of Dublin and Wicklow by St. John Whitty), Dublin, 1924, pp. ix-xv.
24. *Ibid.*, p. xi.
25. *Journal and Proceedings of the Arts and Crafts Society of Ireland*, Vol. 1, No. 3, 1901, p. 200 (described pp. 199-200).

FRENCH INFLUENCE IN LATE SEVENTEENTH CENTURY PORTRAITS

Society in Ireland during the last quarter of the seventeenth century can be broadly divided into three groups: the Old Irish (Gaelic Irish and Catholic), the old English (Anglo-Norman and Catholic) and the New English (recent settlers and Protestants).[1] In the decade 1675 to '85 the groups had polarized into a Catholic and a Protestant division, as it became increasingly clear that land and power were irrevocably changing hands and conflict was inevitable. The Catholic grouping would finally align themselves with the pro-French James, Duke of York, who became King of England on the death of his brother Charles in 1685, while the Protestant New English would put their hopes on the Dutch William of Orange, the eventual victor at the Battle of the Boyne in 1690. William's victory consolidated the position of the New English and thereby destroyed the final bid of the Old English to regain administrative power in Ireland.

The eventual Old English alignment with James II had its beginnings in a series of Anglo-French treaties commencing in 1670 and in his second marriage to the Catholic Maria d'Este (known as Mary of Modena) in 1673. In Ireland, Richard Talbot of Carton, later Earl and Jacobite Duke of Tyrconnell, emerged as spokesman for the Catholic and pro-French Old English faction. These political/religious loyalties can be recognized in portraits painted in Ireland during the last twenty-five years of the seventeenth century, particularly in pictures of Tyrconnell's family circle. In many portraits of members of the Talbot, Molyneux, O'Neill, Wogan and other related families, it is possible to recognize the pro-French Catholic affiliation of the sitter by the mode of costume, style of hair and general appearance of the work. It should be added that this type of portrait probably existed throughout a wider circle but as the property of many of those families who fought for King James II at the Boyne was subsequently dispersed, the greatest concentration of surviving examples happen to have Tyrconnell connections. Another pertinent factor was the religion of the artist – all the portraits of the Old English grouping discussed in this article were painted by Catholic artists.

After 1690, although French influence was superseded by Dutch at the English court, Catholic artists working in Ireland

Here, **Jane Fenlon** examines the state of portraiture in Ireland at the end of the seventeenth century, and reveals the sources and influences involved.

Henri Gascars, James, Duke of York (later King James II), as Lord High Admiral, c. 1675, oil on canvas. Courtesy National Maritime Museum, Greenwich.

Thomas Pooley, Robert Southwell, 1674, oil on canvas. Kings Weston House.

continued to be influenced by French styles in painting and in fact began to draw their inspiration directly from that source. Twenty years earlier, the focus of fashionable French influence in London was embodied in Louise de Keroualle, mistress of Charles II, and the many portraits of her painted by Henri Gascars (1635–1701). She had come to England for the first time in 1670 in the train of Henrietta, Duchess of Orleans, who was visiting her brother, King Charles. The following year, after the death of the Duchess in France, Louise was sent back to maintain the French interest at the English court. This she did by becoming Charles's mistress in 1671 and remaining with him until his death. She bore him a son who was given the Dukedom of Richmond and she was created Duchess of Portsmouth. She was also rewarded by the French king, who gave her the fiefdom of Aubigny in 1673, although she did not retire to France until 1688. During her stay in England, she was painted by a number of the principal court painters such as Sir Peter Lely (1618–1680) and his chief rival, Sir Godfrey Kneller, and, while their depictions of her capture the "baby face" described by John Evelyn in his diaries,[2] it was Gascars's portraits of her and her son which most influenced the Catholic artists who painted in Ireland. A good descripton of Gascars's work is that by Ellis Waterhouse who wrote "His ladies and children wear torrents of lace and simper in the most Frenchified manner."[3] James, Duke of York, was another patron of Gascars, whose portrait of him as Lord High Admiral shows him in Roman armour, with lace-edged cloak and buskins. This is a very busy picture, showing battle scenes, both on land and at sea, and with a plethora of accessories and drapery.

Another French artist whose influence can be traced in Irish portraits was Nicolas de Largillière (1656–1746) who, from 1674, spent about six years in Sir Peter Lely's workshop in London and was patronized by the Duke of York. Motifs from the work of Pierre Mignard (1610–1695) and Claude Vignon (1633–1703) can also be recognized in the paintings of John Michael Wright (1617–1694) and Garrett Morphy (fl. 1678–1716), two important Catholic artists who worked in Ireland.

Only two artists of stature can be named with certainty as painting in Ireland during the decade before 1679. One of them, James Gandy from Exeter (1619–1689), is known to have made copies after the work of Van Dyck, and spent several years working at Kilkenny. He was brought to Ireland by James Butler, 1st Duke of Ormonde, when he arrived as Lord Lieutenant in 1662 after the Restoration. The second was Thomas Pooley (1646–1723), who had spent twelve years in London, and in 1676 returned to Dublin in the train of the Earl of Essex. Pooley painted copies of official portraits of the various sovereigns for Dublin corporation and became the establishment painter for the next twenty years or so. He was also patronized by prominent members of the mainly Protestant administration. Little is known about James Gandy or his work outside the examples attributed to him at Kilkenny Castle.[4] On the other hand, several portraits by Pooley have now been identified and the portrait of Robert Southwell, (1607–1677),[5] painted in London in 1674, is a good example of his early work. It is a straightforward image, set against a charming landscape background and is reminiscent of the work of Sir Peter Lely.[6] His later paintings are all of a similarly restrained nature, following patterns made popular by Lely and Kneller and show little of the flamboyance of the French-inspired style which is prevalent in the work of a number of Catholic artists working in Ireland at the same time. Pooley was a staunch Protestant, his background being that of minor landed gentry from Suffolk; his father had been in Ireland in the 1630s and at the outbreak of hostilities in 1641 seems to have returned to his family in England, as at least two of his sons were born there. The Pooley family was settled in Ireland from the early 1660s. In 1690 Thomas was the author of a letter addressed to King William from the Loyal Protestants of Dublin.[7]

Who else then was painting in Dublin in 1679? We know from the writings of George Vertue,[8] that John Michael Wright and Gaspar Smitz (d.c.1688) were in Dublin at the same time as Thomas Pooley. Further evidence of their stay in Ireland is provided by several portraits painted by them while in this country. Their reasons for being here at this time were linked to events taking place in England. The advent of the 'Popish plot' and the rantings of Titus Oates in Lon-

John Michael Wright, Lady Catherine Cecil and James Cecil, 4th Earl of Salisbury, c. 1670, oil on canvas, 159.4 × 129.5. Marquess of Salisbury.

don in 1678 caused a wave of hysteria to sweep England, and resulted in lists of Catholics being drawn up so that various restrictive measures could be taken against them. One such measure was the proclamation commanding "all Papists to retire from the Cities of London and Westminster",[9] for a radius of ten miles and a like ban applied to other cities in England as well. It is also worth noting that the Catholic court of James, Duke of York, and his new Duchess, Mary of Modena, retired to the Low Countries at the same time and then moved to Scotland, not returning to London again until 1683, thus removing a source of potential patronage for Catholic artists. It is not therefore surprising to find some of those Catholic artists seeking the comparative safety of Ireland. Vertue also tells us that James Maubert (d.1746)[10] was here, and that he was instructed in painting by Smitz.

While Vertue does not inform us that Smitz was a Catholic, he was Flemish and said to be from Antwerp which, combined with the fact that he painted several members of the staunchly Catholic Nugent family of Westmeath,[11] indicates that he was. There is ample evidence that John Michael Wright was a Catholic. Born in London, apprenticed in Edinburgh to the Scottish artist, George Jameson, Wright went to Italy early in

the 1640s and enrolled in the painters' Academy of St. Luke in Rome in 1648. He returned to England in 1656, having first travelled to Antwerp where he remained for two or three years. It may be that he became more familiar with the Catholic circle at court after the marriage of Maria d'Este (Mary of Modena), to James, Duke of York. Evidence for this is provided by his dedication of the English version of his book, *An Account of His Excellence Roger Earl of Castlemaine's Embassy. From His Sacred Majesty James the IId . . . To His Holiness Innocent XI.*, published 1688, to the then Queen, Mary, and the earlier Italian version of the same book to her mother, the 'late Duchess of Modena'. Wright also acted as Steward on this Embassy, which left England in 1685 and on his return in 1687, he brought back gifts to the Queen from her mother, the Duchess.[12]

An examination of the work of these two artists is revealing, in that Smitz's known Irish portraits display only superficial features associated with the French style,[13] while this influence is more obvious in the work of John Michael Wright. Smitz's portraits are painted in a dry manner, are not particularly ornate and are all half-lengths within painted ovals. His surviving portraits are of Catholic Old English patrons, although we do know that Smitz also had contacts with the Percevals, who were of the Protestant New English grouping.[14] At Hatfield in England, there is a full-length and more ornate example of his work, a portrait of the Countess of Kinnoull and her son, Lord Dupplin, painted before 1679. The figures are set in a landscape, with a dolphin fountain and some statuary in the background. The Countess is shown with her right breast bared, holding a garland of flowers; the child wears diaphanous draperies in a manner that could be called classical, and carries flowers in a corner of this drapery. In view of this, it is possible that Smitz also painted a number of similarly ornate portraits during his stay in Ireland that have either been lost or have yet to be recognized.[15]

Wright's work, on the other hand, always has a rich texture, and there is to be considered his use of the very French feature of plumed hats in the earlier portraits he painted in England. His use of this accessory in an early picture, the double portrait of 'Lady Catherine Cecil and James Cecil, 4th Earl of Salisbury'

FRENCH INFLUENCE IN LATE SEVENTEENTH CENTURY PORTRAITS

painted c.1670, shows an awareness of current French fashions in portraits.[16] This can be seen as part of his obvious interest in costume and texture, an interest, however, which did not overwhelm his various sitters, who continue to display strong individuality in their features. After 1672 and the advent of Henri Gascars in London, Wright's work became still more ornate and his portrait of 'The Family of Sir Robert Vyner', c.1673, illustrates this. It is much busier in detail than earlier works, with a dog, flowers, architectural features, drapery and a profusion of ribbons, bows and lace on the costumes. Also his portrait, 'Unknown Lady with a riding crop', c.1676, again with the same plumed hat as James Cecil, bears a close resemblance to 'La Marquise de Sévigné' by Pierre Mignard of approximately the same date. Wright's portrait of 'The Ladies Catherine and Charlotte Talbot', daughters of Sir Richard Talbot, painted in Dublin in 1679, is outstanding for its distinctly French feeling and is uniquely so in his Irish work.

Pierre Mignard, Françoise d'Aubigné, Marquise de Maintenon, *oil on canvas. Private collection.*

A comparison between it and the portrait of the two Cecil children, painted some ten years earlier, high-lights this. It can be seen that the figures of the girls in the later picture are more doll-like, and lack the solidity of flesh that is noticeable, particularly in the painting of the hands and arms of the Cecil children. The costumes in the Cecil picture, while elaborate and carefully painted, do not overwhelm the children in flounces and fringes, as is the case in the Talbot picture. Catherine, the elder Talbot girl, is depicted wearing a dress which is undoubtedly French, as are the red stockings and red-heeled shoes. The younger girl's dress and Roman sandals appear to be an approximation of classical costume and resemble costumes used by Henri Gascars in his paintings of the Duke of Richmond as a young boy with his mother, the Duchess of Portsmouth.[17] Versions of both these portraits by Gascars were in the Talbot collection at Malahide. In these two portraits, the general style of the thong-belted costume

William Gandy, James Butler, Lord Ossory, later 2nd Duke of Ormonde, c. 1685, *oil on canvas. Courtesy National Maritime Museum, Greenwich.*

Garret Morphy, Lady Jane Chichester, c.1677, *oil on canvas. Private collection.*

FRENCH INFLUENCE IN LATE SEVENTEENTH CENTURY PORTRAITS

on the young Duke and the diaphanous striped material in the draperies about his mother combine in the dress of Charlotte Talbot. But it is not just the similarity to Gascars in costume details which illustrates the French influence in the Talbot picture: it is also to be seen in the affected gesture of the hands, a feature found in the work of other French painters, such as Nicolas de Largillière and Pierre Mignard. Indeed, the baby faces and curled hair resemble those features of the Duchess of Portsmouth herself. Wright painted many other portraits during his five-year stay in Ireland. Of these, only Sir Neil O'Neill stands comparison with Gascars's work, in its superficial resemblance to that artist's portrait of James, Duke of York. No other portraits are as ornate or display as much French influence in costume and handling as that of the Talbot children.

Several of Wright's portraits were of members of the Butler family; one of these, a plain image of 'Lady Clancarthy' with little added ornateness, displays a costume used by this artist in several of his earlier paintings[18] and, while it includes the same affected gesture of the right hand as that found in the Talbot portrait, does not in any other way come close to the essentially French style of that picture. Other portraits painted by him at Kilkenny include the very simple widowed 'Lady Thurles', and 'James Butler, 1st Duke of Ormonde' and 'King Charles II', which are both richly painted with lots of silver lace and bunches of ribbons, but without the mincing overtones found in Gascars's male portraits.

A portrait of 'James Butler, Lord Ossory', later 2nd Duke of Ormonde, was painted by the Protestant artist, William Gandy (d.1729),[19] son of James Gandy. This portrait, painted in Dublin before 1686, shortly after Ossory's return from the French army, shows him wearing his lace cravat over large red bows, in the latest French fashion. It may be compared with a similar portrait of the Duke of York by Nicolas de Largillière painted at about the same date, where it can be seen that, while Gandy's rendering of the red ribbons and lace is detailed and quite fine, it does not approach the *bravura* of de Largillière's handling, which has at least a dozen folds to the bows. It is also worth noting that at this date, wigs are worn long and flowing, but quite low on top and unpowdered; not until the next

Garret Morphy, Frances Molyneux, Lady Neil O'Neill, *c. 1700, oil on canvas. 126.9 × 101.6, Private collection.*

decade do wigs become very high and divided with a distinct parting between two peaks.

We now come to the work of the Irish-born artist Garrett Morphy[20] (Murphy), a Catholic,[21] who painted portraits of many of the Jacobite English and Old English families just before 1690. In London in 1673 Morphy had worked for Edmund Ashfield (fl.1670–75),[22] another Catholic artist who had been apprenticed to John Michael Wright. Perhaps it was during the time he was working for Ashfield and attending an academy in London[23] that he had contact with Gaspar Smitz. His earliest known work, a rather meagre portrait of the Protestant Lady Jane Chichester, painted c.1677, bears some resemblance to Smitz's dry manner in the handling of the paint, but also comes close to Ashfield's style in the construction of the head and the way it sits on the very sloping shoulders. The costume details and pearl clasp used in the Chichester portrait resemble those which appear in a similar head and shoulders depiction of Madame de Maintenon by Pierre Mignard.[24]

Morphy is documented as working in the north of England from about 1686, when he painted the signed portrait of Anne Greville, Lady Kingston-upon-Hull. A year later he was paid £24 for painting a portrait of Henry Cavendish, the pro-Jacobite and Tory 2nd Duke of

Newcastle, and two years after that he was in Yorkshire. During the three years from 1685 to 1688 he also painted the Danby,[25] Bland and Finch families, and his portraits of Viscount Preston and his wife, Anne Howard, are also from this period.[26] With the exception of the portrait of Anne Greville, which displays a Flemish/Dutch influence, these portraits are similar to the work of Henry Gascars's in their approach to costume—in the lavish use of lace and silver lace on the ladies' dresses and the brocades, fringes and plentiful laces of the gentlemen—although the poses can be paralleled in the work of Smitz. The portrait of the 'Duke of Newcastle' is particularly over-decorated with ribbons and bows and the pose is almost mincing. Likewise, young 'Master Danby' is dressed in an extraordinary approximation to classical costume with draperies and silver-lace-trimmed buskins, topped off with a plumed brocaded hat of the type used by Wright.

But it is in Morphy's work from the next decade following the Boyne, and hence after the defeat of the Catholic and pro-French influence in England, that more direct borrowings from French artists and fashions can be demonstrated. There is, however, a problem in that this artist used a number of patterns for his portraits, which provide his sitters with identical costumes, although their gestures are varied. This makes the dating of some of his works extremely difficult. In his 1696 portrait of Anne Boyle, Lady Mountjoy, a Protestant, Morphy takes the pose and costume details from an engraving by Etienne Baudet (1639–1711), after the portrait of Louise de Keroualle, Duchess of Portsmouth, and her son, by Henri Gascars. Of interest is the fact that the costume worn had nothing to do with current fashions, being some twenty years out of date. It is, however, one of Morphy's most ornate and charming works though unfortunately, rather dark from old varnish. It shows Anne Boyle, seated, with bared right breast, wearing lacy undress[27] and holding a dove, with a small winged cupid, complete with quiver and arrows, to her left; the buildings and drapery present in the engraving are repeated in the background of the painting. Another ornate portrait of approximately the same date is that of Arthur Chichester, 3rd Earl of Donegall (1666–1706),[28] notably

Nicolas de Largillière, *King James II, 1685, oil on canvas*
Courtesy National Maritime Museum, Greenwich

Nicolas de Largillière, Portrait of a Lady, oil on canvas
Courtesy National Gallery of Ireland, No. 1735.

After Henri Gascars, The Duchess of Portsmouth,
Engraved by Etienne Baudet, London. Courtesy British Museum.

Garret Morphy, Lady Anne Boyle, 1696,
oil on canvas, 98.75 × 125. Private collection.

richer in costume and background details than the earlier male portraits. The pose can be found elsewhere in Wright's work,[29] the coat, with its fashionable deep-buttoned cuffs, and the finely pleated linen finished with lace is, however, very up-to-date and can be compared with French fashions of that time, as are the breeches tucked into the rolled stocking tops.

Later in the same decade, Morphy painted the two oval portraits of Rose and Anne O'Neill, daughters of Sir Neil O'Neill and grand-nieces of Richard Talbot. They appear to have been taken from miniatures, as the figures are on a much larger scale than is normal for this type of portrait. The sitters' hair is worn drawn up into two peaks, with curls, known as favourites, on the forehead, a fashion much favoured in France c.1695.[30] They are very richly dressed with a profusion of lace, jewelled clasps and fur, which may indicate that the original miniatures were painted in France[31] in 1694/5, when the winter was very severe, making ermine and other furs very fashionable; this date would also fit in with the ages of the girls. Of a

William Gandy, Richard Parsons,
1st Earl of Rosse, c. 1698, oil on canvas.
Private collection.

later date are the portraits of Frances Molyneux, Lady Neil O'Neill and her sister-in-law, Bridget Lucy, Lady Molyneux. Lady O'Neill's soft, plain velvet wrapped gown worn over a flounced bodice is identical to that used by Morphy in his signed and dated portrait of Mrs. Poole painted in 1704,[32] and the bright red of Mrs. Poole's dress matches the drapery in the O'Neill picture, while Lady Molyneux is similarly dressed in blue velvet. The hair-styles in all three portraits are fashionably French and worn heavily powdered. It is tempting to suggest that the last two portraits were painted at the same time as the sitters' relatives, Caryll and William, 3rd and 4th Viscounts Molyneux respectively. These two noblemen both wear very high French-style powdered wigs. Their neckcloths are of the Steinkirk style[33] which can be dated after 1692, while the richly embroidered vest and cuffed velvet coat of the 4th Viscount is of a type worn around the turn of the century and later. These portraits may have been painted in England.[34] They are, however, relevant to the argument as they were painted by an Irish-born Catholic

FRENCH INFLUENCE IN LATE SEVENTEENTH CENTURY PORTRAITS

Garret Morphy, Caryll, 3rd Viscount
Molyneux of Maryborough, *c. 1700, oil on canvas, 75 × 61.*
Courtesy National Gallery of Ireland.

Attributed to Hyacinthe Rigaud, Richard Talbot,
Duke of Tyrconnell, *oil on canvas, 130 × 103.*
Courtesy National Gallery of Ireland.

artist and, moreover, the sitters were members of the family circle of Richard Talbot, Jacobite Duke of Tyrconnell.[35] Morphy produced a large number of portraits in the period 1690–1704, and it can be seen that those painted for Tyrconnell's circle depict their sitters wearing powdered hair or wigs in the fashionable French mode. Few portraits painted in England before 1715,[36] display such heavily powdered hair on female sitters or such profuse and high powdered wigs on the male sitters.

On the other hand, the evidence gathered from paintings by unknown artists working in Ireland during the same period 1690–1705, shows the majority following the current Dutch-influenced fashions of the English court, which patronized Sir Godfrey Kneller and his followers. One notable exception to this trend is the portrait of Sir Richard Talbot, by an unknown artist, of which there are several versions in Ireland. The best is that which came from the Malahide Castle collection and is now is the National Gallery in Dublin,[37] where it is attributed to 'unknown artist, after Rigaud'. However, it was the plainer and

more schematic portraits of Kneller and his imitators in Ireland, which found favour among the New English administration in Dublin. In these portraits, the sitters are generally depicted wearing restrained and usually unpowdered or lightly powdered wigs. In this same style are the later portraits painted by Thomas Pooley. One of his pictures, commissioned in 1700 by the Duke of Ormonde for the Royal Hospital, Kilmainham, is of 'Prince George of Denmark'. This is a copy, after Kneller, with the pose taken from a portrait of 'King William III' by that artist. The wig, while full, is not particularly high and is worn unpowdered. The other known Protestant artist, William Gandy, was also painting in Ireland during the decade 1690–1700. His portrait of Richard Parsons, 1st Earl of Rosse, shows that sitter in a modest unpowdered wig (or his own hair) and, even though Parsons is also depicted wearing an embroidered waistcoat, the whole effect is one of restraint.

From the above it can be seen that a number of French-influenced portraits were painted for Irish patrons during the period 1675–1705. Most portraits of this

type were painted for the family circle of Richard Talbot, Jacobite Duke of Tyrconnell, who was leader of the Catholic Old English. These French-influenced portraits can be contrasted with those painted for the New English, where costume, wigs and general style display the more austere fashions favoured by the Dutch-influenced court in London. While the range of examples drawn upon is rather narrow, the concentration of Old English portraits showing extensive and up-to-date French influence in fashions used for costume, wigs and hair-styling is quite remarkable. These, then, were the portraits painted by Catholic artists for Catholic patrons and they provide the evidence of the strong pro-French sympathies held by the Old English grouping in Irish society during the last quarter of the seventeenth century. *Jane Fenlon*

ILLUSTRATIONS OVERLEAF
NOTES ON PAGE 168

ACKNOWLEDGMENTS

I would like to thank my colleagues Noreen Casey and Catherine Marshall for their careful reading and comments on this article and Professor Anne Crookshank for her encouragement in this area of research.

Henri Gascars, Louise de Keroualle, Duchess of Portsmouth and Aubigny, *c. 1678, oil on canvas, 103.5 x 80,*

Garret Morphy, Mrs. Poole, 1704, oil on canvas, 107.8 × 88.9.
Private collection.

FRENCH INFLUENCE IN LATE SEVENTEENTH CENTURY PORTRAITS

NOTES

1. Brendan Fitzpatrick, *Seventeenth-Century Ireland: The War of Religions*, New Gill History of Ireland, 1988.
2. John Bowle (ed.), *The Diary of John Evelyn* (World Classics), Oxford University Press, 1985, p. 231.
3. Ellis Waterhouse, *Painting in Britain 1530–1790*, The Pelican History of Art, Penguin Books, 4th ed. 1978, p. 106.
4. At Kilkenny Castle, there are three portraits attributed to James Gandy, two are of Queen Henrietta Maria and one of King Charles I; all are copies after Van Dyck.
5. Still in the collection at Kings Weston, it is documented; Mellon Collection Dering Mss., an 'Inventory taken of pictures in Kings Weston, 1695,' "In the Drawing Room No. 4. Robert Southwell, Esq., done by Mr. Pooly at Spring Garden 1674".
6. *Ibid.* "In the Drawing Room No. 7. Elizabeth Dering, Lady Southwell copied by Mr. Pooly from an original done by Sir Peter Lely etc. . ." It can be gathered from this quotation that Pooley was a known copyist of Lely.
7. Historical Mss. Commission, 'Finch Papers' II, p. 33.
8. George Vertue, MS. Notebooks (in the British Museum) published by The Walpole Society. 'Vertue I', p. 31.
9. Historical Mss. Commission, 'House of Lord Mss. 1680', p. 223, in HMS Rep. II, Appendix II.
10. George Vertue, loc. cit., 'Vertue IV', p. 120.
11. The eldest son of Christopher Nugent, Lord Delvin (portrait by Smitz, NGI, No. 4142) was a Capuchin friar in France.
12. Sara Stevenson & Duncan Thomson, *John Michael Wright The King's Painter*, Exhibition Catalogue, 1982, Trustees of the National Galleries of Scotland, 1982, p. 29.
13. Oliver Millar, 'Catalogue of Malahide pictures; 1953, unpublished work; under entry for portrait of 'General William Nugent' by unknown artist, (Smitz, NGI, No. 4144), "it is painted in a frenchified style".
14. Anne Crookshank and the Knight of Glin, *The Painters of Ireland*, London, 1978, p. 21.
15. Sheffield Grace, *Memoirs of the Family of Grace*, London, 1823, plate VI shows engraved portraits of Oliver Grace and his wife, Elizabeth Bryan. These are more ornate than the Nugent group of portraits.
16. Millia Davenport, *The Book of Costume*, New York, Crown Publishers Inc., 1948, (1979 ed.). See illustrations Nos. 1392 and 1393 and discussion of costume *c*.1670, pp. 526-528.

17. Came into Talbot family from the Wogans, when they inherited the Wogan estate in 1783.
18. Stevenson and Thomson, op. cit., see Lady Vyner's dress, p. 80, also illus. pp. 76, 77.
19. B.M. MSS. Addit. 28, 876, ff. 1.3. 'Letter from William Gandy, Dublin to John Ellis [sec. to Earl of Ossory], Jan. 17th 1686/7'. Note for payment and receipt on same date. Background information on William Gandy is very scarce. Apart from one signed picture of Henry Stewart (see Anne Crookshank and the Knight of Glin, op. cit., p. 21) and another similar note and receipt for the remainder of the account quoted above, this is the only documented evidence, found as yet, of his presence in Ireland.
20. As the two known signed portraits by this artist ('Mrs. Poole' and 'Anne Greville, Lady Kingston-upon-Hull') bear the signature, 'G. Morphy', without the 'e', and his will was also listed in the name 'G. Morphy', this would seem to be a more correct spelling of the name. It is a form of Murphy, used especially in Cork and Kerry.
21. Walter Strickland, *A Dictionary of Irish Artists*, Vol. II, p. 131.
22. B.M. MSS. Addit. 22,950 'Memoranda Book of Ozias Humphrey, 1777–1795', p. 8.
23. *Ibid.*, p. 8.
24. Francoise d'Aubigné, Marquise de Maintenon, by Pierre Mignard. Private Collection.
25. The inscription 'fecit . . . 87' can be seen on the scroll of paper in the portrait of Sir Abstrapus Danby, Witt Library, Courtauld Institute of Art, Neg. No. B71/637.
26. Viscount Preston was an eminent Jacobite. In 1682 he was appointed Envoy Extraordinary to France, in 1688/9 he was created Baron of Liddall and Viscount Preston in the English peerage, from St.–Germain en Laye. In 1690/1 he was arrested on his way to France with treasonable papers, tried for high treason and forfeited his English baronetcy and estates.
27. It should be noted that although female sitters rarely wore the actual dress of the day, there were constantly changing styles of costume used for fashionable portraiture. Also, hair-styles tended to be of the latest fashion. In this portrait the costume and hair-style taken directly from an engraving of a picture painted in the mid-1670s.
28. This is an uncertain identification, although Morphy did paint his sister, Lady Jane

Chichester. This picture is one of Morphy's 'patterns'; there are at least two other versions of this pattern also by Morphy, in similar costume and pose, one which has been wrongly attributed to Verelst – 'Unknown Man', attributed to Verelst, Christie's, 15 May 1959, lot 23; another attributed to Morphy, Philips', 10 May 1983, lot 35. The whereabouts of both of these portraits is unknown.
29. Very similar to pose of Sir Richard Vyner, see notes 12 and 18.
30. The double portrait of Mademoiselle de Blois and Mademoiselle de Nantes by Claude Vignon, Musée Versailles, No. 3645.
31. It is possible that the two sisters left this country in the mass exodus of Catholic nobility after the Boyne. Other members of the Talbot family were in Paris at that time. Also, their mother Lady Neil O'Neill, did not regain title to her lands until 1700.
32. Private collection, Dublin.
33. 'Steinkirk', a more casual arrangement of the neckcloth, named after the battle of the same name in 1692.
34. Although implicated with James II and tried for their actions on his behalf in 1694, the Molyneux family managed to hold onto their lands and houses at Sefton and Croxteth in Lancashire.
35. Frances Molyneux, daughter of Caryll, 3rd Viscount, and sister of William, 4th Viscount Molyneux, was married to Sir Neil O'Neill, whose mother was Eleanor, sister of Richard Talbot, Jacobite Duke of Tyrconnell.
36. It has recently been verified that the Netchers, Caspar and Constantin, were Catholic. (See letter from Mr. F. Simmons in Netcher file box, Witt Library). These artists, whose pictures show strong affinities with Morphy's also display strong French traits in their work; of particular interest is a signed and dated portrait of 1705, by Constantin, of an unknown lady. The sitter is dressed in an elaborate if out-of-date French style, her hair is heavily powdered and is arranged in a style also favoured by Morphy. Witt Library, Courtauld Institute, 'Unknown Lady', Constantin Netcher, A.F. Mondschein, New York, 1946.
37. At least six versions of this portrait are known, three in NGI, Nos. 1138, 4167 and 4164, one in a private collection in Ireland, one in the National Portrait Gallery in London and one more in a private collection in England.

ROBERT HUNTER

Robert Hunter is an extremely difficult painter to write about. It is not just that practically nothing is known about him (neither his birth nor his death dates), it is not that we do not have signed works (we have a number), but rather because it is impossible to grasp him stylistically. He is a sort of chameleon who reflects the passing fashions of the great artists of his time. This sounds derogatory but that would be unfair as, at his best, as in his portrait of Lord Newbottle, he is very good indeed (No. 49). He avoids the pitfall of weak pot-boilers, though that may just be that he didn't sign them and we don't recognise them. Unlike Latham, he does not have strong, obvious characteristics. I feel quite unable to see my way through the maze of mid-/to late-eighteenth-century portraits picking out Hunters as in the earlier part of the century, one can pick out Lathams.[1]

Pasquin, writing in 1796, and therefore in the lifetime of Hunter, said that he was born in Ulster and 'studied principally under *Mr Pope*, senior'.[2] The Ulster birth is, thus, not proven but is likely since Pasquin could have had the information directly from Hunter himself. A number of families called Hunter lived in the North, and though I have checked many genealogical trees I have been unable to find any Robert of the correct period. As far as I can judge, most of these families were Presbyterians, and I have tried to find Hunter in Presbyterian records in Dublin but this, too, has been in vain. Mr. Pope senior is an artist about whom very little is known. His children included one of his own name and the only paintings known – some portraits of the Reillys of Scarvagh Co. Down – are more likely to be by the son than the father, as they were painted late in the century; one is actually dated 1773.

William Carey, a Cork critic of reliability, makes some comments which help to date Hunter's early years. In discussing the foundation of the Dublin Society, he quotes Hunter a great deal and says that he "was intimate with Madden and Prior".[3] Prior died in 1751 so that, if Carey is correct, Hunter must have been an adult by the late 1740s and one can assume that he was born between 1715 and 1720. This would account for his education not being with Robert West or the Dublin Society Schools. West was teaching in Dublin from the late 1730s, and a boy born c. 1715/17 would, at this

Another artist brought to light by the Irish Portraits Exhibition in 1969 was Robert Hunter, whose ability and long career made him one of the leading portrait painters in eighteenth-century Ireland. **Professor Anne Crookshank** here presents her research to date into this artist.

period, have been apprenticed by 1730. These dates, in fact, fit with the earliest pictures that can be attributed to Hunter, a series of portraits of the King family which are of c. 1748 and show Hunter to have been already a very accomplished painter, by no means a student or beginner. So it is not surprising that by 1753 he was commissioned to paint a large baroque portrait of Dublin's Lord Mayor, Sir Charles Burton. Hunter was old enough to marry by c. 1750 as he had a daughter Mary Anne who, as she was 13 when she exhibited in the Society of Artists in 1765, must have been born c. 1752. (She later married in 1774, John Trotter, the portrait painter).

One might assume from the fact that Hunter borrows poses from several English artists, from Hudson to Reynolds, that he paid a visit to London. However the variants of other artists' work that he makes, where I have spotted them, have always been taken from engraved works. It is also true that I have yet to find a sitter who did not visit Ireland, though one such attibution has recently been made (see No. 60). I think Hunter probably did visit England but not to paint or to live there. As a personality he comes over in Carey and in W. B. Sarsfield Taylor,[4] as a pleasant, cultivated person and by the end of the century the *doyen* of Dublin artists. Carey says that he "was a walking chronicle of everything relative to the Irish artists and arts";[5] and Taylor that "Hunter was a mild amiable man, liberal in communicating what he knew, and generous in estimating the works of his brother artists".[6] He also said that Hunter "had collected many old pictures, some of which were very fine; upon these he formed his style of colouring: hence it happened that his works, though sometimes low and dingy in tone, are never raw or crude."[7] Taylor's estimate of the quality of Hunter's work indicates that he knew them well and he gives a fair criticism if a bit begrudging. He said "Hunter was a portrait painter

who had a large and profitable practice, his exhibition pictures were either whole or half-lengths of the nobility and gentry, a proof that he must have possessed a certain fair portion of talent. His works command respect, although he cannot be spoken of as a very able artist. He took excellent likenesses, and his practice was extensive; he was truly a gentleman in feeling, and had he practiced his art at a time, or in a country where the arts were better understood, he would have been very eminent in his profession."[8] I think Taylor makes one mistake: Hunter was very eminent in his profession in Ireland during his lifetime – and with justification.

One unusual feature of Hunter's work is the number of small whole-lengths that he painted. In the exhibitions of the Society of Artists,[9] where he showed regularly between 1765–73, he exhibited eighty-three pictures, all but one portraits, none of which are named, but of which eight are described as small whole-length, small half-length or 'metzotinto' size. As he presumably will always have shown his life-size work in preference to the small examples, this ten percent of his out-put may well be an underestimate. These small pictures are simply large pictures in small, not miniaturist in technique, and in photograph it is impossible to tell whether you are looking at a large or a small scale work. They are mostly of single figures and are nowadays often attributed to Arthur Devis, though they in no way share Devis's doll-like manner. Neither is there any evidence that Hunter painted conversation pieces of the Devis type, though he did occasionally paint double portraits. Some of Hunter's small whole-lengths may have been made as duplicates for other members of the sitter's family – for instance small whole-lengths of the life-size Marquess of Clanricarde and the Marquess of Buckingham (Nos. 18, 12) are known. But in the case of most of the small scale works they seem to have been an end in themselves. I have only found small scale half-lengths up to 1764 and, I deduce, he may not have painted them later.

The one picture not a portrait, which was exhibited in 1765, was entitled "Susannah and the Elders". One other work may count as a subject picture, a portrait of Miss Woollery, presumably an actress, as Sigismunda, which Strickland says was exhibited in 1800 (No. 76). It must surely have been painted some years earlier as he would then have been at least

Gentleman of the La Touche family, 1775 (No. 47). Courtesy National Gallery of Ireland, No. 4034.

Samuel Madden, *1755 (No. 53). Courtesy the Board of Trinity College, Dublin.*

ROBERT HUNTER

–172–

Lord Newbottle, later 5th Marquess of Lothian, 1762 (No. 49).
Courtesy the Marquess of Lothian. Photograph courtesy National Galleries of Scotland.

ROBERT HUNTER

eighty. Subject picture painting clearly did not pay in Dublin.

As Hunter kept in touch with the work of London artists through engravings it is interesting that certain mannerisms, which must reflect the habits of London society, do not occur in his work. It was obviously not the done thing in Dublin for a man to stand with one hand tucked into his jacket, as it was in London, and it was clearly much more common in Ireland for a gentleman to be depicted out shooting. Slaughter seems to have introduced the shooting pose into the Irish repertoire just at the time that Hunter was developing his own style in the late 1740s, so that one finds the men in the King family are all holding guns (Nos. 39, 42, 44), though they are hardly dressed for shooting but rather for the drawing-room. Hunter also develops an interest in the navy, for he paints an extraordinary number of naval officers. Society had enlarged in Dublin by the mid-century, for while Latham's sitters come from closely connected families, Hunter paints a more varied clientele including professional people as well as landed families.

Obvious examples of borrowing from London painters are the small portrait of a middle aged woman (see No. 79) dated 1760 which, with slight variations, derives from the Hudson portrait of Mrs Faber, engraved by John Faber and published not later than 1756 when her husband died. There is an even more direct link between his portrait of Elenor Morres, Countess of Ormonde (No. 67), painted c. 1766 and the Reynolds portrait of Lady Caroline Russell, engraved by McArdell in 1760. The portrait of Lady Margaret Lowry Corry (No. 51), a portrait dating c. 1769/71, is also a direct version of Reynolds's portrait of Lady Anne Dawson, which was engraved by McArdell c. 1755. As Lady Anne Dawson lived in Co. Cavan, the sitter may have known her and asked for the pose to be copied; only the clothes are different. Many other portraits are closely connected with Reynolds, Francis Cotes, Tilly Kettle (a good English painter who visited Ireland briefly in 1783) and even Gainsborough. Oddly enough, I have not found a male portrait which is a direct version of another painter's work—Hunter may have found

himself less confident when painting women and hence more inclined to use engraved poses.

The portraits of the King family (Nos. 39–44), six in all, are remarkable for their liveliness, depth of colour, and overall complexity of composition, with elaborate costumes and props. They must have made a considerable impact on a Dublin starved, since the death of Latham, of a first class artist. Unlike the Slaughters, on which they may be based, the figures are integrated into their backgrounds. Slaughter often sets his figures in front of, and not *in* their setting. Hunter's figures are set centrally on the canvas and are well modelled. In fact they must have been the young artist's show pieces from which he aimed at getting more sitters. Sir Edward O'Brien (No. 62) who, like Sir Charles Burton must have been painted in the early 1750s, has the same richness of effect and well painted accessories. Sir Charles, now only known through an engraving (No. 91), is full-length and the painting displays all the bravado of a young painter showing off.

Three-quarter length was a size Hunter

Thomas Hudson, Mrs. John Faber, engraving, c. 1756, British Museum, photo Witt Library, Courtauld Institute of Art.

Unknown lady, 1760 (No. 79), photo Witt Library. Courtauld Institute of Art.

William Digby (No. 29). *Courtesy Sotheby's.*

ROBERT HUNTER

was good at and he painted them throughout his career, but in the 1760s and '70s, the costume and setting are very much simpler, and he begins to show a real talent for landscape in the backgrounds. Of this period the portrait of Lord Newbottle, dated 1762, is his masterpiece (No. 49). The sitter, despite his war-like accoutrements (a bayonet is attached to his gun) has a contemplative air and is set in an overcast landscape which backs up his mood. As always, the details of dress are very carefully handled, the leather gloves, the black ribbon in the frill of his shirt and his carefully brushed hair held by a black bow. Armar Lowry Corry, later Lord Belmore, a work of the next decade, c. 1771 (No. 8), has a similar quietness and authority and again a splendid sky and landscape. He is a much finer picture than his wife, who has a stiffness which comes from being a copy after Reynolds (No. 51). Hunter has not allowed himself the luxury of setting her in his own type of background or even of keeping her in scale with her

Esther Crookshank (No. 27).

husband, though he does use his own modelling for the drapery. The fact that the scale is different may indicate that they were not painted as a pair. In the Society of Artists exhibition in 1769 Hunter exhibited 'a lady in the character of Diana' which may be Lady Margaret Butler, later Lady Margaret Lowry Corry, who is depicted as Diana. If so, after her marriage to Armar Lowry Corry in 1771, her husband must have been painted to make up the pair. The finest landscape background is in the La Touche portrait of 1775 where the sitter, full-length, reclines on the ground and gives Hunter the chance to unfold a distant view, perhaps of the lake at Luggala, to the right of the picture. All Hunter's sitters seem to have been great dog lovers and their adoring, expectant eyes gaze up at their owners in the majority of the outdoor pictures.

The passion for fancy dress, common enough in English portraits, was also popular in Ireland. Both Tom Conolly and Lord Milltown (Nos. 20, 55) were

Armar Lowry Corry, Earl of Belmore, c. 1771 (No. 8).
Courtesy the Earl of Belmore. Photograph courtesy the National Trust.

Lady Margaret Lowry Corry, c. 1769 (No. 51).
Courtesy the Earl of Belmore. Photograph courtesy the National Trust.

ROBERT HUNTER

depicted in Van Dyck costume; Esther Crookshank has a ruff of Elizabethan proportions, and several other sitters are also exotically dressed. This is particularly marked in the small whole-length of the so-called Charles Cameron who, despite his later architectural activity in Russia which has led to his costume in this picture being called Russian, is certainly not in Russian dress. Nonetheless the outfit is warm, dashing and not Irish (No. 15). Uniform helped to give colour to many of Hunter's sitters but the interest in some of his portraits lies in their landscape backgrounds. This is particularly so in his small whole-lengths where the landscapes are often extensive and an important part of the picture; William Digby and Lord Langford are excellent examples of this (Nos. 29, 46).

The Society of Artists' Catalogues give three addresses for Hunter; 1765 Bolton Street; 1766 Stephen Street; 1769 Stafford Street. The *Dublin Directory* from 1789–1803 shows him still to be living in 16 Stafford Street and describing himself

John Burke, Baron Naas, engraving *(No. 59).*

as a painter. He did not exhibit with the Society after 1773 though Strickland says he showed in 1800. He must have been at the height of his fame in Dublin in 1763 when Sleator's *Gazateer* for the 12th March has a long poem about Hunter provoked by "Seeing Mr Hunter's Paintings with Mr Dixon's Engravings which obtained premiums from the Hon. the Dublin Society." The poem, which is an appalling panegyric, can only be quoted in part;

> Hunter, step forward, like thy Picture stand
> Out from the canvas, with unrival'd hand;
> Let all thy modest, matchless merit see,
> Shine forth without a shade, sublim and
>   free;
> Throw envy's dark eclipsing cloud aside,
> Stand forth, great genius, with becoming
>   pride. . . .
>
> Thy Picture speaks the language of each
>   eye, . . .
>
> The parts compose one energetic whole,
> Which seems to think, and breathe a living
>   soul,

Thomas Conolly, *1771 (No. 20).*

Charles Cameron, *1773 (No. 15).*
Photograph courtesy Witt Library, Courtauld Institute of Art.

ROBERT HUNTER

*Could Hogarth, Reynolds, view the bold
design,
They'd gladly wave their richest wreaths
with thine . . .*

Hunter's three-quarter length portraits of notabilities, like Lord Baron
Naas, Samuel Madden and Lord Ely are,
as one expects, based on Reynolds but
nonetheless they are dignified and com-
petently painted (Nos. 59, 53, 31). His last
works show quite a marked change of
brushwork especially in the painting of
hair, which is dabbed on in little thin
strokes, as in the Henry Haughton dated
1790 (No. 37). It looks as if he had finally
seen Gainsborough though, of course, he
has nothing of the freedom of the latter
artist. His drawing of Queen Charlotte
(No. 16) is based on the head of Gainsborough's whole-length which was exhibited in the Royal Academy in 1781. The
date on the Hunter drawing is not easy to
read though it looks like 1781, in which
case Hunter must have visited the
exhibition and been overwhelmed by the
great Englishman. It is true that several of
his works of the '80s show this method of
painting hair, for instance his Admiral
McBride of 1783.

A few double portraits survive, that of
Lady Powerscourt and her daughter being particularly successful (No. 69), and
the amusing study of Lord Belvidere and
his cousin being a remarkably good
character study. The latter is a typical
example of the neat, careful style that one
expects of Hunter in the 1770s and '80s.
The one I do not like is Sir Robert Waller
and his son which is curiously lacking in
proportion (No. 74). Both the figures
look stilted and the artist was clearly
unhappy in this scene. He is good with
children, for instance Christopher
O'Brien and Owen O'Malley, so that
cannot have been the trouble (Nos. 61,
64). Perhaps it was movement that
Hunter found difficult to convey, for he
certainly avoids this in his pictures.

I have tried to check Strickland's information about Hunter by going through
the newspapers, but have failed. However
there is a lot of evidence that Strickland
had sources now not available, and I
think we have to rely on his facts. He
states, and this is accurate, that Hunter
was paid £7.7s 10d. in 1788 for repairing
the portrait of Charles II for Dublin
Corporation.[10] What is much more interesting, and unprovable, is that he says
that Hunter had a sale of his pictures in

Sir Robert Waller and his son *(No. 74).*
Courtesy National Gallery of Ireland, No. 4191.

ROBERT HUNTER

1792. This would be one of the first such sales held, not just in Ireland, but in the British Isles and, in my opinion, it indicates that Hunter had decided, due to his age, to give up painting except perhaps for a very flattering commission or for a friend. If I am correct that he was born between 1715 and 1720 he was well over seventy and it seems quite reasonable for him to retire. The latest work known is the Henry Haughton (No. 37), which is dated 1790. Pasquin and Strickland both say Hunter gave up because of the arrival of Robert Home in 1780 and that this "eclipsed his reknown".[11] I suspect age was the cause of his reduced out-put, if this is so. In fact, as many works from the '80s are known to me as from any other decade. However there was competition: Home was in Ireland from 1779–89; Gilbert Stuart, who was enormously successful, from 1789–1793 and Hugh Douglas Hamilton returned from Italy in 1791 and undoubtedly, from the number of his portraits painted in the decade, took over from Hunter as *the* man in Dublin. No doubt all these factors helped to make up Hunter's mind to retire but it may also have provoked him initially into advertising himself. His name

Henry Haughton, *1790 (No. 37).*
Courtesy Christie's.
Photograph A.C. Cooper Ltd, London.

appears in the *Dublin Directory* for the first time in 1789. It continues to appear annually till 1803 though I do not think this indicates that he painted much after his 1792 sale. Like many people who

don't change names in telephone directories nowadays, I suspect he simply forgot to take it out.

One interesting point is that Hunter does not seem to have been employed by the Dublin Establishment at any time during his career, though they immediately commissioned Home. There is no Hunter in Trinity College, Dublin, except the Madden which was given to the College; there is one Hunter only in the College of Physicians, and none in the collections of Dublin Hospitals. This is a strange fact and must mean that he got enough work from his aristocratic patrons, country gentlemen, lawyers, army and naval officers to avoid the tiresome arguments which usually bedevil corporate patronage. Strickland also says that Hunter was still alive in 1803, and that he knew no death date. No doubt he based this opinion on the fact that in 1804 Hunter's name ceases to appear in the *Dublin Directory*, though this is by no means a certainty. Hunter would then have been in his mid-to late-eighties and I assume he died in 1803 or shortly afterwards.

Anne Crookshank

NOTES

1. My interest and search for Hunters again dates back to my work with Desmond Fitz-Gerald, the Knight of Glin, for the exhibition of Irish Portraits held in 1969. To him I owe a big debt for topping up our file of Hunter pictures over the years and for help of every kind. To my other colleagues in the art history world in Ireland and to the librarians I owe a lot, and particularly to Rosemary ffolliott who has provided me with several useful pieces of information. To all the long-suffering owners, who have had visits from me in the last few months, I must

give my thanks and to Jane Fenlon who is masterly in finding Hunters for me and for putting up with my despairing requests for help in attributions. In the *Painters of Ireland* Desmond Fitz-Gerald and I summarized all that is known of Hunter and, try as I have, I can find hardly anything more.
2. Anthony Pasquin, *Memoirs of the Royal Academicians and an Authentic History of the Artists of Ireland*, London, 1796, p. 13.
3. William Carey, *Some Memoirs of the Patronage & Progress of the Fine Arts in England and Ireland*, London, 1826, p. 226.

4. W.B. Sarsfield Taylor, *The Origin, Progress and Present Condition of the Fine Arts in Great Britain & Ireland*, London, 1841, 2 vols.
5. Carey, *ut supra*, p. 226.
6. Taylor, *ut supra*, Vol. 2, p. 283.
7. *ibid*, Vol 2, p. 283.
8. *ibid*, Vol 2, p. 284.
9. George Breeze, *Society of Arts in Ireland Index of Exhibits 1765–80*, Dublin, NGI, 1985, pp. 15/16.
10. *Calendar of the Ancient Records of Dublin*, Dublin, 1909, Vol xiv, pp. 59/60.
11. Pasquin, *ut supra*, p. 13.

A LIST OF ROBERT HUNTER'S WORKS FOLLOWS OVERLEAF

ROBERT HUNTER

This list is by no means exhaustive. Hunter's long career must mean that he painted a great many pictures. Some of those I list are tentative attributions but most are unquestionable. Where I do not have measurements I put bust size; half length; three-quarter length as an indication of their size.

1. John Alexander of Milford, Co. Carlow. Half length in painted oval. It is difficult to decide which member of the family this is, one John has dates 1736–1821, and the second 1764–1843. As the sitter appears to be middle aged and from his hair and costume to date c. 1780, the first of the two seems most likely. Private Coll.

2. William Flower, 2nd Lord Ashbrook (1744–1780). Three-quarter length, m. 1766 Elizabeth Ridge. He succeeded to the title in 1752 and is wearing parliamentary robes holding a coronet. It is not certain that this is a Hunter and it could have been painted in England. Private Coll.

3. Charles Aylmer (b. c. 1715–d.c.1772), bust size in painted oval. m. 1749 Elinor Tyrrell of Clonard. Private Coll.

4. Sir William Barker (1704–1770), 115.4 x 106.47 cms, m. Mary, daughter of Valentine Quin of Adare in 1736 and succeeded his father in 1746. The picture is inscribed with the date Sept 1756 which is probably correct. It has suffered a lot in earlier cleaning and its attribution can only be regarded as tentative. Private Coll.

5. Mary Barker (d. 1776). 115.4 x 101.4 cms, wife of No. 4. This picture is definitely by Hunter and is in better condition than her husband's portrait with which it is a pair. Private Coll.

6. Nathaniel Barry (1724–1785), three-quarter length, s. 'Robert Hunter'. This signature was read as Hickey by Strickland, but there is no doubt that it is Hunter and a fine example. Barry was President of the College of Physicians of Ireland. Coll. Royal College of Physicians of Ireland.

7. Rowland Bateman, of Oak Park, Co. Kerry (d. April 1803). Three-quarter length. The name Rowland is common in this family, but from the date of the picture it is probably the Rowland b. c. 1728, m. 1758 Letitia Denny and was High Sheriff in that year. Coll. The Knight of Glin.

8. Armar Lowry Corry (1740–1802), c. 127 x 101.5 cms. Created Baron Belmore 1781, Viscount in 1789 and Earl in 1797, m. firstly 1771, Margaret Butler, d. of the Earl of Carrick (see No. 51). This may be a marraige portrait c. 1771 but see No. 51 when the problem of the date is discussed. Coll. The Earl of Belmore.

9. Robert Rochfort, 1st Earl of Belvidere (1708–1774), 126 x 100.5 cms, three-quarter length, standing in peer's robes. He may well have been painted to celebrate his Earldom to which he was raised in 1756. The extravagant flow of his robes also indicates an early work. Christie's Belvedere Sale, 9 July 1980, Lot 272.

10. Hon. John Beresford (1738–1805), bust size, second son of Marcus, Earl of Tyrone, m. 1760 Anne Constantia de Ligondes. Appointed Commissioner of Revenue in 1770 and was a most important figure in the arts as well as politics in late eighteenth century Dublin. Coll. Newbridge House.

11. John Hobart, 2nd Earl of Buckinghamshire (1723–1793), 237.1 x 147.5 cms. This whole-length was painted in 1780 when the sitter was Lord Lieutenant of Ireland, 1777–1780. Coll. The Mansion House, Dublin.

12. George, 2nd Earl Temple, created 1784 Marquess of Buckingham (1753–1813), c. 237.1 x 147.5 cms. He was Lord Lieutenant of Ireland in 1782 and 1787. He is shown, whole-length standing in the robes of the Order of St. Patrick which was founded largely by his efforts in 1783 to which year the picture probably dates. It was engraved in mezzotint by William Sadler and is recorded in the *Dublin Chronicle*, Jan. 22–24, 1788, "The Marquess of Buckingham a few years ago sat for his picture to Hunter. Mr. Cuffe bought it after the departure of that nobleman from the Kingdom. The same artist is now to be employed by the city to make another." This second version is not now known as if it was for the Mansion House it would surely have been a full size whole-length not the small picture in the NGI (see No. 13). Coll. The Deanery, St. Patrick's Cathedral, Dublin.

13. George, 2nd Earl Temple (1752–1813). A small scale version of No. 12, 77 × 56 cms. It came from the Malahide Castle Sale, 1976, Collection NGI. 4165.

14. Sir John Caldwell, 128.3 x 102.9 cms. Painted in the 1780s and the attribution is by no means certain. Sir John was Lt. Col. of the 8th Foot and served in Quebec 1768–85. During this period of service Sir John was elected an Indian chief by the Ojibways and given an Indian name which meant "the Runner". In the picture he is dressed as he appeared at a grand council at the Wakeetomike village of the tribe in Jan. 1780. Exh. at the National Maritime Museum in 1976 in an exhibition entitled *1776, The British Story of the American Revolution*, No. 328, Private Coll.

15. Charles Cameron (1745–c. 1803), s. and d. 'R. Hunter 1773'. Portrait of an architect in exotic clothes, pointing at a plan entitled 'Sett of Baths'. From the Townshend sale, Christie's 1904. See George K. Loukomski, *Connoisseur*, March 1936 and the same author, *Journal of the Royal Institute of British Architects*, August 1936, where the identification with Cameron is discussed. There is considerable literature on this

portrait which is variously dated 1771 and 1773 and called whole-length and small whole-length. It is possible that there are two works. One was certainly painted in 1771 when Lord Townshend was Viceroy. Strickland says that the work was signed 'R. Hunter pinxit Dublinii 1771'. I have a photograph of the work signed 1773. One is now in Moscow according to Nigel Gosling, *Leningrad*, 1965.

16. Queen Charlotte, wife of George III (1744–1818). Drawing in pastel 61 x 43.5 cms. Signed in monogram 'R. Hunter 1781'. This portrait is a version of the head of the whole-length Gainsborough portrait of 1781, which was engraved by Gainsborough Dupont. However as the dating is so very close it may indicate that Hunter saw the picture itself when it was exhibited at the Royal Academy in 1781. Puttick and Simpson Sale, 31 May 1932.

17. Henry de Burgh, 12th Earl and created in 1789 1st Marquess of Clanricarde (1742–1797), 222.0 x 147.5 cms, s. and d. 'R Hunter pinxit Dublin 1783'. The Earl is shown full-length in robes as a Knight of St. Patrick. According to Strickland the picture was owned by the Countess of Cork in 1916. However, as it was inherited by the present owner directly from the last Marquess of Clanricarde, it is more likely that she owned the small version, see No. 18. Engraved by William Sedgewick. Coll. The Earl of Harewood.

18. Henry de Burgh, 12th Earl of Clanricarde (1742–1797). A small scale version of No. 17, 66.5 x 51 cms, s. 'R. Hunter Pinxit'. This small picture was probably the one owned by the Countess of Cork as mentioned in Strickland, see above. Sotheby's, 9 March 1988, Lot 40. It was wrongly identified as a portrait of the Marquess of Buckingham.

19. Colonel Eyre Massey (1719–1804), c. 127 x 101.5 cms, created 1st Baron Clarina in 1800, m. Catherine Clements in 1767. Coll. The Knight of Glin.

20. Thomas Conolly (1738–1803), of Castletown, Co. Kildare, 72.4 x 59.6 cms, s. and d. 'R Hunter pinxit Dublinii 1771'. In this small whole-length the sitter is shown standing by a column wearing Van Dyck costume. Full details of its provenance is given in the catalogue of the exhibition of Irish Portraits 1660–1860, Dublin, London and Belfast, 1969/70, No. 46. Private Coll.

21. John Conroy, 65 x 53.5 cms. Mr. Conroy is seated, unusual in a small whole-length. Christie's, 24 June 77, Lot 78.

22. Admiral Philips Cosby, three-quarter length. Admiral of the White, inherited Stradbally Hall from his cousin in 1774 and m. 1792 Eliza Gunthorpe. Sotheby's, Nov. 1988.

23. William Cradock, Dean of St. Patrick's 1775-93. Half-length. The Dean was a friend

ROBERT HUNTER

of John Wesley (see No. 75) and we owe him the Bindon portrait of Swift which he saved during a fire in the Deanery. Coll. The Deanery, St. Patrick's Cathedral, Dublin.

24. Alexander Crookshank (1736–1813). Bust size. Probably painted to celebrate his marriage in 1768 to his cousin Esther Kennedy (see No. 26), though from the hair-style of his wife the pair may date into the early 1770s. Private Coll.

25. Alexander Crookshank (1736–1813), 101.5 x 76.2 cms. s. and d. 'R H 1784'. Another portrait of the above where the sitter is painted in robes as a Judge of the Court of Common Plea, to which position he was appointed in 1783. There is a version of this portrait in the King's Inns Library and another in a Private Coll. in Ireland. It is a pair with No. 27. Coll. The Author.

26. Esther Crookshank née Kennedy (1746–1826), bust size. A pair with No. 24. Private Coll.

27. A second portrait of Esther Crookshank, 101.2 x 76.2 cms. Not signed but a pair with No. 25. She is wearing Elizabethan fancy dress. Coll. The Author.

28. Sidney Davis, dau. of Joshua Davis, m. Thomas Acton of West Aston, Co. Wicklow in 1780. Bust size, unsigned. The sitter is wearing fancy dress. Private Coll.

29. William Digby, 74.5 x 63 cms. The Rev. William Digby of Lackan, son of Simon Digby, Bishop of Elphin, m. Olivia French of French Park. This small whole-length shows the sitter in a park and is an early example of Hunter's excellent treatment of landscape. The companion picture of William Digby's wife is by Digby who attempted to follow Hunter's style quite successfully. Sotheby's Sale, 21 Nov. 1984, Lot 35.

30. Mrs Ellis, 74 x 61.4 cms. In riding habit and hat facing right, must be a 1780s picture because of the hair-style. Christie's, de Steiger Sale Anon Coll., 25 Nov 1932, No. 50.

31. Nicholas Loftus (d. 1766) created 1751 Baron Loftus; 1756 Viscount Ely and Earl of Ely 1766, three-quarter length seated. Private Coll.

32. Lord Charles FitzGerald (1756–1810), 68.8 x 56 cms, created Baron Lecale in 1800. Lord Charles was the third son of the 1st Duke of Leinster. He entered the navy and became a Rear Admiral 1799. He was an M.P. from 1776. This small whole-length must be quite late in Hunter's working life as it must date into the mid 1780s. Christie's Sale, Castle Hacket, Co. Galway, 2 July 1986, Lot 278.

33. A member of the Forbes Family, c. 76.5 x 51 cms. A small whole-length, man standing in a landscape holding a gun and leaning against a tree with his legs crossed. The size is large for a small whole length by Hunter. Private Coll.

Lord Harcourt, engraving, 1775 (No. 35). Photograph J&S Harsch, Dublin.

Sir John Cauldwell, 1780s (No. 14). Photograph E. Stacy-Marks Ltd, Eastbourne.

34. General James Gisborne (d.1778), 76.5 x 63.5 cms, s. 'Hunter Pinxit 1771'. The general was M.P. for Lismore, C–in–C in Ireland, and married the daughter of Alexander Gordon in 1799 in whose family it has descended. Private Coll.

35. Simon, Lord Harcourt (b.c. 1721–1777). Succeeded his grandfather as 2nd Viscount Harcourt in 1727, created 1749 Viscount Nuneham and Earl Harcourt, m. 1735 Rebecca Sambourne Le Bas. Ld. Lieutenant of Ireland 1772–77, Hunter's head and shoulders portrait in a painted oval was engraved by Edward Fisher, 1775. There are numerous versions with slight differences such as different coloured coats.
a. Ulster Mus. No. 47 given in 1892, 76.7 x 64 cms.
b. Christie's 30 Jan. 1987 Lot 173, 76.2 x 63.5 cms.
c. Private Coll. in red coat, 74 x 62 cms.
d. NGI No. 1002. Purchased 1938, 76 x 63 cms. There may be other versions: it is very difficult to be certain from photographs that the work is one of the above four examples or yet another.

36. Simon, Lord Harcourt (b.c. 1721–1777) Three-quarter length in robes. Perhaps the picture mentioned in Strickland as being finished by William Doughty, who came to Ireland in 1778. Known only through a reproduction in the Witt Library.

37. Henry Haughton, 76.2 x 53 cms, s. and d. 1790. In painted oval dressed in a brown coat and white lace jabot. The latest work by Hunter that is currently known. Christie's, 1 March 1985 Lot 113.

38. Member of the Hickie family of Slievoie, Co. Tipperary. Three-quarter length standing with dog and holding gun. This portrait has been much over cleaned. Private Coll.

39. Edward King (1726–1797), 124 x 98.4 cms. Inherited baronetcy from his brother Robert (see No. 44) in 1755. Created Baron Kingston, 1764; Viscount Kingsborough, 1766 and Earl of Kingston, 1768. Three-quarter length standing, with gun, dog and game. Private Coll.

40. Eleanor King, 124 x 98.4 cms. m. 1740 William Stewart of Killymoon and is depicted seated with her son, James Stewart (b.1741.) with his dog and in front of a curtain (see No. 44). Private Coll.

41. Frances King, 124 x 98.4 cms, m. Hans Widman Wood of Rosmead, Co. Westmeath. Shown seated holding a rose and in front of a curtain (see No. 44). Private Coll.

42. Henry King of Belleek, Co. Mayo, 124 x 98.4 cms. Depicted with gun and dog in a field of corn (see No. 44). Private Coll.

43. Isabella King, (d. 1794). 124 x 98.4 cms. Married Earl of Howth 1750. Depicted as a shepherdess with crook and a lamb (see No. 44). Private Coll.

ROBERT HUNTER

44. Sir Robert King (1724–1755). 4th baronet, created Baron Kingsborough 1748. 124 x 98.4 cms. Three quarter length with gun and dog. These six portraits Nos. 39–44 are of six of the seven children of Sir Henry King, 3rd Bt. The seventh, Anne, who married in 1750 John Knox of Castlereagh, Co. Mayo is not included. She may have taken her portrait with her on her marriage. These six pictures must have been commissioned by Robert King, perhaps to celebrate his peerage, 1748. Even his married sister Eleanor, was included in the set with her son, James Stewart. None of these pictures are signed; they all have an old attribution to Robert Hunter though some have been incorrectly ascribed to Allan Ramsay. They are very unlike Hunter's later work but fit in well with such examples as Sir Edward O'Brien (see No. 60) or Samuel Madden (see No. 53) and represent Hunter's earliest developed manner. They must, from their ages and costume, have all been painted about 1748/9. They are a very elaborate set, all in magnificent clothes, unsuited to shooting or even to playing as a shepherdess. Most of them still preserve their superb, rococo, gilded frames. They must have established Hunter as a major painter. Private Coll.

45. Robert, 1st Baron Kingsborough, 247.3 x 147cms. Another portrait of No. 44. A whole-length probably painted in the early 1750s, Kingsborough is seated, his legs stretched out leaning against an elaborate baroque table. Formerly in the collection of Sir Cecil King Harmon and sold after the fire at Rockingham.

46. Hercules Rowley, 2nd Viscount Langford (1737–1796), 73.8 x 62.3 cms. Small whole-length, Lord Langford is seated in a landscape holding a book. Previously attributed to Arthur Devis and said to be Hon. Robert Pakenham, brother of the 2nd Lord Longford. This identification is no longer accepted by the Pakenham family who think it is almost certainly Lord Langford who was the brother-in-law of the 2nd Lord Longford. Formerly in the Collection of the Earls of Longford. For further details see No. 48. Private Coll.

47. Gentleman of the La Touche family, probably Peter. 151.7 x 198.1 cms; s. 'R Hunter pinxit' and dated 1775. Whole-length reclining with dog and gun in a magnificent landscape. This portrait is probably the one listed in Strickland as "A Gentleman with a dog and a gun seated in a landscape" which had come from the La Touche sale, Bellevue, Co. Wicklow, 1906. W. T. Whitley (British Museum, Whitley Papers, VI, p. 792) describes what is probably the same picture in a Christie's sale, 15 Nov. 1918, Lot 17. Coll. NGI No. 4034.

48. Edward Michael, 2nd Baron Longford (1743–1792), 73.8 x 62.3 cms, small whole-length, Lord Longford is standing on the beach with a dog, leaning against a rock with a ship in the background. He is dressed, according to the National Maritime museum, in the uniform of a Captain of over three years seniority and because of his uniform he can only have been painted between 1769–

74. During those years family diaries prove that Lord Longford was residing in Ireland so that the traditional attribution to Arthur Devis is untenable. There is no evidence that Devis ever came to Ireland and the picture is fully acceptable as a Hunter. It is a pair with No. 46 a portrait of Lord Longford's brother-in-law, Lord Langford. Both pictures came originally from the Longford collection, though it is now in an English private coll.

49. William John, Lord Newbottle, later 5th Marquess of Lothian (1737–1815). 127 x 99 cms, engraved by E. Fisher 1769 and according to Strickland it is signed, 'Robertus Hunter Dublinii pinx^t 1762'. Lord Newbottle is shown in uniform with gun and bayonet. He married Elizabeth, daughter of Chichester Fortescue of Dromisken, Co. Louth, in 1762. Presumably it is a marriage portrait as the sitter does not appear to have visited Ireland except at the time of his marriage, when it was recorded in the press. Hunter does not appear to have painted his wife. Private Coll.

50. Galbrath Lowry-Corry (1706–1769). Bust size in painted oval. Father of the 1st Earl of Belmore, M.P., Co. Tyrone and High Sheriff 1733 and 1743. Probably a work of the late 1750s. Coll. The Earl of Belmore.

51. Lady Margaret Lowry Corry, née Butler, as Diana (d. 1776), c. 127 x 101.5 cms, first wife of the 1st Earl of Belmore (see No. 8) and daughter of the Earl of Carrick. Lady Margaret died before her husband was raised

Edward King (No. 39).

Frances King, c. 1748 (No. 41).
Photograph The Green Studio Ltd, Dublin, AF/23B.

ROBERT HUNTER

to the peerage. The portrait was probably painted in 1769, as a portrait by Hunter of a 'Lady in the character of Diana' was exhibited in that year in the Society of Artists No. 34. It might be a marriage portrait, c. 1771, but as the scale is different between this portrait and that of her husband I am inclined to favour the earlier date. The portrait of her husband was presumably painted after their marriage as a companion piece. Posing a figure as a Goddess is not unusual in English portraiture at this time but quite rare in Ireland. Diana, Goddess of the Moon, usually represents chastity. The pose of this picture is taken directly from the Reynolds portrait of Lady Anne Dawson. Coll. The Earl of Belmore.

52. John McBride (d. 1800). Rear Admiral 1793, Vice Admiral 1794 and Admiral 1799, signed RH and dated 1783. Son of a Presbyterian minister from Ballymoney, Co. Antrim, he entered the navy in 1754. In the early 1780s he was stationed in Ireland. There are two versions of this picture, one known only through a photograph, the second version is in a private collection and it appears to have been overcleaned at some time.

53. Samuel Madden (1686–1765). 117.5 x 101.5 cms. Rector of Newton Butler, Co. Fermanagh. Madden's mother was a Molyneux from Castle Dillon, a family noted for their scholarship and patriotism and so it is not surprising that Madden became one of the founder members, with Thomas Prior of the Dublin Society. According to W. Carey he was a close friend of Hunter. An engraving by Richard Purcell, dated 1755 and signed 'Robert Hunter delineavit', shows the sitter in reverse, in a wig and more formally dressed sitting in a library with books, picture, curtain etc. However it is, I think, based on the Trinity College picture which in its informality, showing Madden in a cap and no wig, and a plain dressing-gown was probably not considered suitable for public display. The background is very similar in both, though in reverse in the print. The oil probably dates from the early 50s as the picture has much the same richness of colour and handling and crowded baroque composition as that found in the King pictures. It was also engraved by W. Wilkinson, 1755, and the head was used as an illustration in the *European Magasine*, April 1802, Coll. Trinity College Dublin. Probably part of the bequest of pictures given by Madden to TCD, though not listed as such in Strickland's *A Descriptivie Catalogue of the Pictures . . . in Trinity College, Dublin . .*, Dublin, 1916.

54. John Meredith of Templeraney, Co. Wicklow, 122 x 97 cms. Mr Meredith married Martha Jones of Ballytrana in 1740. He is seated wearing a brown coat and petting his whippet. A landscape shows to the right. This picture was attributed to William Hoare in the Sotheby Parke Bernet Sale, London, 20 July 1983, Lot 19, but I think it is quite possibly a Hunter.

55. Joseph Leeson, 2nd Earl of Milltown (1730–1801). 74 x 61 cms. Leeson succeeded his father as Earl in 1783. He is in Van Dyck costume and dates before he inherited. This picture, which is usually called a Devis, is certainly by Hunter and so close to the signed and dated Thomas Conolly (see No. 20) that one wonders if they represent the result of the same fancy dress party. Private Coll.

56. Robert, Viscount Molesworth, probably the 5th Viscount (b. c. 1727–1813). Half-length. Coll. R. McDonnell.

57. Daniel Mussenden of Larchfield, Co. Down, 75 x 62.3 cms. m. Frediswid, sister of Sir Stewart Bruce in 1782. He is in a black cloak with slashed sleeve and white Van Dyck lace collar holding a scroll. Sadler Sale, Christie's 16 June 1950, Lot 153, one of a pair with his wife (see No. 58).

58. Frediswid Mussenden, 75 x 62.3 cms. She is in a yellow dress and the pair of portraits may well be marriage portraits dating c. 1782. Christie's, 16 June 1950, Lot 153. A pair with her husband (see No. 57).

59. John Burke (1705–1790), created Baron Naas 1776, Viscount Mayo 1781 and Earl of Mayo 1785. Painted as Baron Naas 1776, three-quarter length with curtain and books on table. Engraved in mezzotint by W. Dickinson 1777. Strickland said the original belonged to Lord Mayo.

60. Robert Neale of Shaw House, Wiltshire, 75 x

Sir Robert King, *c. 1749 (No. 44)*.

John McBride, *1783 (No. 52)*.

61.5 cms; half-length in a blue velvet jacket with a white stock and jabot. Prov. J A Neale Mansion House, Corsham, Christie's, April 9 1937, Lot 2; Parke Bernet New York, 28 Nov. 1978 Lot 129. I can find no evidence that Mr. Neale had any connections with Ireland and if it is by Hunter it is a late work.

61. The Hon. Christopher O'Brien, 148.5 x 113 cms. Probably son of Murrough, 1st Marquess of Thomond who married in 1753, Mary, Countess of Orkney. Insc. Christopher O'Brien/Aetatis May 1766. Sotheby's Sale, 15 July 1987. Coll. Dromoland Hotel.

62. Sir Edward O'Brien, 2nd Bt. of Dromoland (1705–1765) m. 1726 Mary Hickman of Fenloe c. 127 x 101.5 cms. A fine velvety picture showing Sir Edward carrying a driving whip, his gloves tucked into his belt, and with a dog. Probably a picture of the early '50s as it is stylistically close to the King portraits. Though a portrait of Lady O'Brien is listed, no picture by Hunter of her survives in Dromoland. On loan to the Dromoland Hotel.

63. Member of the O'Hara family probably Charles O'Hara (b. 1746). Three-quarter length, standing. Private Coll.

64. Owen O'Malley of Spencer Park, Co. Mayo (b. 1771), son of George O'Malley of Burrishooole, Co. Mayo, 124.5 x 99.5 cms. The sitter is shown full-length, standing as a child of 6 or 7, holding a shuttlecock and racket, wearing a red coat. Sotheby's, 13 July 1988, Lot 39.

65. Col. William Odell, M.P., of The Grove, Ballingarry, Co. Limerick (1752–1831), 94.5 x 70 cms, High Sheriff 1789. The small whole-length may date shortly after his marriage with Aphra Crone in 1773. The face in this picture is painted in a very direct manner and not particularly like Hunter. It is possible that it has been somewhat overpainted. Private Coll.

66. John Butler, 15th Earl of Ormonde, (d. 1766), 49.5 x 38 cms. This small three-quarter length shows the Earl standing with a spaniel and holding a gun. John Butler was the son of Thomas Butler of Kilcash and succeeded *de jure* to the title on the death of his second cousin once removed, Charles Earl of Arran in 1758. This picture dates after his succession to the title. Sotheby's in Ireland Sale, 3 Nov. 1981, Lot 616.

67. Elenor or Ellen Morres (1711–1793), wife of Walter Butler, 16th Earl of Ormonde, three-quarter length seated holding a dog. In pose and even in costume, this is a direct version after the portrait of Lady Caroline Russell by Sir Joshua Reynolds engraved by McArdell in 1760. See No. 68. Coll. Kilkenny Castle.

68. Walter Butler (1703–1783), three-quarter length, succeeded his cousin, John Butler (see No. 66) in 1766 as *de jure* 16th Earl of Ormonde. In 1732 he married Elenor Morres (see No. 67). He is shown seated with his dog, in a garden with a circular temple in the background. Probably painted in the 1760s, a pair with No. 67. Coll. Kilkenny Castle.

69. Dorothy, Viscountess Powerscourt, née Rowley (d. 1785), with her daughter Isabella who later married Sir Charles Style Bt., 200.5 x 153 cms, dated 1767. Lady Powerscourt was the second wife of the 1st Viscount Powerscourt. From the Powerscourt Sale 1984. On loan to Newbridge House.

70. Edward, 2nd Viscount Powerscourt (1729–1764), 73.6 x 63.5 cms. Succeeded his father in 1751, probably dates later and is not certainly by Hunter. Originally from Lord Charlemont's collection. Christies, Powerscourt Sale 24 Sept. 1984, Lot 36.

71. Richard, 3rd Viscount Powerscourt (1730–1788), 121.8 x 96.5 cms. Succeeded his brother (see No. 67) in 1764, but probably dates from the same period, 1767, as the portrait of his mother and sister (see No. 69). Originally from Sir Charles Domville's collection. Christies, Powerscourt Sale, 24 Sept. 1984, Lot 37.

72. Capt Charles Ruxton, of the Red House, Ardee (c.1726–1806), three-quarters standing with gun leaning against the trunk of a tree. Private Coll.

73. Sir Annesley Stewart, 6th Bart. (1725–1801), three-quarter length, standing holding papers. There is a signature on this picture and the attribution to Hunter may prove inaccurate. Private Coll.

74. Sir Robert Waller (d. 1780) and his son Robert (1768–1826), 107 x 81 cms. Sir Robert was created a Baronet two months before he

William Odell, *1773 (No. 65)*.

George Rochford, Lord Belvidere and Mr. Handcock *(No. 77)*.
Courtesy Christie's. Photograph A. C. Cooper Ltd, London.

died. This picture must date from the mid -1770s given the age of his son, who is presumably his eldest son and heir. He is standing alarmed by the behaviour of the child who is standing on a table pulling books off the library shelf. Coll. NGI No. 4191.

75. The Rev. John Wesley (1703–1791), half-length. Engraved in mezzotint by James Watson with the inscription, "Done from that much esteemed picture painted at Dublin now in possession of William Weaver. Published by William Weaver, Ross Court, Covent Garden 1773." The information on the print does not altogether agree with the tradition that the present picture was given to Wesley's Chapel in City Road, London, by a Mr Battress who had commissioned it. It is possible that two pictures were originally painted. In Wesley's *Journal* (ed. N. Curnock 1909–1, 6 p. 139) for 31 July 1765 the preacher describes sitting for Hunter when he was in Dublin. He says he sat "from about ten o'clock to half an hour after one, and in that time he (Hunter) began and ended the face, and with a most striking likeness." Coll. Wesley's Chapel, City Road, London.

76. Miss Woollery as Sigismunda. Seated whole-length. Listed by Strickland as ex Society of Artists, 1800. There is an old reproduction in the Witt Library of this picture.

DOUBLE PORTRAIT OF SITTERS WITH DIFFERENT NAMES

77. George Rochford, Lord Belvidere (1738–1814) and Mr Handcock, his cousin, who is in uniform. 151.2 x 133.2 cms. Lord Belvidere succeeded to the title in 1774. The picture was formerly called Hugh Douglas Hamilton (see Strickland) and came from the collection of William Rochford, Cahir Abbey, Co. Tipperary. The attribution to Hunter seems correct to the author. Christie's, 17 March 1978, Lot 83.

LIST OF UNIDENTIFIED PICTURES

78. Portrait of a man with book, on panel, 25.8 x 20.5 cms. S. and d. 1760, a pair with No. 79. Prov. Puttick and Simpson, 18 April 1928, Sotheby's Lucas sale, 10 April 1929, Lot 56.

79. Unknown lady, on panel, 25.8 × 20.5 cms. s. and d. 1760, a pair with No. 78 and a version of Thomas Hudson's portrait of

Mrs Faber, the wife of the engraver, John Faber. Sotheby's, 10 April 1929, Lot 56.

80. Portrait of a young officer, bust size in painted oval, s. and d. 1764.

81. Portrait of a man. 76.2 x 62.5 cms. In brown coat with gold trimming seated on a red chair. Probably a work of the '80s. Advertisement by Vicars Brothers, *Burlington Magazine*, July 1930, CCCXXVIII 57.

82. Unknown man formerly called Francis Hutcheson M.D., 76 x 63 cms. Christie's Sale, 5 June 1925, Lot 29, Coll. NGI No. 905.

83. Unknown group of two young men in Van Dyck dress, one seated at a table in front of an open book, the other standing looking at him and placing one hand on his shoulder. Phillips, Edinburgh, Nov. 1984.

84. Portrait of a Lady, 75 x 62.2 cms. In yellow dress holding scroll. Sold as a Robert Hunter, Christie's Curzon Sale, 10 July 1931, Lot 121. The reproduction is poor but if it had not been given to Hunter I would have suggested Tilly Kettle. It may therefore date from Kettle's visit to Ireland, 1783.

85. Portrait of a Lady, 63.5 x 45.8 cms. In a white silk dress with a yellow head dress with feathers, nearly profile; judging from the reproduction it was in very bad condition. Christie's, Crawford Sale, 11 Oct 1946, Lot 83.

PICTURES LISTED BY STRICKLAND BUT NOT KNOWN TO THE AUTHOR

86. John Bowes, Lord Chancellor of Ireland (1690–1767). Listed by Strickland who says it was sold at auction at 17 Pembroke Place, Dublin, 27th April 1847.

87. Capt. L. Brabazon, RN. Listed by Strickland who says it belonged to A. Cunningham Robertson, 142 Prince's Rd., Liverpool, in 1884.

88. Arthur Dobbs, M.P. (1689–1765). This portrait is listed in Strickland as belonging to S.M. Dobbs of Glenariffe Lodge, Co. Antrim.

89. George, Earl Macartney (1737–1806) as a young man, owned according to Strickland by C. G. Macartney, Lissanoure, Co. Antrim. Lord Macartney was one of the most

eminent diplomats in the late 18th century, famous for his mission to China in 1792/94.

90. Portrait group of children blowing soap-bubbles. In Strickland's day this picture belonged to Captain Durham Matthews and had formerly belonged to John Tracey of 13 Heytesbury St., Dublin.

PICTURES ONLY KNOWN FROM ENGRAVINGS

91. Sir Charles Burton, M.P., Lord Mayor of Dublin in 1753, d. 1775. Engraved in mezzotint by James McArdell. This picture is no longer in the Mansion House and its whereabouts is unknown.

92. Tom Echlin, engraved and published by Edward Lyons of Essex Street in 1752. Print advertised in *Faulkner's Dublin Journal* 4th November 1752, "A half-length of the facetious Tom Echlin, from an original painting extremely like". Echlin was a noted Dublin wit and may have been a member of the Echlin family of Ardquin, Co. Down. The original painting is not known to the author.

93. W. Todd Jones, engraved in stipple by A. McDonald. The original of this work is not known to the author.

94. John Mears (1695–1767), Presbyterian Minister, who, after a chequered career working as a minister in Cos. Down, Antrim and Tipperary, moved to Dublin in 1746 where he was first minister in Strafford Street meeting house and later after 1762 at the new meeting house in Strand Street. Engraved in mezzotint anonymously. The original was not known to Strickland.

95. Nicholas, 6th Viscount Taaffe (1677–1769). Known only in the undated engraving by John Dixon which is inscribed as follows "The Right Honourable Nicholas Lord Viscount Taaffe of Corran, Baron of Ballymote, Count of the Holy Roman Empire, one of the Lords of the Bed Chamber to their Imperial Majesties and Lieu t Gene 1 of their armies–To His Excellency John Ponsonby Esq. Speaker of the Honourable House of Commons and one of the Lords Justices and Gen¹ Govenours of the Kingdom of Ireland This Plate is most humbly Inscribed by his Excellency's most obedient humble Servant John Dixon". It was also engraved by Sylvester Harding 1801 when the original was dated 1763.

LOOKING BACK

Rosc 88, the sixth Rosc and the second in the converted Guinness Hop Store, managed to avoid the initial flurry of dissent which marred its predecessor. The problems facing Chairman, Patrick J. Murphy, and his team of organizers were, however, the same – how to go about displaying the diversity of current activity in the visual arts to an audience which, although receptive and at least willing to be entertained, is relatively untutored in the particularities of international contemporary art even if to nothing like the extent of the first Rosc in 1967. Add to this the exercise of coping with a limited budget and limited space. (In fact, eventually two locations were used, with the Royal Hospital at Kilmainham being brought into use).

It was Patrick Murphy's catholic enthusiasm for a variety of means and media which decided the form of Rosc 88, a hugely eclectic affair which made spirited forays into many different branches of endeavour, from the outer reaches of conceptualism to gutsy figurative painting. The result was undoubtedly a stimulating and, sure enough, entertaining show, but one that carried no passengers in the sense that every participating artist had to fight for attention.

Given this, it is perhaps surprising that the German Wolfgang Laib did very well indeed in terms of audience response. His delicate, pristine rice houses and pollen jars at the RHK won him a host of converts to their passive, ascetically understated celebration of life and beauty. Laib's artistic strategy is one of minimal interference. He nudges us gently in the direction of extraordinary aspects of natural processes and then quietly stands back to let us see for ourselves.

Laib has obvious links with the ethos of *arte povera*, and Italians associated with that movement were present in some force. Giovanni Anselmo's precariously poised stone slabs, mammoth blocks defying gravity by somehow clinging to a sheer wall, were particularly striking. The Japanese Shigeo Toya, a sculptor who gouges robust chunks of wood with chainsaw and hatchet, then rubs coloured pigment and plaster of paris into the surfaces, also made a strong impression. Toya's work, particularly his big 'Woods', a row of hacked, jagged pillars, vividly evoked the feelings of wonder and mystery that form the core of his

Art critic, **Aidan Dunne** looks back over the year's exhibitions and events in the Republic of Ireland, while **Liam Kelly,** lecturer in the Faculty of Art and Design, University of Ulster at Belfast, covers Northern Ireland.

inspiration: childhood memories of the magic and terror of woodlands by night.

Hiroshi Sugimoto, who makes technically brilliant, conceptually based, taxonomic series of photographs, also stood out. British artist, Ian McKeever, an interesting figure who works on an ambitious scale, gave the impression that he would need to be experienced in greater depth to get the measure of his powerful, critical, landscape-based diptychs.

More immediate in their impact were American painters Terry Winters, with casual images characterized by thick, clotted textures and sombre colour, relating to stages of organic processes, and Elizabeth Murray with her loudly coloured, shaped paintings. Others who impressed were Argentinian Ricardo Cavallo, Spaniards Jose Maria Sicilia and, among the Irish, veteran Tony O'Malley and Mary Fitzgerald, whose spare, linear, abstract compositions bespeak a fruitful Japanese influence – and Francis Tansey, who hearkens back to hard-edge colour abstraction.

One of the first Swedes to exhibit in Rosc – thanks, presumably, to the presence of Olle Granath of Stockholm's Moderna Museet on the jury together with Murphy and Kynaston McShine of MOMA – was Rolf Hanson, who showed powerful, visionary, abstract landscapes, epic in scope and richly surfaced. In quite a different vein, Jenny Holzer's 'chapel of doom' was extremely effective, as were Jeff Wall's "Cindy Shermanesque", disorientating, back-lit transparencies.

There was a distinct feeling, however, that Rosc was at heart a miscellaneous survey of a miscellaneous scene, that post-modernist promiscuity raged with the freedom of an uncontrolled forest fire, and any effort at discerning a pattern, at putting order on the direction of the flames, was futile.

The exhibition's original criterion, simply one of excellence, makes little sense when one person's excellence is another's aesthetic confidence trick. Rosc 88 emphasized the need for a serious

look at the nature and scope of the exhibition. Should it, for example, aim for a concerted structure along thematic or historical lines? There are surely persuasive arguments, to do with its national and international effectiveness, for at least seriously considering such an alternative approach. Virtually everyone did agree on one thing: the remarkable quality of the George Costakis Collection of Russian Avant Garde art which was quite an eye opener.

•

1988 was a big year for the Sculptors' Society of Ireland. Around a major international conference which took place at Trinity College at the end of August and which addressed the formidable subject of public sculpture, the SSI organized an incredible range of related exhibitions and events, many of them tied in to Dublin's Millenium celebrations.

In the family of contemporary Irish art, sculpture has been in many respects the poor relation, disadvantaged through circumstance, forever on the point of decisively making good but never quite getting there. Individual bright sparks never coalesce into a blaze of concerted brilliance. Clearly, the activities of the SSI Sculpture Festival were the big push, the campaign that was meant to put Irish sculpture on the map.

As it happened, the conference was a success and, in terms of logistics alone, given the staggering amount of work that found its way into the public arena, the umbrella Sculpture Festival has to be judged a spectacular success as well. It could be plausibly argued, however, that the numerous exhibitions and installations served to underline the troubled condition of Irish sculpture rather than to effectively change it.

This condition might be summed up in these terms: a heartening amount of individual talent and technical ability in search of a coherent language of form – though it should be stressed that there are several Irish sculptors whose work displays both technical verve and formal sophistication, Eilis O'Connell being one prominent example.

The big, sprawling 'Sculpture Open' at the Gallagher Gallery served to enhance the standing of the best. Among the best must be O'Connell, who for several years now has been producing mature work in a confidently developing language of

LOOKING BACK

form, rich in metaphor and suggestion; Kathy Prendergast, who switches media with abrupt and startling ease but is always assured and fastidious in her grasp of the relationship between different materials and forms.

John Kindness's dogs, ingeniously fashioned from a diverse range of mosaic materials, have gained a stubborn, intriguing foothold on the stage of contemporary Irish art. They have a real *chutzpah* of their own, and a vivid, realer than real presence that suggests something much more than the work of a slick technician. There were other high notes, but the overall impression was one of desperately variable quality. In addition to temporary sculpture trails, leading through the city centre and also out at Dublin Airport (with the help of Aer Rianta, the Irish airports authority, who in February 1989 mounted an ambitious exhibition of paintings and sculpture at the airport as part of Aer Rianta's second arts' festival), both conceived on an ambitious scale and both enjoyably diverse, the Festival also left the city with ten permanent outdoor public sculptures.

One of the best, and certainly the least visible is Rachel Joynt's 'Oileán na nDaoine', which consists of patterns of footsteps sunk flush with the paving slabs on the pedestrian island between Westmoreland Street and D'Olier Street. Grace Weir's 'Trace', a fragmented stone and metal arch construction on St. Stephen's Green in front of the Shelbourne Hotel, also blends well with its setting and refers us obliquely to images of the city's past, present and potential future. Michael Bulfin's 'A Walk Among Stones', a formidable arrangement of imposing monolithic slabs sited close to the monolithic slabs of Ballymun's tower blocks, also conflates past and present by juxtaposing granite and cast concrete. It is impressive, yet in its context seems almost cruel. Jakki McKenna, with her straightforwardly naturalistic 'Meeting Place' in Liffey Street, in which two bronze women sit and chat on a bench, manages to be direct and involving of her audience without any feeling of condescension.

Through pressing so many sculptors into direct public contact—since the effect of seeing one's handiwork thrust under the public gaze is pretty sobering—the SSI Festival should have a profound long-

term effect on the course of Irish sculpture. Another, related encouraging development was the 'Pillar Project', an exhibition sited right in O'Connell Street's GPO. It featured collaborative proposals from architects (members of the Architectural Association of Ireland, which has been very active in organizing exhibitions) and sculptors for a new monumental focal point for O'Connell Street that might take the place of Nelson's Pillar. The proposals, many of them genuinely exciting and practicable, are recorded in a handsome book published by Gandon Editions.

Co-incidentally with the Festival, one young sculptor, Liadin Cooke, mounted her first one-person show at the Project Arts Centre. 'Making a Dream' turned out to be a bracingly ambitious, thoroughly individualistic set of linked installations and drawings which treated a core of metaphysical concerns with considerable conceptual skill and resourcefulness. It was easily one of the best one-person shows of the year and Cooke went on to win a GPA Emerging Artists Award.

•

The commercial gallery scene in Dublin has been in a state of relative flux. The Hendriks, which never really got into its stride again after the death of David Hendriks, closed late in 1988, and the event created a shockwave which affected the entire balance of the gallery network. Fortunately, by no means all developments have been negative.

The Kerlin Gallery, which looked from the start a confident newcomer, has convincingly consolidated its position, taking on board such substantial figures as Barrie Cooke (scheduled to have a show there in late spring 1989) and Basil Blackshaw, both longtime exhibitors with the Hendriks. The Kerlin also managed a busy, fairly ambitious exhibitions programme including, for example, a prestigious Stephen McKenna show which, in the event, suggested that he was resting on his laurels rather than seriously stretching himself. Another Kerlin show, by young Northern artist Ross Wilson, in the latter half of October, was one of the year's best. His densely textured, highly charged, mythically cloudy images of animals displayed real power and ingenuity.

Early in 1989, Eve Linders opened a handsome new venue, the Mount Street

Gallery. Her first show featured a vivid series of animal paintings by Margaret MacNamidhe. Nor was that the only development. The Graphic Studio opened a small but propitious gallery behind the Central Bank and in the same part of town, Brid and Gerry Dukes of Limerick's Riverrun acquired a handsome, spacious building on the corner of Parliament Street with the intention of opening a gallery later in 1989. They meanwhile enlisted Eithne Jordan and Michael Cullen, formerly with the Hendriks.

Limerick's Exhibition of Visual Art, which is usually selected from an open submission by a single, invited juror, someone uninvolved in the Irish art scene, came up with an innovation: two jurors, Florent Bex from Holland and Alexander Rozhin, editor of the magazine of the Soviet Artists' Union, who selected separate, complementary shows from the same submission.

There was an overlap in their selection, but one of less than twenty per cent. This is interesting in itself. Two selectors from different backgrounds essentially chose quite different shows from the same body of work, and different prizewinners: Eamonn Coleman (whose potently atmospheric paintings of a kind of modern-mythic industrial underworld were shown *en masse* to great effect in March 1989 in a one-person show at the Mount Street Gallery) and Peter Power, in the case of Bex, and Tom Fitzgerald and T.J. Maher (a good textural abstract painter whose work presents dense, rugged surfaces reminiscent of Tapies or Alberto Burri and a whole strand of modern painting), in the case of Rozhin.

Both judges did, however, select shows of crowded, hectic diversity, following up every line of enquiry, emphasizing the freedom of creative expression. They both tried to let people have their say. There was some very good painting and drawing by, among others, Richard Gorman (a fine Irish painter with terrific colour sense, based in Milan), Jill Dennis, James O'Connor (who held an impressive one-person show at the Taylor Gallery), Andrew Coombes (powerful, apocalyptic drawings of city-scapes), Gwen O'Dowd and William Crozier. In a substantial photographic contingent, Rory Donaldson's ambitious mixed-media composite was notable, as was one of Willie Doherty's photo-texts explor-

LOOKING BACK

ing the ideology of words and landscape. There was, perhaps inevitably given the openness of both selections, a lot of distinctly loose work that gave an impression of being inadequately thought through, contributing to a feeling of muddle.

Dorothy Walker chose the presentation of the GPA Emerging Artists Awards to announce her virtual departure from critical and administrative activity to concentrate on longer term projects. Besides Liadin Cooke, the awards went to Pakki Smith, Patricia Hurl, Locky Morris and Finbar Kelly.

'Clean Irish Sea' at the City Centre, Dublin, in November was a concerted, well chosen group exhibition of work by sixteen artists with clear motivation if slightly uncertain aims. That is, the stated aim was to focus attention on the state of the Irish Sea, one of the dirtiest in the world. The cause was manifestly sound and the co-organizers, the Irish Visual Arts Association and Greenpeace, mounted a creditable show. It has to be said, though, that relatively few people pay much attention to any art event, and there was nothing about this show that would serve to alter that fact. Or maybe this is too cynical a view.

There was a clear sympathy of attitude about the concurrent 'Celtic Vision II' at the Bank of Ireland in Baggot Street, Dublin, a spirited, exuberant show which boasted a great deal of fine painting and which encompassed more artists than the nominal Celtic tag might suggest, including, for example, Albert Irvin, Nick Miller (a young, London-born, Irish resident artist who had a good one-person show earlier in the year at the Project); and no less than Sidney Nolan himself.

Throughout December 1988, a major quite spectacular exhibition of Islamic calligraphy occupied the RHK. Selected and catalogued by David James of the Chester Beatty Library, the show marshalled an incredible richness of sacred and secular Islamic writings, covering a vast geographical spread and about one thousand years. Such exhibitions are particularly useful in that they offer insights into alternative traditions of parallel richness.

In 1988 the Galway Arts Festival got around to doing something long overdue in the Irish art world, that is, staging a retrospective of the work of Brian

Michael Mulcahy, Water Gipsy 4, *1989.*

Bourke. This extensive show, featuring some twenty-five years of paintings, drawing and, latterly, sculpture, also found its way to the RHK in the early part of 1989.

Bourke is a fluent and prolific artist, and he emerged well from the enterprise. His landscapes, particularly, looked often sensational, brilliantly capturing intensities of colour and transient effects of light and shade with great feeling for the spirit of place and an almost palpable love of the physical world. The drawings, notably the many series of portraits, also looked strong.

What of his limitations, his failings? Well, he is wary of large scale work, preferring to cut large spaces down to size with elaborate border patterns. Successful big paintings are rare. His liking for illustrative caricature, taken with his otherwise fruitful habit of working in almost repetitious series, can become wearing. But set against the measure of his achievement, these are minor quibbles. One real regret is that the exhibition budget clearly did not extend to a well-produced, well-illustrated catalogue.

To celebrate the "official", 150th anniversary of the invention of photography, the Gallery of Photography, Dublin, hosted two shows that originated in the extraordinarily productive Ffotogallery Cardiff. 'Regarding Photographic possibility as currently perceived, and 'True Stories and Photofictions' marshalled representative samples of the work of makers of staged or otherwise manipulated photographs.

Exciting in terms of revealing photography's expressive potential, 'Photofict-

ions' was a very entertaining affair as well, from Les Krims's meticulously arranged, dementedly detailed, *kitsch*-crowded *tableaux* to Joel-Peter Witkin's disturbing, eerily surreal images. It also featured the innovative work of two young Scots, Ron O'Donnell and Calum Colvin. Though somewhat lost in the cluttered, limited space of the Gallery of Photography, it was a valuable, consistently challenging exhibition.

One of the highlights of the National Gallery's calendar, the annual showing of the Turner water-colours, was marked this January by the publication of the long-awaited catalogue of the collection, illustrated in colour in a handsome book compiled by Barbara Dawson. The gallery in general battened down the hatches to begin the enormous job of drastic refurbishment.

Julian Campbell's 'Frank O'Meara and his Contemporaries' which opened at Dublin's Municipal Gallery, went on to the Crawford in Cork and then visited the Ulster Museum. It explored the work of the short-lived, sadly none-too-productive Carlow-born artist. O'Meara (1853–1888) was a central figure in the social life of the artist's colony at Grez-sur-Loing in the forest of Fontainbleau. His best known painting, the sweetly melancholic 'Towards Night and Winter', is also his best. He went to Grez as a student and succumbed to its listless charm, for he more or less remained there for the rest of his life, a perpetual student who never fulfilled his considerable potential. Campbell's catalogue is rich in detail, a veritable mine of information, valuably illuminating an important era in Irish art history.

Wexford sculptor, Michael Warren, has carved out quite a substantial reputation for himself with a series of commissions for publicly sited sculptures which have formed a major part of his output since the late 1970s. He has consistently developed his own severe, almost ascetic style, working on an often monumental scale, in wood augmented by steel and iron. A major exhibition of his work at the Douglas Hyde Gallery in January spelled out the parameters of his art.

Although in general appearance his work has many of the hallmarks of mainstream minimalism, Warren's aims quickly diverge from those of minimalist aesthetic. 'Silence and Necessity', a catalogue essay by John Hutchinson,

LOOKING BACK

*Michael Warren, Obelisk of oak, 1987–1988, oak, 505 × 46 × 51 cms.
Collection of the artist. Photograph John Donat, London.*

elucidated Warren's claim to a spiritual dimension to his work. It is certainly true that his great planks of raw wood, cracking and buckling as they dry, often stained with rust from iron or steel frameworks and bolts, read as being representative of titanic energies and, in the combination of their straining upwards and their terrestrial weathering they have a very human poignancy, bespeaking a longing towards transcendence that is given a tragic edge by their tremendous materiality. The concerted effect of these big pieces, with their tightly contained energies, was touching and impressive.

Since Michael Mulcahy began, in the early 1980s, to devote his mercurial energies to painting, he has produced a uniquely exciting body of work. He is very prolific, working in long, impassioned bouts, entirely possessed by the images he makes. His travels – to Australia, Papua New Guinea and most recently to Africa – have always been important, not merely because a change of locale is stimulating but because he is drawn to places and people that embody certain qualities that are central to his art.

His major exhibition at the Douglas Hyde Gallery, which ended in June, comprised his largest, and probably his best paintings to date, inspired by time spent among the Dogon people of Mali in sub-Saharan Africa.

Mulcahy's profligacy has often told against him, his prodigious energies seeming widely dispersed. His new work, however, is marked by its fierce concentration. The paintings are lovingly made, with a determined, sustained intensity. They are the most abstract of his works. Although they employ a small range of distinct, almost calligraphic marks and symbols which are emphatically delineated against surging, liquescent, superheated backgrounds, these signs are ambiguous. They suggest certain things: phallus, vagina, wall, gateway, flower, spear, but they always stop short of commitment to any real representational job. The nett result is a feeling of ethereal freedom. We float freely in the paintings' majestic, celestial spaces. Oddly enough, despite their seething surfaces, they also possess a virtual serenity. They made up what was one of the most spectacular exhibitions of the year.

Aidan Dunne

LOOKING BACK

The past year was very mixed in the quality and range of its exhibitions and art events. By comparison the art year in the Republic of Ireland seemed positively bustling with activity. Particularly in Belfast there was little evidence of enterprise, innovation and risk-taking. The Greater Belfast area is at present badly served by suitable public spaces; arts policy and planned infrastructure stagnates while arts funding especially by the city fathers is curiously idiosyncratic. And it almost seems at times that Derry has adopted U.D.I. and seceded.

At the Fenderesky Art Gallery, Belfast, the early part of 1989 seemed the more rich, David Crone (Jan./Feb.) showed new works where surface interest in the best sense appealed in painterly subtle encrustations and light dark passages. In March Jeremy Henderson's liquid landscapes delighted the eye. Diarmuid Delargy followed with a series of paintings, drawings and etchings. The paintings were Neo-Renaissance (Leonardesque) reworkings in a heightened, shot *sfumato* effect in oranges, yellows and earth reds. They made an uneasy homage to mediterranean visual culture typified by *grandes baigneuses*, nude youths or a reclining Venus. The silence of these lyrical *pastorales* is upset by a small painting of crubeens (also worked as etchings) and tend to hint at some cultural subversion at work. His etchings were as assured as ever and Venus, in particular, slept soundly on her metal plate.

Earlier, in November 1988, Stephen McKenna (exhibited also at the Kerlin Gallery, Dublin, and the Orchard Gallery, Derry, in August '88), showed 'Works on Paper' at the Fenderesky and comparisons with Delargy's changes in direction are inevitable. But while McKenna's paintings have a beautiful neo-classical poise, his drawings at Fenderesky were disappointingly lightweight and plain bad rather than camp bad.

Fenderesky also organized the G.P.A. sponsored 'Ulster Art in the 80's'—a golden jubilee celebration of the Irish Association for cultural, economic and social relations. It was a solid enough exhibition with no selection surprises, but untimely in that it followed so soon after 'Directions Out' (on Northern Art) at the Douglas Hyde held the previous year.

Like Fenderesky, the 'On the Wall' Gallery (now The Kerlin Gallery, Belfast) continued to establish a 'stable' of artists. In Sept. '88 Mark Ainsworth showed his

Diarmuid Delargy, Sleeping Venus, 1988, *etching edition 50.*
Courtesy Fenderesky Gallery, Belfast.

LOOKING BACK

abstract colour imaginings where colour, unfashionably, supports and interacts with colour. Ross Wilson (Nov./Dec.) proceeded to experiment both with ideas and media in his animal motifs. And Simon Reilly's 'No-Thing' exhibition promised more to come.

To trot out Louis le Broquy's 'Heads of Writers' series as an associated Belfast Festival event was more commercial than risk-taking and added nothing to what we already know of this series despite breaking the Irish mist with Shakespeare. Both Fenderesky and Kerlin combined to take part in the Cologne Art Fair in November 1988. The visit was supported by the Arts Council of Northern Ireland, the Department of Foreign Affairs (Republic of Ireland) and Aer Lingus. Some twelve artists from Ireland were represented.

The knock-on effect of the sculptural conference and related activities in Dublin provided us with 'The New North' exhibition of sculpture organized by the Corridor Gallery in Lurgan. Sounding like a policy statement from the S.D.L.P., it tended to show the paucity of good sculpture in the North (as compared to the south) and failed to sustain a belief in any substantial body of work emerging. The Corridor Gallery, however, has to be admired for putting on an exhibition programme on a shoestring budget.

The Peacock Gallery in Craigavon in July/Aug. took 'The Birches', new photoworks by Victor Sloan, an exhibition initiated by the Octagon Gallery, Belfast, in June that year. In his exhibition, the artist applied his now familiar overlay technique to explore the landscape of rural Ulster—landmined as it is with relics of history, religion and conflict. An apparently beautiful and peaceful region of small farmhouses near Portadown, 'The Birches', like other areas of Ulster, has deep traces laid down that Victor Sloan brought to the surface.

Like the Peacock Gallery, the Flowerfield Art Centre in Portstewart hosted Arts Council of Northern Ireland touring exhibitions—'Lilies among the Hats', recent acquisitions by A.C.N.I., and 'Rendez-Vous with Nature' dealing with landscape.

Back in Belfast, Art Advice Gallery in September '88 showed the work of Gerry Gleason, who also declared his dexterity in the 'New North' sculpture show. Fin-

John Aiken, Torres Vedras, 1988. Courtesy Octagon Gallery, Belfast.

bar Kelly, a G.P.A. Emerging Artists prizewinner in 1988, showed in November, followed by Philip Blythe with his illustrations in 'American Travel Diary'.

In nearby Shaftesbury Square, Jenny Holzer (Dec. '88) beamed her slogans and messages as a public screen work. One reminded us that 'Your Oldest Fears Are The Worst Ones'. Anne Carlisle (formerly of CIRCA magazine and now living in Wales), also festooned Piccadilly Circus in 1988 with her variations on the cultural deployment of the Union Jack.

As part of its efforts to take art out of the gallery and into the community, the Octagon Gallery, Belfast, collaborated with John Kindness on 'NEWSPRINT'. For two weeks in June '88 the Belfast artist made a daily response to the Northern Ireland news in the form of a screen printed image. These 'prints' were then despatched to fifty sites throughout the province and clamped into sandwich boards, the way that news headlines are displayed to the public. The stories covered by Kindness ranged from the shooting down of an army helicopter to a survey by school children on the amount of dogs' dirt on the streets of their seaside town. The prints were made in full public view at the Octagon where an exhibition accumulated as the event progressed.

Dorothy Cross and Vivienne Roche had their first showings in the North at the Octagon, while 'Based In Berlin' included the work of two young Irish artists working in that city. The gallery also

brought in from Paris work by Sheila Hicks and Cristina Rubalcava. Hicks came with a considerable international reputation to show her work as part of the Belfast Festival at Queen's. As part of the exhibition the artist constructed especially for the gallery space a 'Textile' wall which was created by an ingenious use of pillow cases knotted together with natural linen.

Cristina Rubalcava, a Paris-based Mexican artist and General Secretary of the International Association of Artists (UNESCO, Paris) showed five large canvases—figurative erotic works loaded with Latin American panache and humour. The artist also gave a public lecture about her work.

The Octagon also shared 'Ocean's Edge' with the Arts Council Gallery, in Belfast. This new sculptural work by John Aiken was seen at the Douglas Hyde Gallery, Dublin in May/June '88 and came to Belfast during Oct./Nov. Aiken's use of geometrical grids persisted from his former sand bar installations of the early 1980s. But his work is now less sytematic and finds new relationships with the organic nature of stone. The materials were stone, steel and wood—cool, elegant mixtures and compounds of materials. Assemblages of creamy purbeck stones were incised, marked and often arranged in wooden/steel devices. In the work entitled 'Return', a wall piece in purbeck marble and steel, we saw the impregnation of marble by steel, wedged gasket tight: a synthetic implant.

Among other exhibitors at the Arts Council Gallery during the year were Lance Wright and Richard Hamilton. Hamilton's illustrations of Joyce's *Ulysses* spanned the years 1948–88. During that time he made a series of works, drawings, paintings and prints based on episodes from Joyce's book. I visited this exhibition entitled 'Work in Progress' expecting a substantial body of work, only to find many of the works tentative sketches searching out but not substantiating an *oeuvre*. Nevertheless, individual works stood out; I still think 'Finn MacCool' ('Maze Hunger Strike'), a photogravure, aquatint and engraving of 1983, a very powerful and evocative image.

The exhibition was organized by Declan McGonagle and first shown at the Orchard Gallery in Derry where the director continued his impressive programme of exhibitions, public artworks

LOOKING BACK

Sheila Hicks, Nuages Blanc, *1988, textile wall, installation.*
Courtesy Octagon Gallery, Belfast.

and publishing. The total output is conceived within the spirit of the gallery director as *auteur* and *metteur-en-scene*—his ongoing theme being politically and socially engaged art.

McGonagle invites artists to respond in one way or another to a location—the city, the place. In this way Edgar Heap of Birds, a North American Indian, was invited (during the N.W. Arts Festival) to show his photographs and drawings as well as to work in the city; as was Michael Peel by way of his posterworks.

The Orchard Gallery space held exhibitions often in collaboration with other U.K. and European galleries. These included exhibitions of Bernard Prinz (Germany), Imants Tillers (Australia) and Glenys Johnson and Terry Atkinson (England).

The Armada Exhibition at the Ulster Museum ran from October 1988 to January 1989, and clearly the expense involved must have curtailed their programme for the visual arts. The

Ireland-German Exchange Exhibition was their only large offering. Like all work selected by committees (albeit a small committee, in this case: Sean McCrum, Anya Von Grösseln, Klaus Honnef) it was something of a mixture but certainly reached some complementarity in the balance of works selected from the two countries. Among the expressionist/figurative/painterly concerns of artists like David Crone, Andrew Coombes and Michael Mulcahy in the Irish selection, Willie Doherty (photographic conceptualism) and Micky Donnelly (symbol searching) stood out. The German selection erred more on the photographic side with works by Axel Hütte, Jurgen Klanke and Thomas Smith. The exhibition was housed in two rooms; works in the smaller room suffered greatly from a variety of wall coverings designed more for salon painting.

Andrew Coombes and David Crone were also included in the opening exhibition (July/Aug. '88), called 'The

Expressive Image', at the new Narrow Water Gallery, Warrenpoint. This non-profit making space is housed in the Narrow Water castle basement. Their programme proceeded with student work from the Faculty of Art and Design, Belfast; Chris Wilson (collage drawings), Hazel Neil and Debbie Coombes (photography); and contemporary crafts.

In November they staged recent paintings, prints and sculpture by Paul Neagu which proved a rich showing.

It is important that challenging exhibitions come into Ireland and Irish art gets out and about abroad. And while the smaller spaces in N. Ireland are attempting to bring in international artists, Belfast clearly needs a much larger gallery space to accommodate the larger thematic and avant-garde exhibitions. And not just to receive them but to initiate and curate them as well.

Liam Kelly

GARDEN STATUARY IN IRELAND

The use of statuary as a decoration in gardens, common in ancient Rome, was revived during the Italian Renaissance. A garden in the Renaissance style is first recorded in Ireland at Youghal[1] where, at the beginning of the seventeenth century, the Great Earl of Cork laid out a formal terrace garden with fountain. However, no statuary is recorded although there is likely to have been some, nor is it recorded in the garden at Lismore Castle[2] to which he later moved. The first firm evidence of statuary in an Irish garden that has yet been discovered is in 1664 when a fountain, in the form of a Triton[3] and shell with water spilling from his mouth, is recorded at Kilkenny Castle, the seat of the Duke of Ormonde. The Triton, a minor sea-god represented as a man with a fish's tail

*The architect, garden designer and author, **Patrick Bowe**, traces the history of the use of statuary in Irish gardens and draws attention to the best collections, some of which are still intact.*

carrying a shell trumpet, is a classic fountain figure-type in the European garden tradition.

The Duke had been in exile at the court of Louis XIV at Versailles with the future Charles II. When the latter was restored to the throne of England in 1660, the Duke became the Viceroy of Ireland. His experience of the gardens of Versailles influenced his laying out of an elaborate garden at Kilkenny Castle on his return to Ireland. His contract with a London

statuary maker, John Bonnier, to copy in lead four pieces—Diana, The Sabine Women, Hercules, and Commodus and Antoninous (sic)—which stood in the King's Privy Garden in London—is dated 1689. A clause in the contract stipulated that the Duke, or his wife, could require Bonnier to provide at no extra cost, "draperies for the privy parts" of the figures, should they desire them. In addition, they ordered the figures of sixteen Cupids, emblems of The Four Seasons, and The Twelve Signs of the Zodiac, all in lead.[4] Much of this statuary may have been ordered for The Lead Terrace on the west front of the castle, which was replaced by the present terrace in the nineteenth century.

In the eighteenth century it was a common desire to have good copies rather

Powerscourt, Co. Wicklow. An overall view of the garden after completion with its maker, 7th Viscount Powerscourt standing in the middle. Flanking the steps in the foreground are, on the left, a copy of Diana the Huntress, the original of which is now in the Louvre, Paris, and, on the right, a copy of the Apollo Belvedere, the original of which is in the Vatican Museum.

GARDEN STATUARY IN IRELAND

than original work by contemporary sculptors as explained in a letter from Lisson to Lord Molesworth who, in 1721, was laying out a garden at Brackenstown, Co. Dublin:

> It is of them (statues) as of pictures that good copies are better than scurvy originals. 500ᵗᵗ would go but a little way if such were made by the best hands here, besides which, freight would mount very high; whereas there are very many tolerable things to be purchased at Hyde-park corner (the John Cheere workshops), near at hand, and of which the very lead will yield something in case the figures chance to be spoiled. I remember some Niches at the corners of the walls in the parterre: if Yr. Ld. intend to place any statues there, I suppose they will be Fauns and Satyrs or at least some of those Pastoral figures of Shepherds and Shepherdesses which I see in the road to Hyde-Park; the same will also fit the centres of the wilderness, for I not know whether any Dii Terminii are to be had ready made.[5]

He also thought a Venus would do well for the centre of a grass plot.

Accounts of early eighteenth century Irish gardens provide many references to such copies from original statues. The gardens at Garryhunden, Co. Carlow,[6] and at Doneraile, Co. Cork,[7] boasted figures of a gladiator, copied from one at Hampton Court Palace, near London, which was in turn a copy of The Borghese Gladiator (now in the Louvre). Copies of Giambologna's Mercury (now in the Bargello Museum, Florence), that perennial subject for garden statuary, survive on the domed rotunda which remains of the great formal garden which was laid out at Dromoland Castle, Co. Clare, and on top of a column at Furness, Co. Kildare, which was recently transferred from the derelict demesne at Dangan, Co. Meath. The latter must have had one of the best collections of the early eighteenth century. Mrs. Delany, that eagle-eyed chronicler of Irish eighteenth-century life, records her visit there in 1749:

> In his garden there is a fir-grove dedicated to Vesta, in the midst of which is her statue; at some distance from it is a mound covered with evergreens, on which is placed a Temple with the statues of Apollo, Neptune, Proserpine, Diana, all have honours paid to them and Fame has been too good a friend to the mentor of all these improvements to be neglected; her Temple is near the house, at the end of the terrace

near where The Four Seasons take their stand, very well represented by Flora, Ceres, Bacchus and an old gentleman with a hood on his head, warming his hands over a fire.[8]

Those not versed in the sculptural themes of the classical world often misunderstood them, Protestants in particular, sometimes suspecting their Roman origin. The Earl of Orrery, who was making a garden at Caledon, Co. Tyrone, wrote to a friend in 1747 after he had placed a statue of Diana in his woods:

> To tell you the truth, my tenants have a notion that I am atheistically inclined, by putting up heathen statues and writing upon them certain words in an unknown language. They immediately suspected me for a papist, and my statuary had been demolished, my woods burnt and my throat cut had I not suddenly placed a seat under a holly bush with this plain inscription, SIT DOWN AND WELCOME. I have assured them that all the Latin mottos are to this purpose, and that in places where they cannot sit down, I have desired them in the old Norman dialect, to go to the lodge and drink whiskey.[9]

He may have exaggerated the situation for dramatic effect in the letter to his friend, for at least some of the offending statues were still there in 1794 when they were described in O'Connor's journal:

> On the banks of the River Blackwater in a sort of sloping Green, the Statue of Minerva, having her right brest bare . . . she stands on a pediment on which rests opposite to her right knee her shield on which is portrayed the head of Medusa with her wide tongue outdropping saliva, a thick Roman nose, a flat haggard complexion, lank cheeks marked with furrows, large terrible eyes, as if staring out of their sockets—makes (sic) I thought the sight would petrify me.[10]

This kind of statuary was invariably imported either by a garden-owner himself or through a mason's yard. An advertisement which appeared in the *Munster Journal* on the 5th February 1750 proclaimed the financial advantage of the latter:

> Just imported from London, by John Daly, Marble-Mason, a large quantity of Ornaments of Stone and Lead, such as Statues, Urns, Flower-potts, Vases, Pines, Lions, Eagles, Foxes, Hares, Rabbets and Sun-Dial Pedestals, which goods he will sell cheaper than any gentleman can import.

Figurative statuary was too small in

scale to act on its own as a focal point in the big landscape parks which were being created in the latter half of the eighteenth century. Statuary bought or commissioned during that period was intended as an adjunct of a bigger architectural focal point—temple, folly or grotto. The shell grotto at Curraghmore, Co. Waterford, for example, contains a marble statue of Lady Tyrone in flowing garments, holding a shell, which was sculpted by John van Nost the Younger.[11] The Casino at Marino, Co. Dublin,[12] boasted lions *couchants* sculpted by Joseph Wilton and based on the lions in the Villa Borghese in Rome. The gates to Castletown House, Co. Kildare, were crowned with sphinxes taken from a design in Sir William Chambers's *A Treatise on Civil Architecture* (1759) for which Lady Louisa Conolly paid John Coates of Maynooth £16 18s. 6d. according to a bill still preserved in the house.[13] In 1772, the future Lord Aldborough was erecting a "Temple with little Mercury" at Belan, Co. Kildare. Contrary to the prevailing trend, however, he seems still to have been using isolated statuary figures as focal points in his garden for in the same year he was arranging for the cartage of a statue of Hercules with some difficulty. (This was probably a copy of the Farnese Hercules, now in the National Museum, Naples. It has been frequently erected in gardens throughout Europe.) In 1792, he recorded in his diary the purchase in a statuary yard in London of a "Diana and Vertumnus in marble for 10 guineas."[14] (The god Vertumnus was connected by the ancient Romans with the growth of plants and so his figure was often chosen as a decoration for gardens).

The above examples should not be taken as the norm, however, for most garden owners eschewed the use of statuary in their gardens on account of the difficulty in harmonizing its frankly artificial aspect with the beautiful, natural appearance of much of the countryside. This difficulty found expression in Joseph Cooper Walker's *Essay on the Rise and Progress of Gardening in Ireland*, published in 1791, where he criticized the over-use of statuary in gardens in the past:

> Thus did our ancestors, governed by the false taste which they imbibed from the English, disfigure with unsuitable ornaments, the simple garb of nature.[15]

GARDEN STATUARY IN IRELAND

The revival in popularity of formal gardens in the first half of the nineteenth century, however, paved the way for a renewal of interest in statuary to decorate it. Two Irish collectors were buying statuary not from London but direct from Rome, the Lords Cloncurry and Powerscourt. Both enterprises were unfortunately tainted with disaster. Lord Cloncurry, who had been forced into exile because of his support for the United Irishmen, lived in Rome from 1803 to 1805, when he assembled a major collection of statuary.[16] Sadly, much of it was lost when the ship carrying it went down in Dublin Bay. Some pieces on another shipment did arrive, including a tall column which now sits in the centre of the parterre at Lyons, Co. Kildare, with a figure of Venus on top. Lord Powerscourt purchased copies of the Apollo Belvedere and the Laocoon (both in the Vatican Museum) and of Diana the Huntress (now in the Louvre) when

Powerscourt, Co. Wicklow. The winged figure of Fame *commissioned from Professor Hagen of Berlin in 1866.*

he was in Rome on his Grand Tour. Although the statuary arrived home, he himself died in France during his return journey in 1844. (The statuary lay in packing cases at Powerscourt until his son came of age and had it erected on the upper terrace of the garden where it stands to this day).[17]

Three great collections were made in the latter half of the nineteenth century—at St. Anne's, Clontarf, Co. Dublin, Kilruddery, Co. Wicklow, and Powerscourt, Co. Wicklow, the latter two being extant. St. Anne's, the estate of Lord Ardilaun, had a statue walk and included among its pieces a copy of G.L. Bernini's Jupiter and Thetis.[18] His passion for the antique found further expression in the construction at St. Anne's of a replica of a Roman house excavated at Herculanaeum, near Naples (furnished with a full-sized bronze figure of a soldier, also unearthed in the excavations) and nearby, a replica of the

Powerscourt, Co. Wicklow. The winged figures of Pegasus cast in zinc by Professor Hagen of Berlin which are now painted to look like bronze. In the centre is the fountain designed by Lawrence Macdonald and cast in cement by Sir Thomas Farrell of Dublin. The design is based on Bernini's triton fountain in the Piazza Barberini in Rome.

famous Roman tomb of the Julii, surviving at St. Rémy in the south of France.

The collection of garden statuary at Kilruddery divides itself into that displayed in the conservatory, once indeed known as The Statue Gallery, and that in the gardens which is mainly of cast iron from the great European manufacturers of the nineteenth century, Kohl of Potsdam, Geiss of Berne and Barbezat of Seine-et-Oise.[19]

The finest collection is at Powerscourt, assembled by the 7th Viscount who followed in his father's footsteps by buying and commissioning pieces in Rome. He commissioned Lawrence MacDonald, a sculptor living in the Piazza Barberini in Rome, to make a plaster copy of Bernini's Triton Fountain in the middle of that square. This he had remodelled in cement by Sir Thomas Farrell the Dublin craftsman, and placed in the centre of the pond at Powerscourt. Likewise, he commissioned Alexander MacDonald, also living in Rome, to design two large plaster groups representing Hercules and Antaeus, and Ajax with the body of Patroclus which were then remodelled in Portland stone by Mr. Kirk in Dublin. He also bought copies of busts of Michel-

Powerscourt, Co. Wicklow. Thomas Kirk, Ajax with the body of Patroclus. Photograph George Mott.

angelo, Leonardo da Vinci, Benvenuto Cellini and Raphael, then in the Vatican Museum. However, wherever he travelled, he bought souvenir sculpture for his garden. Thus, on his visit to Naples in 1883, he purchased copies in bronze of The Sitting Mercury (of which there is also a stone copy at Fota, Co. Cork) and The Sleeping Faun, which had been unearthed during the excavations at Herculanaeum and are now in the National Museum in Naples. From his visit to Berlin in 1866 came figures of Fame and Victory, and the great figures of *pegasi* by the pond which were all commissioned from Professor Hagen. From France came a group of bronze *putti* by Joseph Marin, a sculptor employed by Louis XV, and urns and vases in bronze, copies of originals in the gardens of Versailles. The most important pieces in the gardens were also bought in Paris where they were for sale after the Palais Royal, the residence of Napoleon III's nephew, Prince Jérome-Napoleon, had been burned down by the communards at the end of The Franco-Prussian War. Figures of Aeolus, the god of the wind, they had originally been in the Duke of Litta's great garden, the Villa Arese,

Kilruddery, Co. Wicklow. The Conservatory, formerly called the Statue Gallery.

north of Milan. When Prince Jérome-Napoleon had them erected in Paris he had them connected to a gas main so that they breathed fire and water spouted from under their arms![20] Although some pieces have been sold in recent years, including The Italian Shepherd Boy by the Irish sculptor, John Hogan, the collection remains substantially intact.

Apart from these three great collections, most Victorian gardens of any size had some statuary. At Killakee, Co. Dublin,[21] there was a bronze fountain of Nepture, in his car of shells drawn by sea horses, on the main terrace. There were figures of Venus and Diana, Sappho and Flora on other terraces. The whiskey magnate, Sir James Power had figures of Terpsichore (perhaps a copy of the Farnese Flora in Naples), Ceres (the Mattei Ceres in the Vatican was the one usually copied for gardens) and Cupid in his garden at Edermine, Co. Wexford.[22] The Gerrard family of Gibbstown Park, Co. Meath, on the other hand, had a great urn with relief carving representing Night and Day (after Thorvaldsen) in the middle of their garden.[23] (It now stands outside the premises of the Royal Dublin Society in Ballsbridge, Dublin).

Kilruddery, Co. Wicklow. Winged Putti *supporting a vase cast in iron by Kahl of Potsdam, Germany.*

Apart from the taste for copies of antique statuary, new themes for garden sculpture were emerging, particularly in the mass-produced lines of cast-iron statuary displayed at the Great Industrial Exhibitions of the second half of the nineteenth century. The gardens of the Dublin International Exhibition (1863) were decorated with figures representing The Goddesses of the Arts and Industries holding torches aloft.[24] The 4th Marquis of Waterford had a fountain with representations of the same goddesses which he bought at the Paris Exhibition (1867) erected at Curraghmore, Co. Waterford. Sadly, it was sold by his son for scrap as on a windy day its central jet showered the windows of the house with water.[25] Statuary on a more sentimental theme was also popular. Alderman Roe, another distiller, had a fountain with cast-iron herons standing looking, we are told, as if they had "apparently invidious designs on the goldfish in the basin".[26] *Putti* groups were frequent. Examples were in the gardens at Headfort, Co. Meath,[27] Castle Blayney, Co. Monaghan,[28] Palmerstown, Co. Kildare,[29] Johnstown Castle, Co. Wexford[30] and many others. Commem-

Kilakee, Co. Dublin. The Neptune fountain depicting the sea-god holding his trident and sitting in his shell-chariot.

GARDEN STATUARY IN IRELAND

Curraghmore, Co. Waterford. The cast-iron fountain representing the goddesses of the arts and industries bought by the fourth Marquis of Waterford at the Paris exhibition of 1867.

orative statuary also began to appear with increasing frequency in public parks but that is outside the scope of this article.

The opening of the twentieth century saw a much more cosmopolitan approach to garden statuary, particularly with regard to statuary from the Far East. The only nineteenth century use of Far Eastern statuary in an Irish garden was at Powerscourt where one of the terraces had a Hindu figure in soapstone, representing the two aspects of Parvati, the consort of Shiva (now in the Victoria and Albert Museum, London). The opening up to visitors of Japan, and the Japan-British Exhibition in London in 1910 provided opportunities for many garden-owners to buy pieces. For the Japanese garden at Tully, Co. Kildare, a boat was chartered to bring back from Japan to Ireland not only trees, shrubs and bonsai, but also lanterns and a tiny model village carved in Fujiyama lava.[31] Sadly, another boat was later chartered to take away from Ireland a collection of garden statuary which had been assembled at Garnish Island, Co. Cork,[32] but which was sold due to a change in the owner's circumstances. Some sitting Buddhas and Chinese Dogs of Fo, however, remain in this outstanding garden.

The Dublin international exhibition, 1865. The cast-iron fountain displayed by Barbezat et Cie., Seine et Oise, France.

Formal, compartmented gardens, conceived as a series of outdoor 'rooms' became a popular approach to garden design in the 1920s and statuary was needed by way of furniture for these 'rooms'. The new garden at Castletown Cox, Co. Kilkenny, had statuary import-

ed from Clearwell Court, Gloucestershire.[33] That laid out at Heywood, Co. Laois,[34] to the designs of Sir Edwin Lutyens, had a figure of a woman holding an infant by the Irish sculptor, John Hughes. The new material, concrete, was used by the local craftsman, Thomas Beattie, to make for Lady Londonderry at Mount Stewart, Co. Down, a riotous assembly of gnomes and gryphons, cats and kittens, dogs and dodos, horses and hedgehogs, a baboon, rabbits, squirrels, a crocodile and much else besides.[35]

In recent years, the centuries-old tradition of using statuary of Italian origin has continued. The late John Hunt, the mediaevalist, had a figure by or after Bernini in his garden at Drumleck, Co. Dublin.[36] Busts of Roman Emperors and Italian bucolic figures were imported for the garden at Glenveagh Castle, Co. Tyrone.[37] Painted lead figures from the Italian *Commedia dell'Arte* feature in the garden at Mount Congreve, Co. Waterford.[38] But there has also been a welcome development in the use of contemporary abstract sculpture as a focal point in the garden. That, however, lies outside the scope of this article.

Patrick Bowe

NOTES

1. A.B. Grosart (Ed.), *The Lismore Papers*, London, 1868-8, Vol. 1, (1613) p. 50, (1615) p. 98, (1617), p. 146, (1619), p. 243.
2. Ibid., Vol. IV, p. 121, p. 185, p. 206, p. 218.
3. Bodleian Library, Oxford, Carte Ms. 220 f. 102.
4. C. Litton Falkiner (Ed.), *Calendar of Ormonde Mss.*, London, Vol. VI, 1911, p. 150, p. 169, p. 282-3, p. 292, p. 465.
5. PRONI (Belfast) MS. D 638/82/2. John Cheere was the chief producer of lead statuary in England at the time, exporting even to Portugal. Fauns, rural deities with horns and a tail, and Satyrs, woodland deities with horse's ears and tail have always been regarded as appropriate subjects for garden statues. The writer of the letter seems to have been confused as to the correct use of Dii Termini, or herm or term figures which, being carved on one side only, were designed to terminate a vista, not occupy the centre of it.
6. William R. Chetwood, *A Tour through Ireland*, 1748, p. 208.
7. James Grove White, *Historical and Topographical Notes on Buttevant etc.*, Vol. 3, Cork, 1913-4, p. 20. Philip Luckombe, *A Tour of Ireland*, London, 1780, p. 181.

8. Llanover (Ed.), *The Autobiography and Correspondence of Mary Granville, Mrs. Delany, Vol I*, 1861, pp. 406-7. Vesta was the goddess of the hearth in ancient Rome.
9. Orrery Papers, Houghton Library, Harvard College, Ms. Eng. 218.2, Vol. 5 p. 7.
10. Trinity College, Dublin, Ms. 539.
11. Edward Malins and the Knight of Glin, *Lost Demesnes*, London, 1976, p. 41.
12. Ibid., p. 141.
13. Ibid., p. 64.
14. Diary quoted by Ethel M. Richardson, *Long-Forgotten Days*, London, 1928, pp. 297-300.
15. J. Cooper Walker, *Essay on the Rise and Progress of Gardening in Ireland*, Dublin, 1791.
16. Cloncurry, *Personal Recollections of the Life and Times, with extracts from the correspondence of Valentine, Lord Cloncurry*, 2nd ed., 1850.
17. Viscount Powerscourt, *A Description and History of Powerscourt*, 1903.
18. *The Irish Farmer's Gazette*, 1864, p. 389; *The Gardeners' Chronicle*, 1873, p. 46 and p. 77.
19. John Cornforth and the Knight of Glin, 'Kilruddery, Co. Wicklow', *Country Life*, London, July 14, 1977, p. 78.
20. Viscount Powerscourt, op. cit.
21. William Robinson, *The Gardeners' Chronicle*, 1864, p. 1179.

22. Thomas Lacy, *Sights and Scenes in the Fatherland*, London, 1863, p. 472.
23. *The Gardeners' Chronicle*, 1884, p. 459.
24. 'An Ornamental Plan for the arrangement of the Dublin Crystal Palace Garden', *The Irish Farmer's Gazette*, 1863, p. 405.
25. Correspondence with the present owner.
26. *The Irish Farmer's Gazette*, 1862, p. 243.
27. Lawrence Photographic Collection, National Library of Ireland.
28. Ibid.
29. Ibid.
30. Edward Malins and Patrick Bowe, *Irish Gardens and Demesnes from 1830*, London and New York, 1980, p. 55.
31. Ibid. p. 150.
32. Ibid. p. 98.
33. Ibid. p. 159.
34. A.S.G. Butler, *The Architecture of Sir Edwin Lutyens*, London, 1950.
35. The Marchioness of Londonderry, *Guide to Mount Stewart*, January, 1956.
36. Correspondence with the late John Hunt.
37. Edward Malins and Patrick Bowe, op. cit., p. 170.
38. Michael George and Patrick Bowe, *The Gardens of Ireland*, New York and London, 1986, p. 56.

SIR CHARLES LANYON

One hundred years ago on 31st May, 1889, Sir Charles Lanyon, the most important architect of his generation in Ireland, died at his home near Belfast. There have been numerous scattered references to Lanyon in various publications over the years but no full account of his life and career, listing all his buildings, has ever been published.[1] Centenary occasions often seem to provide the spur to reassessment of persons who have been somehow neglected or, as may apply in this case, merely taken for granted. Thus, while this is not the place to try to redress the whole balance for Lanyon, the time may be considered opportune in this the centenary year of his death, to give some brief account of his career and some of his works.

Lanyon was born on 6th January, 1813, at Eastbourne, in Sussex, on the south coast of England, the third son of John Jenkinson Lanyon and his wife, Catherine Anne Mortimer. We know nothing of his early years except that he was educated at a private school in Eastbourne, and then was articled to Jacob Owen of the Irish Board of Works in preparation for the profession of civil engineer. The next thing we know is that he took second place in the first examination for Irish county surveyorships in 1835. Owen, however, was only appointed as principal engineer and architect to the Board of Works in Dublin in May 1832. To have had an adequate period of training, Lanyon must have started his apprenticeship a couple of years before that. It would seem likely, therefore, that Lanyon was actually first articled in Portsmouth where Owen had been Clerk of Works to the Royal Engineers Department, and then moved to Dublin with his master. Lanyon's father had been a Royal Naval purser and so Portsmouth, the south-coast home of a great naval dockyard, would have been an understandable choice for an office for his son.

Following his success in the Dublin examination, Lanyon was appointed to the county surveyorship of Kildare in 1835, but it was not long before the surveyorship of County Antrim became available, on the resignation of John Woodhouse. Lanyon sought a transfer northwards and was duly appointed to the Antrim post in 1836. He first appears in the capacity of County Surveyor of Antrim in October that year when, from an office in Donegall Street, Belfast, he

In this, the centenary year of Sir Charles Lanyon's death, **Dr. Paul Larmour,** who is preparing a fully illustrated book on that great Victorian architect, here tells something of his life and works, with particular regard to his early career.

Portrait of Charles Lanyon.
Artist not recorded.
The Queen's University of Belfast.

gave notice in the press of his intention to visit several baronies that winter prior to the Special Sessions. Incidentally, it has often been assumed that Lanyon first married the boss's daughter before getting the County Antrim appointment, but his marriage to Elizabeth Helen Owen did not take place until 2nd February, 1837. This is, of course, no more than a minor point of fact, and is not to deny that Lanyon's career was probably advanced by his close relationship with the Owen family.

Right from his first arrival in Belfast, Lanyon displayed the business-like approach to professional affairs that was to be the hallmark of his twenty-five years as County Surveyor. John Woodhouse, working alone, had found the post so onerous that he had been quickly tempted away to a railway engineering position in England. Lanyon, however, met the task head on. He successfully made a case

for the appointment of baronial assistants to ease the burden on himself and was soon involved in making all parts of the county accessible by road. Road-making and bridge-building formed a great part of his responsibilities over the years, the execution, by 1842, of William Bald's scheme for the Antrim coast road from Larne to Ballycastle being one of his great achievements in that field. As a road-maker in his own right he was responsible for the series of cross-routes, mainly between the coast road and the mail-coach road from Antrim to Ballymoney. It was due to his persuasiveness, too, that the particularly scenic route that was to be cut around Dunluce Castle was the one adopted in 1844. We can also credit him with what is probably the most unusual feature in the whole road network, the two stretches laid over the bog in 1839–40 at an area known as the Frosses, north of Ballymena, where stability was ensured by planting the raised edges of the road with avenues of Scots Pine trees.

Of the many bridges which he designed as County Surveyor the most notable was also his first. That was the tall, triple-arched viaduct which carries the road from Cushendun to Ballycastle over the Glendun River. Lanyon was only twenty-four years of age when it was started in the summer of 1837. It is an impressive testimony to his youthful ability.

Although traditionally credited with the design of the originally very handsome Queen's Bridge in Belfast, Lanyon was only responsible for its execution. In 1836 the surveyors of Antrim and Down were jointly required to draw up plans for a new bridge to link their two counties over the River Lagan. The design was prepared by Woodhouse, Lanyon's predecessor, and although Lanyon drew up an alternative version in 1840, it was Woodhouse's scheme which was built. Lanyon did, however, provide the design for the Ormeau Bridge in 1860, another joint Antrim-Down affair, and the last significant work of his county post.

The surveyorship also entailed some purely architectural work in connection with court-houses and gaols. Lanyon's first known building was Ballymoney Court-house for which tenders were invited in June 1837. It is a very plain building, entirely symmetrical with a two-storey three-bay block rising from the centre of a five-bay single-storey, the

The central hall at Drenagh, Limavady, Co. Londonderry, c. 1837.

Glendun Viaduct, near Cushendun, Co. Antrim, 1837–9.

only ornament being the Greek key pattern cut into the lintel of the doorway. It is a modest building, very late Georgian in character, and appropriate for a small town of no pretension. How different the treatment and scale at the County Court-house in Belfast a decade later, or indeed at Ballymena Court-house in 1845, but by then Lanyon was an established designer.

The first really large building of Lanyon's career, and carried out in his capacity as County Surveyor, was the new gaol in Belfast, erected in 1843-5, the contractors being Williams and Sons of Dublin. Lanyon was directed to prepare plans for it in August 1840, and he was able to report that task done by spring the next year. It was possibly a more significant building than has yet been realized. It was laid out on the separate system so strongly recommended in reports of Inspectors General of Prisons in England. Its layout was similar to that of the model prison then being built at Pentonville in London and, in fact, Lanyon made a visit to Pentonville in the spring of 1841. That was after his own plans had been drawn, yet the result of the trip was only a minor change to some detail. Stylistically, the gaol on Crumlin Road represents an important moment in Lanyon's development. It ushered in that really vigorous Italian Renaissance Revivalism that was to be the most interesting of all his many modes of working.

At the same time as he was tending to his official duties, Lanyon was building up a private practice which, in time, with the help of partners (first William Henry Lynn from 1854 and later his own son, John, from 1860), was to become very extensive with work carried out in most counties of Ireland. His private practice started early and seems to have developed without any objections from his county masters. There were two early houses, both built over the county border, in County Londonderry. They are Drenagh (or Fruithill as it was then) at Limavady, (reputedly dating from 1837), a really fine house with a superb central hall, and Laurel Hill House of 1841–3 at Coleraine. There were also two manor court-houses, at Larne (no longer standing) and Glenarm, both of 1838; they could have been considered rather appropriate private works. Likewise there could hardly have been any objections to Lanyon designing the series of

SIR CHARLES LANYON

small churches built between 1839 and 1843 for the Church Accommodation Society of the Church of Ireland. The Society had been set up at the close of 1838 to help provide churches in areas where there was a need in the Dioceses of Down and Connor, and Lanyon had offered his services as architect free. This was a gesture which no doubt endeared him to many important and influential people, and it is no surprise that in subsequent years he was employed to design houses for some of those connected with the Society. So long as Lanyon's county duties were carried out in an efficient and business-like manner, there was clearly no ground for objecting to him building up a private practice and indeed a number of members of the Antrim Grand Jury itself were to employ him for country house and other works during the 1840s.

The range of work carried out by Lanyon in his private practice in this early period covering the 1830s and '40s was very wide. There were churches, banks, country houses, institutional buildings, public buildings, school-houses, fever hospitals, colleges, railway lines and stations, speculative housing and some commercial work. There was also surveying and engineering. It is clear that Lanyon must have had great organizational abilities and we have to admire his versatility and business capacity, while accepting that he could hardly have got through the work unaided.

Robert Young, who joined Lanyon as an apprentice in 1841 and left around 1849, having become his chief assistant, has, in his unpublished *Recollections* written in 1906, left us the only account we have of Lanyon's office and staff in the early years. Apart from five other office boys already there when Young joined, we learn from him of Daniel Hanna who was in charge of surveying, engineering and road-making, and of Thomas Turner, who came from Dublin to manage the office as regards architectural work. How much, if any, responsibility for design Turner's position entailed we know not, but an indication of the rather junior nature of his position at that stage is provided by Young's revelation that, when Lanyon needed urgent help to get out the elevations and sections of the gaol in Belfast (for which only plans had been drawn), he brought over from England an experienced man, his brother-in-law,

Raloo Church of Ireland, Glenoe, Co. Antrim, 1840–2.

Trinity Church of Ireland, Kircubbin, Co. Down, 1843.

Thomas Owen, to take charge of the matter. We learn too that Young's role in the office was very much that of engineer on roads and bridges and railway work although he was later to practice on his own as both an architect and engineer.

Particularly valuable is the picture Young gives us of Lanyon himself. Recalling the moment in 1841 when he was first ushered into Lanyon's private office, Young writes of his great surprise at finding him "so much younger than I expected, both tall and with the decidedly good looks of a well educated gentleman", and further refers to Lanyon's appearance and manners as "so prepossessing". He describes Lanyon's private office as "fitted up and furnished as a library and had a really excellent collection of works up to date on Architecture and Engineering and a good many of the classics on Art subjects . . ."

Not only was the scope of Lanyon's practice all-encompassing, but the styles employed in his buildings were very varied. They included Neo-classical, Italianate, Gothic, Tudor, Elizabethan and Scots Baronial.

His two manor court-houses of 1838 at Larne and Glenarm were Italianate in style, each with a triplet of windows in a pyramidal-roofed campanile or tower, but the very next year, in the small churches designed for the Church Accommodation Society, he employed a completely different style. For these he chose a Gothic style of a rather simple, almost impoverished sort, economy being one of the requirements. In all he built sixteen churches or chapels-of-ease between 1839 and 1843 for the Society. They are all variants of two basic types, some running to a western tower, others making do with a bellcote. Good examples, still largely unchanged and standing in rural surroundings, can be seen at Muckamore, Blaris, Ballyclug, Tyrella, Kilwarlin, Glynn, Killagan and Glenoe. Glenoe, in County Antrim, is a particularly nice one with all its furnishings, including box pews, still intact. Only at Trinity Church in Belfast (built in 1841–3 but no longer standing), which looks as though it was inspired by Charles Barry's St Peter's in Brighton of 1824, does Lanyon appear to have had scope to produce anything more ambitious, with a tall tower and spire with finials and traceried windows. Even so, it was still in a rather outmoded style with side galler-

SIR CHARLES LANYON

ies and what must have been cast-iron trusses. Clearly Lanyon was not a committed student of medieval architecture, and yet, here and there in these and other early churches, are nice little details culled from the books of measured specimens or from illustrated glossaries. At Hollymount, County Down, (built 1839–40) we find, for instance, that the little octagonal bellcote, perched on the apex of the gable, is derived from Corston Church in Wiltshire, while at Christ Church in Lisburn (built 1842) we find a particular chamfer detail that is taken from the Abbot's Barn at Glastonbury.

Just as the Church Accommodation Society was wound up, Lanyon built one further small church, not actually under the auspices of the Society but paid for by some of its subscribers, and it shows a truly remarkable departure from the others. At Trinity Church in Kircubbin (1843) in his only essay in the style, Lanyon built one of the finest Greek Revival churches in Ulster. It has a Doric *in antis* façade that is obviously based on the Temple of Diana–Propylaea at Eleusis as represented in *The Unedited Antiquities of Atticus*, right down to the seven sets of triglyphs across the frieze. Although there was occasionally a Neoclassical element of Lanyon's later work

he was never again so reliant on an antique model.

One other rather unique building from Lanyon's early years must be mentioned as it has an importance beyond the merely local. That is the Palm House in Belfast's Botanic Gardens. Early in 1839 Lanyon drew up a rather ponderous classical scheme for a 'range of glass' as it was termed, consisting of three domed pavilions linked by lower blocks. Funds permitted only the low link blocks to be built first. Completed in 1840, these two wings are in fact the earliest known work of the Dublin ironmaster, Richard Turner, pre-dating by some years his Glasnevin Conservatory of 1842–50 and his Great Palm House at Kew of 1844-8. Incidentally, Turner and his partner Walker had been recommended to Lanyon by Jacob Owen. When the project was resumed in 1852, Lanyon set aside his earlier rather 'architectural' design for a central block, and instead linked the two earlier conservatories by a large domical double-curved bulb which exploited more fully the ironmaster's art. This time the construction was by C.D. Young and Co., of Edinburgh.

Next to the Botanic Gardens in Belfast stands the building with which Lanyon's name is most closely associated, Queen's

University. One of the three Queen's Colleges set up in Ireland in 1845 to provide non-denominational higher education (the others were at Cork and Galway), Queen's is probably the high point of early Victorian architectural achievement in Ulster. It is a good example of the Tudor Revivalism that was considered appropriate for a college building. Early Victorian architects depended on historic models but it was not for lack of confidence in their own creative abilities. Indeed, in a way that showed their supreme self-confidence, they often improved on the original, as they thought. Thus the cental tower at Queen's, although based on the Founder's Tower at Magdalen in Oxford, is more strident and assertive than the original. Furthermore, the usual quadrangular collegiate plan was eschewed for a long towered composition that strove for maximum pictorial effect when viewed across its open lawn.

Lanyon had earlier used the Tudor style, intermingled with Elizabethan, in another long-towered red-brick frontage, the Institute for the Deaf and Dumb and Blind of 1843–5 (demolished). There the precise historic models are less obvious than at Queen's. Other Tudoresque works in the 1840s were the schools

Perspective drawing of original design for Queen's College, Belfast, 1846.

attached to Whitehouse and Craigs churches, Gills Almhouses at Carrickfergus and some very plain Fever Hospitals at Belfast and elsewhere. The most interesting stone building in the Tudoresque vein was Ballymena Courthouse of 1845-6. Its central feature of a gabled breakfront with a Perpendicular traceried window over a Tudor arched opening, was a recurring motif with Lanyon. Variations of it were used at Hollymount Church (as originally built in 1840) and Dunluce Presbyterian Church of 1845–7, and can be seen in the gabled projections flanking the main tower at Queen's as finally executed (though not in the original perspective drawings).

On the classical side of Lanyon's practice, which made up the bulk of his work in country houses, public buildings, banks and railway stations, there was plenty of variety. The handling ranges from the refined and simple to the vigorous and bold, in a series of buildings both Neo-classical and Neo-Renaissance.

The 'palazzo' style was a particular favourite of Lanyon's. Made famous by Sir Charles Barry in his London clubhouses, it was an alternative style to Neo-classicism. Its effects were achieved, not by big porticoes or pediments, but by an elaborate cornice, rusticated quoins and aedicule surrounds to windows. The models were not antique temples but the Renaissance palaces of Florence and Rome. Lanyon may not have been the first to bring this astylar treatment to Ireland – his old master Jacob Owen had tried the 'Farnese style', as one commentator termed it, in his Female Training School in Talbot Street Dublin in 1842[2] – but it was certainly Lanyon who built the first full-blooded example here when he remodelled the old Exchange and Assembly Rooms in Belfast for the Belfast bank in 1844–6. It owed a particular debt to the north front of Barry's Travellers Club in Pall Mall, London. Lanyon would have had opportunities to see that building on his frequent trips to London, and it was also well illustrated in W.H. Leeds's book *The Travellers Club-House*, published in 1839. Lanyon was to make this Italianate style his own. He used it for some country houses, usually with cornices over windows rather than full aedicules. The most important examples are Ballywalter Park in County Down and Dundarave in County An-

Stair hall at Ballywalter Park, Co. Down, started 1847.

Central hall at Dundarave, Co. Antrim, started 1847.

SIR CHARLES LANYON

Killyleagh Castle, Killyleagh, Co. Down, enlarged 1849–51.

Gate lodge at Eglantine House, near Hillsborough, Co. Down, 1840s.

trim, both of 1847. Both have very impressive interior halls but differ in their arrangement. At Ballywalter, much of the large central space is given over to a grand stairway with screens of columns and a gallery cutting across the hall, whereas at Dundarave the stairs are tucked off to one side in a separate compartment and the great central hall rises through two floors to a clerestorey above. With its colonnaded gallery around all four sides at first floor level, this hall is clearly based on that of Barry's Reform Club in London, drawings of which were published in the architectural press in 1840.[3] At both Dundarave and Ballywalter there is an almost identical Italianate gate lodge, perfectly symmetrical with a triple-arched portico. The same type was also used at two other houses of the 1840s, Moneyglass House and Eglantine. The *palazzo* style was employed with great majesty in the design of the Custom House in Belfast in 1854-7. It is a very refined building, and a very interesting one in its use of the rather austere 'Farnese' manner for much of the elevations, and a richer, more modelled, rather Venetian Renaissance manner for such parts as the projecting entrance bays. It is a fascinating building which calls to mind aspects of a number of sixteenth-century Italian works.

Other buildings of the 1850s that show Lanyon's increasing partiality for richer surfaces and stronger modelling, with occasional mannerist touches, are the former Northern Bank in Victoria Street, Belfast, of 1851–2, and the former Belfast Banks at Armagh of 1850 and Londonderry of 1853. At the Presbyterian College in Belfast of 1852–3, a really powerful Renaissance Revival set-piece, we find groups of tall keystones, Venetian windows set in vermiculated rustications, and a little balcony squeezed in between giant columns that carry little more than their own entablature blocks. The interior treatment is more conventional, with a Doric-columned hallway, a Venetian stair window, and a really spacious library on the first floor with screens of Corinthian columns and a clerestory of Diocletian windows. The Campanile at Trinity College, Dublin, of 1852–4 is a particularly sculpturesque example of this rich and rusticated Renaissance style. It was built at the expense of the Archbishop of Armagh, Lord John George Beresford, Primate of All Ireland

SIR CHARLES LANYON

and Chancellor of the University of Dublin. From a sturdy rusticated Roman Doric base rise, in successive and diminishing stages, an arcaded belfry and lantern both with domical roofs, all to a height of over ninety-four feet. Comparisons this time are all with English eighteenth-century work. Pierced balustrades, a Corinthian order and four over-life-size Portland stone figures of 'Divinity', 'Law', 'Science' and 'Physic' by J.R. Kirk, complete the elaboration.

Lanyon's classical style is wrought in many forms. There is even a Neo-Palladian strain, as at the York Road Railway Terminus in Belfast, built in stages from 1849 to 1854 (now demolished) where a tall central block has superimposed porticoes below a pediment. Then again, there is a monumental and rather Neo-classical quality about works such as Holywood Non-Subscribing Presbyterian Church of 1847–9 with its Corinthian porch in antis, or the County Court-House in Belfast of 1848–50 (in its original state). When we look at its great hexastyle Corinthian portico, its giant pilasters and its triple-arched screen walls, we can see the influence of Gandon's Four Courts in Dublin.

With all this emphasis on classical styles it is something of a surprise to come across the picturesque and romantic turrets added to Killyleagh Castle in 1849–51. Yet, even here, we find Lanyon's favoured Doric order inside, beneath a layer of Jacobean strapwork. This was, of course, an enlargement and embellishment of a genuine seventeenth-century castle, its skyline now made more exciting than ever.

The picture of Lanyon's early phase would be incomplete without mention of the serious Gothic Revivalism of two churches designed in the late 1840s. The whole handling of St Paul's in Belfast (1849–51) and St Paul's in Castlewellan (1847–53) and the range of carefully studied Early English detail marks them off from anything in this line before. It is obvious that Lanyon himself stood aside here and allowed his assistant, W.H. Lynn, to show what he could do. Gothic of an ecclesiological type was a field that Lanyon himself had no need to enter. This was to be Lynn's domain.

In the years of the partnership with Lynn we notice a swing towards several new styles. There is Italian Gothic, inspired first by Ruskin and then later by Street, used on some banks and warehouses, and Early English and Decorated Gothic, not just for churches but for houses too, as at Old Conna House near Bray in County Wicklow (1857–60), and Shane's Castle at Randalstown in County Antrim (1862). These were no doubt wholly the work of Lynn.

Two other styles, the Jacobean for country houses, first used at Stranmillis in Belfast in 1859, and the Scottish Baronial used for Ballymena Market House in 1852 and Scrabo Tower in 1856, as well as for some county house projects, may have been developed by Lynn but the presence of Lanyon is apparent in some details. Until more can be established of the contribution of Lynn and John Lanyon in the 1850s and '60s there will be uncertainty about the authorship of some works.

A few Italianate designs of the old brand were still coming out of the office in the 1860s, however, and these look like the work of Charles Lanyon himself. They include the Ulster Club in Belfast of 1861–3, Moore and Weinberg's linen warehouse (now The Linen Hall Library) in Belfast (1864), and Stradbally Hall in County Leix (1866–9).

Lanyon's energies were not confined to the immediate affairs of the office. From early on he played a part in the wider community and that involvement increased as time went on. There were worthy causes as well as cultural and artistic interests. He was a Vice-President of the Belfast Fine Arts Society in the 1840s and of the Belfast Classical Harmonists Society in the 1850s and he was also a prime mover to have a Government School of Design established in Belfast. A Vice-President from 1849 he was later to become Chairman of its Board of Managers. There were professional associations and attainments too, most notably the Presidency of the R.I.A.I. and the Vice-Presidency of the R.I.B.A. He was also admitted as an architect member to the R.H.A.

In the 1860s he became prominent in civic affairs. On resigning his county surveyorship, he was invited to serve on the Grand Jury of Antrim. He became Mayor of Belfast in 1862, and then in 1866, Conservative M.P. for Belfast until 1868. That was the year he was knighted, by the Duke of Abercorn, which set the seal on his rise as a public figure.

Charles Lanyon seems to have been blessed with good fortune in his life. Fate was certainly kind to him professionally, if somewhat cruel personally – his wife predeceasing him by thirty years. Fortunate was the connection with the Owen family which seems to have set him on the road to success, and fortunate was the resignation of John Woodhouse, which allowed Lanyon to move from a quiet county in Ireland to one where things were poised to happen and where great opportunities were open to him. How well he took those opportunities is clear to see.

Paul Larmour

All photographs by the author.

NOTES

1. Details of Lanyon's life are given in the obituary article in *The Belfast News-Letter*, June 3, 1889, and in *The Dictionary of National Biography*, London, 1892. Lanyon's Belfast works are described and illustrated in C.E.B. Brett, *Buildings of Belfast 1700–1914*, London, 1967 (revised edition, Belfast, 1985); Brian M. Walker and Hugh Dixon, *No Mean City: Belfast 1880–1914*, Belfast, 1983; Brian M. Walker and Hugh Dixon, *Belfast 1864–1880*, Belfast, 1984; and Paul Larmour, *Belfast, An Illustrated Architectural Guide*, Belfast, 1987. Some houses by Lanyon and his firm are described and illustrated in Mark Bence-Jones, *Burke's Guide to Irish Country Houses Vol. 1. Ireland*, London, 1978. Drenagh is described and well illustrated by Donald Girvan in *Buildings of North Derry*, UAHS, 1975, and Dundarave in *Buildings of North Antrim*, UAHS, 1972. There are good articles by Alistair Rowan on Ballywalter Park in *Country Life*, March 2 and 9, 1975, and on Killyleagh Castle in *Country Life*, March 19 and 26, 1970; and chapters on the architecture of Ballywalter Park in *Ballywalter Park*, UAHS, 1985.
2. See *The Civil Engineer and Architect's Journal*, Jan. 13, 1844.
3. See *The Civil Engineer and Architect's Journal*, May, 1840.

BRONZE BY GOLD, THE WORK OF IRISH WOMEN SCULPTORS

I believe it is correct to say that there is no public perception of the huge body of work by women sculptors in Ireland since the end of the Second World War. The names of women painters come readily enough to mind but there is, somehow, a subconscious idea that sculpture is a male province and preserve. It is incontestable that two women painters, Mainie Jellett and Evie Hone, led the Modernist movement in Ireland, and I think it is equally incontestable that the sculptor, Hilary Heron, led the equivalent movement in sculpture. Lawrence Campbell, Frederick Herkner, and particularly Oisin Kelly, all had leanings towards Modernism but Hilary Heron was the artist whose work was most radical in the years immediately after the war, even if then very heavily influenced by Henry Moore.

Heron quickly developed her own particular style of witty invention, moving from wood-carving to metal and stone. Her most innovative work was in a combination of both, as in the Lithodendron series of stone and copper flower pieces, which combine an innocent, light-hearted spirit with an original, skilful and economic use of materials. She rarely worked to a large scale; her 'Crazy Jane' (1958) welded-steel figure, based on W.B. Yeats's series of poems of that name, stands ninety-two inches high and is probably her largest work, whereas her male contemporaries at the time, such as Ian Stuart, were to take on very much larger works in the following decade.

Another artist working at this time was the sculptor, Melanie le Brocquy, whose small, rather careful, but distinguished bronzes held their own in their quiet way throughout the experimental '60s when three women, Deborah Brown, Alexandra Wejchert, and Gerda Fromel, held a dominant position in the forefront of Irish sculpture. Deborah Brown grew up in Belfast and began her career as a painter, but relief elements gradually began to hold more importance than the picture plane. Initially these relief forms were made in *papier-mâché* mounted on painted canvas; these gave way to fibreglass forms mounted on painted canvas, all in an abstract idiom. The relief forms acted in conjunction or counterpoint to pierced forms cut in the backing canvas, all of this sculptural interaction mingling with the interaction of colour in both the fibreglass itself and the painted can-

In an enthusiastic and sympathetic article, **Dorothy Walker,** a prominent art critic, gives some account of sculpture made by women in Ireland during the past half-century.

vas. The play of light, both sunlight and artificial light, was another factor in these pieces and, understandably, it was not long before the artist developed these relief forms into free-standing, three-dimensional sculpture of pure colourless fibreglass, in which the material was stretched to the limits of its own lacy strength. In the 1980s Deborah Brown has returned to her early use of *papier-mâché* in figurative work of groups of people and animals which, although vested with a keen observation of natural form, are, nevertheless, of very much less interest and strength than her fibreglass abstractions.

Alexandra Wejchert trained as an architect in her native Poland before coming to Ireland in 1965. Her early work consisted of relief constructions of short pegs inserted in a painted background in dynamic rhythms which created effects of wave movements, a cross between Op art and kinetic art, both popular at the time. Later her work became more directly sculptural in the notable series of free-standing pieces she made for the Bank of Ireland in coloured plexiglass. Here her architect's feeling for the use of materials, allied to her artist's imagination, made of the unpromising commercial material a distinguished and lively art based on her grasp of the malleability of the sheet of plastic and the curious fact that the cut edge of the sheet becomes a different colour from the sheet itself. She was therefore able to make almost purely linear sculpture by exploiting the sheet's edge-colour, while holding the sheet's transparent curving plane as the main sculptural element. These baroque pieces influenced younger sculptors like Michael Bulfin, who also produced some interesting plexiglass sculpture during this period.

Wejchert has also worked in metal, as in her giant stainless steel piece at the Allied Irish Bank Bankcentre in Ballsbridge, and her golden wall-relief in the Irish Life Building in Lower Abbey Street, Dublin. One of her most successful pieces was a combination of

chromium and clear plastic tubing which was exhibited some years ago in the Hugh Lane Municipal Gallery of Modern Art and in the Irish Marketing Institute.

Probably the most versatile sculptor working in Ireland in the '60s and early '70s was the Czech-born artist, Gerda Fromel. She and her husband, Werner Schurmann, came to Ireland in 1955. He also was a sculptor and bronze-caster. Schurmann, who had a fine bass voice, eventually abandoned sculpture for operatic singing and returned to his native Germany, while Fromel remained in Ireland with their three sons and developed her own career as a sculptor with great dedication and success. Her early work was in bronze, in a romantic Symbolist style, having much in common with the Italian sculptor, Medardo Rosso, involving tree forms and the heads of small children.

While close to a potentially dangerous area of sentimentality, the delicacy and tenderness of her touch avoided this pitfall and her work developed, in time, to a totally abstract form where her essential gentleness of character was sustained with immense strength by the materials she used, marble and alabaster particularly, but also stainless steel. It is interesting, in formal terms, that her Central European background, and her training as a student in Munich, led her to develop the romantic tendencies of her nature, as in her bronze 'Girl' and her tiny monumental 'Castle'. When she came to Ireland, however, her work evolved towards an abstract mode, echoing not only cup-mark carvings on prehistoric monuments in the Irish countryside, but Celtic ornamentation of positive / negative, inner / outer forms, embodied in large-scale, free-standing and often mobile sculpture. She captured light and movement in her work first by means of the materials she used such as translucent alabaster and polished stainless steel, but also by a hard-earned simplicity won from the forms, 'embodying enjoyment of the spiritual through the materials,' to quote James Johnson Sweeney.

The poetic quality of her sculpture is easily grasped in her small pieces, whether abstract or figurative, but it is even more remarkably evident in the very large sculpture in Carroll's factory in Dundalk: the polished stainless steel has fitting technological overtones suit-

BRONZE BY GOLD, THE WORK OF IRISH WOMEN SCULPTORS

able to the industrial factory building, which is a very fine work of architecture, but the poetic idea of the three tall 'sails' turning in the wind and reflecting in the water of the pool in which they stand, re-affirms the harmony of architecture and sculpture. She has considerable expertise in steel and made many abstract pieces with moveable parts. One of these large-scale steel pieces is unfortunately very badly sited in the Setanta Centre in Dublin, unlike the beautiful siting at the Carroll's factory in Dundalk. Throughout the various media in which she showed her technical skill, a spiritual quality always shone through. Fromel was drowned in a tragic accident off the west coast of Ireland in 1975 at the height of her powers.

Irish sculpture is lucky to have acquired so many foreign artists of talent. Imogen Stuart was born and trained in Germany before marrying the sculptor, Ian Stuart, and moving to Ireland in the early '50s. Her work has largely consisted of church commissions and she has succeeded Oisin Kelly as the leading practitioner of religious art. Inevitably her

Eilis O'Connell, Kendo,
1986, painted steel, 72 × 30 × 10.
Courtesy the Douglas Hyde Gallery.

work shows the German influence of artists like Barlach, although she has profitably browsed in the rich area of early Irish Christian imagery and iconography.

In the early 1970s two remarkable young women, Eilis O'Connell and Vivienne Roche, began to show their work. Both had been students of the Cork sculptor, John Burke, at Cork School of Art and their early work clearly showed his influence in large-scale abstract pieces in painted steel, beautifully made. Whatever else John Burke may have imparted to them and to his subsequent students, he

certainly taught them how to make their work, with impeccably polished, stylish technical skills. They have both won numerous awards and competitions. O'Connell won the competition for a Memorial to the aviatrix, Amelia Erhardt, on the site of her landing near Derry. This tall white marble column acts as a wind instrument at the conjunction of a grid of paths on the site; she also won the first GPA Award for Emerging Artists, a British Council fellowship for a year at the British School in Rome, and the first Mont Kavanagh Award; she represented Ireland at the last Paris *Biennale des Jeunes* in 1982, and recently won the Ireland/PS I Fellowship in New York.

In the late 1970s O'Connell injured her back lifting heavy steel and had to forego using that material. Her work then entered a highly creative phase, in which she freely experimented with other materials, notably her own hand-made paper. She incorporated much organic material into this paper: stones, slate, feathers, shells, so that the material itself was quite sculptural and from this she made further sculptural constructions, often to a large scale, such

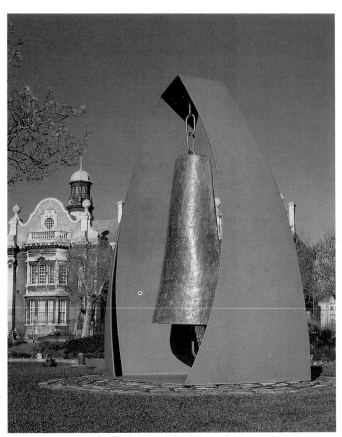

Vivienne Roche, Bell Sound Sculpture, bronze and steel.
Courtesy Sculptors Society of Ireland.

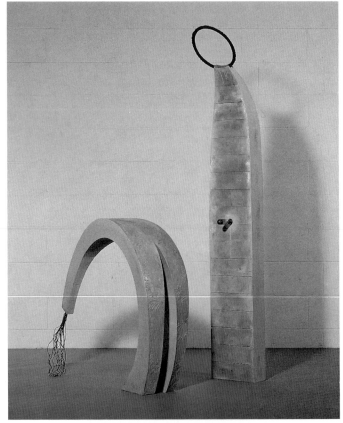

Dorothy Cross, Erotic Couple, 1988, painted wood wall paper
found objects, she 93 × 99 × 32 cms, he 203 × 31 × 11 cms.
Courtesy the Douglas Hyde Gallery.

BRONZE BY GOLD, THE WORK OF IRISH WOMEN SCULPTORS

as her 'Turfing it down to its slender quarry' in the Paris *Biennale*. A trip to Brazil, where she represented Ireland with three other young artists at the Sao Paolo *Bienal* in 1985, also had a distinct influence on her work. She easily incorporated the rich colours and exotic forms of bird and plant life from the tropical jungle into her work, especially a particular blue which she has used to handsome effect in small-scale painted steel pieces, often combined with organic materials, paper, feathers etc. While using organic materials, and balancing them, unusually, against sophisticated painted steel, her work has retained all its elegance and style, with the added interest of organic textures.

Vivienne Roche has remained faithful to the more architectural concerns of clear-cut steel. As she lives near the sea on Cork Harbour, her sculpture is often related to the forms of sailing and boats, beautiful objects in themselves, and easily lending their forms to abstract sculpture. Until 1988, her major public piece was her prize-winning white steel memorial to the late President Cearbhall O Dálaigh, situated on the village green in Sneem, Co. Kerry, near the art-loving President's home. In 1988, she won one of the Dublin Millenium Sculpture Symposium awards for a site adjoining St Patrick's Cathedral in the Liberties, and her large stylized steel bell was one of the first of ten new public sculptures to be installed. Of the ten winning projects, six were by young women sculptors, bringing to public notice a whole new generation of sculptural talent to which I will return later.

Yet another Cork sculptor is the very stylish, witty and subversive artist, Dorothy Cross. Her series of 'Contraptions' were architecturally-based, freestanding spires and towers made of timber or lead, and often combined with wall pieces incorporating antique prints. Again, her work is beautifully made, exquisite joinery work in timber, often allied with gold leaf and bronze. Her 1988 solo exhibition in the Douglas Hyde Gallery during the International Sculpture Conference in Dublin, combined the architectural structures with a new anthropomorphic concern related to men and women and their reciprocal gender fears, all conveyed with a witty surrealism that infused the somewhat dry timber structures with a satirical twist.

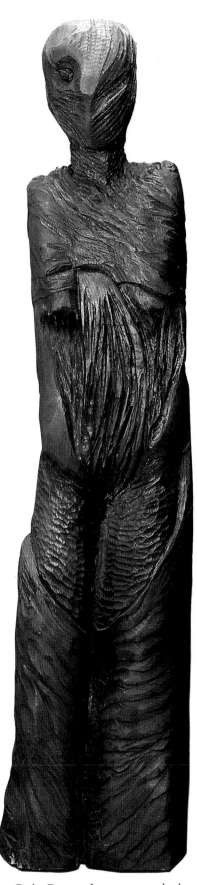

Cathy Carman, I cannot say who he sleeps with now, but I can say he does not sleep alone, *1987, elm, 176 × 36 × 39 cms.*

Craftsmanship of the mind – in Berkeley's words – as well as of the hand, is apparent in the work of a young sculptor, Liadin Cooke, who graduated from the National College of Art and Design in 1987. Her masterly installation at the Projects Art Centre, 'Making a Dream', was a sophisticated *tour-de-force* for a young artist. The installation included several individual works such as the 'Sea-box', a long minimalist steel box filled with blue pigment, with a symbolic sea-to-sky thin bronze ladder on the surface, and a rock-island emerging from the blue. 'Sailing through a closed door' was a wall-drawing handled on a huge scale with certainty and poise, a small bronze boat leading the geometric quadrant-angle through a corner and on to the adjoining wall. The poetic 'Sea envelope' was a lead envelope high on the wall, filled with blue which overflowed down the wall and on to the floor. The poetic theme of a dream journey found surprisingly apt expression in the minimalist style of the steel and lead constructions, animated aesthetically by the rich cobalt blue.

At the other extreme from these concerns is the rough-hewn timber sculpture of Cathy Carman, Sally Houston, and Jackie McKenna. Carman's crudely fashioned squatting women have a deliberate feminist brutality, eschewing the dainty, and celebrating tough, battered survival. Her powerful standing figure, 'I know not who he sleeps with now but I know he does not sleep alone,' is a moving version of the old Irish poem, 'I know not who Eimear sleeps with tonight but I know she does not sleep alone.' Sally Houston has likewise worked in rough-hewn timber with large chisel-marks rhythmically hacking out the surface. Occasionally her pieces are painted in Expressionistic colours which reinforce the Expressionist nature of the carvings; these pieces work unexpectedly well out of doors, particularly the more artificial-looking pieces such as the bright red and green construction in Fernhill Gardens, Co. Dublin.

The Sculptors Society of Ireland, of which all these young women are members, and of which one of the most active is the sculptor, Cliodna Cussen, is an admirable body which has considerably advanced the scope of public sculpture and has organized symposia in different materials – timber, steel, stone, etc. The timber symposium was held in a beautiful

BRONZE BY GOLD, THE WORK OF IRISH WOMEN SCULPTORS

wood, Hazelwood, on the shores of Lough Gill in Co. Sligo. The lifesize figure of an old woman carved in timber by the young sculptor, Jackie McKenna, is one of the best integrated, looking entirely natural in the woodland setting, searching the ground at her feet as if looking for mushrooms, and reminiscent of early Malevich paintings of Russian peasants.

Caroline Mulholland is an artist from Northern Ireland, one of the few contemporary artists who can produce credible bronze portrait sculpture. Her charming bronze chair for the Dublin Millenium is now placed at the bottom of George's Street for the 'walkers' weary shankes' to rest; the back of the chair grows into leafy branches to give shade to the sitters. Other projects for the Millenium which have been realized are Rachel Joynt's bronze, brass, and concrete imprints of runner-soles, shoes and birds on the pedestrian traffic island on O'Connell Bridge in the heart of the city, and Betty Maguire's half-submerged Viking ship

Jackie McKenna, Wood Gatherer, *beech. Courtesy Sculptors Society of Ireland.*

skeleton on Wood Quay, the site of the original Viking settlement on the Liffey in 841 AD.

Kathy Prendergast is one of the most gifted artists of her generation. Although her output is relatively limited, her work is of concentrated exquisiteness that well merits waiting for it. Her small bronzes have a unique poetic quality, both in their unusual dream-like subject-matter and in the concentration of their execution. The larger works, like her white chalk wall in Rosc '88, are equally exquisite. The wall, made like a traditional dry-stone 'lace' wall in the West of Ireland, was made of pure white chalk rocks, but the centre section was shaded by incredibly delicate drawing with a fine mapping pen, making 'contours' on the rock in short straight lines. Her drawing has always been exquisite and has often related to maps or technical drawing related to her own body. Equally exquisite craftsworking, on a tiny scale, is the hallmark of the ceramic sculptor, Marie Foley, who makes minute, com-

Lily van Oost, Growth, *wood and synthetic fibres 20 × 6.5 m, exhibited at the Bank of Ireland Exhibition Hall in 'Fibre Art '88'. Courtesy Sculptors Society of Ireland.*

BRONZE BY GOLD, THE WORK OF IRISH WOMEN SCULPTORS

plex, subtle sculptures combining ceramic elements and natural organic forms like feathers or quills. A whole range of women sculptors work in the area of organic natural materials, which seem to come more naturally to them than the technological materials like steel.

Helen Comerford was one of the first feminist sculptors who, in the mid-'70s made abstract forms in fibreglass very specifically related to the female form. However, she soon veered from these to more subtle, abstract works in layered paper completely covered in graphite, stitched together to form large surfaces. Making paper seems to be an attractive option for women artists, and Comerford has realized successful projects in this area. In fact her most virtuoso work was a life-size environment, 'Molly Bloom's Bedroom' made entirely of papier-mâché, as a memorial to James Joyce in 1982, the year of the Joyce Centenary. In this she achieved a sophisticated paradox in the treatment of colour and pattern: although the entire work was monochrome, the pale muddy colour of the untreated material, by raising all the patterned surfaces, such as wallpaper, clothing etc, into three-dimensional relief, successfully conveyed the idea of colour with which the room was filled. Comerford also worked in a serial vein, using 'bags' of fibreglass filled according to a graduated system of colour.

Women artists also seem to relate more directly to the land and to nature, particularly in sculpture. Although Oisin Kelly was a pioneer in creating landscape sculpture, many women have adopted this approach. Aileen McKeogh has developed a courageous theme of landscape sculpture, using branches and twigs in works which are more successful in a non-objective mode, when using the material in a purely organic manner to create her own individual landscape. When the pieces are more directly narrative or representational, they teeter on a decorative edge which is on the brink of toy- or model-making. Louise Walsh, on the other hand, is a very strong young artist, working in somewhat similar materials, branches, found objects in natural materials, baskets and so on, which all go to be ground in a convincing feminist mill, emerging as telling, poetic, stringent images of women in various guises. Her women are often half-beast,

such as the horse, which enjoys in Ireland an extraordinary status not only as a handsome animal which may also be the means of winning a few pounds, but as a traditional beast of burden, and a mythical Celtic goddess. Walsh combines the equally numerous aspects of woman, including the mythical, with the image of the horse to make a neat feminist point about both; in spite of their mythical status, beauty, etc., they are still widely perceived as useful domestic animals. She does not, however, labour her feminism in a hectoring tone; her work is always poetic, ambiguous, but strong and dynamic. Other artists working in the area of found materials are Betty Oliver-Brown and Éilis Ní Fhaoláin. The former has made more straightforward animal images than Louise Walsh but, as such, they are inventive, dynamic images which catch the basic movement and structure of her life-size animals with precision and accuracy, in spite of the unpromising nature of the plastic bowls, toys, kitchen utensils, clothing and other odds and ends that she uses.

Éilis Ní Fhaoláin's quirky humour in her studies of life-size cows, for example, carries on the witty tradition of Hilary Heron, but again through a medium of genuine arte povera, sections of abandoned cars, chicken wire, papier-mâché, and so on. It may be that women's traditional role of seeking to create harmony and system in the ceaseless chaos of domestic life has given them a gift for this kind of ad hoc solution and making the best of whatever is to hand. Angela Morrissy uses old nylon tights to make expressive stuffed figures. Expressionist sculpture does seem to tend towards being a male preserve, except for Cathy Carman, and to some extent, the blunt carving of Sally Houston; it also tends to be in timber, although ceramic sculpture would seem to be a natural medium for such concerns.

Una Walker, another Northern artist, uses directly domestic elements in her ritual installations, for example, pottery bowls and pottery in the form of soda-bread, offerings of salt, decoration of reeds and leaves. These are assembled, however, in the perpetual geometry of circles, triangles and squares, thus combining the organic and the geometric in these private, home-based, but quite large-scale pieces which, despite their domestic privacy, still have a public

validity. Even more domestic in character are Lily van Oost's amazing knitted sculptures. Van Oost is a Dutch artist living in the Black Valley near Killarney, Co. Kerry; she knits amazing clothing also, wool coats and jerseys which are truly sculptural, but her recent work has increased to a wild scale, vast curtains of spaced-out knitting and crochet, sometimes including whole figures, at other times purely abstract mountainous sculptures of wool.

Teresa McKenna also incorporates tapestry and weaving into her work but in a constructivist fashion, i.e. combined with timber structures. Her wall drawings on cut-out buckram, marouflé on paper were extremely interesting both in technique and in their archaeological subject-matter. Archaeology and prehistory tend to be areas that interest women artists, perhaps in nostalgia for the power-era of the Mother Goddess but also, I think, in a desire to recapture a pre-male-dominated world. There is a dual activity among women artists: one is to start the past afresh, to go back far enough to an innocent equality of male and female; the other is to lay claim to the future in the practice of new media which have not yet become male-dominated, e.g. video, performance, sound, and other new forms. Irish women sculptors have been particularly active in this latter field, and of these the most outstanding is the young woman performance artist, Alanna O'Kelly. She began as a sculptor working in similar organic materials to many of the foregoing artists, using flax, wicker, and other natural materials, as in her installation in the exhibition 'Without the Walls' at the ICA in London in 1980. Another outstanding installation of hers was 'Barriers' at the Project Arts Centre, Dublin, which filled the gallery space with the massive timber posts used to counter land erosion on the Wexford coast. This piece worked on several levels of meaning, both visual and psychological, and was a remarkably powerful, uncompromising work for a young artist. She has also devised more ambitious outdoor installations centred on the midsummer solstice, rather less original in concept. But she has reached a genuine peak of originality in her solo voice performances. While based on traditional Irish keening, she has created a uniquely personal vehicle which she uses in abstract, serial, wordless but in-

BRONZE BY GOLD, THE WORK OF IRISH WOMEN SCULPTORS

tensely moving calls, with all the emotional power of the human voice strictly contained in a structured sequence. Later works, such as 'Chant down Greenham' involved a more complex and more ambitious sound environment in which the recorded sound of approachng helicopters was relayed from various points, filling the space, while O'Kelly's live voice pitched its sequence of chants against the mechanical menace. This is one of the most powerful and most moving live performances of any I have seen in twentieth-century performance art, heart-rending to witness as the live voice rises passionately to hold its human own against the machine, almost failing, but like the highest E-string note of a Heifetz Beethoven sonata, finally, agonizingly, reaching the summit. O'Kelly has also made notable video work and installations at an easier level but none approaching the intensity of her voice performances.

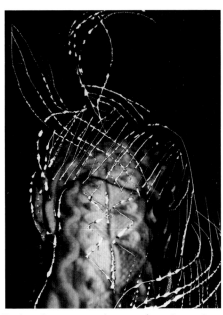

Pauline Cummins, male torso from Inis t-Oírr, slide/sound installation. Shown at the Irish Exhibition of Living Art, December 1985.

Pauline Cummins, on the other hand, is an accomplished video artist, who is also active in organizing women artists' events, exhibitions, seminars etc. Her video piece, 'Inis t-Oirr', unites drawing, knitting patterns laid over a nude male torso, and her own erotic narrative in her distinctly seductive voice. She has also made purely sound works, in a feminist strain, which can be listened to with earphones. She is now beginning to gain international recognition for her work, as indeed is O'Kelly who has performed in the UK, USA, and at Documenta 8 in West Germany. One of the most interesting and inventive younger artists working in this area is the young Derry artist, Moira McIver, who has produced very accomplished and beautifully made video installations, based more on feminist politics than on the expected Derry issues of violence or nationalism. The work of artists like Cummins and O'Kelly in mixed technological media is also

Linda Brunker, Foliose, Bronze. Courtesy Sculptors Society of Ireland.

BRONZE BY GOLD, THE WORK OF IRISH WOMEN SCULPTORS

reflected in more traditional mixed media by other artists. The painter, Alice Maher, for example, has created a spatial environment in her installation 'Maculata' at the GPA Emerging Artists exhibition in the Douglas Hyde Gallery in 1988. Four painted sheets, representing four decades of the Rosary, based on four episodes in the life of the Virgin Mary – the Annunciation, the Visitation, the Nativity, and the Coronation – were hung at varying heights and angles to create an iconographic colour-space. While basically feminist in intent, the work incorporated expert iconographic information in great detail such as the image of the Virgin Mary giving birth with no expression of labour pains. The Church teaching on the matter is that the Virgin, being sinless, did not suffer the ills of this wicked world but gave birth without pain, and in consequence during the Middle Ages and early Renaissance, the most intense period of devotion to the Blessed Virgin, she is never depicted lying-in, at the Nativity. Another detail of Alice Maher's installation concerns the midwife Salome who, in the Apocryphal Gospels, is alleged to have doubted the virgin birth, and to have had her hand withered when touching Mary's genitals.

Drawing is often a preoccupation of sculptors. The Derry artist Mhairi Sutherland has used her considerable drawing skill to make impressive *in situ* wall drawings, or rather, part *in situ*: she commences her drawings on paper, strange hair-line images of satirical animals, often with political overtones, and then pastes them to the wall and continues the drawing across the wall. Catherine Mulvihill has a different technique of commencing a drawing on

the wall and then bringing it out into three dimensions. Since her subject-matter is also concerned with elements of building construction or interiors, the drawing/sculpture often has a further illusionist effect. Mary Farl Powers is one of the best engravers in Ireland, with *virtuoso* skills in etching and lithography. In the last year or two, her engraving has become steadily more sculptural, with embossing and other similar techniques, until last year she produced completely three-dimensional work in water-colour on paper. These very beautiful abstract pieces give hope that she may develop into an interesting sculptor.

Of all the various materials that have been grist to the mill of women sculptors, glass has been noticeably absent. This is curious in a country which has a long glass craft tradition, and also because of the nature of glass itself. It is such a sculptural, malleable, and inherently decorative aesthetic material, capable of taking any shape demanded of it, but also sustaining any number of surface decorating techniques – etching, blasting, cutting etc.– and even having that domestic quality and usage which so many women artists like to exploit in their work. The Cork stained glass artist, Maud Cotter, makes constructivist sculpture with infill panels of stained glass. It is, however, a rather limited use of the material; basically she is making a three-sided window, like a small glass tent, with leaded sections in the traditional method. While this does produce a certain aesthetic effect, it seems to me that a medium of such potential could be taken to more interesting conclusions.

Cork, however, still continues to produce pioneering sculptors, working now in quite different media from the John

Burke school of painted steel. Sheila Long is a very young artist, who has produced large-scale coloured 'monsters', albeit friendly monsters – no doubt she watched the Muppets as a child. These large light-hearted beings have a delightful character and are imaginatively made with, again, many organic, found objects like shells embedded in their painted plaster and fibreglass forms.

On the other hand, a young artist like Geraldine Lucie, also in Cork, has shown very elegant minimal timber sculpture, beautifully carved and finished, quite small in scale, but extremely poised. So the Modernist wheel has turned back to these young women and their traditional skills, and their very wide range of sculptural concerns. In this context I will finish with one of last year's sculpture graduates from the National College of Art and Design, a young girl named Linda Brunker whose poetic bronze figures made of bronze oak leaves astonished not only the foundry where she did her innovative casting but also the public who rushed to buy her work. Her concerns are again based on landscape and nature, and her figures, when shown in the romantic woodland gardens of Fernhill at the foot of the Dublin Mountains, seem to take form from the leafy undergrowth. Seamus Heaney asks in a recent poem 'How habitable is the perfect form?' The perfect form *is* habitable when the underlying idea, the artist's intention, and the medium used to express that intention and idea, coalesce so closely and with such crucial balance that an ardent energy is released, breathing life into inert matter.

Dorothy Walker

FASHION AS A GUIDE TO DATING IRISH PORTRAITS 1660–1880

It is only very recently that any serious attempt has been made to date Irish portraits and miniatures by reference to fashions in dress and hair-styles, and although there is much in print concerning such fashions in England and on the Continent, very little has been published on Ireland. Though the Irish gentry obtained their general sartorial trends from England, which in turn derived them from France, it seems that not only was there a variable time-lag between London and rural Ireland up to 1790 (when it virtually disappeared), but there were also continuous subtle differences between styles in the two kingdoms, as also, of course, between England and France. In some cases what was fashionable in England was not popular in Ireland; in others, the Irish produced a fashion variant of their own.

Ignorance – or neglect – of changing modes of dress has led to many absurd attributions. To this day, the National Gallery of Ireland has a charming portrait of a young woman clad in the distinctive fashions of the later years of James I, which is labelled "Lady Anne Hamilton, Duchess of Hamilton, 1636–1717(?)"! This identification is wholly impossible as people were painted in their smartest clothes and nobody would have been seen in such garments in 1660. The picture probably represents the Duchess's mother, Mary, who was married in 1620. A further complication is that names and dates actually painted on to a canvas are not wholly reliable since many of them were added at a later date and mistakes could – and did – occur. Unless they agree with the clothes, they are wrong. Printed family histories are yet another source of confusion, since these abound with mis-attributions. For instance, *The Leslies of Tarbert* includes a miniature of a divine wearing a wig of c. 1770–80, which it claims is the Rev. John Leslie who *died* in 1700! *The Dublin Tweedys* goes one better, for it even confuses the *gender*; a silhouette it calls "Jane Tweedy" can only be that of a *man*, having regard to the tie-wig and cravat – Jane's husband, perhaps? A little basic knowledge would save a lot of these blunders.

Whilst the better-known portraits of the rich may be already identified – though, as in the case of Lady Anne Hamilton, not necessarily always correctly! – there exists in Ireland a great

In a useful introduction to dating Irish paintings by reference to costume, **Rosemary ffolliott** suggests what to look for and how to avoid misattributions.

Portrait labelled "Lady Anne Hamilton, Duchess of Hamilton, 1636–1717(?)." National Gallery of Ireland, No. 1149. A perfect example of misattribution since the dress is c. 1620.

mass of likenesses which cannot be ascribed to any particular artist, are undated and, due to the general carelessness of the most of the Irish country gentry, lack even a reliable identity for the person portrayed. It is in these instances that an exact knowledge of fashions in hair and dress will, at least, limit the possibilities. This article endeavours to set out the main trends between 1680 and 1830 – the period when confusion seems to be greatest – and draw attention to the chief differences between fashions in England and Ireland. Specifically excluded are the clothes worn by the peasantry and by the Quaker community (who had strange garments) since neither category appears to any extent in paintings.

Before 1670 Ireland was in turmoil; only the very rich were painted at all, and most of them took the opportunity on a visit to England or to the Continent since – due to the turmoil – very few artists were then at work in Ireland. By 1680 the island had settled down sufficiently for portrait painters from outside to consider it worth their while exploiting. The more skilled of these – John Michael Wright, Gaspar Smitz and even Garrett

Morphey – probably confined their activities to Dublin and the Pale, but the less-able painters, out-ranked in the capital, ventured deeper and deeper into the countryside, and continued to do so. These itinerant wielders of the brush signed nothing and dated nothing; if the sitter's name was ever attached to the frame, it was apt to get lost in the process of later re-framing, apparently an all too frequent occurrence in Ireland. After all, at that time everybody knew that the portrait was old Uncle James, who gambled away his patrimony and died of drink. Unfortunately in due course 'everybody' also died (not necessarily of drink) and soon 'Uncle James' was not only artist-less and dateless but nameless as well. Sometimes a family memory of the sitter's Christian name did manage to survive, and there are endless confusions between father and son of the same name, sometimes even between grandfather and grandson, irrespective of the fact that a pretty accurate date – to within ten years – can be put on any portrait by reason of dress.

Fortunately people were painted in their best, newest, clothes, one sometimes even suspects that a flamboyant waistcoat or elaborate gown may have been bought specially for the picture! Thus, by and large, portrait-date and dress-fashion go remarkably well together. Admittedly, in the late eighteenth century one may find a likeness (usually a miniature) of some crusty old country gent sporting an out-of-date wig atop an in-date coat, he being evidently long accustomed to that type of wig and not minded to change. This attitude, however, does not seem to have affected females: ladies' caps and hair-dressing represent current fashion, no matter how aged their owner.

Painters charged for portraits by size, full length being the most expensive, head and shoulders, with no hands showing, the cheapest. The middling Irish gentry, being chronically short of cash, mostly opted for the least costly version they could get and in consequence one tends to have only the upper body for evidence of date. Actually this is less of a handicap than might be expected, since wig or hairstyle is one of the most dateable features of the entire get-up, and fashions in necklines or cravats changed a great deal faster than did those in petticoats or breeches.

FASHION AS A GUIDE TO DATING IRISH PORTRAITS 1660 – 1880

Until the Restoration of Charles II, the sartorial division in Ireland had been between those who wore 'Irish' as opposed to 'English' dress. Thereafter the rift tended more and more to be between the garb of the rich and that of the poor, as the traditional Gaelic garments were abandoned and the Gaelic gentry adopted current fashions. This change was quite obvious to those living at the time. Dr John Lynch, a Galway man, writing in the 1660s, observed "It is only within my own days that English dress has been commonly worn. We never were victims of such fickleness that, like Proteus, we should be constantly changing our dress according to the fleeting fashions daily imported from England."[1]

"Daily" importations may not have been too far wide of the truth. In 1663 periwigs were introduced to London from France, and obviously made rapid headway in smart Irish society, to judge by those shown in the portraits of Sir Audley Mervyn and Lord Delvin.[2] Sir Audley is depicted in a buff coat and the frilled or "petticoat" breeches, which suddenly went right out of favour in London in October 1666, and very soon afterwards elsewhere, being supplanted by a costume of oriental origin, known variously as "Persian dress" or "Turkish dress," consisting of a long, ornamental vest (forerunner of the waistcoat), worn under a coat whose skirts reached to the knee or below, and with shoes and stockings replacing boots save for actual use on horseback, while a knotted cravat at the throat replaced the old falling bands. The full-bottomed periwig suited this costume and, though expensive, was quickly regarded as essential. Its original flat top did not last long and as the century drew to its close, so it rose higher and higher in twin peaks above the forehead. It began as dark brown but before the end of James II's reign a fashion for ash-blonde had developed. In 1690 the will of James Roch of Killgobbane, Co. Clare, mentioned his "two fine hats," his "silver handled sword," his watch, a pair of silk stockings and his "new flaxen wig."[3] A sword was still part of the everyday dress of Irish country gentlemen: in 1665 the will of George Cary of Redcastle, Co. Donegal, mentioned "the sword I always wear."[4]

The outbreak of more hostilities in 1689, heralded by the arrival of the fugitive James II, set the country gentry

Sir Audley Mervyn, of Dublin, knight, probate 1676.
Sold at Cabra Castle 24 Sept. 1968, Lot 235. A good example of the petticoat breeches and elaborate boots that characterized the beginning of Charles II's reign.

FASHION AS A GUIDE TO DATING IRISH PORTRAITS 1660–1880

Stephen Slaughter, Anne (1721–1745), daughter of James O'Brien, M.P., m. 1744 the Right Rev. Michael Cox,
Bishop of Ossory and later Archbishop of Cashel. *A very decorative and elaborate example
of the new type of "morning dress" introduced in the 1740s. Photograph George Mott.*

FASHION AS A GUIDE TO DATING IRISH PORTRAITS 1660–1880

rummaging in their attics and press cupboards for the armour in which they (or their fathers) had fought the Carolean wars. This armour seems mostly to have been in good repair and the old corslets and helmets did duty manfully. Peace came again in 1691 and there was quite a rush to have portraits painted in the newly-burnished armour. These likenesses were mainly of the head-and-shoulders variety and display a wide diversity of barrel wigs – dark, light and medium in shade – but not much variation in the actual armour, which consisted in the main of a breast-plate and riveted sleeves of mail. Many elderly warriors, old veterans of the civil war, also put on armour to sit for a portrait. It was a sort of final triumph before the reign of Queen Anne (despite its military successes on the Continent) fairly swiftly abolished all interest in armour in Ireland, with result that the bulk of surviving armour-portraits date from this grand flourish at the turn of the seventeenth century.

The ladies' clothes of this period were a good deal less remarkable and, strangely, subject to less change. Their low-necked gowns were full-skirted and loosely cut, the waists ill defined, the sleeves elbow-length. They tended to be made of rich stuffs, silk, satin or velvet. Unlike England,[5] there were few, if any, laced bodices. Hair was dressed high above the forehead and at least one long fat ringlet allowed to trail across the shoulder. The tall wire-framed caps of lace and ribbon, so popular in England in the 1690s,[6] do not seem to have been worn in Ireland. A few aristocratic ladies were painted with a black veil or mantilla arranged over their piled-up hair, an example being Mrs Lucius O'Brien.[7]

The cloak had long been the normal female outdoor garment and its seventeenth century form was voluminous and hooded, perhaps because hats were temporarily out of favour. The blue or black hooded cloaks so widely worn by Irish peasant women in the nineteenth century, and which survived in west Cork until the 1950s, were the descendants not of the ancient Irish mantle but of the cloaks worn by country ladies in the second half of the seventeenth century. A portrait of Mrs Bryan Townsend (daughter of Bishop Synge of Cork), painted about 1715, shows her in just such a black cloak, its gathered hood

drawn over her white cap.[8]

It was during Charles II's reign that specially designed riding dress for ladies first appeared in England, having been devised in France. A male-type coat was cut to suit a lady and worn with a long, very full petticoat of heavy material; beneath the coat was a shirt, its neckline finished with a male-type cravat, and on the head – again imitating the male – was worn a periwig and feather-trimmed hat. Apart from riding, ladies at this time never wore a wig, nor was their hair dressed in imitation of one. It is hard to doubt that this smart and practical riding dress took long to reach Ireland, where riding was so universal, but I have seen no portraits of it until the 1740s.

Towards the end of the century come the first indications of what upper-class Irish children were wearing. The enchanting double portrait of Colonel Richard Talbot's daughters was painted in Dublin in 1679. The elder girl, then about ten or eleven, has a dress that is a scaled-down version of current adult fashion, but her hair is curled in the style introduced by Charles II's queen in 1662 and looks decidedly out-of-date. The little one, a mere three year-old, has a much more suitable childish dress, apart from the incongruous black gauze veil trailing down her back, and amazingly modern sandals. Little boys were clad in floor-length skirts until about the age of five or six, differentiated from their sisters by the cut of the bodice, which was more like a doublet, and the fact that their hair was not twisted into ringlets. In 1675 the records of the newly-founded King's Hospital school in Dublin detail the purchase of uniform for the pupils at this charitable establishment, each being provided with a Monmouth cap, two coats and petticoats, two shirts, four pairs of shoes, three pairs of stockings, two small bands or cravats and brass buttons, at a cost of £1 8s. 10d. a head.[9] The portrait of Kendrick Fownes of Dublin, aged twelve, showing the boy as a miniature adult, bears a close relationship to the Wissing and Vandervaart portrait of "Master Montagu Drake"[10] the chief differences being that the Irish child has a periwig instead of a hat and rather stouter boots, whose six rows of double buttons up the front must have been any boy's nightmare to fasten!

There is scant evidence as to the Irish customs in respect of clothes for infants.

Swaddling was still in vogue, and in England upper-class babies were taken to be baptized wrapped in elaborate, coloured mantles; christening robes, worn under the mantle (or shawl) seem only to have developed in the eighteenth century, and in England white christening robes only became commonplace at the beginning of the nineteenth century, though fashionable in France as early as the seventeenth century.[11] Coloured mantles were certainly used in Ireland; the 1683 will of the Rev. Samuel Ladyman, Archdeacon of Limerick, bequeathed to his grand-daughter "one green satin christening mantle with broad gold and sylver lace."[12]

Queen Anne's reign was marked by a general absence of exciting clothes and a lack of changes in fashion amongst even the most wealthy in Ireland. Admittedly, after the latest bout of war and pillage even the wealthy were feeling the pinch: the Catholic aristocracy, as a class, was finished and knew it, while the Protestant aristocracy was trying to tidy up the general mess and consolidate their land purchases following the wave of confiscations, occupations that did not leave them any abundance of spare money for showy clothes. One interesting and long-term development was that the refugee Huguenot weavers, who had settled in Dublin, invented a new fabric, which became known as Irish poplin. It was first advertised in the Dublin newspapers in 1704. Poplin is woven with a silk warp in which is buried a very fine worsted weft, leaving the warp alone visible on both sides of the material. It continued to be manufactured in Dublin for the next two hundred and fifty years, was remarkably hard-wearing and used for a wide variety of purposes, including legal, clerical and academic gowns, as well as, of course, for ladies' dresses.

The reign of George I brought little radical change to Irish fashions. A few men adopted powdered wigs, the majority adhered to the old brown variety, which was gradually becoming flat on the top. The turban-like cap worn over a wigless, shaven head, that was worn in England as a form of undress, seems to be rare to unknown in Irish portraits. Also unlike England, women wore neither powdered wigs nor powdered hair, remaining faithful to the long, trailing ringlet. The necklines of their loose, plain dresses were low, showing the edge

FASHION AS A GUIDE TO DATING IRISH PORTRAITS 1660—1880

of a white underdress beneath, a fashion which persisted into the 1740s.

By the time George II ascended the throne in 1727, the measures taken to repair the Irish economy had met with some success and the Protestant ascendency was again on its feet. This new prosperity produced the greatest extravagance in sartorial fashion ever seen in Ireland. Though the upper classes were once again happily in funds, it had not, as yet, occurred to them to spend the surplus on building themselves smart and comfortable residences (which they badly needed, all too many of them being still cooped up in converted tower houses); instead, they put the money on their backs.

A comparison between English and Irish portraits of the 1730s and 1740s shows how expensively the Irish clothed themselves at a period when clothes were relatively costly. Irish coats and waistcoats were positively stiff with gold or silver (usually gold!) braid and extensive embroidery; the stuffs chosen were of the very richest—heavy satins, glossy velvets, lavish brocades, shimmering silks and abundant, imported (or smuggled) lace. Their English counterparts, who had far more cash to dispose of, were nothing so gaudy, but they were building and equipping splendid Baroque houses. The contrast did not pass unnoticed: in 1735 Bishop Berkeley pondered on "what would be the consequence if our gentry attempted to distinguish themselves by fine houses rather than by fine clothes?"[13] Happily these extravaganzas coincided with a time when two excellent portrait painters were working in Ireland, Stephen Slaughter and James Latham, and it is in their works, particularly in Slaughter's, that these glories are recorded. Slaughter's portrait of Sir Edward O'Brien, M.P., shows embroidery run riot: not only is the entire long waistcoat (fastened by no less than eighteen buttons and with flap pockets in its skirts) solid with decoration, but the coat itself is embroidered down the entire lengths of its fronts and on a panel across the skirt at pocket-level, and is still further embellished by wonderfully worked extra-deep cuffs. One dreads to think what this magnificence had cost. The wig is a descendant of the old barrel, but grown smaller, flatter and generally neater, as well as being pure white in colour, as befitted a man of such taste. It

Henrietta Deering, Sir Emanuel Moore, 3rd Bart., (d. 1733), M.P. for Downpatrick, m.1707 Catherine Alcock, *painted in Dublin 1707. Sold at Belvedere House 9 July 1980, Lot. 249. The high barrel wig and plain, tied cravat are very typical of early 18th century. Photograph Pieterse-Davison International.*

FASHION AS A GUIDE TO DATING IRISH PORTRAITS 1660–1880

Giles Hussey, Edward O'Brien (d. 1787), *signed on back "Hussey Pinxt April 1746."*
Collection Lord Inchiquin. An interesting picture of a child dressed as a miniature adult.

seems that in Ireland of the 1720s and '30s, the rich and smart wore white wigs and the less rich and less smart retained the brown. However, the barrel wig was finally on its way out. Slaughter's portrait of John Rogerson in 1741 shows him (still stiff with embroidery) sporting a short white Ramillies wig, tied at the back with a bow.

The new-found magnificence spilled over even into riding dress. There is a sharp contrast betwen Latham's portrait of Charles Tottenham, M.P., in 1731 and Slaughter's portrait of Windham Quin in 1748. Though Tottenham's long, crimson waistcoat is heavily laced, his rich, slate-blue velvet frock coat with deep, turned-down collar, is unadorned and worn with a plain cravat. Particularly interesting are the knee-length jack boots with their bucket tops and square toes. His white wig is a transitional form between O'Brien's hang-over from the periwig and Rogerson's new tie-wig. The full new splendour of Irish riding dress emerges in Windham Quin, weighed down with gold braid. This was a final fling in the late 1740s, for such extravagance was already starting to decline.

The ladies were slower in the uptake, and apart from richness of fabric, including a lot of lace, their dresses in the 1720s and 1730s were relatively plain. They still wore their unpowdered Dutch coiffure with curls over the shoulder, and their low-cut neckline revealing the ruffle of a white underdress, which could also be glimpsed between the fastenings of the fitted bodice, a fashion which does not seem to have been favoured in England. Jewellery, long out of fashion, made something of a come-back: a variety of brooches, earrings and even choker pearl necklaces may be seen in portraits of the late 1730s, though wedding rings, condemned by the Puritans in Cromwellian times, were not generally worn again until the nineteenth century. Bodices were often fastened with jewelled or enamelled buttons. Young women were usually bare-headed, except for an occasional jewelled hair-ornament; married women might wear a little pinner on the backs of their heads, its lappets falling almost to their waists. In the 1740s there appeared a new type of morning dress, as worn by Anne Cox in her portrait by Slaughter in 1744, formed by a matching jacket and petticoat, the jacket body ending on the hip, its edges curved and

FASHION AS A GUIDE TO DATING IRISH PORTRAITS 1660–1880

often rimmed with a ruffle. This garment seems to have been virtually unknown in England. Similarly–though possibly due to a shortage of full-length Irish portraits (but possibly not)–there is no evidence of the wide side-hoops which are such a feature of Gainsborough's pictures in the late 1740s and early 1750s. Only a few of the Irish ladies have embroidery on their dresses, and fewer still are trimmed with gold or silver braid; in general the effect is muted as compared to the male birds of paradise. Hats, totally *démodé* since Carolean times, crept back into use during the 1740s. Descended from the French *bergère*, they were fetching, narrow-brimmed straw creations, perched on top of the head and sometimes decked with flowers.

The portrait of Mrs. Windham Quin, painted about 1748, shows how female riding dress aped the current glory of the male, its pale grey jacket encrusted with silver braid on its fronts, pocket-flaps, collar, cuffs and lower parts of the sleeves. Rather amazingly, the braid design on the two cuffs does not match. On her head is a brown Ramillies wig, closely resembling that which might have been worn by a man. Until the 1780s, riding seems to have been the sole occasion when Irish ladies wore wigs.

As well as a large gallery of portraits, the 1740s and '50s produce the first surviving inventories that give some indication of the clothes possessed by the middle classes, though unfortunately all those I have been able to find stem from Munster. The inventory of Dr. John McKeogh, a Catholic physician in Nenagh, Co. Tipperary, taken in May 1751, lists his garments as "1 Brown cloath body coat, 1 Ratteen body coat, 2 pairs of Breeches, 2 waist coates, 2 shirts and 8 stocks, 5 pairs of stockings, 1 Hatt and Wigg," as well as boots.[14] The 1756 inventory of the goods of Richard Ryan of Anamalle, in the same county, included "1 Crimson Velvet weastcoat, 1 Brown Laced Body Coat, 1 Olive coat with Velmholes, 1 Riding Coat, 1 Night Gown, 3 Leace Hatts, 1 Scarlett pair of Britches."[15] In this context, of course, lacing means trimmed with braid.

A most detailed list of her clothes appears in the 1751 inventory of Alice, widow of Neptune Blood of Borshalagh, Co. Clare. Reading the contents of her extensive wardrobe, it is quite hard to credit that she was aged between sixty

James Latham, Catherine, Daughter of John ffolliott, m. Owen Wynne 1690.

and seventy, since the garments might well have belonged to a young matron. Perhaps it was the accumulation of a lifetime, every garment she had ever owned carefully squirreled away! The numerous "handkerchiefs" were for neckwear, not pocket handkerchiefs in the modern sense. She had "33 caps 8s. 3d; 15 caps 18s. 6d; 5 Pair of Ruffles 5s. 8d; 22 caps 18s. 6d; 5 Cambrick Handkerchiefs 15s; 1 worked Handkerchief 12s. 6d; 9 cambrick Handkerchiefs 18s; 8 old shifts 2s; 2 old wastecoats 1s. 1d; an old stuff Gown 1s. 4d; 6 Cambrick aprons £2 14s; 7 shifts £4 11s; 9 cloath Aprons £3; 4 yards of Cambrick ruffles 6s. 6d; 1½ yards of Cambrick 9s. 10d; Remnants of thin Cambrick ruffles 2s. 8d; 3 Flannen Petty coats 2s. 4d; a striped silk Gown 18s. 6d; A Blue Taffety Gown £1 15s; a black old Poplin Gown 1s. 1d; a scarlet laced cloak 10s; a velvet cloak 8s. 1d; a Capusheen a riding hood with a deep cape 3s. 4d; a Velvet cap 6s. 6d; 2 Hoops 2s. 2d; a Bedgown £1 13s; a China Gown 6s; Another Gown 6s; a Gown 7s; 5 Petty Coats 7s; 3 Bed Gowns 3s. 4d; a pair of shoes 3d; Black Gause & white lining

1s. 1d; White Gingam for a gown £1 1s; a Quilt 3s; a pair of stockings 1s. 4d; 7 Handkerchiefs 16s. 6d; 4 Handkerchiefs 6s; 1 Handkerchief 2s; 1 Handkerchief 3d; 7 Handkerchiefs 9d; a pair of Black stockings 3d; 3 remnants of Lace 16s; 2 old muslin Aprons 2s. 6d; 4 pair of stockings 5s. 6d; a muslin worked Apron 2s. 2d; 2 gold rings £1 6s. 9d; 4 Fans 1s. 6d; Mowhair 6d."[16]

The 1748 will of Ellen Cumberford of Clonmel, a Catholic lady, mentions quite an array of garments, all bequeathed as specific legacies–a 'lase brade cap and lase handkerchief, a pair of lase ruffles, 2 lase caps, a blue damask gound, a blue Ludstris petty cote, a small rose dymond ring, 2 cambrick caps, 2 poys with my velvet poys, 2 best cloth aprons, 2 night gounds, a corsett with some of my quilted petty cotes and a dymond hoop ring.'[17] Night gowns, which had begun as a sort of dressing-gown in the early eighteenth century, had soon come to mean a plain open robe worn as casual undress. They were exceedingly popular, indeed Mrs. Jane Macnamara of Ballyvelly, Co. Clare, had nothing else, according to her 1758 inventory, which listed her attire as "1 Dimitty Night Gown 4s., 2 Callicoe Night Gowns 18s., 3 shifts 3s., 1 Lutestring Night Gown 11s., 6 Aprons 6s., 1 plad Night Gown 6s."[18] In contrast, the widowed Ellinor Warham of Ennis, Co. Clare, had a far more varied collection in 1756 when her inventory enumerated, "2 silk gowns, 1 silk petticoat, 1 cross band apron, 1 cambrick handkerchief, 2 single handkerchiefs, 1 pair of stays," the lot valued at £3. 16s. 3½d. The list continued with "4 suites of cambrick caps, 1 crape gown, 1 pair of rib roys shoes 17s. 6d. 1 velvet capushine 11s. 4½d. 2 pair of ruffles and 2 single Handkerchiefs 5s. 5d. 1 pillion, pillion cloath and riding coat £1 2s. 2d. 1 callicoe gown 10s. 10d. 1 callimancoe petticoat 4s. 4d. 1 bonten apron and 2 pair of ruffles 6s. 4d. 1 shift and an apron 3s. 3d. 1 cap an apron and a handkerchief 2s. 8½d. 3 shifts 8s. 1 ditto and an apron 4s. 6 shifts more £2."[19]

Pictorial evidence for the dress of children only resumes in the 1740s. The swaddling of infants gradually died out during the eighteenth century, to be replaced by the more practical 'long clothes.' The inventory of the "Things belonging to Master Daniell McMahon" drawn up by his mother in 1747, lists "a Cradle with a bed and quilt and two

FASHION AS A GUIDE TO DATING IRISH PORTRAITS 1660–1880

Stephen Slaughter, Frances, daughter of Richard Dawson, m. 1748 Windham Quin of Adare,
Co. Limerick, M.P. *Formerly at Adare Manor. Even dressed for riding, Mrs Quin boasts a wealth
of elaborate braid and embroidery. Courtesy Courtauld Institute of Art.*

FASHION AS A GUIDE TO DATING IRISH PORTRAITS 1660—1880

pillows, a Gown, two frocks, 4 petticoats and six capps, six binders, 4 bibbs, four hundred pound in Money – three Cradle blankets – two pillows – three pair of Shekins and one pair of shoes."[20] The combination of binders and shoes makes it hard to assess the age of the dead child.

There are quite a number of child portraits from the 1740s. Hussey's likeness of Edward O'Brien in 1746, when aged about eleven, shows him with all the adult attributes – tie-wig, scarlet waistcoat, long bright blue coat lined with scarlet, the lot. However George Quin, at much the same age, is simply and suitably clad in a pale grey collarless coat with silver buttons whose long buttonholes are trimmed with silver braid, and his own hair brushed back to resemble a wig. He is going after game and like an adult is shown holding his fowling piece. The 1765 portrait of "Master D. Daly Aged one year three quarter"[21] shows the toddler in a wondrously waisted, short-sleeved, round-necked white dress worn over a pale pink petticoat, bare-headed and with his hair clipped short. In portraits, caps seem to be the badge of female children, even though in real life little Daniel McMahon owned six.

The 1750s brought a decided change in the shape of both male and female heads. Gone were the old full-bottomed wigs and trailing ringlets. An elegant gentleman wore a close-fitting tie-wig with a rolled curl above each ear, and the tail of the wig secured by a ribbon bow at the nape of the neck. Other variants were a bag-wig, where the tail was encased in a silk bag, or a Ramillies wig that finished tidily in a pigtail, or a *toupée*, where a small wig was worn in addition to the natural hair. The ladies' heads likewise became small and neat, with the hair drawn tightly off the face and knotted at the back instead of falling in long curls over the shoulder. Exotic embroidery and flashy brocades were no longer seen and the general trend of even the richest clothes was much less outwardly extravagant. (Now, at last, money was being spent on house-building and furnishing.) The actual cut of the male garments changed little, save that frock coats increased in popularity and cravats steadily gave place to a stock neatly folded about the throat. Waistcoats became rather plain and somewhat shorter, their buttons now seldom extending below the waist; they were frequently made in white

George Quin, of Quinsborough, Co. Clare (1729–1791), inscribed "Master George 3rd son of Valentine Quin of Adare Esqr." Formerly at Adare Manor. Courtesy Courtauld Institute of Art.

or a buff colour, contrasting with the coats, which continued in shades of blue, red, black, brown or plum. Coats could be either collarless or collared, this being a time of transition between the two.

Unlike their hair-styles, ladies' dresses did not alter over much in the 1750s and '60s, remaining low-necked, waisted and with elbow-length sleeves. The white underdress, however, had ceased to show. In England there was a great vogue for decorative muslin aprons. These did make their way to Ireland but were never universally popular, and only a small minority of portraits – mostly from Ulster – show them. The Irish ladies may have thought them too close to the dress

of the peasantry to be a suitable garb for a portrait. A far more acceptable innovation was the *sac* dress, fitted in front but falling in loose folds at the back. This had been worn in England since the time of Queen Anne but seems to have become widespread in Ireland only about 1750. It retained its attraction, however, and as late as 1773 featured as her best dress in the will of Ellen Walker of Doneraile, Co. Cork, who bequeathed "to my niece Mary Cook my Red and White Sack and Petticoat, my green and white Poplin Night Gown, my White Sattin Cloak, a Blue Sattin Petticoat and a Suit of Broad Lace."[22]

By the middle of the century shoes had

FASHION AS A GUIDE TO DATING IRISH PORTRAITS 1660 – 1880

Jeremiah Barrett, inscribed "Master D. Daly
Aged one year three quarters: Jer Barrett pinxt A.D. 1765."
National Gallery of Ireland, Cat. No. 1319.

lost their square toes, becoming pointed for ladies, round-ended for gentlemen and boys. Though coats, waistcoats and breeches for little boys were still miniature versions of those for adults, a concession had crept in by way of a frilled-neck shirt: this could be closed by a ribbon bow as in the case of the Batesons,[23] or worn as an open neck as by Sir Robert Waller's small son.[24] It was only during the late 1760s that a modified form of clothing was adopted for little girls: this consisted of a simple, semi-fitted, ankle-length white dress with short sleeves and no trimmings beyond, perhaps, a ribbon or scrap of braid. Worn with a be-ribboned round cap, it strangely fore-

shadowed the plain, all-white dresses that would be universally worn by ladies in the 1790s.

All through the eighteenth century the clergy dressed in the current fashions for laymen, save when actually attired to perform their office (or to sit for their portrait!). For these formal occasions they donned a full-length, flowing black gown, normally made of the heavy Irish poplin, and covered by a voluminous white surplice. With this, they retained a form of falling bands, known as tabs, for which a fashionable stock was never substituted. Likewise, they tended to retain a conservative form of wig, presently termed a "physical wig" (being also fav-

oured by the medical profession), which was inevitably white and a good deal fuller than anything worn by Society after 1750. It seems to have been only in the closing years of the century that the everyday dress of the Protestant bishops (though not, of course, of their clergy) began to differ slightly from that of ordinary gentlemen. The Chevalier de Latocnaye noted in 1796 that "the Bishops of the Established Church wear, as a mark of their dignity, a little petticoat, which does not go below the knee, like the Scotch Highlanders, with this difference that I believe they wear a breeches under them."[25] They did indeed!

Some of James Healy's chalk drawings of the late 1760s show clothes otherwise not often depicted – gentlemen attired for skating (wearing shoes, not boots), or hunting (in smart peaked caps), and two sketches of Lady Louisa Conolly which provide interesting evidence of how a riding habit might be used by a fashionable lady for country walks and outdoor pursuits. This type of riding habit, a far cry from the splendour of Mrs. Quin twenty years earlier, was an exceedingly practical garment, composed of an easy-fitting petticoat with a matching hip-length waistcoat, cut with revers and secured at the waist by a sash, over which was worn a thigh-length jacket, cut like a man's frock coat with a collar and narrow sleeves.

The sort of wardrobe possessed by a country gentleman is recorded in the diary of William Stackpoole of Anagh, Co. Clare, who, on 26th March 1769, wrote "A List of Cloaths &c. 1 Full trimmed suit black; 1 do crimson velvet; 1 do full mourning; 1 do mourning frock; 1 white coat and britches; 1 blue coat and waistcoat; 1 silver tessera waistct; 1 purple silk waistcot and brickens bound with gold; 1 crimson with ditto; 1 pr blk silk britches; 1 pr Linnen with 2 waist; 36 shirts with 15 stocks; 6 pr fringed muslin ruffles; 4 do broad hemmed do; 5 pr white silk and 1 pr black; 2 pr weepers; 8 pr grey thread stockings; 6 handkerchiefs; 2 Night caps and bandowes; 3 pr woolen stockings and a shaving box; 2 case pistols."[26] Hats and shoes seem to have been outside his reckoning but he must have had both, and presumably a wig or two.

The late 1760s and early 1770s are the one time when a sort of "fancy dress" was worn for portraits. This originated in the sudden popularity of "Vandyke dress", as painted in England by Gainsborough and others. A good example of this is Robert Hunter's portrait of Thomas Conolly of Castletown, painted in Dublin in 1771.[27] It is notable, however, that the hair-style is contemporary and not that of the reign of Charles I, so there is no real danger of confusing its date.

By the late 1770s, ladies' hair had started to rise above their foreheads, probably dressed over a wire frame, but it remained neat, largely uncurled and, in Ireland, still unpowdered. Jewelled hair-ornaments were again popular. By the end of the decade, this neatness was suddenly supplanted by bouffant curls, achieved either with curling-irons or a wig, and powder, used to produce either a grey or pure white effect, had become all the rage. In the early 1780s there was a short vogue—and possibly only in Cork—for a dark brown wig, very full and ending in long ringlets trailing across the

shoulders. With this bouffant hair-do went a low-necked, long-sleeved, full-skirted white dress, nipped in with a sash at the waist; blue was a favourite sash-colour and sometimes a matching blue ribbon would be threaded through the hair or wig, particularly in the case of young married women. Sensibly, not all the older ladies adhered to the white dress, considering blue, plum or some other colour more flattering to their years. Their high-piled, powdered hair was topped with magnificent caps of lace and ribbon. A great deal of lace was worn, as caps, fichus, sleeve-ruffles and general trimmings. Pretty hats were fashionable too, high-crowned (of necessity!), broad-brimmed and always tastefully decorated.

The 1870s saw a great increase in the number of miniatures painted in Ireland, many of them designed to be actually worn as jewellery, either as a pendant on a ribbon or gold chain around the neck,

or as a bracelet on a black wrist-ribbon; very occasionally a tiny version might be set as a finger ring. This rise of miniature painting—so much less costly than the oil portrait—meant that far more people were painted than ever before, and from a much wider spectrum of merchant and county society. This was particularly so in Cork, where Frederick Buck worked industriously for nearly forty years.

Women were always married in their best dresses, and since many of them were painted about the time of their marriage one suspects that the dress of their portrait may well have been their wedding dress. Anne Cox is a case in point. What is now regarded as traditional bridal dress only came into general favour in the nineteenth century, its popularity being ensured by Queen Victoria who was married in 1840 in white satin and lace with a lace veil secured to her head by a chaplet of white flowers. Dorothea Herbert's *Retrospections* describe the get-

James Worsdale, The Hellfire Club, Dublin, c. 1735.
Courtesy National Gallery of Ireland.

FASHION AS A GUIDE TO DATING IRISH PORTRAITS 1660–1880

Dorothy, daughter of Hercules Rowley (d. 1785), widow of Richard, 1st Viscount Powerscourt, with her daughter,
the Hon. Isabella Wingfield, who m. 1770 Sir Charles Style, Bart., *dated 1767. Sold at Powerscourt 24 Sept. 1984, Lot 35.*
A useful example of the dress of a middle-aged widow and that of a young lady in the 1760s.
Photograph Pieterse-Davison International.

Stephen Slaughter, Elizabeth, daughter of William Brownlow of Lurgan, m. 1732 Sir John Vesey, later 1st Baron Knapton,
inscribed *"Lady Vesey by Step*ⁿ *Slaughter Dublin 1744."*
Private Collection, photograph George Mott.

John Michael Wright, Lady Catherine and Lady Charlotte Talbot, *inscribed on back*
"James Mich. Wright, a Londres, pictor Regina/pinxit Dublin anno 1679."
National Gallery of Ireland, No. 4184.

FASHION AS A GUIDE TO DATING IRISH PORTRAITS 1660–1880

up on no less than three Protestant brides in 1785. In June, the eighteen-year-old daughter of Dr. Carshore was married at Carrick-on-Suir, Co. Tipperary, in "an azure sarsnet with white ribbons," attended by two bridesmaids, one "dress'd the same way but for fear of Mistakes wore brown Ribbons," while the other—Dorothea herself—"sported my straw colour Lustring." A few weeks later, Charlotte Blunden, marrying in Co. Kilkenny, was "dress'd in a white sarsnet and a white silk Bonnet with a very long Veil to it—Her Dress was very rich with Fine Lace and costly trinkets," while "Emma Mathews and I were dress'd in white as Bridesmaids." The third bride, Fanny Blennerhasset, older than the others, was married in Dublin clad "in a plain, thin Muslin trimmed with fine Lace and blossom colour Ribbon—with a Handkerchief elegantly pinned on her head—with flowers and ornaments of that delicate hue."[28]

In marked contrast to this trio is the description of her wedding clothes given by Mary Frances, daughter of Augustin Fallon, a Catholic from Co. Roscommon. In 1791, aged sixteen, she was married in London, straight from her convent school, to James Kelly, another Roscommon gentleman. She told her granddaughter, "people in those days not troubling themselves with elaborate and extravagant *trousseaux*, it was then the fashion for brides to wear a riding habit on that important day of their lives to intimate that that they were about to change all their habits on entering the holy state of matrimony."[29] Since no such custom prevailed in England,[30] and according to Dorothea Herbert was not the practice of the Irish Protestant gentry, the only explanation seems to be that this was a tradition followed by Catholic gentry in Connaught, to which they adhered even when being married in England. Unless her grand-daughter got the story all wrong, Mrs. Kelly can hardly have been mistaken as to what she had worn at her own wedding!

Dorothea Herbert also gives a vivid picture of the evening dress worn by herself and her sister and their cousin Edward Eyre when attending the Cashel Assembly Rooms in 1789. "Fanny and I wore pink Lutestrings with thin muslin trains, and Black silk Bodices, all handsomely trimmed with black lace and green ribbon with white plumes and

Charles William Bury, 1st Earl of Charleville (1764–1835).
Sold at Belvedere House 9 July 1980, Lot 247.
This depicts the high-coat collar and brushed-back hair of the 1780s.

other ornaments on our Heads . . . Ned Eyre was one blaze of Brilliants from Top to Toe and cut a most curious figure in a pink Lutestring suit adorned with quantities of Double Paste Buttons—with Buckles and knee Bucles (*sic*) to match."[31]

The unprecedented abundance of middle-class miniatures that exist dating from the forty years that followed 1780 emphasizes the need for precise dating of clothes, since sadly so many of these are nameless and the only hope of guessing their identity is through their date. As only the head and shoulders are shown, there is additional stress on the importance of wigs, cravats, coat-collars and hair-dressing. Fashions changed with remarkable rapidity at this period, which

is a considerable help, apart from older men who might not follow it slavishly. This was observable even at the time; in 1780 Dorothea Herbert watched her relative, Sir John Blunden, reviewing his troop of Volunteers near Carrick-on-Suir, and 'a most curious figure he cut, dress'd in an old greasy suit of blue Cloth, an old shabby Hatt And a Wig Twenty Years old," while his wife "trudged after him in a plain flower'd cotton."[32]

To take the men first. By the late 1780s the trim tie-wig had softened out into a certain fulness on either side of the face and in many cases was even being replaced by the owner's natural locks, brushed out and powdered. In the years 1785–90, coat-collars rose high behind the neck and waistcoats were also made with col-

FASHION AS A GUIDE TO DATING IRISH PORTRAITS 1660–1880

*Stickland Lowry, Sarah Jellett (1724–1805), wife of Robert Holmes of Dublin, goldsmith,
signed on back "Strickland Lowry pinxit 1780." Private collection.
A splendid instance of the elaborate clothes of the 1780s – a
plum-coloured silk dress, abundant imported lace, high-piled powdered hair
and a bracelet-miniature of her husband. Photograph J. & S. Harsch.*

lars, to accommodate which coats were left unbuttoned. Coats were mainly dark blue or black, and striped waistcoats very popular. Early in the 1790s wigs were abandoned by natty young men (though *not* by our proverbial crusty old gent, who might retain any sort of elderly wig on top of his new coat), and for a few years the brushed-out natural hair continued to be lightly powdered. Men were rarely portrayed in hats, though, of course, they possessed and wore them. Coat-collars came down quite rapidly in the 1790s to lie flat upon the shoulders, while waistcoats ceased to be collared, allowing the coats to be buttoned so that only a tip of them showed. The throat was unvaryingly encircled by a plain stock, finished with an ornamental bow

in front. This was the heyday of the Irish militia, and many young men were painted in their smart new red jackets, and they can only be dated by reference to their hair and cravat, though very often the uniform jacket enables their regiment to be determined. By the end of the century powder was gone; hair regained its natural shade with its ends lightly curled and even combed into intentional disarray. Stocks became stiffer, their bows smaller and presently nonexistent. By 1810 two little collar-points had pushed out of the stock towards the chin, these points getting bigger and higher between 1815 and 1825, by which latter date the white stock was being replaced by a coloured or black one. Short sideburns had appeared in the

1790s, and gradually grew longer and more noticeable, though they were never obligatory; many of the natty young militia officers eschewed them entirely, and they are no evidence of date.

The ladies, too, went through a metamorphosis. The 1790s produced drastic changes in fashionable female dress, originating in the political upheavals of the French Revolution, and these revolutionary fashions swept into Ireland with hardly any time lag. Indeed, their coming proved to be the end of the Irish time-lag. Out went the bouffant curls or wigs (powder was dead by 1795), hooped petticoats, the tight waists, neck ruffles, jewellery and rich fabrics. Hair was now plainly dressed, at first still lightly curled, but by the turn of the century, for the first time ever, girls were seen with bobbed hair and fringes! It was a most extraordinary sight. Stays were hastily dispensed with and waist-lines rose to directly beneath the bust (highly unflattering to the stout or elderly, who nevertheless valiantly wore it), while the materials used for dresses became extremely thin, muslin or the finest cambric, sometimes almost transparent, and reputedly even put on while damp so as to adhere more closely to the figure. White alone was permissible, colours being frowned upon for almost a decade, even for old ladies. Remarkably little was worn beneath these diaphanous gowns; at best, only a shift and a flimsy petticoat, at worst, apparently, nothing at all! Given the Irish climate, it must have been all very chilly. Drawers, which hitherto had been a wholly male preserve, by the turn of the century were being worn by women for the first time, but were regarded as fast and really rather scandalous. By about 1806 the presence of such nether garments was generally condoned in smart society but they took a long time to win acceptance amongst the ranks of the country gentry: as late as 1839, drawers are not listed among the clothes required by a girl at a good boarding-school in Waterford.

The bobbed hair was short-lived and seems to have vanished by 1806. A centre parting dividing short, tight curls was the new craze. White dresses at last ceased to be *de rigueur*; pink, blue, grey or mauve became fashionable alternatives, cut with square necks and short, puffed sleeves, and even decked out with a bit of lace or a braid trimming. Waists, how-

Robert Fennell Crone (1819–1853), only child of John Robert Crone of Byblox, Co. Cork.
Private Collection. Interesting both for the wide-necked divided tunic worn over trousers and the large hat.
Photograph George Mott.

James Latham, Charles Tottenham, of Tottenham Green, Co. Wexford, M.P. for New Ross, "Tottenham in his Boots" (1685–1758), dated 1731. National Gallery of Ireland, No. 411. This shows the flat-topped white wig and long waistcoat (worn even with riding dress) of the first years of George II.

FASHION AS A GUIDE TO DATING IRISH PORTAITS 1660–1880

ever, remained high. These dresses persisted to the end of the Napoleonic Wars, with the hair steadily becoming more curly and rising at the back of the head, until by 1820 it was once again a highly elaborate *coiffure* with "puffs" and "bangs" and ringlets. In 1821 George IV's visit to Ireland (where no reigning monarch had set foot since Richard II's disastrous excursion which cost him both his throne and his life) called forth a great display of female magnificence, and portraits of this date show ladies with ornate feathered hats set on their ornate hair, wearing superb dresses and dripping with jewellery – all in marked contrast to the Empire-style simplicity of a mere twenty years earlier. Pictures suggest that during the 1820s Irish hem-lines may have been slightly longer than was then fashionable in England where an ankle-length gown was suddenly the rage.

As with their elders, so the late eighteenth century brought a decided change in children's clothes. In the case of little boys, it came earlier than for men since, from the 1770s, instead of imitating their fathers by wearing breeches and stockings, they were given a radical innovation in the shape of trousers, which would not be adopted by the very smartest adults until the turn of the century. With these narrow-legged trousers, boys wore a frill-necked shirt and round jacket, so they ceased entirely being miniature versions of the grown-ups. For younger girls, the simple white dress and ribboned cap that had appeared in the 1760s was retained, the dress acquiring a waist-sash in the 1780s, when the girls' hair was curled

though not powdered. Dorothea Herbert gives some details of her clothes in 1780, when aged about thirteen (admittedly a very precocious thirteen). Staying at her aunt's house in Dublin, she "received from the Milliner . . . a beautiful pink Sattin Slip, pink Satin shoes and a Suit of rich Gawse trimm'd with blond Lace and plenty of Marechale Powder and Rose Pomatun – thus equipp'd I figured away at the Childrens Balls, the finest Young Lady in the room – Add to this I had always the one of the 6 or 7 Pearl Pins, as She [the aunt] mostly wore a fine Set of Diamonds and insisted on my wearing her Pearls – my Aunt Cuffe too had a very fine set of Garnets which she lent me occasionally for a change."[33] Later that year, the generous Aunt Cuffe paid Dorothea's family a visit in Co. Tipperary, bringing "Me a New White Cloth Habit, a gold Lace Hat and Feather, A fine Side saddle Bridle etc – Grace Cuffe a chip Hat and a Suit of Gawse fully Trimmed with quantities of Lilac and Straw colour Ribbon – Fanny Hasset a Straw Coloured Lutestring gown." Very shortly afterwards, in anticipation of a *Grand Fête Champêtre*, Grace Cuffe "cut up a piece of Buff Sarsnet between us – We got them made into Shepherdesses a picturesque sort of short Jacket then worn – hers was Mitred with Lilac persian, Mine with blue – the Mitring quill'd with White Love Ribbon – we wore small white chip chapeaus at one side of our Heads with bunches of Natural Flowers."[34]

The wearing of caps by fashionable little girls seems to have gone out by the

1790s, though it persisted much longer among the merchant and gentry classes. Though white and pastel colours predominated in the children's clothes at this period, such colours were by no means rigidly prescribed, as may be seen in the portrait of Robert Crone, where the child is shown wearing a dark, tunic-like garment over his trousers. Brightly coloured shoes were often a feature in the get-up of small girls, even as they had been in the seventeenth century, though not since.

From about 1830, the sartorial differences between England and Ireland seem to have become almost negligible; there was virtually no time-lag and the "Irish look", so observable in the earlier period, has vanished. This was doubtless due to the increasingly rapid communication between the two countries, further facilitated by the coming of the railways.

It is hoped that by studying this article – and in particular its illustrations – and using it, if necessary, in conjunction with one of the many good books on English dress, that a fairly accurate date may be ascribed to any Irish portrait. If the garments shown bear scant resemblance to anything here, then the likelihood is that the painting is of Continental origin. One of the best readily-available books on English fashions is John Peacock's *Costume 1066–1966*, published in 1986 by Thames and Hudson at £4.95. This excellent book is entirely pictorial, with no text, and is extremely informative and easy to follow.

Rosemary ffolliott

NOTES

1. John Lynch, *Cambrensis Eversus*, ed. by Rev. Matthew Kelly, Celtic Society, Dublin, 1848.
2. Reproduced in *Irish Portraits 1660–1860*, Catalogue by Anne Crookshank and the Knight of Glin, 1969.
3. John Ainsworth, *The Inchiquin Manuscripts*, Dublin, 1961.
4. Amy Isabel Young, *Three Hundred Years in Inishowen*, Belfast, 1929.
5. John Peacock, *Costume 1066–1966*, Thames and Hudson, London, 1986.
6. *Ibid*.
7. Reproduced in *History of the O'Briens*, by Hon. Donough O'Brien, London, 1949.
8. Reproduced (badly) in *An Officer of the Long Parliament and his Descendants*, by Richard and Dorothea Townshend, London, 1892.
9. Lesley Whiteside, *A History of the King's Hospital*, Dublin, 1975.
10. Reproduced in *The Portrait in Britain and America*, by Robin Simon, Oxford, 1987.

11. Phillis Cunnington and Catherine Lucas, *Costume for Births, Marriages and Deaths*, London, 1972.
12. Rev. William Burke, *History of Clonmel*, Waterford, 1907.
13. Rev. George Berkeley, *The Querist*, 1735.
14. Rosemary ffolliott, 'Household Stuff', *The Irish Ancestor*, Vol. I, 1969.
15. *Ibid*.
16. *Ibid*.
17. Rev. William Burke, *ut supra*.
18. The Killaloe Court Book, British Library Add. Mss. 31–882.
19. *Ibid*.
20. Rosemary ffolliott, "Children's Clothes 1679–1867", *The Irish Ancestor*, Vol. II, 1970.
21. *Ibid*.
22. "Mallow Testamentary Records", *The Irish Ancestor*, Vol. I, 1969.
23. Reproduced in *The Painters of Ireland, 1660–1920*, by Anne Crookshank and the

Knight of Glin, London, 1978.
24. *Ibid*.
25. Chevalier de Latocnaye, *Rambles through Ireland*, Cork, 1798.
26. T.J. Westropp's "Notes on Co. Clare", Royal Irish Academy Mss., 3A.39, p. 65.
27. Reproduced in *Irish Portraits 1660–1860*, Cat. No. 45. *ut supra*.
28. Dorothea Herbert, *Retrospections 1789–1806*, London, 1930.
29. "What my Grandmother told me: Reminiscences of Mrs. James Kelly of Newtown, Co. Roscommon (1782–1876)", National Library of Ireland, Ms. 9903.
30. Cunningham and Lucas, *ut supra*.
31. Dorothea Herbert, *ut supra*.
32. *Ibid*.
33. *Ibid*.
34. *Ibid*.

IRISH HISTORY PAINTING

Dr. John Turpin, of the National College of Art and Design, records examples of history painting in Ireland and the world views they reflect.

History painting was regarded as the highest form of art in classical academic theory. It aimed at an heroic and morally uplifting subject drawn from the Bible, mythology and classical history, although national history was also possible. In this article I am concerned with paintings of classical mythology and of Irish history, including the painting of contemporary events. All these categories are linked by the desire to tell a story, sometimes with a serious moral and ideological purpose. By their very existence, paintings of historical subjects can have a political resonance, even if intended as pure reportage. The reason for a lack of mythological or religious history painting, either as wall decoration or easel pictures, during the seventeenth century in Ireland, was the constant warfare and insecurity of the period. This was in marked contrast to Italy, France, Spain, the Low Countries, or even England, where there were several series of history paintings in palaces and public buildings such as the Amsterdam Town Hall. In general the most fruitful periods for paintings of contemporary Irish history were usually those periods of greatest political crisis and excitement such as the Jacobite Wars, the Volunteers, the Land War and the War of Independence; the great exception was the Famine which only produced alienation and horror.

There existed in the seventeenth century a European high art tradition of battle paintings celebrating national victories. The 'Surrender of Breda' by Velazquez and Van der Meulen's paintings of Louis XIV's battles, are examples of this. It is in such a context of Netherlandish battle-pieces that we can place Jan Wyck's 'Battle of the Boyne', dated 1693.[1] This and other pictures, like W. Van der Hagen's 'The Landing of King William of Glorious Memories at Carrickfergus 1690' (1730s),[2] celebrated the 'Glorious Revolution' as it applied to Ireland, in establishing the political power of 'The Protestant Nation'. The important role of prints in multiplying various images of the Williamite victories is indicative of the need of Protestants of all classes in Ireland to have visible icons symbolizing their status and identity apart from the Catholic majority.[3] Such images, notably of William of Orange on horseback, have continued to be produced, mostly as murals on the gable ends of terrace houses in Belfast. Twin tapestries woven by Van Beaver were installed in the Irish House of Lords in 1733, the 'Battle of the Boyne' and the 'Siege of Londonderry'. These commemorated the two canonical events in the fight for Protestant 'liberties' against Catholic 'arbitrary power and tyranny', as the Whig theory would have it. These victories were the guarantee of the power and land titles of the Protestant parliamentarians.

There are some isolated examples of decorative history painting in the late seventeenth century, such as a series in a County Wicklow house of equestrian portraits with a Royalist reference with allegorical subjects (painted on planks) in a provincial Baroque style. These, and a baroque allegory of the arts in County Kilkenny (also painted on planks), were based on engravings of French, Dutch and Italian art. The tradition of decorative history painting was continued by William Van der Hagen, the Dutch immigrant artist, who worked in various country houses during the 1730s and 1740s.[4]

Personal experience of Italy gained through the Grand Tour was important in shaping the taste of wealthy noble patrons, as well as artists, to an appreciation of the European tradition of history painting. Mythological subjects drawn from Greek and Roman literature were commonplace in European history painting of the eighteenth century, which was virtually confined to decorative ensembles in Great Britain and Ireland.

Examples of this are the lunettes 'Bacchus', 'Vulcan', 'Diana' and 'Mercury' painted by the Irish artist, Jacob Ennis, in the house of his patron, Arthur Jones Nevill, at 14, Rutland Square, Dublin.[5] Ennis had been to Italy in 1754 and these paintings were in the baroque style after Pietro da Cortona at the Palazzo Pitti, Florence. Ennis was important in that as Master of the Dublin Society's Figure Drawing School, in succession to Robert West, he introduced young students to the heritage of Italian and French art of the sixteenth and seventeenth centuries, through copying original drawings and engravings. By this means he communicated the narrative language of European history painting.

Nevertheless, most of the historical subjects painted in Ireland in the eighteenth century were by foreigners. Giambattista Cipriani, who was brought to Ireland by Lord Charlemont, decorated the vestibule of the Casino at Marino with a 'chiaroscuro' (now gone).[6] He was also to have painted a ceiling of the Rotunda Hospital Chapel in the 1750s but this was not done.[7] The most extensive decorative scheme to incorporate history painting on a miniature scale was the long gallery of Castletown House, Co. Kildare, by Charles Reuben Riley and Thomas Ryder, both from England.[8] It was decorated during the 1770s in the Neo-Classical Pompeian manner, which the patron, Tom Conolly, probably came to appreciate on his visit to Italy. These are mostly small-scale panels copied from engraved pattern books of classical antiquities. The large semi-circular lunette of 'Aurora', whose authorship is uncertain, was copied from Guido Reni's painting in the Palazzo Rospigliosi, Rome. The choice of subjects was probably a combination of the taste of the artist and of Tom Conolly. The print room at Castletown is itself an anthology of conventional Anglo-Irish Grand Tour Taste for old master history painting.

Grisaille subjects of a mythological nature were favoured in the eighteenth century. Filippo Zafforini, an Italian scene painter, did the elegant series of grisaille wall and ceiling paintings of Greek subjects for Aldborough House in 1798, now all destroyed. The greatest exponent of grisaille in Ireland was Peter de Grée, who came in 1785, having been a pupil of Gheerarts. He worked at several Irish country houses and at 52, St. Stephen's Green, the town house of David La Touche, who had invited him to Ireland. One native artist who attempted to imitate these foreigners was Nathaniel Grogan, whose 'Minerva Throwing away the Spears of War' at Mount Vernon, Cork, shows that he did not have the necessary talent, or training in figure work, to create grand history painting.[9]

The leading Irish history painter of the eighteenth century, although he worked in England, was James Barry (1741-1806), whose paintings can hold their own in

Jan Wyck, The Battle of the Boyne, 1693, oil.
Courtesy National Gallery of Ireland, No. 988

IRISH HISTORY PAINTING

European terms. Barry, a Roman Catholic of modest origins from Cork, studied at the Dublin Society Schools before going to Italy under the patronage of Edmund Burke. Barry was one of the most intellectual and idealistic of all Irish artists, becoming totally committed to Neoclassical ideas while in Rome. His aim was to reform modern culture through the revival of the principles of classical art. Equally, he believed that since one of the purposes of art was to instruct, the artist should be an advocate of social reform. In the words of his biographer, Pressley, 'Barry's identity as an Irish Roman Catholic provided the driving force behind his productions; his devotion to the principles of equality, justice and religious toleration gave meaning and energy to his entire career'.[10] For him, history painting was a demonstration of a nation's worth and public character. His masterpiece, the series on 'The Progress of Human Culture' at the Society of Arts, Adelphi, London, (1777–1783), illuminated the power of civilization in the past, and how contemporary England could be improved, but there were also hidden illusions to the role of Catholicism. Since Barry believed that an artist should be wholly free of the dictates of patronage, he painted the murals free of charge. In his seriousness he can be compared to Jacques Louis David, rather than to his British contemporaries.

Of particular Irish relevance was Barry's early painting of 1763, 'St. Patrick Baptizing the King of Cashel',[11] a subject to which he returned in 1800 when he was intensely interested in Irish politics, which were then at a crisis point. Like many Irish Catholics, including the bishops of the hierarchy, he was a supporter of the Act of Union, believing that England's justice would be preferable to Anglo-Irish intransigence. He made about 1800 an allegorical design of 'The Act of Union between Great Britain and Ireland'.[12] In it Hibernia and Britannia place their hands over a crown on an antique altar; an angel holds their attributes of a harp and shield while, above, an even scales of balance is crowned by the dove of peace (Peace and Justice over all). In the background are personifications of Destruction and Envy banished by thunderbolts. It is an optimistic and idealized allegory of the Union.

Apart from Barry, two other Irish artists, Hugh Douglas Hamilton and

James Barry, Study for The Act of Union between Great Britain and Ireland, *c.1801. Courtesy the Trustees of the British Museum.*

Henry Tresham, were significant, if conventional, Irish painters of mythological history paintings, but neither painter had any of Barry's didactic and reforming zeal. Hamilton was in Italy from 1779 to 1792 where he absorbed Neo-Classical ideas. His paintings, 'Diana and Endymion' (1783) and 'Cupid and Psyche in the Nuptial Bower' (1793)[13] have traditional amorous themes, now couched in the antique-inspired Neo-Classical mode. The glorification of youthful beauty has analogies to French erotic painting of the period. Both pictures are heavily dependent on antique bas-reliefs and publications on Herculaneum and Pompeii. Hamilton was a friend of Henry Tresham, an Irish artist who had spent fourteen years in Rome. He painted standard Neo-Classical subjects, such as 'Brutus sentencing his Sons to Death' and 'The Death of Julius Caesar'. He had links with Fuseli, Romney and the Roman artists, Appiani and Cammucini.[14] He also made historical illustrations for publication.

Classical mythological subjects could carry an allegorical political meaning. This is certainly the case with the great ceiling paintings by Vincent Waldré in St. Patrick's Hall, Dublin Castle, which are the culmination of the grand style of

history painting in Ireland in Renaissance aesthetic terms. Waldré, an Italian, came to Ireland in 1787 with his patron the Duke of Buckingham, the Lord Lieutenant.[15]

The central circle of the Dublin Castle ceiling depicts George III flanked by Britannia with the Union flag, and Hibernia with her harp, attended by Justice and Liberty; an olive branch and cornucopia with two crowns and sceptres lie nearby, while Minerva and other mythological figures are included. Clio, the Muse of History, blows her trumpet, the Regalia of the Prince of Wales is carried aloft and the crown of St. Edward is held above the King's head. It is an allegorical propaganda piece arguing for the closest possible political unity between the two kingdoms, just as the Rubens ceiling in the Banqueting Hall, Whitehall, London (whose composition influenced Waldré) celebrated the Act of Union between England and Scotland.

Accompanying the central circle are two rectangular narrative subjects, 'St. Patrick lighting the Paschal Fire at the Hill of Slane', showing discredited Irish druids and indicating how native Ireland was being improved by outside christianity. 'Henry II meeting the Irish chiefs and receiving the Surrender of Dublin' is the clearest possible political statement of the power of England over Ireland, particularly in the 1790s, when this connection was coming increasingly into question by the Anglo-Irish Parliment and by more radical voices in the United Irishmen, stemming from the French Revolution.

There is uncertainty as to when Waldré painted the ceiling; it was begun in the 1790s but was still unfinished at his death in 1814. The initial conception is preserved in the model in the Royal Dublin Society. These were typical later eighteenth century history paintings, in that suggestive theatricality was favoured over exact historical reconstruction of costume and setting. A few details such as an Irish round tower and the mantles of the Irish chiefs were pointers to the later 'accurate' Victorian approach to history painting. Medieval subjects were becoming common at the Royal Academy in the late eighteenth century. Stylistically, the R.D.S. model was a good deal more baroque than the painted ceiling which reflected Neo-Classical taste. Iconographically, it is the official British Government interpretation of Ireland's past, whereby civilization, brought to Ireland by English law and religion, would dispense the benefits of liberty and justice.

The conventional academic approach to history painting began to break down in the late eighteenth century. In England, Benjamin West's 'Death of Wolfe' (1770)[16] had dealt with a contemporary British historical subject in a style which partook of ideal art, a tendency which J.L. David was to bring to completion in France. Consequently, scenes of contemporary historical reportage became more common in England. Events from history, either recent or remote, were interpreted in a new *genre*, or everyday, manner, combining elements of typography, portraiture and traditional historical composition. There was a new more 'realistic' view of the past which was to command general acceptance in the nineteenth century, in accordance with Victorian ideas on the nature of writing history as accurate factual reconstruction.

Francis Wheatley, the English artist who visited Dublin in 1779, applied the new historical *genre* approach of the American artists, West and Copley, to a series of paintings relating to the Volunteer movement in Ireland. (The Volunteers sought greater legislative and economic freedom for the Irish Parliament). Wheatley's 'The Dublin Volunteers in College Green' (1779)[17] was not a history painting in the Renaissance sense, but it marked a break-through in Irish art to a new, more immediate, artistic response to contemporary Irish events. 'The Interior of the Irish House of Commons' (1780)[18] with Henry Grattan speaking on legislative independence on 19 April 1780, was painted by Wheatley on public subscription, and retrospectively, through the engraving by J. Collyer, was seen as the visual correlative of 'Grattan's Parliament', important in the constitutional Nationalist canon of Irish history. Wheatley also did a series of commissioned subjects, usually with a Volunteer reference, for Lord Aldborough, for Sir John Irwin and for Lord Carlisle, the Lord Lieutenant.[19] These pictures correspond to the aristocratic Anglo-Irish 'Patriotic' viewpoint,

to which Wheatley responded opportunistically but also sympathetically.

Thomas Robinson, another English artist who came to Ireland in 1790, was much less talented than Wheatley, but he used the same fresh approach to history painting, notably in 'The Battle of Ballinahinch', signed and dated 1798, a few months after the battle, which was a British victory over Irish rebels, mostly Presbyterians, in County Down.[20] Robinson was unable to sell his 'Review of the Belfast Volunteers and Yeomanry by the Earl of Hardwicke the Lord Lieutenant in 1804', so he judiciously purged it of its Volunteer references by altering the picture to become a 'Procession in honour of Lord Nelson', more in keeping with Unionist thought.[21] The United Irishmen movement and the various rebellions found more ready commemorations in terms of prints, which the Nationalist market could afford to buy.

The Romantic movement in Britain, with its overwhelming stress on nature and the imagination, was a stimulus for

Thomas Robinson, The Battle of Ballinahinch, *oil. Courtesy Aras an Uachtaráin. Photograph John Searle.*

*Thomas Ryan, The Flight of the Earls, c.1960, oil.
Courtesy the Artist.*

Daniel Maclise, The Marriage of the Princess Aoife of Leinster with Richard de Clare, Earl of Pembroke (Strongbow), *1854, oil.*
Courtesy National Gallery of Ireland, No. 205.

IRISH HISTORY PAINTING

history paintings which combined landscape and figures, notably in the work of J.M.W. Turner and John Martin. Both artists influenced the Irish painter, Francis Danby, who settled in Bristol. He made his name with great Biblical history paintings such as 'The Delivery in Israel out of Egypt' (1825), 'The Opening of the Sixth Seal' (1828), and 'The Deluge' (1839).[22] These appealed to the popular taste for Gothic horror and mass spectacle as in popular entertainments, like dioramas. The 'grand manner' was also sustained by Richard Rothwell in works like 'The Blinding of Cupid' after Titian, and 'Callisto' from Shakespeare.[23]

The Victorians were interested in scenes from medieval history which had to be both imaginative heroic evocations, as well as accurate factual descriptions of the past—in reality, an impossible combination. Daniel Maclise, the Irish artist who settled in London in the 1820s, began in the fashionable *genre* approach to history with pictures such as 'Merry Christmas in the Baron's Hall' (1838),[24] which was a glossy idealization of English medieval social relations, reflecting Disraeli's 'Young England' ideas. Of special Irish relevance was Maclise's 'Captain Rock' (1834)[25] depicting an oath-taking by an Irish rural secret society which originated in some scenes Maclise himself had witnessed in Ireland; it includes a nationalist orator at a wake set in a Gothic ruin. One reviewer felt that Maclise might be mistaken for a radical. (The 1830s saw the heyday of O'Connell and the radicals in Parliament.)

Under the influence of contemporary German art, Maclise adopted a more serious approach to history painting in the 1840s. The antiquarian movement was the most visual aspect of Irish Romanticism, and Maclise's interest in Irish history, legends and archaeological artefacts developed under the influence of Crofton Croker and Thomas Moore, as in the highly fanciful 'The Origin of the Harp' (1842).[26] 'The Marriage of Strongbow and Eva' (1854)[27] was a subject initially specified by the Government as part of a programme of paintings in the Houses of Parliament to glorify British history and institutions. However, Maclise painted it outside that context, not as a Unionist, but as a nationalist picture. It clearly defines his sympathies with the defeated Irish warriors and the bard, symbol of Gaelic Ireland, all the emphasis being on trag-

edy and sacrifice. The subject relates to other pictures by Maclise on the agression of the Danes, the Normans and the English, such as the volume of engravings on 'The Norman Conquest of England' (1866). These are scenes from British history,[28] combining a grandiose sweep of historical narrative, with precise antiquarianism of costume and accessories. It is a form of public historical theatre analogous to the historical novel and costume drama concentrating on heroic and tragic themes, forerunners of Irish 'historical' melodrama in the Dublin theatre of the 1900s and of countless 'historical' films of the twentieth century.

From the 1840s, Irish history painting largely reflected the nationalist viewpoint as articulated by Thomas Davis, the spokesman for art in the Young Ireland movement. Davis complained that "Irish history has supplied no subjects for our greatest artists", and he suggested the writings of Thomas Moore and Geoffrey Keating as sources: "We have Irish artists, but no Irish Art." In his 'Hints for Historical Painting' he argued in conventional terms that "for any good painting the marked figures must be few, the actions obvious, the costume, arms, architecture and rank of the characters should be observed".[29] He published a long and visually unexciting list of subjects. The paintings by Joseph Patrick Haverty, 'Father Matthew receiving a repentant Pledge Breaker' relates to the Davis list and is a typical example of Victorian anecdotal moralizing. Also relating to Davis's list was Haverty's 'O'Connell and his contemporaries: the Clare Election of 1828'.[30] Maclise's final painting, 'The Earls of Ormond and Desmond' (1870) probably originated in the slightly different Davis subject, 'Kildare on the necks of the Butlers'. The same romantic view of Irish history informed the book illustrations of the period.[31]

The *genre* approach to reporting Irish historical events is equally evident in William Sadler's inconsequential paintings like 'The French in Killala Bay 1798' (commemorating General Humbert's invasion), and 'The Search for Michael Dwyer 1803' (the United Irishman, captured in that year).[32] Henry McManus, who was sympathetic to the ideals of Davis, painted the anecdotal picture 'Reading *The Nation*', while 'The Emigrant ship' (1853) by Edwin Hayes

has a Turneresque pathos.[33]

Other painters recorded events like journalists and, intentionally or not, gave support to the British *régime* by giving it pictorial visibility. Examples of this are Joseph Peacock's 'The Installation of a Knight of St. Patrick in St. Patrick's Cathedral 27 May 1819' (1821); Michaelangelo Hayes's 'The Changing of the Guard, Dublin Castle' (1844), James Mahony's large water-colour 'Queen Victoria and Prince Albert opening the 1853 Dublin Great Exhibition' and Richard Moynan's 'The Death of the Queen'.[34]

Davis was disappointed that Frederick William Burton did not become the painter of Irish history that he had hoped for, since Burton, through his friendship with Petrie, was very interested in Irish antiquities. Burton's 'Aran Fisherman's Drowned Child' (1841) is a *genre* scene, but is important in that it points to a new pictorial and moral emphasis on the west of Ireland. Although it is inaccurate in several details, it has a gravity of treatment and reliance on old master devices which raises it above the numerous petty anecdotal scenes of peasant life in so many Victorian books on Ireland. Burton argued that a national art could not be forced. His painting, 'The Meeting on the Turret Stairs', in the National Gallery of Ireland, belongs more to the orbit of English Pre-Raphaelitism.[35]

For Dr. Cyril Barrett, "not every historical painting with a national subject is a nationalist painting". It was his view that "if in the context of a nationalistic movement, an artist chooses to paint heroes or events of a national significance then this must be regarded as nationalistic art".[36] One could say that the crucial issue is the presence, even by implication, of a moral or ideological political meaning in the work. Despite the propaganda of Davis in *The Nation*, there was no demand for such subjects from the rising Catholic middle class, who wished to be socially assimilated into established Protestant social conventions and taste. Accordingly, prints of seascapes, townscapes and British military subjcts were most common. However some historical prints by artists like the Brocases were made of events from the Williamite wars and the rebellion of the United Irishmen.

In the 1845 Royal Hibernian Academy exhibition, there were four historical paintings, three from medieval Ireland, and one by N.J. Crowley, 'O'Connell in Prison'.[37] This small number still encouraged *The Nation* to state that "the attention of artists is directing itself to the right road". In the succeeding major exhibitions of art and industry in Ireland, very few Irish historical pictures appeared in the art sections. The exception was the Irish exhibition at South Kensington in 1888, which was at a time when the Land League agitation had already proved to be successful as a mass rural movement. Five paintings related to either evictions or boycotts.[38] This exhibition demonstrated the close connection between the production of historical paintings and the emotion generated by contemporary political movements.

The Famine was the central historical event of nineteenth century Ireland, but its deeply socially destructive nature to all classes made it repellent to artists and patrons alike. It is noteworthy that it was G.F. Watts, the celebrated English artist, who painted 'The Great Famine' (1850), a stark portrayal, which was originally titled 'Irish Eviction'. This work reflects not only the individual humanity of Watts, but also the newspaper publicity on the depressed state of rural Ireland since the Famine of 1845–47, which was affecting English public opinion.[39] One of the results of the Famine, the emigrat-

ion of Irish peasants to work in England, was recorded in Walter Deverell's 'The Irish Vagrants' (1853) which shows a poor Irish labouring family at harvest time on an English farm, a critique of British as much as Irish rural society.[40]

Erskine Nicol, a Scotsman, painted realistic peasant subjects such as 'Scene in an Irish Cabin' (1851),[41] but in general, depictions of Irish rural life were sentimental and anecdotal stereotypes, as in the work of Samuel McCloy, Joseph Haverty or the illustrations of Irish travel books. However, the naturalistic movement in art and literature in France or England, began to result in a new more realistic type of painting by the 1880s. Two paintings by the English artist, Lady Butler (born Elizabeth Thompson), 'Listed for the Connaught Rangers' (1879) and 'Evicted' (1890)[42] mark a turning point towards a closer description of Ireland's contemporary social realities. Her husband, an Irish officer in the British army, was an enthusiast for Home Rule and for political reform in Ireland which views she shared. 'Listed' shows two young peasant lads walking with the recruiting sergeant, leaving behind their beautiful but poverty-stricken landscape. 'Evicted' was a comment on the land war in Ireland showing a woman thrown out of her unroofed cottage. With her upturned glance and proud demeanour, she is depicted as the victimiz-

ed heroine. Critics in London avoided the political indictment of England, implicit in both pictures. 'Evicted' was significant in that it marked a departure towards a more realistic description of Irish peasant life, yet equally it pointed to a heroic idealization of the modern Gaelic peasantry.

In the late nineteenth century most Irish artists came from upper class Protestant backgrounds; they studied in France where they were drawn to a modern aesthetic approach which rejected the moralizing of Victorian art. They were interested in landscape, portraiture, still life and conventional *genre*, but not in pictures of Irish social or political significance for which there would have been no market. Jack Yeats, who also came from the upper class, was reared in Sligo, and went with John Synge to make drawings in the West of Ireland, was to be the great exception. He marked the pictorial turning point to a new moral revaluation of people of the West.

In the early twentieth century large scale decorative painting enjoyed a renewed life. Sir William Orpen painted three large pictures between 1913 and 1916 which are his own ironic and sardonic comments on the Irish literary and cultural revival of those years: 'Sowing the Seed' (1913) is an allegory of the changes in Irish art education promoted

George Frederick Watts, The Irish Famine, 1849–50, oil on canvas. Courtesy the Trustees of the Watts Gallery, Compton, Surrey, England.

Walter Deverell, The Irish Vagrants, 1873, oil on canvas. Courtesy the Johannesburg Art Gallery.

IRISH HISTORY PAINTING

by the new Department of Agriculture and Technical Instruction; he may also have intended the girl to represent the spirit of *Sinn Fein* sowing the seed. The 'Holy Well' (1915) with its nudes, and 'The Western Wedding' (1914), with its bride and groom kneeling in the roadway, are strange and unreal celebrations of Irish peasant piety, sexuality and customs. Yet in another way they are modern anti-romantic comments by an Anglo-Irishman on the gushing idealization of western peasant culture.[43]

Municipalities in Britain and Ireland, proud of their history, sometimes commissioned murals as in the case of Ford Madox Brown's series on the history of Manchester in the City Hall. Between 1913 and 1917, James Ward, headmaster of the Dublin Metropolitan School of Art, directed the painting of a set of twelve frescoes in the rotunda of the City Hall, Dublin, assisted by Harry Clarke and other students.[44] The eight narrative subjects came from medieval Ireland, with three of them relating to the Danes, all sufficiently remote so that Unionist and Nationalist could agree. The subject matter and style was in the tradition of Maclise with some echoes of Burne Jones. Similar in style, but with a greater debt to Puvis de Chavannes, was Frederick Cayley Robinson's 'The Landing of St. Patrick' (c. 1912)[45] which was commissioned for Sir Hugh Lane's new art gallery.

Emotionally and stylistically it belongs to the nineteenth century. The romantic mythological paintings of George Russell (AE) are within the European *Fin de Siècle* symbolist movement but also relate to the writers of the 'Celtic Twilight'. One of his finest achievements was a series of decorative 'Parnassian' murals painted for Horace Plunkett's house in Merrion Square and later transferred to the National Gallery of Ireland.

The country was convulsed by the War of Independence and Civil War between 1916 and 1923. For nationalists, it was the heroic modern moment in the age-old struggle with England. Several artists responded to the violence of the day in creating images from a national point of view. Kathleen Fox's 'The Arrest' (1916) depicts the surrender of Countess Markievicz and Michael Mallin outside the College of Surgeons after the Rising. She was moved by this scene, which she herself witnessed, and she included herself

William Orpen, Sowing the Seed, *1913, oil. Courtesy the Mildura Arts Centre, Victoria, Australia.*

as an onlooker in the painting. To do such a picture was a clandestine act and she sent it to New York for safety on completion. She was patriotically inclined, having known several of the leading revolutionaries, and her painting, 'The Ruin of the Four Courts' (1922), portrays an incident which marked the beginning of the Civil War.[46] These pictures expressed her feelings at the time, although in later years she was to stress a purely painterly justification. A more conventional 'official' approach is that of Wal. Paget's drawing, 'Scene at the General Post Office Easter Week, 1916', which is an imaginative reconstruction showing the leaders, Patrick Pearse, J.M. Plunkett and Thomas Clarke surrounding James Connolly on a stretcher as a 'martyr'.[47]

Jack Yeats made the finest pictorial response to the historical events of the day. He was a romantic idealist in his commitment to Irish self-determination but he was also deeply sympathetic to the predicament of individuals caught up in tragic events. Thomas MacGreevy makes large claims for Yeats as an historical painter: "Those years constituted a tragic and heroic phase of Irish history. And in the pictures commemorating them, Jack Yeats lifted the art of painting in Ireland to a place of heroic tragedy it had never before attained to. There is nothing grandiose or pompous about his historical pictures. There is no flourish in them". For Hilary Pyle they are 'elegies'.[48] Certainly there is no sense of propaganda. They are deeply personal and human statements expressing the artist's intense

patriotism and human sympathies, yet also they are products of a Modernist outlook.

Yeats was himself an early witness to public events, as when he recorded a meeting of the Irish Republican Brotherhood, probably in Mayo, in 1905. His painting 'The Public Orator' was inspired by Pearse speaking at a Volunteer rally in Drumcondra in 1914, and he sketched 'The Lying in State of the Fenian O'Donovan Rossa' in 1915. In 'Batchelor's Walk in Memory' (1915), a girl scatters flowers in memory of people shot by the British military in 1914. The theme is historical although the incidentals are commonplace, and Yeats's strategy is to describe the larger historical tragedy through a small poetic detail. He recalled the role of women in the independence movement in 'Communicating with Prisoners' (1924) where women in the foreground wave to women prisoners inside Kilmainham Jail. A telling detail is the advertising hoarding with a poster which reveals what is available to us but not to the prisoners. 'The Funeral of Harry Boland' (1922) commemorates a man who took the Republican anti-Treaty side in the Civil War and died of wounds while resisting arrest;[49] Yeats, too, as an idealist, rejected the treaty; he included the IRA uniforms, the round tower of O'Connell's tomb, Cumann na mBan carrying wreaths and the priests, all glimpsed from the position of an onlooker in the crowd, the artist as individual sympathizer, not as official recorder or mouthpiece.

Yeats's sensitive interpretations of Irish history are remarkably dissimilar to those of Sean Keating whose paintings came exclusively in reaction to the post-1916 Republican movement. 'The Men from the West' (1917), with the ethnic Aran islands costume, is a highly romanticized and unreal image. It is more instructive to interpret it as an allegory of the ideological link between the remote West of Ireland, as 'true' repository of ancient Irish culture, and the new Ireland, being born by force of arms. In addition, the self-portrait aspect dramatizes the idea of artist as revolutionary. 'The Men of the South' (1922), is more realistic and less powerful, showing the trench-coated Republicans, in the heart-land of the IRA, waiting in ambush. Keating was not interested in Modernist conventions, which were used elsewhere in Europe to

IRISH HISTORY PAINTING

express revolutionary ideas, but fell back on traditional realism with a Spanish reference as best suited to be a vehicle for the Republican message. His style and imagery had interesting similarities to the official realism favoured by Communist and Fascist states between the Wars as the only comprehensible style for ideological mass communication.[50]

Far closer to observed reality was Keating's series of pictures commissioned in 1926 to illustrate the development of the hydro-electric scheme on the river Shannon.[51] It was the first instance of a major public commission by a government agency of the new State, seeking to describe its operations. The modern world had hardly touched rural Ireland before electrification and the Shannon scheme had immense symbolic importance for the vitality and success of the independent Irish State. This vast in-

dustrial project was seen by government, the E.S.B. and by Keating as a major heroic national challenge. In 'Night's Candles are burnt out' (1929),[52] according to the artist, "The stage Ireland and the stage Irishman" are symbolized by the skeleton, the new order by the young family and by the capitalist engineer (with his massive turbines behind him) who disregards the gunman as *passé*, like the out-dated oil lamp. The heroic gunmen of Keating's earlier works are overtaken here by the modern technology of the new Ireland. "The dim candlelight of surviving medievalism in Ireland is fading before the rising sun of scientific progress."[53] However, the literal realism damages the credibility of the allegory. '*Der Obermann*' (late 1920s)[54] showing a German engineer eating his lunch, turned away from the Irish girl who has brought it, may be seen as a comment on

the mutual incomprehension and hostility between the German and Irish workers in the scheme.

In a number of other paintings such as 'The Aran Fisherman and his Wife' (1920s), '*Slán Leat a Athair*' (1935), and 'Brethren So Run' (1938),[55] Keating raises Aran *genre* subjects to the level of heroic statements where he promotes a particular view of the normative excellence of western culture. Although most civil servants, parliamentarians, teachers and priests of the new Ireland did not come from Aran, they did come from rural parts, and Irish was the first official language of the State; in that sense the traditional religious and social values expressed by Keating's Aran pictures are a symbolic expression of the psychological reality of the Irish Free State and of its dominant ideology.[56] The same could be said of pictures like Patrick Tuohy's 'A

Sean Keating, Night's Candles are burnt out, 1929, oil. Courtesy Oldham Art Gallery, England.

IRISH HISTORY PAINTING

Mayo Peasant Boy' (1918) and Charles Lamb's 'Dancing at a Northern Crossroads' painted in 1920 at the height of the Anglo-Irish War[57] which encapsulated what Lamb called the 'national essence' and what the *Taoiseach* Eamonn de Valera later immortalized in the famous radio broadcast about 'frugal comfort' and 'rural pastimes'.

Sir John Lavery, despite his English residence, retained a life-long interest in Irish affairs. Both he and his wife, Hazel, identified strongly with Michael Collins, who visited their studio in Cromwell Place during the Treaty negotiations. When Collins was killed in the Civil War, Lavery painted 'Love of Ireland' (1922) showing him lying in state, which is a closely focussed study of the 'martyred hero'. It relates, as McConkey points out, to a number of nineteenth century records of death chambers.[58] The close connection between the Catholic Church and the Irish Free State, so unlike the cool nineteenth century relationship between that Church and the state is implicit in Lavery's 'Blessing of the Colours' (1920s)[59] where a Bishop blesses the tricolour held by an officer. Lavery painted other pieces of historical reportage such as 'The Ratification of the Treaty in the House of Lords' (1922) and 'Casement on Trial' (1916)[60] which commemorated an event viewed by nationalists as the classic case of British vengeance towards Ireland.

A high point in the nationalistic approach to history painting was the inauguration in 1944 of the collection of historical pictures by Dr. Douglas Hyde, first President of Ireland, "Illustrative of the Struggle of Ireland throughout the centuries to assert its nationhood and the right of its people to develop its own culture".[61] The nationalistic canon of Irish history stressed certain key events such as the Flight of the Earls in 1607, which marked the end of the Gaelic order. Tom Ryan, a former pupil of Keating, did a painting of this subject.[62] He said that he painted it "as a consequence of a feeling that Ireland had not been well provided for in the area of history painting and that we had not the benefit of pictorial commentary, so much a feature of the art of other European states." He viewed the painting as "a patriotic and national gesture, a contribution to an Irish historical calendar and perhaps a worthwhile artistic exercise as well".[63]

Robert Ponsonby Staples, Shipbuilding in Belfast, *1904–24. Triptych. Courtesy Ulster Museum.*

IRISH HISTORY PAINTING

He aimed to include the *genres* of figure, portraiture, costume study and still life; he worked with arms from the National Museum and costume specially made up. It shows Hugh O'Neill departing for Rome, blessed by a Dominican, symbolizing the belief that although the Gaelic order was departing, the Catholic Church would remain with the people. The painting is realistic in detail, but couched in a neo-Baroque composition in a style strongly against the emerging Modernist consensus of Irish State patronage of the 1950s. It is a very belated nationalistic counterweight to the Battle of the Boyne paintings, and an affirmation of Ireland's links with Catholic Europe.

In nationalistic theory, the Fenians were of the greatest importance as they initiated the underground physical force movement, the Irish Republican Brotherhood, which eventually led to the 1916 Rising. Maurice MacGonigal, a former member of the I.R.A. and a former pupil of Keating, painted 'Rescue of the Prison Van, Manchester' which recalls a vivid event of 1867 in Fenian history. Yet, in another work, 'Dockers' (1935),[64] MacGonigal created a powerful image of labour, with dockers standing to be hired, almost a socialist subject, which raised moral issues about the men on to a level of history painting far beyond descriptive *genre*.

In contrast to the nationalistic viewpoint was the triptych 'Shipbuilding in Belfast' (1904–24) by Sir Robert Ponsonby Staples, depicting the turbine makers, a liner on the stocks and the Bangor boat, which all celebrated the Belfast Unionist heritage. In Joan Fowler's view, "The visual codes of 'Unionism' are in popular culture rather than in fine art, a divide which William Conor managed to cross".[65] Certainly, Conor's scenes of Ulster life which showed the British army, the War and the shipyards, are largely a record of various aspects of the life of the Unionist community. Belfast's industrial heritage was celebrated in the mural by John Luke in the City Hall, Belfast, to mark the Festival of Britain in 1951 which depicts the shipbuilding, pottery and linen industries in the seventeenth century with a background of Protestant churches. To a far greater extent, however, it was in the popular, heraldic, outdoor murals that the Ulster Unionists celebrated their history.

Robert Ponsonby Staples, Shipbuilding in Belfast, *1904–24. Triptych. Courtesy Ulster Museum.*

IRISH HISTORY PAINTING

The traditional romantic nationalistic approach to Irish history painting could be said to have ended with the celebrations in 1966 to mark the fiftieth anniversary of the Rising. It was an occasion of much revisionary and critical re-appraisal by Irish historians of the earlier certitudes and the infallibility of Pearse's teachings. The competition for an historical painting saw the top prizes go to Modernist pictures by John Kelly, James Nolan and Charles Harper, rather than Tom Ryan's more identifiably realistic and nationalistic painting of the GPO's interior or John Coyle's large scale-mural which included the executed signatories of the Proclamation.[66] The exhibition demonstrated that, with the advent of the Modern Movement in art, the traditional nationalistic narrative or allegory based on a publicly-shared ideology had become marginalized by individual subjective response. Modernist formalistic priorities and preference for abstraction left little room for ideological art of any stripe. Within the international Modern Movement, historical paintings like Picasso's 'Guernica', 'Massacre in Korea' or 'War' and 'Peace' (Vallauris), were isolated examples. Only the Mexican muralists and the Russians made significant statements of history painting since 1930 but these were in locations remote from the fulcrum of the art world. In Ireland, the sophisticated treatment of themes from history, in an ironic and self-questioning mode using artistic quotation, by such artists as Robert Ballagh, has opened new possibilities. Nevertheless, in Northern Ireland, with its strong tribal identities, the age-old political crisis continues, and the making of images relating to Irish history still has power as a means of public communication.[67]

John Turpin

NOTES

I have included paintings by foreigners and work by Irish abroad within a broad definition of Irish history painting.

1. Oils by Jan Wyck are in The National Gallery of Ireland and in the Ulster Museum.
2. In the Ulster Museum; see Anne Crookshank and the Knight of Glin, *The Painters of Ireland*, London, Barrie and Jenkins, 1978, illustrated p. 58. They stated that William Van der Hagen was commissioned in 1728 to take six prospects of scenes in the Williamite Wars, to which the Ulster Museum picture relates.
3. See 'Cuimhneachan 1916', Catalogue of an exhibition at the National Gallery of Ireland (Nos. 3, 6, 7, 8, 9, 10) which included a number of prints of the Williamite Wars. (This exhibition was separate from the Municipal Gallery one, of 1966, cited at the end of these notes).
4. See Crookshank and Glin., op. cit., pp. 31, 32 and 55-57.
5. Three of these are in the National Gallery of Ireland, 'Vulcan ends the manufacture of Arms', 'Diana Suspends Hunting', 'Mercury announces Peace to Mankind'.
6. David Newman Johnson, 'The Casino at Marino', *The Irish Arts Review*, Vol. 1, No. 3, Autumn 1984, p. 20.
7. C.P. Curran, *Dublin Decorative Plasterwork*, London, Tiranti, 1967, p. 52.
8. Ann Margaret Keller, 'The Long Gallery of Castletown House', *Bulletin of the Irish Georgian Society*, XXII, 1979. She lists the Italian publications which were the sources of the Castletown images.
9. Crookshank and Glin, op. cit., Ch. 9 'Foreigners in Ireland and Decorative Painters'.
10. 'James Barry, the Artist as Hero', Catalogue of exhibition at the Tate Gallery, 1983, compiled by William L. Pressly, p. 18. For comprehensive catalogue information, see William L. Pressly, *The Life and Art of James Barry*, New Haven and London, Yale, 1981.
11. National Gallery of Ireland, on loan from Terenure College, see Pressly (1981), pp. 3 and 228.

12. The British Museum, Pressly (1981), p. 252 (No. D. 43). A preliminary version in the Ashmolean Museum, Pressly (1981), p. 251 (No. D. 40).
13. Respectively, in private collection, England, and in The National Gallery of Ireland. For recent information on the artist, see Fintan Cullen, 'Hugh Douglas Hamilton in Rome, 1779–92', *Apollo*, CXV, February 1982, pp. 86–91, and 'Hugh Douglas Hamilton's Letters to Canova', *The Irish Arts Review*, Vol. 1, No. 2, Summer 1984.
14. Walter Strickland, *A Dictionary of Irish Artists*, Dublin and London, 1913, II, pp. 453-457; also Crookshank & Glin, op. cit., pp. 94, 95.
15. See John Gilmartin, 'Vincent Waldré's Ceiling Paintings in Dublin Castle', *Apollo*, XCV, January 1972; and Edward McParland 'A Note on Vincent Waldré' which discusses the dating problem, *Apollo*, XCV, November 1972, p. 467.
16. The National Gallery of Canada.
17. The National Gallery of Ireland. See Ross Watson, 'Francis Wheatley in Ireland', *Bulletin of the Irish Georgian Society*, IX, No. 2, April-June, 1966. It is not clear whether the picture was commissioned since it was raffled; the preparatory water-colour is in the Victoria and Albert Museum.
18. Leeds City Art Gallery, Lotherton Hall.
19. 'Lord Aldborough on Pomposo, a Review in Belan Park, Co. Kildare' (National Trust, Waddesdon Manor); 'Review of Troops in Phoenix Park by General Sir John Irwin' (National Portrait Gallery, London); 'Lord Carlisle, Lord Lieutenant, Riding in Phoenix Park' (Coll. George Howard).
20. Arus an Uachtaráin, see Catalogue, 'Collection of Historical Pictures etc. established by Dr. Douglas Hyde, President of Ireland, 1944' (No. 41). I am grateful for information from the President's Secretary.
21. The Belfast Harbour Office.
22. On these see Eric Adams, *Francis Danby: Varieties of Poetic Landscape*, New Haven and London, Yale, 1973.
23. In the Ulster Museum and the National Gallery of Ireland respectively.

24. The National Gallery of Ireland, 'Daniel Maclise 1806–1870', Catalogue of an exhibition at the National Portrait Gallery, London, compiled by Richard Ormond and John Turpin, The Arts Council of Great Britain, 1972.
25. Strawberry Hill, Twickenham; on 'Captain Rock', see John Turpin, *The Life and Work of Daniel Maclise 1806–1870*, unpublished Ph.D. thesis, The University of London, 1973, pp. 87-90. Maclise also made a drawing, 'A Catholic Association' (Victoria and Albert Museum) − a satirical commentary on one of the meetings of Daniel O'Connell's political organization.
26. Manchester City Art Gallery.
27. The National Gallery of Ireland.
28. cf. Maclise's 'King Alfred in the Camp of the Danes', 1842, Laing Art Gallery, Newcastle-upon-Tyne (Maclise Exhibition 102), 'Edward I presenting his infant son, the first Prince of Wales, to the Welsh People', c.1848–53 (Maclise Exhibition 103, Victoria and Albert Museum).
29. Davis published his articles at intervals in the 1840s in The Nation, but these were collected and published posthumously, *Thomas Davis, Literary and Historical Essays*, Dublin, James Duffy, 1854, p. 153 'National Art', and p. 169 'Hints for Historical Painting'.
30. Both Haverty pictures are in the National Gallery of Ireland.
31. See Thomas Wright, *History of Ireland*, 1854, drawings by Henry Warren, engraved by J. Rogers; C.F. Cusack, 'The Nun of Kenmare', *The Illustrated History of Ireland from Early Times: 400 AD–1800 AD* with illustrations by Henry Boyle, 1868, Kenmare, republished, Dublin, Manfield Publishing Co., 1986.
32. Both Sadler pictures are in the National Gallery of Ireland. Nicholas Pocock's 'Pursuit of the French Squadron after the Surrender of *Le Hoche 84* . . . *Oct. 12, 1798*' (Ulster Museum) commemorates the defeat of Wolfe Tone and French support for the United Irishmen.

33. Both MacManus's and Hayes's pictures are in the National Gallery of Ireland.

34. The location of the pictures are as follows: Peacock (Brabourne Coll.); M. Hayes (Army Museum, Ogilby Trust and Cavalry Club, London); J. Mahony and R. Moynan (National Gallery of Ireland). See 'Irish Art in the 19th Century', Catalogue of an exhibition at the Crawford Municipal Art Gallery, Cork, 1971, compiled by Cyril Barrett.

35. Both Burton pictures are in the National Gallery of Ireland, see Marie Bourke, *The Aran Fisherman's Drowned Child by Frederick William Burton RHA*, Dublin, 1987 and 'The Aran Fisherman's Drowned Child', *Irish Arts Review*, 1988.

36. Cyril Barrett, 'Irish Nationalism and Art', *Studies*, Winter 1975, p. 398 et seq.

37. At the 1845 RHA exhibition the subjects were, G.F. Mulvany: 'St. Patrick Baptising the King of Munster' (188); Samuel Watson: 'The Battle of Clontarf' (335); J. Mc Nevin: 'The Surprise of Turgesius' (432); and N.J. Crowley: 'O'Connell - Painted in Prison' (192). In the classification of occupations in the 1861 Census of Ireland, four persons described themselves as 'Historical Painters' and of these, three were Roman Catholics and one was a Protestant. (Information from Brian de Breffny.) A reasonable interpretation of this is that the Catholics, for nationalistic reasons, had more interest in subjects from Irish history. However, these 'Historical Painters' were a tiny fraction of the total number of artists recorded.

38. At the Irish Exhibition at South Kensington the five 'land war' paintings were, 'A Boycotted House' by Georgina Borrer; 'Boycotted' by M.D. Webb-Robinson; 'Notice to Quit' by James Brenan (Headmaster of the Cork School of Art); 'An Impending Eviction' by R. Staunton Cahill; 'The Eviction' by J. Tracey.

39. It is in the Watts Gallery, Compton, Surrey. Watts visited his friend, the Irish poet, Aubrey de Vere, in Ireland in 1850, after he had painted the picture in his London studio. It is one of a quartet of pictures depicting social problems (the others being British scenes). I am grateful for information from Richard Jeffries, Curator of the Watts Gallery.

40. Deverell's painting is in the Johannesburg Art Gallery. I am grateful for catalogue information sent by Mrs. Gillian E. Carman of the Gallery. See Robin Ironside, with a descriptive catalogue by John Gere, *Pre-Raphaelite Painters*, London, The Phaidon Press, 1948, Plate 24. See quotation from Deverell's Diary, p. 28; also *Letters of Dante Gabriel Rossetti*, Oxford, Clarendon Press, 1965, Vol. I, p. 198, letter 172 of 14 May 1854. The painting is extensively noted in the art historical literature of the 1980s.

41. Erskine Nicol recorded the Famine in a series of sketches; see also 'Irish Art in the 19th Century' Exhibition Catalogue, 1971, Nos. 92, 93 'Notice to Quit', and 94.

42. See Paul Usherwood, 'Lady Butler's Irish Pictures', *Irish Arts Review*, Vol. 4, No. 4, Winter 1987, pp. 47–49, with colour illustrations of both pictures, 'Listed' (Bury Art Gallery and Museum England), and 'Evicted' (Depart-

ment of Irish Folklore, University College Dublin).

43. See Bruce Arnold, *Orpen. Mirror to an Age*, London, Jonathan Cape, 1981, pp. 290-296. 'Sowing the Seed' (Mildura Art Centre, Victoria, Australia); 'The Western Wedding' (destroyed); 'The Holy Well' (The National Gallery of Ireland).

44. See John Turpin, 'The Dublin Metropolitan School of Art, 1900–1923', part 3, *Dublin Historical Record*, XXXVIII, June 1985, No. 3, p. 86. See Headmaster's Annual Reports for 1912–13 and 1913–14; also Reports of the Department of Agriculture and Technical Instruction, 1916–17 and 1918–19. See also *Frescoes on the City Hall* (leaflet), Dublin Public Libraries, Archives Division, City Hall, Dublin. (The dates in the Headmaster's Reports are probably the most reliable.)

45. 'Irish Renascence', Catalogue of exhibition, Pyms Gallery, London, 3–29 Nov. 1986, introduction by Kenneth McConkey, which illustrates F.C. Robinson's 'The Landing of St. Patrick', p. 10. McConkey's introduction, 'Cultural Identity in Irish Art', is a valuable overview.

46. 'The Arrest' (Sligo Art Gallery); 'The Ruin of the Four Courts' (University College Dublin, Newman House). See Lynda Johnson Fox 'An Artist of the Rising, the Life and Work of Kathleen Fox-Pym, 1880–1963, Ms. thesis, Dublin, The Institute of Professional Auctioneers and Valuers, May 1988, pp. 33-37.

47. In the National Museum, see Catalogue, 'The Collection of Historical Pictures etc. established by Dr. Douglas Hyde, 1944' illustrated in James Carty, *Ireland from the Great Famine to the Treaty of 1921*, Dublin, C.J. Fallon, 1958, p. 184. On the Anglo-Irish War, see also two paintings by Archibald McGoogan, 'The Burning of the Custom House' (New Ireland Assurance Co.) and 'Easter Week after the Bombardment'.

48. Thomas MacGreevy, 'Three Historical Pictures by Jack B. Yeats', *The Capuchin Annual*, 1949, pp. 238-251; and Hilary Pyle, *Jack B. Yeats*, London, Routledge and Kegan Paul, 1970, pp. 117, 119.

49. The locations of the Yeats pictures are as follows in the order of mention, 'A Political Meeting in the West of Ireland' (Sligo Art Gallery), 'The Public Orator' (Pyms Gallery), 'Lying in State of the exiled Fenian O'Donovan Rossa' (National Gallery of Ireland), 'Batchelor's Walk' (Hugh Lane Municipal Gallery of Modern Art, Dublin), 'Communicating with Prisoners' (Sligo Art Gallery), 'The Funeral of Harry Boland' (Sligo Art Gallery). See 'Jack B. Yeats and his Family', Catalogue of an Exhibition at Sligo County Library and Museum, 29 Oct.–29 Dec. 1971.

50. See 'Critics Choice', Catalogue of an Exhibition by the Association of Irish Art Critics at the Hugh Lane Municipal Gallery of Modern Art, September 1988, article by Joan Fowler, 'Sean Keating, The Men of the West', pp. 16, 17.

51. See 'Keating and the ESB', Catalogue of an Exhibition of paintings by Seán Keating, Royal Hibernian Academy Gallagher Gallery, Ely Place, Dublin (insert in the RHA Exhibition Catalogue, 1985). Texts by Thomas Ryan

PRHA and Patrick Gallagher.

52. Oldham Art Gallery (currently on loan to ESB offices, Dublin). See 'The Problem Picture: End of the Stage Irishman', *The Irish Times*, 6 May 1929; see Brian Kennedy, 'Irish Art and Modernism, 1920–1949', unpublished Ph.D. Thesis, T.C.D., May 1987.

53. Quoted by Hugh Butler in 'Ireland's Industrial Renaissance', *The Sphere*, 9 May 1931; I am grateful to Deirdre Haywood, Director of Cultural and Information Services, Oldham, for information.

54. Pyms Gallery, London, 1986. See 'Irish Renascence', op. cit. (27), illustrated; see also Kenneth McConkey, 'Paintings of the Irish Renascence', *The Irish Arts Review*, Vol. 3, No. 3, Autumn 1986, p. 21.

55. These Keating pictures are located in order of mention as follows, the Crawford Art Gallery, Cork; the Ulster Museum; Coll. John P. Rehill.

56. Keating also did some religious works such as 'St. Patrick lights the Paschal Fire at Slane', commissioned by the Haverty Trust, to mark the 1932 Eucharistic Congress (Irish College, Rome); he developed his allegorical work in commissions for the Irish Hospitals Trust, 1938, and for the New York World's Fair, 1939. See also Brian Kennedy. 'RHA Modernism and Living Art', *Circa*, 14, p. 28, which refers to 'Slán Leat a Athair'.

57. The Tuohy picture is in the Hugh Lane Municipal Gallery, Dublin. The Lamb picture was in Pyms Gallery, London in 1986 (24).

58. Hugh Lane Municipal Gallery, Dublin. See 'Sir John Lavery RA, 1856–1941', Catalogue of an Exhibition, The Ulster Museum and The Fine Arts Society, London, 1984–85, compiled by Kenneth McConkey, pp. 86, 87.

59. H.L. Municipal Gallery, Dublin. W.B. Yeats referred to it in his poem 'The Municipal Gallery Revisited'.

60. The final version of 'The Ratification' is in the Glasgow Art Gallery; the study is in the National Gallery of Ireland; 'Casement' is in the H.L. Municipal Gallery, Dublin.

61. 'Collection of Historical Pictures' etc., op. cit. It was opened on 26 May 1945 and it is housed in a special Museum room.

62. Collection of the artist, on display in Kennedy's art shop, Harcourt St., Dublin. It was exhibited at the *Oireachtas* Art Exhibition on the insistence of Sean Keating. According to Tom Ryan, other selectors were reluctant to exhibit it.

63. Letter from Tom Ryan to the Author, 9 September 1988.

64. Both MacGonigal pictures are in The H.L. Municipal Gallery, Dublin. See also 'Critics Choice' (1988), op. cit., article by Noel Sheridan, 'Maurice MacGonigal, Dockers', pp. 30, 31.

65. Joan Fowler, 'Art and Independence, an Aspect of Twentieth Century Irish Art', *Circa*, 14, Jan.-Feb. 1984. p. 7.

66. See Catalogue of 'Cuimhneachan 1916', Art Exhibition at the Municipal Gallery of Modern Art Dublin, Easter 1966, which includes lists of prizewinners and illustrations.

67. For a most stimulating study of the relation of imagery particularly in Northern Ireland to political circumstances, see Belinda Loftus, 'In Search of a useful Theory', *Circa*, No. 40, June-July 1988.

BELVEDERE HOUSE, GEM OF THE IRISH MIDLANDS

Belvedere House. *Front view showing terraces to good effect.* Photograph Olive Sharkey.

Ireland can boast few enough stately homes and gardens which are open to the public. However, near the town of Mullingar in County Westmeath, Belvedere House and gardens, more famous today, perhaps, for the splendour of the gardens and the fine setting on the north-east shore of Lough Ennell than for the stateliness of the house, are certainly worth a visit.

The house, one of the most distinguished in Ireland, is one of the few examples of a moderately-sized house built during the eighteenth century for pleasure rather than show. It appears to have been originally built in the 1740s as a fishing lodge on the shore of the lake by the 1st Earl of Belvedere as an adjunct to his mansion at Gaulstown, some five miles away.

The most remarkable feature of the building, and still in evidence today, is

Belvedere House, near Mullingar, County Westmeath, is one of Ireland's fine medium-sized eighteenth century houses. **Olive Sharkey** has investigated the history of the house and its furnishings and recalls the eccentricities of the 1st Earl of Belvedere.

the Rococco plaster-work on the ceilings in the drawing-room, dining-room and hall, quite untypical of Irish work, which is usually overwhelmingly ornate and profuse. The Belvedere ceilings possess a lightness of touch and character that puts them in a class of their own. In one of the two ceilings which form the hall, Jupiter sits astride an eagle scattering lightning across the clouds from the

thunderbolt in his hand, and in the other there is a skyscape sprinkled liberally with stars. The drawing-room and dining-room ceilings possess much more elaborate representations, with scrollwork, as Mark Girouard says, "that flickers and crackles like flames across the edge of the ceiling".[1] Medallions of Juno, Venus and Minerva centre the drawing-room ceiling, while the dining-room ceiling is adorned with clusters of fruit and flowers, a chimera, and cherubs puffing exuberantly among the billowing clouds.

Similar work was featured in Mespil House, Dublin, which was demolished in 1952. However, the plaster-work in the two houses may not have been the work of the same man, although both exhibited the same generous use of billowing clouds, as well as the presence of delicately executed cherubic figures and an effigy of Jupiter. The French stuccodore,

Cramillion, who decorated the chapel of the Rotunda Hospital in Dublin, is generally thought to be a likely executant of such fine work.

Sadly, today, Belvedere possesses none of its original eighteenth and nineteenth century furniture or paintings. When Westmeath County Council acquired the property from its last private owner, Mr Rex Beaumont, in 1981, the furnishings had already been auctioned by Christie's and have not been replaced. The visitor can but admire the ceilings, the fine joinery and, of course, the architecture of the building itself, which is quite unique.

Belevedere is more of an elaborate pavilion than a mansion, and this was all the more so when it was built, as the rear wing, which today makes the house L-shaped, was a later addition. A vaulted basement contains the offices, and the ground floor consists of the hall, the dining-room to its left, and the drawing-room to the right. An elegantly curved staircase leads to the first floor where there are two main bedrooms and two smaller ones.

The architect of Belvedere was Richard Castle, Ireland's leading Palladian architect of the time. The cut limestone façade is a restrained composition, today rather spoiled by the squaring off of the original semi-circular therm windows that surmounted the pair of Venetian windows which decorate the two breakfronts. It is thought that the use of bow windows at either end may well be the earliest example of this feature in the country. The interior is expensively and tastefully finished with quality woodwork including carved timber chimneypieces, bold cornices and the curving balustraded staircase. The building is composed of three bays forming a recessed centre between two projecting breakfront end-bays. And the terraces, which add such distinction to the overall picture, are very much in keeping with the architectural style, their rounded-arch balustrade reflecting the central rounded heads of the Venetian windows and the skylight above the door. Brinsley Marley, the third-last private owner of Belvedere, was responsible for the erection of the terraces during the nineteenth century.

In its hey-day Belvedere was richly furnished, its walls adorned with beautiful paintings and gilded mirrors, its hallway alive with a splendid array of tropical

The hall, ceiling detail, showing Jupiter riding eagle and scattering lightning from his tightly held thunderbolt. Photograph Keaney Photographers, Carrick-on-Shannon.

French mahogany and marquetry commode with moulded serpentine brèche violette *marble top. Courtesy Christie's of London.*

plants, and its rooms filled with beautiful furniture. In the hall, for instance, there were some fine Georgian gilt mirrors, a selection of tables, including a Regency mahogany breakfast table and Victorian satin-wood Sutherland table with a moulded rectangular fall-flap top on turned legs and bar feet. There were brass and copper *jardinières* and a variety of lamps, including a middle-eastern brass trumpet-shaped lamp whose baluster stem and domed base were pierced and engraved with hieroglyphics. A selection of mounted animals' heads adorned the walls, including that of a kudu which still survives today.

The most notable feature of the drawing-room was probably the ornate Victorian over-mantel which measured 66in×44½in (1.6m×1.1m). Known as 'Lo Sposalizio' it was after Raphael and very much reflected the great master's style. Among the other items of interest in this

The Duchess of Rutland *by Richard Buckner. Courtesy Christie's of London.*

room were the Austrian gilt-wood and white painted over-mantel mirror, richly decorated with cherubs, and enhanced with floral arrangements and a Chinese figure in a shrine-like attitude, and a pair of Italian white-painted plaster gilt console tables with waved serpentine damask-covered tops on naturalistic bases moulded with *putti* supporting foliate branches. In the corner of the room close to the fireplace stood a fine mahogany cylinder bureau of Louis XVI design, and at the other side of the room was a beautiful French mahogany and marquetry commode by G. Durand after a design by Riesener. Its moulded serpentine *brèche* violette marble top, which incidentally was the base for the aforementioned Austrian gilt-wood mirror, complemented the colourful central marquetry panel below with its graceful urns and basket of flowers and fruit terminated by scrolling ormolu foliage.

The drawing-room, showing the fireplace with Lo Sposalizio *above. Photograph Keaney Photographers.*

BELVEDERE HOUSE, GEM OF THE IRISH MIDLANDS

The dining-room boasted such treasures as a Victorian white-painted sarcophagus-shaped wine-cooler carved with dolphins, birds and sea-horses, a set of six George III dining chairs with seats covered in 'William Morris' pattern cotton chintz, and a set of four George III dining chairs of similar design to the other six, except for the legs which were square chamfered with stretchers.

Among the paintings which were hung about the house was a portrait by Robert Hunter of Robert Rochfort, 1st Earl of Belvedere, in his peer's robes, and two portraits of Charles William Bury, 1st Earl of Charleville, one by Hugh Douglas Hamilton, and the other by G. Stuart. There were other family portraits, some religious pictures and some fine seascapes, unsigned, from the English school. Two of the finest paintings were Richard Buckner's representation of the Duchess of Rutland standing in an open

The Blessed Herman Kneeling Before the Virgin *by Van Dyke. Courtesy Christie's of London.*

landscape, and Van Dyke's 'The Blessed Herman Kneeling before the Virgin'. Only one painting remains at Belvedere today, that of Brinsley Marley in a blue coat, unsigned but believed to be from the nineteenth century French School.

The Belvedere gardens are a delight to the eye at any time of year, and the view of the lake is quite magnificent, especially at sunset when the orange brilliance of the sun seems to burn its way into the water, its warm glow reflected on the building. The gardens are a mixture of the formal and the informal. All about the house are avenues and walks with stately parkland trees and a variety of shrubs that flourish in haphazard abandon. Many of the trees and shrubs in the arboretum are rare specimens. Apart from the flowering magnolias, Japanese cherries and several beautiful species of rhododendron, there are fine examples of *Thuga Plicata* (Western Red Cedar)

Drawing-room detail. The Austrian gilt mirror. Photograph Keaney Photographers.

BELVEDERE HOUSE, GEM OF THE IRISH MIDLANDS

introduced during the 1800s, some Caucasian wingnuts and a fine *Sequoiadendron* (the 'Mammoth' tree), a member of the redwoods. The *Pyndelus Smitiana* (Morinda Spruce) adds distinction to the collection; and there are also some fine examples of indigenous trees and shrubs.

The formal walled garden, entered by an arched gateway, is a pleasant surprise, especially between June and October when the roses are in bloom and their heady fragrance fills the air. A tiny wooden sanctuary hidden away in the corner of the garden was once a dove-cote, and a charming wishing well adds a touch of quaintness. There is also a tiny fishpond and the estate peacocks promenade about the garden in a graceful manner.

North of the house, the woodland walk follows the shore of the lake to the Gothic Arch, built in the mid-eighteenth century as a mock entrance and eye-catcher at the northern end of the estate. Its eerie-looking facade easily conjues up visions of Dracula venturing through its archway in search of blood! The walk continues on back towards the house by a different route, passing the old ice-house, once an important feature of the estate, but which was abandoned with the advent of freezers. A well-insulated underground chamber was the main feature of the ice-house; at Belvedere the ice would have been carted in blocks from the lake in winter-time. Foodstuffs likely to decay quickly were stored for lengthy periods in the ice-house throughout the year.

A striking ruin which backs on to the stableyard might be taken for the remains of some old abbey, but this curious architectural folly, which has become known as 'The Jealous Wall', was built as a ruin. Local tradition has it that it survives as mute testimony to the bitterness and contempt that existed between the 1st Earl of Belvedere and his brother, George. George built nearby Rochfort House (later known as Tudenham House, and which at that time of its completion was clearly visible from Belvedere). The Earl was apparently jealous of the fine mansion (also said to be the work of Richard Castle) across the fields, so in order to block his view of the offending building he had an Italian architect named Barrodotte design an abbey ruin which he had built in 1760 in just the right strategic position. There is a school of thought, however, which suggests that

The Gothic Arch folly at the northern end of the estate. Photograph Olive Sharkey.

the Earl had the folly constructed to his own design, probably on a whim after seeing follies on English estates, and that Barrodotte did not exist at all because there is no evidence of his existence.

A second story which surrounds Belvedere – an indisputably true one this time – serves to reinforce the reputation of the 1st Earl, Robert Rochfort, as a cold, vindictive man. In 1736 he married his second wife, Lady Mary Molesworth, eldest daughter of Richard, 3rd Viscount Molesworth, then Commander-in-Chief in Ireland, who resided with his family in Dublin. Robert Rochfort was then a young man of twenty-eight, a widower without a family. He was handsome, a man of considerable talent and ability, with expensive tastes and polished manners. But at the same time he possessed a haughty and vindictive temper, was utterly selfish and unprincipled, and quite dissipated in his way of living. However, his manners and charm, his wealth and his prospects impressed Lord Molesworth, and Mary, his eldest daughter, was handed over in marriage. She was sixteen when Robert Rochfort took her as his bride to Gaulstown, where she was blissfully ignorant of the fate that was to befall her at the hands of her handsome husband. The marriage is recorded as having taken place on August 7th, 1736,

and in 1738 Rochfort was created Baron Belfield.

In Lord Halifax's *Ghost Book*[2] Mary is described as the victim from the outset. According to the narrator, the young Mary had a rival in the shape of an older woman who had for some time wielded her influence over Robert and was now jealous of his young wife. With the passing of time, the periods he spent away from Gaulstown became longer and when he returned he wore a constant look of suspicion that frightened his wife, now the mother of four children. She began to suspect that his close friends, and in particular her female rival, were poisoning his mind against her. Seven years after the marriage the storm broke. Lord Belvedere arrived home one day and charged his wife with adultery, the partner being none other than his younger brother, Arthur. At no time in the narrative are we led to believe that she might have been guilty. The *Ghost Book* depicts her as an innocent, almost naive young woman who was clearly astonished by her husband's charge.

However, in the book, *Some Celebrated Irish Beauties of the Last Century*,[3] Mary is depicted as a conniving and devious little madam, cold and unloving towards her husband, and not averse to flirting with his brother. The woman who is described in the *Ghost Book* as a mischief-making rival, is here said to have discovered a bundle of love-letters sent from Arthur to Mary declaring his undying passion for her. The woman gave them to Robert who recognized the handwriting, and although he had had suspicions, he had not challenged his wife with the issue previously. After he brought the charge against his wife, she is said to have somehow forewarned her paramour, who "fled precipitately and without making any defence". He apparently fled to London and Robert is said to have followed with the intention of killing Arthur if he caught up with him.

This account is supported by contemporary evidence, in the shape of Mrs Delany who, in March 1743–4, wrote of Lord Belfield that "he has discovered an intrigue, and they say he has come to England in search of *him* . . . he is very well bred and very well in his person and manner; his wife is locked up in one of his houses in Ireland, with a strict guard over her, and they say he is so miserable as to love her even now; she is extremely hand-

BELVEDERE HOUSE, GEM OF THE IRISH MIDLANDS

some and has many personal accomplishments."[4]

Whatever the truth of the preliminaries, the outcome itself varies little in the telling. Lord Belvedere's all-consuming jealousy had been badly thwarted and he felt justified in punishing his young wife as he saw fit. He decided to lock her up in Gaulstown. She had access to the grounds and had servants at her disposal, but was deprived of human companionship in the shape of family and friends. The presence of the servants probably prevented her from becoming insane.

The Earl grew more and more vindictive with age. Whenever he visited Gaulstown his arrival had to be announced well in advance so as to avoid a direct confrontation with his wife. On one occasion, however, when this precaution was relaxed the two came face to face in the garden. Had he been alone he might have ended the punishment there and then. Begging mercy, Mary fell before him on her knees, and for a second or two he almost weakened. But he had a close friend with him who is recorded as having said: "Remember your honour, my lord", thus reminding him of his resolve to punish his wayward wife. He walked on, his determination more pronounced than ever. He then ordered that a servant accompany his wife during his future visits to the house, but more importantly, that a bell be sounded constantly to advise him of her whereabouts.

Mary endured twelve years of enforced solitude before some faithful servants risked their jobs and possibly their lives by helping her to escape her bondage. She made her way to Dublin, to her father's house, but Lord Molesworth, persuaded by his son-in-law of her guilt, refused to shelter her. Panic-stricken, she did not know what to do, but the decision was taken out of her hands. Within twenty-four hours she was tracked down and taken prisoner by her husband once more. Back in captivity, she was a lonely broken woman. Her children were then no longer allowed to visit her, her movements were even more restricted than before, and what comforts she had previously enjoyed were curtailed. Her only pleasure – if it could be so described – was to walk in the gallery conversing with the figures in the paintings.

In 1774, some eighteen years after her futile bid for freedom, she was finally released from her prison when the Earl died. Her son, the new Earl, was appalled by her appearance, for she wore a haunted, unearthly look and spoke with a low harsh whisper. When she realized that she was at last free her only words were: "Is the tyrant dead?" She is said to have protested her innocence most strongly, even on her deathbed some years later. Her final years were spent with her daughter who was married to the Earl of Lanesborough, and every care and attention was bestowed upon her by all of her children. But her strange story always haunted her. It was the very Nemesis of her existence, pursuing her even when she was free. She dreaded publicity and shrank from notice, vehemently declaring her innocence, whilst at the same time conversely oppressed by a curious remorse.

Arthur Rochfort, her alleged paramour, had returned from England in 1757 expecting to find that time had cooled his brother's anger. But the moment Robert learned of his return, he sued him for damages resulting from the alleged adultery. Unable to pay the damages, Arthur spent the rest of his life in gaol.

Throughout Mary's imprisonment her husband adopted a gay bachelor lifestyle at his new, comfortably furnished lakeside villa from which he took the title of his earldom. A visitor in 1773, not long before the Earl's death, described a dinner with His Lordship as an extravagant and most elegant affair with "two soups, two removes, a dessert in the highest taste. All sorts of wine, Burgundy and Champagne, a load of meat on a side table, four valets-de-chambre in laced cloths, and seven or eight footmen".

In 1774 the Earl's son, George, took possession of Belvedere. A much more responsible adult, he had to correct the finances which were in a parlous state due to the 1st Earl's extravagant life-style. The 2nd Earl left no issue and the Earldom and other titles became extinct. The estates went partly to George Augustus Boyd (a son of the 2nd Earl's widow by her second husband) and partly to the descendants of the 2nd Earl's sister, Jane, Countess of Lanesborough, from whom Belvedere passed to her great-grandson, Charles Brinsley Marley. He died in 1912 and left the property to his cousin, Lieutenant-Colonel Howard-Bury.

Colonel Howard-Bury, a keen traveller, big game hunter, photographer and plant collector, became famous throughout the western world in 1912 when he led a party of climbers to within 2,000 ft of the summit of Everest. Lack of oxygen prevented the climbers from getting to the top.

Colonel Howard-Bury was responsible for coining the term 'the abominable snowman' for it was he who sent back reports to British newspapers during the climb, and in some of these he described the footprints of some creature which they could not identify. He wrote about the local "bogeyman", a mythical pookah creature that the locals warned their children about, and jokingly suggested that it might have been responsible for the large footprints. Alternatively, they could have been made by large animals such as monkeys or wolves, some species of which can exist at very high altitudes; or they could have been made by solitary outcasts who made a living by hunting and stealing.

Colonel Howard-Bury, who was born at Charleville Forest Estate near Tullamore, County Offaly, brought some fine plant specimens back to his lakeside villa. During his frequent absences abroad his friend, Rex Beaumont, looked after his interests there. The colonel bequeathed the Belvedere estate to his friend who, for some years, opened it to the public once a year.

Today Belvedere is being developed into a major tourist attraction in the midlands. Most recently a pet's corner has been established for the delight of visiting children, and a well-stocked nursery offers plants for sale. Currently there are plans afoot to establish a folk museum in the stable buildings. There is a coffeeshop there already, and a craft shop offering handmade crafts and paintings for sale. Occasionally there are temporary exhibitions mounted in the house itself, including the Howard-Bury Exhibition, mounted and launched in 1987.

Olive Sharkey

NOTES

1. Mark Girouard, *Country Life*, 22 June 1961.
2. Lord Halifax, *Ghost Book*, Geoffrey Boles, London, 1936 (4th ed.).
3. Frances Gerard, *Some Celebrated Irish Beauties of the Last Century*, Ward and Downey, London, 1895.
4. George Edward Cokayne, *The Complete Peerage*, Alan Sutton Publishing Ltd., Gloucester, 1982 (microprint ed.).

THE LYNN BROTHERS, ARCHITECT AND SCULPTOR

William Henry Lynn (1829–1915), who lived to be eighty-six, was probably the most successful architect ever to work in Belfast, where he spent his entire career. Certainly he was the first Belfast-based architect to score repeated successes in competitions well beyond the boundaries of Ulster. The impressive list of his executed buildings includes Scrabo Tower (1858), St. Andrew's Church, Dublin (1860), the Parliament Buildings of New South Wales, Sydney (1861), Unitarian Church, St Stephen's Green, Dublin (1862), Chester Town Hall (1864), Queen's University Library (1865–8), Richardson Sons and Owden's Warehouse, Donegall Square North (1867–9), Belfast Castle (1868–70), Carlisle Memorial Methodist Church, Belfast (1872-5), Chateau St. Louis, Quebec (c.1875–78), Clark Halls, Paisley (1876), Barrow-in-Furness Town Hall (1877), Belfast Central Public Library (1883), Belfast Harbour Office enlargement (1891–5), and Campbell College (1892–4). As late as 1910, at the age of eighty-two Lynn defeated fifty-seven other entrants in a competition for the extension of Queen's College, Belfast, which was completed only months before his death five years later. Yet Lynn was a reticent, self-effacing character. Until 1872 he played second fiddle in the architectural firm of Sir Charles Lanyon (1813–89), though it would appear that Lynn was the firm's most versatile designer, its most able draughtsman, and its main winner of competitions. Kyle Knox, who, along with Thomas Drew, had been an apprentice in Lanyon's office when Lynn was the junior partner, wrote some interesting biographical notes on the brothers Lynn, published in 1916,[1] in which he recounts some telling details of this last competition for the extension of Queen's after the College had been elevated to university status. According to the rules, Lynn had submitted his designs anonymously, but in addition he absented himself from Belfast to avoid the possibility of meeting the assessor who was to select the winning drawings. The assessor, Sir Ashton Webb (architect of the facade of Buckingham Palace, the Mall and Admiralty Arch, and of Birmingham University), pronounced Lynn's drawings for Queen's College "very masterly, and the best submitted in the competition". Knox, who happened to be chairman of the buildings committee,

Martyn Anglesea, Assistant Keeper at the Department of Art in the Ulster Museum, writes of the talented Lynn brothers, and their contribution to the arts of architecture and sculpture.

William Henry Lynn.

broke the news that the winning designs were "those of an Irishman and a Belfastman", to which the Senate responded with "loud applause and manifest pleasure".

Lynn's architectural achievements began and ended with projects for Queen's College. The son of a Royal Naval Lieutenant, Henry Johnstone Lynn, who was attached to the coastguard service, William Henry had been born at St. John's Point, Co. Down, but had spent much of his childhood in Bannow, Co. Wexford, one of those curious dead towns (like nearby Clonmines) that survived the middle ages only as parliamentary rotten boroughs. The abundance of mediaeval remains in the locality must have stimulated Lynn's appetite for antiquarian scholarship. Apprenticed to Charles Lanyon in Belfast, at the age of eighteen he served as Lanyon's clerk of works on the new Queen's College (1846–7). This Tudor Gothic design in red brick with stone dressings is generally regarded as Lanyon's masterpiece, but much of the detail must have been by the scholarly Lynn. The draw-

ings came into the possession of the College in 1910, and are still there. They were received from the Board of Works by Kyle Knox as chairman of the buildings committee, in the unassuming presence of the aged Lynn. "Among them was an elevation of the West Front, showing in minute detail all the ornamental work on the Main Tower, the great entrance and the entire facade. I could not refrain from expressing to Mr. Lynn, who stood behind my chair, my regret at seeing this beautiful piece of work spoiled by neglect. 'Well', said he, 'Knox, I could not do it now, but that is my work. I drew it in 1846'. That is to say, sixty-four years before".[2]

In a period when architects tended to be classical men, italianate men or gothic men, or indeed church men or house men, Lynn distinguished himself by his adaptability, earning himself the dubious title of "an eclectic of the eclectics".[3] He must have lapped up Ruskin's *Stones of Venice* and *Seven Lamps of Architecture*, and also George Edmund Street's *Brick and Marble Architecture in Italy*, as many of his buildings show an affinity for Venetian, French or English Gothic. "Structural polychromy", as exemplified in the coloured brick buildings of William Butterfield, appears in Lynn's Queen's University Library of 1865–8. His Italian Gothic masterpiece is the linen warehouse of Richardson Sons and Owden (1867), in Donegall Square, Belfast, admired alike by Alfred Waterhouse, Oscar Wilde and John Kells Ingram,[4] now part of Marks and Spencer's. Lynn had his office in this building, on the Callender Street side. But he could also turn his hand with assured ease to *Beaux-Arts* classicism, as demonstrated by the Belfast Central Library of 1883. It was customary for Victorian architects to spend their summers on walking tours of England, France and Italy, sketching and measuring buildings and collecting motifs. The Ulster Museum has a long series of such sketches made in the 1860s by the minor Belfast gothicist Anthony Thomas Jackson. Though Lynn's tours are not documented, they must have taken place.

Perhaps Lynn's best asset was his skill in drawing and handling water-colour. Apart from his architectural perspective drawings, he was a most accomplished landscape water-colourist, having a free liquid style rather like Andrew Nicholl's

THE LYNN BROTHERS, ARCHITECT AND SCULPTOR

remarkable amateur pupil, the Belfast surgeon Dr. James Moore (1819–83). Lynn owned some of Nicholl's water-colours. In the Ulster Museum are several of Lynn's water-colour views in the Glens of Antrim, and one of the 'Britannia Tubular Bridge' over the Menai Straits, which had been built by Robert Stephenson in 1845-50. Lynn turned his ability to handle paint to his greatest advantage in his large perspective water-colours, the function of which was to sell the design to the client. It is likely that the selection of the winner in an architectural competition would have been decided by the appeal of the perspective impression. In many instances Lynn's drawings must have tipped the scales and carried the day. In his winning design for St. Andrew's Church, Dublin, he ignored the congested site and surrounded the church with mediaeval buildings like an old Norman town. But he did not always succeed. His design for the Albert Memorial Clock in Belfast (1865), which exaggerates the size of the existing square and introduces Canalettesque sunlight from a northerly direction, was defeated by a design from the office of William James Barre (see below). Among Lynn's most ambitious and beautifully-worked perspective impressions are two huge water-colours of a design for Carlisle Bridge (now O'Connell Bridge), Dublin, submitted to Dublin Corporation in 1862. These show an elaborate *Beaux-Arts* scheme with domed pavilions, rather like Lanyon's campanile in Trinity College, and the statue of O'Connell (laboured on by Foley for many years after 1866) placed in the centre of the bridge. While it was agreed that these were the best designs in the competition, the Corporation delayed the issue for two years and then settled for someone else's design. Lynn's background views of Sackville Street (without the neon signs), delicate aerial perspective and cast shadows, and the group of figures to provide lively incident, counted for nought.

Lynn's numerous successes in competitions for buildings outside Ireland began in 1858, when he won an international competition for Trinity College Church, Edinburgh, but his winning design was not used. He designed the chapel of the British Embassy in Constantinople. But his most prestigious international success came in 1861 with

William Henry Lynn, Richardson Sons and Owden's warehouse, Donegall Square North, Belfast, 1867–9. Detail. Photograph the author.

William Henry Lynn, Robert Stephenson's Britannia Tubular Bridge over the Menai Straits. Water-colour.
Ulster Museum, Belfast.

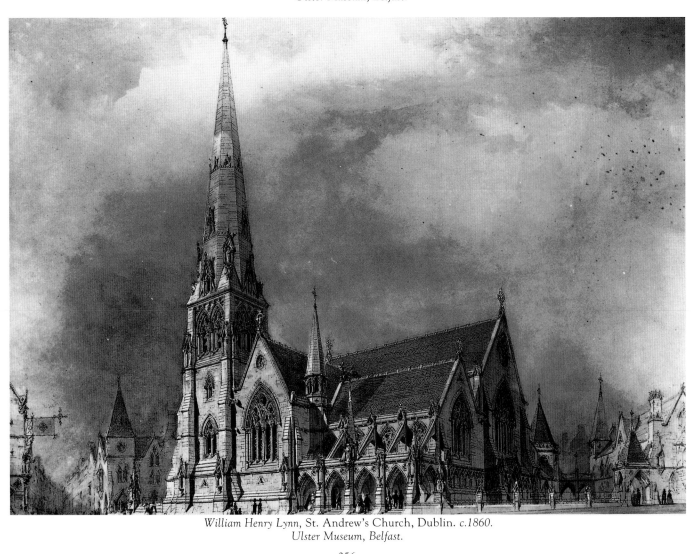

William Henry Lynn, St. Andrew's Church, Dublin. c.1860.
Ulster Museum, Belfast.

William Henry Lynn, unsuccessful competition design for Carlisle Bridge, Dublin, *1862.*
Ulster Museum, Belfast.

William Henry Lynn, design for Chateau St Louis, Quebec. *c.1875.*
Private collection.

THE LYNN BROTHERS, ARCHITECT AND SCULPTOR

the Houses of Parliament of New South Wales, in Sydney. This is a very complex Gothic design with many towers, including a clock tower positioned in a way which recalls the placement of Sir Charles Barry's clock tower on the Westminster Houses of Parliament. It is evidently a close relation of the unsuccessful design for the Albert Clock, which Lynn submitted to Belfast Corporation four years later. Knox (1916) describes Lynn's drawing for the Sydney Parliament Buildings as "by far the best architectural drawing I have ever seen". In 1916 it belonged to the Belfast architect R. Miles Close.[5] A large sketch design was among the group of Lynn drawings presented to the Belfast Museum in 1916 by Lynn's cousin, Mrs. Ellen Cooper. The design was awarded a gold medal at the Universal Exhibition in Paris in 1867. In 1872 Lynn left Sir

Charles Lanyon's firm (Lanyon, Lynn and Lanyon) and continued winning competitions on his own into his old age. His other major colonial commission, the Chateau St Louis in Quebec (c. 1875–78), the Vice-Regal summer residence, was obtained through the influence of Lord Dufferin, who was Governor-General of Canada. There are three water-colour views of the Niagara Falls in a private collection,[6] which appear to be from a sketchbook used by Lynn while in Canada working on this commission. Lynn's friend, Sir Thomas Drew, who was given the commision for St. Anne's Cathedral, Belfast, was moved by Lynn's suggestion to change his design from Gothic to Romanesque in the interests of economy. Characteristically, Lynn refused to have his name mentioned along with Drew's in connexion with this building, though he paid for the west

window himself. His antiquarian interests culminated in a historical and architectural survey of Dunluce Castle, written in collaboration with the Belfast solicitor and antiquarian dabbler Francis Joseph Bigger (1863–1926). He made his observational sketches on the spot on a sheet of common wallpaper, "all I could get of sufficient size in Bushmills".[7]

The artistic career of William Henry Lynn's younger brother, Samuel Ferres Lynn (1836–1876), did not reach its maturity, as he died at the early age of forty. Born at Fethard-on-Sea, Co. Wexford (mistakenly given by Strickland as Fethard, Co. Tipperary), in 1836,[8] Samuel first worked with his architect brother in Belfast. Their personalities made a strong contrast. Kyle Knox describes him as "a bright, happy and pleasant companion, not too much my senior, always ready for jokes", while, on the other

William James Barre, winning design for
the Albert Memorial, Belfast, *c.1865. Ulster Museum, Belfast.*

William Henry Lynn, unsuccessful competition design for
the Albert Memorial, Belfast, *c.1865. Ulster Museum, Belfast.*

THE LYNN BROTHERS, ARCHITECT AND SCULPTOR

hand, "of William Henry Lynn we stood too much in awe, and felt too great respect to venture on such things". While studying architecture, Samuel also attended the short-lived Belfast School of Design, headed by Claude Lorrain Nursey, and here he won prizes for modelling, offered by two of the patrons of the school, Lord Dufferin and Sir Hugh Cairns. Deciding to abandon architecture and to study sculpture, he left for London in 1854, and in 1855 entered the Royal Academy Schools. The following year, 1856, he first showed work at the Royal Academy Summer Exhibition, from an address at 5 Albert Street, Pimlico. He continued to exhibit there every year until 1862, and again every year between 1867 and 1875. It was possibly through his elder brother's position in Lanyon's firm that in 1857, Samuel's designs were used for the pediment and spandrel sculptures on the seaward side of Lanyon's Belfast Custom House, though the carvings were executed by a mason-sculptor, Thomas Fitzpatrick, who finished them in 1860.[9] That same year Samuel Ferres Lynn won a Royal Academy Gold Medal for a group 'Achilles and Lycaon', with a quotation in the catalogue from the *Iliad:* "Die then, he said: and as he spoke, the fainting stripling sank before the stroke". He was then living at 6 Ranelagh Street. In 1864 he signed and dated a pediment group representing 'Commerce and Agriculture', on the Provincial Bank (now the Allied Irish Bank), College Street, Dublin.[10] The National Gallery of Ireland has a pair of sandstone heads of Palmerston and Gladstone, carved by Lynn, which came from either side of the entrance of Gilbey & Sons, 46–49 O'Connell Street, built in 1865–67 and demolished in the early 1970s.[11] Another of Lynn's schemes of architectural sculpture, done in 1861, was a pair of figures for the interior of the Lancashire Insurance Office in Manchester, representing personifications of 'Life Insurance' and 'Fire Insurance'![12]

Victorian sculptors spent much of their working time in large draughty wooden sheds, surrounded by heaps of wet clay, plaster, blocks of marble and buckets of water. Physically arduous in the extreme, the work demanded strength and fitness of a kind equalled only in the navy. Weaklings could not survive. Because of the sheer size and expense of the

Samuel Ferres Lynn.

Samuel Ferres Lynn, The Reverend Dr Henry Cooke. *Bronze, dated 1875, unveiled 1876. Wellington Place, Belfast. The traffic cone is a modern addition.*

materials needed, the life of a young sculptor at the beginning of his career was also financially very risky. The only possibility of security open to most of them was to earn a meagre living in the studio of some established sculptor. At some time Samuel Ferres Lynn worked in the London studio of the Belfast-born sculptor Patrick MacDowell, R.A. (1790–1870), whose main patron was the Belfast M.P., Sir James Emerson Tennent, though he also received commissions from the family of the Marquess of Donegall. Potterton[13] sees MacDowell's influence on Lynn in an angel on a monument to Joseph Makesey (1868) in Waterford Cathedral, Lynn's only known church monument in Ireland. For two years, about 1862–63,[14] Lynn worked as a studio assistant to one of the most successful sculptors in London, the Dublin-born John Henry Foley R.A. (1818–1874). Most sculptors employed assistants for practical studio work, though some others did not. Foley himself had been one of the many studio pupils of William Behnes. Besides the gaining of essential technical hand-skills, such as the making of armatures, the use of pointing machines, the manipulation of large quantities of wet clay, and not least, the lifting of heavy weights, none of which could be taught in the Royal Academy Schools, the pupils had the incentive of eventually taking over the master's studio, clients and commissions. Of course, there was no guarantee that this would happen. Lynn was by no means exceptional as a pupil of Foley, who had as his studio assistants at various times Thomas Brock, Mary Grant, G. F. Teniswood, George Mossman, F. J. Williamson, Albert Bruce-Joy (another Irishman), C.B. Birch and still more. Of these, only Brock could be said to have inherited Foley's practice and some of his commissions, such as the O'Connell monument in Dublin.[15] Having reached the peak of his profession, after 1861 Foley refused to send works to the Royal Academy because of a dispute over the positioning of his sculpture in the gallery. Gilbert Scott's design for the Albert Memorial in Kensington Gardens was accepted in 1863, and Foley and MacDowell were among the team of sculptors selected to adorn it. Indeed, Foley was given the prime commission, the colossal seated bronze statue of Albert, originally allocated to Queen Victoria's favourite,

THE LYNN BROTHERS, ARCHITECT AND SCULPTOR

Baron Marochetti. Lynn assisted Foley in the modelling of this figure. Foley was also commissioned for the marble group 'Asia' on this monument, and it was while working on the full-size clay model for this that he contracted pleurisy from the damp clay, which led to the illness from which he died—a tragic example of the occupational hazards associated with the strenuous art of sculpture.

When in 1865, Belfast Corporation announced a competition for its own Albert Memorial in the form of a clock tower, William Henry Lynn submitted competition drawings, but was defeated by his arch-rival, William James Barre of Newry. After Barre's death in 1867 it was discovered that he had ensured the victory of his own design by conniving with a contractor to furnish the lowest tenders.[16] Another, perhaps malicious, story was told by John Vinycomb in a talk given to the Belfast Art Society in 1899, when he alleged that the winning competition design for the Albert Clock was actually drawn by three of Barre's assistants during his absence over a weekend—the perspective outline by Sherrie, figures by Goodman and colouring by Perry. They submitted the drawing, Vinycomb stated, without Barre's knowledge, but when it won the competition Barre got the credit![17] Strangely enough, Samuel Ferres Lynn was given the commission for the life-size white marble figure of Prince Albert, placed in a niche high on the west face of the tower towards High Street. Wearing his Garter robes, Albert stands on a round corbell supported by three demi-angels. While totally different in concept from Foley's seated figure of Albert on the Kensington Gardens memorial, Lynn's figure bears some similarity to some of Foley's other statues of Albert, notably the one on Leinster Lawn, Dublin (1871), and the one originally in the Fitzwilliam Museum, Cambridge (1866) and now at Madingley Hall. It is quite possible that W.H. Lynn had his brother in mind for his own unsuccessful design, which has groups of statuary at the corners, as well as a seemingly smaller niche and statue on the west face, above a fountain.

Foley's influence on Lynn, particularly in his skilful handling of period or contemporary costume, can be seen in two plaster models in the Ulster Museum (presented by Sir Thomas Drew in 1907), studies for the full-length statues of Dr.

Samuel Ferres Lynn, model for statue of The Reverend Dr Henry Cook. *c.1875. Plaster, painted white, 32ins. high. Ulster Museum, Belfast.*

THE LYNN BROTHERS, ARCHITECT AND SCULPTOR

Samuel Ferres Lynn, model for statue of Lord Farnham. Dated 1869. Exhibited London Royal Academy, 1872. Plaster, painted white, 32ins. high. Ulster Museum, Belfast.

Henry Cooke in Belfast and Henry, 7th Baron Farnham in Cavan town. These recall Foley's models (among the Foley bequest to the Royal Dublin Society) for his much-admired bronze figures of Edmund Burke and Oliver Goldsmith, which flank the main entrance to Trinity College, Dublin. The statue of Lord Farnham, who was killed in a railway accident near Abergele, North Wales, on 20 August 1868, was subscribed for by his Cavan tenantry and executed in marble, unveiled in 1871. The plaster model in the Ulster Museum, dated 1869, was possibly the one exhibited at the Royal Academy in 1872 (No. 1506). The figure wears the robes of a Knight of St. Patrick. In July 1912 the statue in Cavan was daubed with tar. It has since been moved to the front of the Farnham Hall across the street from its original site, and more recently it has been subjected to yet more vandalism, the nose having been broken off and red paint daubed down the front.[18] Another full-length statue of a landowner, paid for by his tenantry, is that of Arthur, 4th Marquess of Downshire (1812–68), which stands opposite the church gates in Hillsborough, Co. Down. This bronze figure is over life size, but wears casual outdoor clothes – gumboots, vigorously modelled corduroy trousers, a huge shawl and a substantial walking-stick. The model for this, presumably in plaster, was in the Royal Academy Exhibition of 1873. The bronze was cast by Prince of Southwark. The twelve-foot-high statue of the Presbyterian hard-liner Dr. Henry Cooke, said to be a speaking likeness, was not erected in College Square, Belfast, until 1876. It replaced a bronze figure of the young philanthropic Earl of Belfast (1855), by Patrick MacDowell, which was removed to the Town Hall, then to the Free Library, and may now be seen in the City Hall. This, the first statue to be erected in Belfast, acquired the nickname of "The Black Man", which had been transferred to its successor, even though the bronze patina of Lynn's statue is green. The plaster model in the Ulster Museum differs in several ways from the finished bronze, chiefly in that the plaster figure of Dr. Cooke carries his gown and mortar-board over his left arm, whereas in the final version Cooke wears his doctoral gown and hood, and holds a bible in his right hand and his mortar-board in his left. For stability, the back of Dr.

THE LYNN BROTHERS, ARCHITECT AND SCULPTOR

Cook's gown is supported by a pile of books, a mechanical necessity, forming a tripod with his legs. The bronze is signed and dated on the left side of the base "S. F. LYNN ARHA Sculpt. LONDON 1875", while the name of the bronze-founder, H. Prince of Southwark, appears on the right side of the base.

S.F. Lynn's portrait busts can be impressive. Particularly so is a posthumous marble bust of John Clarke in the Belfast Harbour Office (signed and dated London 1867, in which year it was exhibited in the Royal Academy), which shows a grave and modern-looking head emerging from classical drapery rather like a voluminous dressing-gown. Clarke (1793–1863), a former Mayor of Belfast, was a would-be art patron, and a friend of the Pre-Raphaelite collector, Francis McCracken. Also in the Harbour office is a marble bust of another Mayor of Belfast, John Lytle, signed and dated London 1872. A model for this bust was exhibited in the Royal Academy in 1874. Less successful than the bust of Clarke, this has a somewhat incongruous chain of office creeping out of the folds of a Roman toga, while Lytle's amiable bearded features are unmistakeably mercantile and Victorian.[19] Queen's University has a marble bust of its first President, the

Rev. P. Shuldham Henry, commissioned from Lynn for the College Library and exhibited in the Royal Academy in 1869.

In spite of his attendance at the Royal Academy Schools, S.F. Lynn never made it into the ranks of academicians or even associates of the Royal Academy. He was, however, elected an associate of the Royal Hibernian Academy in October 1872. Soon after, he appears to have come to live in Belfast. His last exhibit at the Royal Academy, in 1875, was a statuette in white marble of Lord Lurgan's prize-winning greyhound, Master McGrath (whose name lives on today as a brand of dog-food). Since Master McGrath was a black dog, the owner had the white marble statue painted black. Strickland states that S.F. Lynn's last works were four panels, 'The Seasons', installed in 1873 under the dome in the central hall at Gibbstown House, Navan, Co. Meath. He died suddenly at his brother's house, 3 Crumlin Terrace, Crumlin Road, on 5 April 1876, apparently of an infection picked up while travelling abroad. Therefore, as he survived his master Foley by only two years, S.F. Lynn never had the chance of developing his full potential. As I have said, the only one of Foley's pupils who inherited his clients and practice was Thomas Brock. Brock went on to

develop in the direction of "the New Sculpture", a tendency inaugurated by Lord Leighton's 'Athlete Struggling with a Python', exhibited at the Royal Academy in 1877. Benedict Read[20] identifies Foley as a precursor of '"the New Sculpture" in its aesthetic of individualized, ungeneralized modelling and detailed treatment of contemporary costume rather than classicizing drapery. But he places Foley's 'Prince Albert', not unveiled until 1876, at the end of an era. Had Samuel Ferres Lynn lived, he might well have worked along the lines of Alfred Gilbert, George Frampton, Onslow Ford, F.W. Pomeroy, Goscombe John and the rest of the "New" sculptors. Dying as early as he did, his remaining works belong to a different ethos than, say, Brock's 'Victoria Memorial' (1903), Pomeroy's 'Marquess of Dufferin and Ava' (1906), or Brock's 'Titanic Memorial' (1913), which subsequently were to be set up in central Belfast.

Active to the end, William Henry Lynn lived on until 1915. He remained a bachelor. After a very short final illness, he died and was buried in the Belfast City Cemetery, with his mother and brother, under a refined monument designed by himself.

Martyn Anglesea

NOTES

1. R. Kyle Knox, *Notes on the Brothers Lynn*, Belfast Museum Quarterly Notes, No. XXXII, Spring 1916, p. 7. This article accompanies the catalogue of a memorial exhibition of work by the Lynn brothers held in the Belfast Museum and Art Gallery that year.
2. Knox, op. cit., p. 8.
3. Paul Larmour, *Belfast: an illustrated architectural guide*, Belfast, Friar's Bush Press, 1987, p. 35, No. 71.
4. Waterhouse described it as the most beautiful commercial building he had ever seen; Wilde, lecturing in Belfast on 1 January 1884, described it as "beautiful in colour and very beautiful in design"; while Ingram, mathematician, economist, poet, Fellow and Librarian of Trinity College, Dublin, asked Kyle Knox "What Duke built this?" and received the reply: "Duke Linen, and it is one of his Palaces". (Knox, op. cit., p. 9).
5. The Lynn drawings which had belonged to R.M. Close were re-located in 1978 in the possession of Mr. P.J. Mulvenna of Carrickfergus. Some of them were loaned to the exhibition in the Ulster Museum, 'William Henry Lynn (1829–1915): Watercolours and Building Perspectives', catalogue by Hugh Dixon, April 1978. The

collections of Lynn drawings belonging to Kyle Knox, Robert M. Young and William Swanston, all loaned to the 1916 exhibition, have not been re-located.
6. Exhibited Ulster Museum 'William Henry Lynn', 1978 (No. 28).
7. Knox, op. cit., p. 10.
8. Knox, who knew S.F. Lynn, gives his birth year as 1836 and his age at death as forty, but Strickland (*Dictionary of Irish Artists*, Dublin and London, 1913) while stating that he was born in 1834, curiously also says that he died at the age of forty!
9. According to a manuscript note ascribed to Isaac W. Ward ("Belfastiensis") in the annotated copy of Strickland's *Dictionary* in the Art Department of the Ulster Museum.
10. See Benedict Read, *Victorian Sculpture*, Yale University Press, 1982, p. 222 and pl. 284, and Anne Crookshank, *Irish Sculpture from 1600 to the present day*, Dublin, Department of Foreign Affairs, 1984, p. 50.
11. Adrian Le Harivel (ed.), *Illustrated Summary Catalogue of Prints and Sculpture*, Dublin, National Gallery of Ireland, 1988, p. 575, Nos. 8235-6. They were presented by the English Property Company Ltd. in 1974.
12 Obituary notice: 'Death of Samuel Lynn,

Esq., ARHA.' *Belfast News Letter*, Fri. 7 April 1876. His death was announced in the births, marriages and deaths column on the previous day.
13. Homan Potterton, *Irish Church Monuments 1570–1880*, Belfast, Ulster Architectural Heritage Society, 1975, p. 58.
14. Obituary, see note 11.
15. See Read, op. cit. note 10, p. 69.
16. An account of the conflict over the Albert Clock is given by C.E.B. Brett, *Buildings of Belfast*, London, 1968, revised edition Belfast, 1985, pp. 40-41. See also Hugh Dixon, *Ulster Architecture 1800–1900*, (catalogue) Belfast, Ulster Museum, 1972 (No. 139), and Hugh Dixon, 'William Henry Lynn', *Irish Georgian Society Bulletin XVII*, 1–2, Jan.–June 1974.
17. See Martyn Anglesea, *The Royal Ulster Academy of Arts: a centennial history*, Belfast, 1981, p. 8 and p. 25, note 4.
18. See William Garner, *Cavan*, Ulster Architectural Heritage Society and An Taisce, 1978, p. 12.
19. See Eileen Black, *Paintings, Sculptures and Bronzes in the Collection of the Belfast Harbour Commissioners*, 1983, Nos. 87, 88.
20. Read, op. cit., note 10, pp. 289-91.

BOOK REVIEWS

SPANISH PAINTINGS IN THE NATIONAL GALLERY OF IRELAND
ROSEMARIE MULCAHY
National Gallery of Ireland, Dublin, 1988

This *catalogue raisonné* by Dr. Rosemarie Mulcahy, the fifth in the series published by the National Gallery of Ireland, presents, in an exhaustive analysis, the Gallery's magnificent Spanish holdings. The fifty paintings represent masters from Nicolás Francés in the fifteenth century to our contemporaries, Juan Gris and Pablo Picasso, with a heavy concentration of the great painters of the Golden Age, Navarrete el Mudo, Morales, El Greco, Ribera, Velázquez, Zurbarán, Murillo—nor is Goya absent!

The critical apparatus accompanying the actual catalogue makes it a scholar's ideal tool: there is a chronological sequence of acquisitions, an index of previous owners, a listing of changes of attribution (and here Dr. Mulcahy's impeccable and reasoned scrutiny of paintings allows her to re-establish long disputed attributions such as Murillo (No. 33), or Zurbarán (No. 479)). A judiciously selected bibliography ranges from Siguënza's . . . *Escorial* (1605) to Brown's *Velázquez* (1986), covering essential sources of information and research on Spanish painting. Another enlightening and very useful element is Dr. Mulcahy's painstakingly established list of related works. Finally, eighty-five plates show not only the paintings themselves, but revealing X-rays thereof, enlargements of details, signatures, illuminating data on the verso of the canvases (seals, dates, labels, even a photograph of the original armour as worn in one of the paintings, pl. Nos. 47 and 48, *et al.*). While the plates are black-and-white, Dr. Mulcahy knows how to translate colour into words ("The colouring of the panel is striking in the evocative subtlety in which vibrant colours are juxtaposed—the red of Aliatar's tunic, the turquoise, pink and cinnamon of the soldier on the left, and the acid green and white of the executioner's garb", the Alcira Master's series, p. 72).

However, best things last: the catalogue itself! Updated and well-documented biographies of each painter are followed by a thorough study of his works presented here, in which Dr. Mulcahy not only gives the usual data of iconography, attribution, antecedents, provenance, etc., but also shows herself keenly aware of cultural, literary, psychological, even political overtones—or undercurrents! Thus Murillo's 'Prodigal Son' series, Nos. 4540 to 4545, with its 'feeling of hope and serenity . . . emphasizing the theme of repentance" (p. 51), causes Dr. Mulcahy to evoke another repentant sinner, who like Murillo, came from Seville, namely Don Juan de Manara (p. 47), the original Don Juan. Similarly, in Núñez del Valle's 'Jael and Sisera', she hears contemporary political allusions, beyond the Old Testament subject (pp. 58/59) and Juan Gris's recurrent use of the guitar symbolizes the expatriate's longing for his Spain (p. 28).

Thus Dr. Mulcahy's scholarly know-how and sensitivity to her subject matter have provided not only a researcher's ideal tool, but also fascinating reading matter for the *aficionado*. Thank you, Dr. Mulcahy!

Ilse Hempel Lipschutz

NATIONAL GALLERY OF IRELAND – ACQUISITIONS 1986–88 INCLUDING THE BEIT COLLECTION

Exhibition Catalogue
National Gallery of Ireland, 1988, Ir£9.00.

This is the fifth catalogue published by the Gallery since 1980, and is by far the most remarkable because it features the Beit and Sweeney bequests. Also acquired during the same period were several paintings by Frederic W. Burton and a series of drawings of heads by Ivan Opfer. Opfer (Nyborg, Denmark, 1897–1980), is remembered as a portrait draughtsman and these eight portraits (bought from his widow) are of De Valera, G.B Shaw, Edward Carson, Oliver St. John Gogarty, Charles Vane-Tempest-Stewart, 7th Marquess of Londonderry, Edward Chichester, 6th Marquess of Donegal, William Butler Yeats and James Stephens. Twelve prints of Irish scenes, including Waterford city, Lismore Castle, Dunbrody Abbey, Carrick (-on-Suir) Castle, Blarney Castle and Cork city, by Thomas Sautell Roberts (born Waterford 1760, died 1826), were also bought.

The Máire MacNeill Sweeney bequest, which "celebrates the contribution of her husband to poetry and the spoken and the visual arts", includes the work of Barrie Cooke, Evie Hone, Jack B. Yeats, John Butler Yeats, Seán O'Sullivan, Picasso, Klee, Modigliani and Juan Gris. This is a very fine collection, but is inevitably overshadowed by such names as Goya, Hals, Metsu, Vermeer, Hobbema, Murillo, Gainsborough, von Ruisdael, Jan Steen and Velazquez, who are represented in the princely gift of the Collection of Sir Alfred and Lady Beit. The Director (in June 1988), Homan Potterton, expresses in a preface his thanks, his delight, his almost disbelief; however, his and our satisfaction must be tempered by the fact that four of these great paintings, the Vermeer, the Goya and two by Metsu, have not been recovered since being stolen from Russborough House, the Beit home in Co. Wicklow.

THE IRISH HERITAGE SERIES SAINT MARY'S PRO-CATHEDRAL DUBLIN HISTORIC DERRY SAINT EUNAN'S CATHEDRAL LETTERKENNY

DERMOD McCARTHY, BRIAN LACY
GRAHAM HARRISON
Dublin, Eason's, 1988.

All must welcome three additions, Nos. 60, 61 and 62, to Eason's wonderful little library, which uphold the high standards set by the earlier booklets while maintaining the wonderful value of Ir£2.75 each. This series is one of the best things in Irish publishing, as before, the format attractive and the quality of text and illustrations excellent.

DICTIONARY OF ART AND ARTISTS

General Editor: DAVID PIPER
London and Glasgow, Collins, 1988, Stg£4.95.

This is one of the Collins series of reference dictionaries, which deals also with such subjects as biology, electronics, economics, music and mathematics. This book has over 2,700 entries, on artists, materials, techniques, groups and movements, even writers on art. David Piper is Director of the Ashmolean Museum in Oxford, and is well-known as one of the presenters of the television series, "100 Great Paintings". Up-to-date, concise, authoritative and easy to carry around, this is a very useful guide.

BOOK REVIEWS

FOUR IRISH LANDSCAPE PAINTERS

THOMAS BODKIN
Introduction by Julian Campbell
Dublin, Irish Academic Press, 1987, IR£35.

In a photolithographic facsimile edition of the original published in 1920, this is a handsome book, with illustrations in black and white and four colour reproductions of work by each of the four painters, George Barret, R.A., James A. (James Arthur) O'Connor, Walter F. Osborne, R.H.A., and Nathaniel Hone, R.H.A. Also included are catalogue entries and appendices.

Julian Campbell considers the chapter on Hone to be the most valuable of the four, partly at least because of Bodkin's personal acquaintance with Hone. It is intriguing that Mildred Butler, now popularly regarded as a recently-discovered and previously unknown artist, is mentioned by Bodkin, in 1920, as one of only three Irish artists to have their work bought by the Chantry Bequest, the others being Edwin Hayes and Walter Osborne.

It is good to have this authoritative early book available again, though it is expensive, considering its size and the number of illustrations. Some of Thomas Bodkin's judgments have been modified by later studies but his book remains a basic reference work. It is also a book for the non-expert. His style of writing is simple and of admirable clarity, and this is a pleasant contrast to much art criticism which so often is expressed in language that results in more confusion than illumination.

A complete full-colour facsimile of the Book of Kells, in a limited edition of one thousand four hundred and eighty copies, is due to be published in 1989, by Faksimile-Verlag Luzern, Switzerland. A separate commentary by J.J.G. Alexander, art historian and author, will accompany it. A facsimile this will certainly be as it faithfully copies all the irregularities (and even the holes) in the six hundred and eighty pages; the finished book will measure 9½ x 13 inches and weigh more than twenty pounds.

There is very little more that can usefully be said by the layman or woman about our great book, written twelve hundred years ago. Even experts will continue to be baffled by aspects of this, "the great Gospel of Columcille, the chief relic of the western world", now known as the Book of Kells. They answer some of our questions, others remain. We do not know where the book was between the time of its composition and the year 1006, when it was stolen from the great stone church of Kells. About three months later, the book was found buried near the church. It remained at Kells until it was brought to Dublin by Henry Jones, Bishop of Meath, about 1661, and entrusted to Trinity College Dublin.

Like all masterpieces it has its mysteries: its conception and origins; the influences that moulded it; the fortunate accident of its preservation; and, not least, the high organization and sophistication of the society which produced it, shown by, for instance, the immense quantity of high-quality leather needed, the importation of such precious substances as lapis lazuli and other dyes and inks, the skill and dedication of the artists. Nowhere have line and colour been better combined; brilliant colour, and calligraphy that has not been surpassed (the Latin text is written in superb, insular majuscule script and depicts the life of Christ as narrated in the four New Testament Gospels), are organized with assured mastery.

The facsimile, bound in white goatskin, and the commentary volume, both in a presentation box with mountings and embossed surfaces in silver, brass and gold, cost approximately $15,000, and are, therefore, intended for libraries, collectors and connoisseurs. Trinity College Dublin imposed the most stringent conditions with regard to the safety of the original. The technical problems posed necessitated the invention of very special and sophisticated photo technology.

Trinity College agreed to this edition by Faksimile Verlag, who have produced other facsimiles, including one of *The Book of Hours of the Duke of Berry*, so that "the entire manuscript can be shared with the world".

Rosemary Ryan

Additions to the list of paintings by James Latham published in *The Irish Arts Review 1988*.

1. The Hon. James Carmichael, M.P. (d. 1754), c. 77 x 64 cms. Third son of the 2nd Earl of Hyndford. There is no evidence that the sitter came to Ireland but his sister married Charles O'Hara of Annaghmore and he could have been painted on a visit to her. Private Coll.
2. Richard Lambart, 4th Earl of Cavan (d. 1742), in painted oval, c. 75 × 62 cms. The assured handling indicates that this is not an early portrait but the size and length of the wig cannot date much later than 1730. Parke-Bernet Sale, 21/22 Nov. 1958, Lot 267.
3. A Lady of the de Poer family, c. 75 × 62 cms. A typical early work. Private Coll.
4. Lady Mary Forbes (d. 1797), in painted oval, c. 75 × 62 cms. Daughter of the 3rd Earl of Granard, she married James Irvine of Kingcaussie. Private Coll.
5. Lady Mary Levinge' (d. 1756), three-quarter length seated, wearing a superb brocade dress. This magnificent portrait may not be of Lady Mary, whose husband, Sir Richard Levinge, died in 1724, as, from the costume, the portrait dates into the 1740s. She may be another member of the family. Private Coll.
6. Portrait of an unknown lady, three-quarter length seated holding a rose and wearing a hat. A late portrait, c. 1740. Recently purchased in Australia. Private Coll.
7. Portrait of an unknown gentleman, in painted oval, 76.2 × 63.5 cms. Christie's, 18 March 1988, Lot 186.

Anne Crookshank

ERRATA

In the *GPA Irish Arts Review* 1988, an unfortunate omission was made in 'James Latham 1696–1747'. Column two on page 68 should read . . . the Bishop. But this is not so with the Leslie girls or the Cosbys. One portrait, the General Wade, is an indication . . .

In 'Sackville Street/O'Connell Street' by Maura Shaffrey, the illustration on page 147 entitled "H.A. Baker, Architect, New Shop Fronts. Intended for Westmoreland Street, signed, 1799, executed design. Dublin Corporation Archives, Doc. No. WSC/Maps/195/1" is, in fact, an earlier design proposed for the street; the scheme that was finally built does not have a colonnaded ground floor.